BREAD FROM HEAVEN

The Johannine Monograph Series
Edited by Paul N. Anderson and R. Alan Culpepper

THE VISION OF THE Johannine Monograph Series is to make available in printed, accessible form a selection of the most influential books on the Johannine writings in the modern era for the benefit of scholars and students alike. The volumes in this series include reprints of classic English-language texts, revised editions of significant books, and translations of important international works for English-speaking audiences. A succinct foreword by one of the editors situates each book in terms of its role within the history of Johannine scholarship, suggesting also its continuing value in the field.

This series is founded upon the conviction that scholarship is diminished when it forgets it own history and loses touch with the scintillating analyses and proposals that have shaped the course of Johannine studies. It is our hope, therefore, that the continuing availability of these important works will help to keep the cutting-edge scholarship of this and coming generations of scholars engaged with the classic works of Johannine scholarship while they also chart new directions for the future of the discipline.

Volume 1: *The Gospel of John: A Commentary*, by Rudolf Bultmann
Volume 2: *The Composition and Order of the Fourth Gospel*, by D. Moody Smith
Volume 3: *John's Gospel in New Perspective*, by Richard J. Cassidy
Volume 4: *Bread From Heaven*, by Peder Borgen
Volume 5: *The Prophet-King*, by Wayne A. Meeks
Volume 6: *The Testament of Jesus*, by Ernst Käsemann

BREAD FROM HEAVEN

AN EXEGETICAL STUDY OF
THE CONCEPT OF MANNA IN THE GOSPEL OF JOHN
AND THE WRITINGS OF PHILO

BY

PEDER BORGEN

WIPF & STOCK · Eugene, Oregon

Wipf and Stock Publishers
199 W 8th Ave, Suite 3
Eugene, OR 97401

Bread From Heaven
An Exegetical Study of the Concept of Manna
in the Gospel of John and the Writings of Philo
By Peder Borgen, and Paul N. Anderson
Copyright © 1965, 1981 E. J. Brill
ISBN 13: 978-1-4982-8885-9
Publication date 4/1/2017
Previously published by E. J. Brill, 1965, 1981

*TO
MY PARENTS*

CONTENTS

	Page
Foreword by Paul N. Anderson	IX
Preface to the New Printing	XXXV
Preface to the First Edition	XLV
Preface to the Second Edition	XLVII

I. The Use of A Haggadic Tradition 1

Thesis	1
The present stage of the research	4
The six relevant texts for the tradition about bread from heaven and earth	7
Versions of the same haggadic tradition	8
Fragments of this haggadic tradition used in Philo's exegesis	14
Fragments of haggadah used in John's exegesis, John 6, 31-58	20

II. A Homiletic Pattern 28

The state of research. Homilies in translation	28
The exegetical paraphrase. The similarity between opening and closing	34
Subordinate quotations from the Old Testament	38
The homilies and their literary contexts	43
Parallel homilies elsewhere in Philo and in Paul	46
The same pattern in Palestinian midrash	51

III. Midrashic Method, Patterns and Terminology . . 59

Approach	59
John 6, 31-33	61
John 6, 34-40	69
John 6, 41-48	80
John 6, 49-58	86

IV. The Heavenly Philosophy of the Synagogue and the Encyclia. Mut. 253-263 99

The analysis of different homilies, a relevant approach to the ideas of Philo	99
The encyclical education and philosophy	100
Teaching and the selftaught by nature	103
Agriculture and selfgrown fruits	105

	Page
Encyclia on the borderline between Judaism and paganism	108
Manna, wisdom and the Sabbath.	111
The nation of vision	115
Heaven and earth	118

V. THE HEAVENLY ORDER OF THE JEWS AND PAGAN CAREER. LEG. ALL. III 162-168 122

Stoic thoughts	122
The situation in Alexandria	124
Platonic thought patterns	127
Terms from natural science	130
The heavenly quality of the Jewish nation	133
Heavenly principles embodied in the Jewish laws	136
The heavenly measures	141
God's care, men's trust	145

VI. THE UNIQUE VISION OF GOD IN JESUS, THE SON OF JOSEPH. JOHN 6, 31-58 147

Judaism as background for John 6	147
Bread, Torah and Sinai	148
Bread and wisdom	154
Bread and the commissioned agent	158
Bread and eternal life	165
Bread, external and spiritual, given to Israel	172
Perishable and imperishable food; flesh and spirit	179
Incarnation proves docetic spiritualists to be externalists	183

PERIODICALS, SERIES, ETC.	193
REFERENCE WORKS	196
INDEX OF AUTHORS	197
INDEX OF REFERENCES	201
INDEX OF SUBJECTS	213

Peder Borgen's *Bread from Heaven*—Midrashic Developments in John 6 as a Case Study in John's Unity and Disunity

A Foreword by Paul N. Anderson

AMONG THE WEIGHTY TREATMENTS of the Gospel of John over the last half-century, one of the most significant has been *Bread from Heaven*, by Peder Borgen.[1] As the unity and disunity of the Fourth Gospel had been debated extensively among Johannine scholars for the previous half-century, approaching this issue from a text-based comparative standpoint posed a new window through which one could assess key issues and contribute to the larger discussions. Whereas Rudolf Bultmann and Wilhelm Bousset had envisioned the context of John's composition as Hellenistic Christianity leading into Gnostic trajectories, Borgen focused on particularly Jewish writings as John's primary backdrop—albeit within a diaspora Hellenistic setting.[2] More specifically, the writings of Philo and the

---

1. Peder Borgen, *Bread from Heaven: An Exegetical Study of the Concept of Manna in the Gospel of John and the Writings of Philo*, NovTSup 10 (1965; reprint, Leiden: Brill, 1981).

2. Rudolf Bultmann, in volume 2 of his *Theology of the New Testament*, Kendrick Grobel, trans. (1955; 2nd ed., Waco: Baylor University Press, 2007), situates the historical position of John as being situated within Hellenistic Christianity (3–14). Wilhelm Bousset in his *Kyrios Christos: A History of the Belief in Christ from the Beginnings of Christianity to Irenaeus*, John E. Steely, trans. (1913, 5th ed. 1965; Nashville: Abingdon, 1970) had done the same, separating Palestinian Christianity from Hellenistic Christianity (69–152) and locating Johannine Christology within the latter sector of the early Christian movement (211–44). These moves, of course, assumed Johannine movements into Gnosticism rather than taking seriously the facts of John's Jewishness and Palestinian affinities.

Palestinian midrashim offer a text-based way forward in discerning the origin and development of John's presentation of the feeding and sea-crossing in the ministry of Jesus in John 6, followed by ensuing discussions and the confession of Peter. Given the numerous explicit and implicit cases of John's citing of Jewish biblical motifs, if the case could be made for the Johannine narrator's following Jewish patterns of thinking and writing, then implications would extend to understandings of the Johannine tradition's origin and contextual development, elucidating also its character and meaning.

If John 6 can be considered "the Grand Central Station of Johannine critical issues,"[3] Peder Borgen's 1965 monograph, *Bread from Heaven*, proved to be one of the most incisive and important monographs on that pivotal chapter.[4] With extensive implications for addressing a host of other New Testament issues—including the unity and disunity of John's narrative, relations between Johannine and synoptic traditions, and the socio-religious context of the Fourth Gospel—Borgen's work augurs hard for a unitive view of the Johannine text. Rather than seeing John's story of Jesus as an amalgam of disparate sources, or as dependent on the Synoptics, Borgen explores a number of commonalities between contemporary Jewish writings, including the writings of Philo and the haggadic midrashim. In so doing, new glimpses are also availed onto the dialectical Johannine situation, including an antidocetic thrust in addition to Johannine-synagogue engagements. The enduring impact of Borgen's work shows the Fourth Gospel to represent a self-standing Jesus tradition, combined with Jewish engagements of biblical texts, contributing to homiletic expansions upon memories of the ministry of Jesus for later generations. The implications are extensive, indeed.

---

3. Paul N. Anderson, "The *Sitz im Leben* of the Johannine Bread of Life Discourse and Its Evolving Context," in R. Alan Culpepper (ed.), *Critical Readings of John 6*, BINS 22 (Leiden: Brill, 1997) 1–59, here 1.

4. This is the judgment of Robert Kysar, who regards it to be the most significant study of John 6 at the time, in his *Fourth Evangelist and His Gospel: An Examination of Contemporary Scholarship* (Minneapolis: Augsburg 1975) 124. For an analysis of his treatment, see Paul N. Anderson, *The Christology of the Fourth Gospel: Its Unity and Disunity in the Light of John 6*, WUNT 2.78 (Tübingen: Mohr, 1996; 3rd printing with a new introduction, outlines, and epilogue, Eugene: Cascade, 2010) 52–61.

Borgen's Approach

In addition to noting John's literary features and their religious background, Borgen also gives special attention to the existential application of these concerns in addressing the needs of later audiences. In a fuller treatment than Bultmann's work had earlier provided,[5] Borgen examines the exegetical writings of Philo as a means of comparing John's presentation of Jesus within a diaspora context. Borgen also does something similar to what J. Louis Martyn performed three years later, analyzing Johannine history and theology as a two-level reading of the narrative.[6] Unlike Martyn, however, Borgen gives special attention to Palestinian midrashim as a means of analyzing grounded parallels with the origin of John's narrative, and his engaging the writings of Philo provides a parallel analysis in a Hellenistic context. In these ways, Borgen's work not only sheds light on the operations of the Fourth Evangelist as a Jewish purveyor of written tradition, but it also delivers an advance upon historical understandings of the ministry of Jesus, despite the Johannine Gospel's being finalized several decades later. That being the case, Borgen's work bears implications for understanding the Jesus of history as well as the Christ of faith.

Borgen's interest in the subject, however, came about somewhat by accident. Feeling that recent interpreters had not taken seriously the degree of authority commanded by Jewish Scripture in the Johannine narrative, Borgen began examining biblical quotations—in particular, John 6:31, "He gave them bread from heaven to eat." In his own words, Borgen describes his initial intrigue and emerging hypotheses to be tested:

> Interestingly, an important observation was made in the waiting room at the Main Railroad Station in Copenhagen. I had to wait for some time on a train, and sitting on a bench I looked at the text of John 6 in my Greek New Testament. I noticed that words from the Old Testament quotation were also found in the *subsequent* verses. I picked up a pencil and underscored the repeated words and learned how each word and phrase was interpreted. The last word in the Old Testament quotation in John 6:31, "to eat," was added in v. 49, and it was then in the center of the exposition in vv. 49–58. Thus, an element of a systematically structured exposition

---

5. Rudolf Bultmann, *The Gospel of John: A Commentary*, G. R. Beasley-Murray, trans. (1971; reprint, Johannine Monograph Series 1, Eugene: Wipf & Stock, 2014).

6. J. Louis Martyn, *History and Theology in the Fourth Gospel* (1968, 1979; 3rd ed., Louisville: Westminster John Knox, 2003).

can be traced. With these observations made, I searched for examples of parallel expository activity, in the Jewish *midrashim*, and particularly in the expository writings of Philo of Alexandria. It can also be examined how various biblical traditions may be alluded to and also may be woven into the exposition. In this way it is seen how a received and given text is applied and used in a meaningful way in new situations to new persons and groups. On this basis received and applied aspects of meanings are brought together.[7]

That earlier set of insights is clearly visible in the ways Peder Borgen then developed his research project as evidenced in his first major monograph. At the outset (chapter 1), he declares his thesis in the light of previous history-of-religions approaches to John: "This study is based on the fact that Philo and John both interpret the Old Testament, and that in so doing they both expand on the pericope of manna—the bread from heaven."[8] As a means of posing a comparison/contrast with John 6:31–58, Borgen lays out six relevant Palestinian midrashic texts for analysis: *Exodus Rabbah* 25:2 (linking Ps 104:14; Deut 11:11; Num 21:17 and Exod 16:4); 25:6 (linking Num 21:17 and Exod 16:4); *Moses I* 201–202; *Exodus Mekilta* 16:4 (linking Deut 33:28 and 14); *Petirat Moses* (linking Exod 16:4 and Num 21:17); and *Moses* II 267. Borgen first compares these texts with each other, noting similar ways they address the "bread from heaven" motif, and he further compares these findings with haggadic traditions featured in Philo's exegesis: *Mut.* 258–260a (Exod 16:4); *Congr.* 170, 173–174 (Deut 8:2); and *Leg. All.* III 162, 168 (Exod 16:4). Borgen then performs an analysis of John 6:31–58, showing similarities and differences between these three sets of midrashic expansions upon a key manna text (Exod 16:4, "he gave them bread from heaven to eat"), demonstrating similarities and differences, followed by their implications.

Borgen goes on to explore commonalities in contemporary homiletical patterns in the writings of Philo and Paul, and also the Palestinian midrashim, noting instances of exegetical paraphrase and subordinate quotations from Hebrew Scripture (chapter 2). Identifying commonalities in terms of midrashic method in patterns and terminology in John 6 (vv. 31–33, 34–40, 41–48, 49–58), Borgen thus demonstrates Jewish exegetical operations within the Johannine Bread of Life discourse (chapter 3). From

---

7. Shared in personal correspondence, September 2016.
8. Borgen, *Bread from Heaven*, 1.

there, Borgen performs detailed analyses of the heavenly philosophy of the synagogue and encyclical schools in Alexandria (Philo, *Mut.* 253–263; chapter 4) and of the heavenly order of the Jews in contrast to pagan life in Hellenistic culture (Philo, *Leg All.* III 162–168; chapter 5). Upon those bases, Borgen explores the unique vision of God in Jesus as the son of Joseph in John 6:31–58, elucidating the Jewish background of John 6 and its sharpened rhetorical thrust as a challenge to emerging Docetists, who are unwilling to accept the fleshly humanity of Jesus (chapter 6).

Within the context of contemporary New Testament scholarship, it is notable that Borgen builds upon the work of his mentor, Nils Alstrup Dahl, who had also levied a pointed set of critiques against the Hellenization and Gnosticization of the Johannine tradition. Pushing back against Bultmann's minimizing the Jewish and Old Testament background of the Fourth Gospel, Dahl argues that the evangelist represents the Jewish idea that "Israel is the center of the world."[9] The Fourth Evangelist, however, reinterprets that Jewish missional identity, showing Jesus as the King of Israel—of whom Moses and the prophets wrote—constructing a christocentric and forensic view of history. In the distinguishing of those who are from above and from below, however, John's dualism is closer to Qumranic Judaism than full-blown Gnosticism. It reflects affinity with the ethos and operations of Jewish Merkabah mysticism, which builds upon Scripture in its rhetorical appeals.[10] In constructing his argument on the Jewishness of John, Dahl builds on the work of Eduard Schweizer, while also flagging the danger of separating the universalizing Christ of faith from the Jewish Jesus of history, especially within docetizing Christian developments. According to Dahl,

> The christological interpretation of Old Testament visions and theophanies, therefore, seems to have a polemical note directed against a type of piety which made the patriarchs and prophets heroes of the mystical visions of the heavenly world. Even a docetic Christology may have been supported by allegorical interpretations of the Old Testament. Over and against such tendencies, John bears witness to the true humanity of Jesus and to the reality of his death (6:41–2, 61; 19:35).[11]

---

9. Nils Alstrup Dahl, "The Johannine Church and History," in John Ashton (ed.), *The Interpretation of John*, 2nd ed. (Edinburgh: T. & T. Clark, 1997) 147–67, here 152; first published in W. Klassen and G. F. Snyder (eds.), *Current Issues in New Testament Interpretation* (New York: Harper & Row, 1962) 124–42.

10. Ibid., 160–64.

11. Ibid., 164.

Behind the constructive work of Borgen, the formative work of Dahl is thus evident. Rather than seeing the Fourth Gospel as truncated from a Palestinian context, John's presentation of Jesus as the Jewish Messiah/Christ is foundationally rooted in Jewish typological and exegetical engagements of Scripture, and its ethical dualism reflects a Jewish worldview, albeit developed in a diaspora context. While earlier tensions with Jewish leaders in Judea and later tensions with Jewish communities among the mission churches are evident, Borgen also notes the fact that John's incarnational motifs are designed to target docetizing members of the Johannine situation, implying a multiplicity of rhetorical thrusts. Like the letters of Ignatius, which target Judaizing and docetizing threats within the context of Roman imperial pressures, John's crafting of the Bread of Life discourse not only invites true adherents of Moses to receive the true heavenly manna that Jesus gives and is; it also challenges Gentile members of the audience to embrace his real suffering and death.[12]

Therefore, in performing the most intensive investigation of Jewish exegetical and midrashic practices underlying any text within the Gospel of John, Borgen makes significant advances not only in Johannine studies but also in showing how the writings of Philo and the Palestinian midrashim might serve as a backdrop for understanding the writings of Paul and other writings of the New Testament. Additionally, in illuminating the existential targeting of audiences within the Johannine situation, Borgen shows the dialectical character of Johannine Christianity to be more complex and polyvalent than recent studies had imagined.[13] These and other strengths

---

12. Thus, the emerging Johannine situation reflects a highly dialectical set of engagements within the evolving Johannine situation. See treatments of Samaritan and Galilean-Judean tensions—Wayne A. Meeks, *The Prophet-King: Moses Traditions and the Johannine Christology*, NovTSup 14 (1967; reprint, JMS 5, Eugene, OR: Wipf & Stock, 2017); Johannine-Jewish tensions—J. Louis Martyn, *History and Theology*; Johannine-emperor cult tensions—Richard J. Cassidy, *John's Gospel in New Perspective: Christology and the Realities of Roman Power* (1992; reprint, JMS 2, Eugene, OR: Wipf & Stock, 2015); Johannine-Docetist tensions—Udo Schnelle, *Antidocetic Christology in the Gospel of John: An Investigation of the Place of the Fourth Gospel in the Johannine School*, Linda M. Maloney, trans. (Minneapolis: Fortress, 1992); Johannine-hierarchical Christian tensions—Ernst Käsemann, *A Testament of Jesus: A Study of the Gospel of John in the Light of Chapter 17*, Gerhard Krodel, trans., New Testament Library (1968; reprint, JMS 6, Eugene, OR: Wipf & Stock, 2017). Borgen's work thus supports and corroborates most of these developments in sketching contextual factors affecting what R. Alan Culpepper refers to as *The Johannine School* (1975; 2nd ed., Atlanta: SBL, 2007) and what Raymond E. Brown refers to as *The Community of the Beloved Disciple* (Mahwah, NJ: Paulist, 1979).

13. In addition to C. K. Barrett's essay "The Dialectical Theology of St John," in his

are among the advances made by Peder Borgen's important monograph, *Bread from Heaven*.

The Significance of John 6: A Showcase of Johannine Critical Issues and Their Solutions

Borgen's selection of John 6 as a case study for his work proved a pivotal move in New Testament scholarship, as it is within this chapter that a number of critical issues converge. Given that Rudolf Bultmann's commentary identified four of John's five major literary sources being discoverable within this chapter, including aspects of the text's disordering and reordering, assessing the literary unity and disunity of John 6 bears several weighty implications.[14] Likewise, John's theological tensions within this chapter demand critical consideration. If John 6 presents signs-narratives deriving from an alien source that are existentialized by the evangelist, or if the revelation-sayings material reflects the Gnostic Redeemer-Myth countered by the evangelist's incarnational thrust, or if a redactor has added Eucharist-cultic material to counter the evangelist's purportedly antisacramental stance, these issues would be important to address.[15] In analyzing similarities and differences between John and the Synoptics, John 6 also gives the most extensive set of parallels outside of the Passion Narrative. Therefore, John's relation(s) to the Synoptics would also hinge upon a close analysis of this text.[16]

New Testament Essays (London: SPCK, 1972) 49-69, see also Paul N. Anderson, "From One Dialogue to Another: Johannine Polyvalence from Origins to Receptions," in Stephen Moore and Tom Thatcher (eds.), *Anatomies of Narrative Criticism: The Past, Present, and Future of the Fourth Gospel as Literature*, Resources in Biblical Studies 55 (Atlanta: SBL, 2008) 93-119.

14. Bultmann, *Gospel of John*, 209-37; cf. my overview in the foreword to Bultmann's commentary (2014, i-xxviii) and a more extensive analysis in *Christology*, 33-251.

15. Therefore, as Robert Fortna has argued, it is not simply the stylistic unity of the Fourth Gospel that requires consideration; it is also the contextual and theological Johannine tensions that must be engaged critically, if the full spectrum of John's riddles is to be addressed. R. T. Fortna, *The Fourth Gospel and Its Predecessor: From Narrative Source to Present Gospel* (Philadelphia: Fortress, 1988) 6, 16-22.

16. C. K. Barrett, for instance, argues that the similarities between John 6 and Mark 6 and 8 point to the possibility that John may at least have had access to Mark, and perhaps other synoptic traditions. Barrett, *The Gospel according to St. John: An Introduction with Commentary and Notes on the Greek Text* (1955; 2nd ed., Philadelphia: Westminster, 1978). A similar case was argued by B. H. Streeter in *The Four Gospels: A Study of Origins* (London: Macmillan, 1924).

These are some of the reasons John 6 is so pivotal, not only in Johannine studies but also in terms of gospel-relations studies, New Testament theological analyses, the history of early Christianity, and even historical-Jesus research overall. John 6 offers the most solid bases for examining what Ashton named the two great Johannine riddles addressed by Bultmann: (*a*) *John's place in the development of early Christianity*, and (*b*) *John's central governing thrust*.[17] It also serves as a basis for ascertaining the keys to many of the other Johannine riddles, and thus John 6 provides a number of planks on which to base a solid overall Johannine theory with extensive implications.[18] This is why John 6 is so central to understanding the panoply of Johannine critical issues, as findings on this pivotal text bear within themselves extensive implications.[19] These may also be reasons as to why Borgen was directed by Dahl to consider the socioreligious provenance of John 6 as a means of posing alternative ways forward in the critical addressing of the Johannine riddles. Some of these key issues are as follows.

First, as the water-of-life and bread-of-life themes are propounded by Jesus in Galilee in John 4 and 6, and as the Jerusalem healing of the lame man in John 5 is referenced also in John 7, Bultmann infers *a transposition of these chapters*. He thus assumes the original order was chapters 4, 6, 5, 7, which requires an inference of disordering followed by a theory of rearrangement—probably by another hand.[20] Assuming that such a re-positioning of major sections of John may have taken place, Bultmann extends a disordering-rearrangement set of inferences to dozens of other

17. John Ashton, *Understanding the Fourth Gospel* (1991; 2nd ed., Oxford: Oxford University Press, 2007) 2–11, argues that the greatest contribution of Bultmann's magisterial paradigm was that it addressed these two great Johannine riddles, and yet he fails to note that John 6 is the classic text upon which these and other riddles must be explored and tested. See, for instance, a fuller treatment of thirty-six of the Johannine riddles (a dozen theological, historical, and literary riddles displayed and assessed) in Paul N. Anderson, *The Riddles of the Fourth Gospel: An Introduction to John* (Minneapolis: Fortress, 2011) 25–90.

18. Added to the 2010 third printing of Anderson, *Christology*, is a series of solid planks upon which to base a new overall Johannine theory regarding John's dialogical autonomy (xxxv–lxxxix). See also Anderson, *Riddles*, 125–55.

19. Note for instance, that in contrast to Martyn's identifying a single partner in dialogue between the Johannine leadership and its audience (synagogue leaders), no fewer than four partners in dialogue can be inferred when performing a history-and-theology reading of John 6; cf. Anderson, "Johannine Bread of Life Discourse," 1997, 24–58.

20. The transposition of John 5 and 6 was followed by Schnackenburg and a few others: Rudolf Schnackenburg, *The Gospel According to St. John*, Kevin Smyth, trans. (New York: Seabury, 1982) 2:73.

texts (a total of ten with relation to John 6 itself),[21] which avails him license to rearrange other sayings material as a means of "exposing" the poetic and strophic character of an inferred Gnostic-sayings source.[22]

Second, within Bultmann's *source-critical approach*, assuming there was no self-standing Johannine tradition on its own, Bultmann infers the evangelist's making use of a *Sēmeia* Source and a Revelation-Sayings Source as a means of constructing the feeding narrative and its ensuing discussions and discourses in John 6. Building, then, on the other signs material in John, Bultmann infers a self-standing miracle source designed to convince audiences that Jesus was the Jewish Messiah/Christ. This hypothetical source is inferentially parallel to Mark, accounting for the origin and character of John's distinctive presentation of Jesus's works. Additionally, Bultmann extends his theory of disordering and rearrangement, allowing for the rearranging of more than half a dozen units of material within the sayings of Jesus in John 6, which, when rearranged, appear more similar to what one might imagine a Gnostic poetic discourse to have sounded like. Assuming the Johannine Prologue was also a part of this Mandean tradition, Bultmann accounts for the origin and character of John's distinctive discourses and sayings of Jesus, accordingly. He then poses stylistic evidence to support his identification of these two sources, arguing that the signs source displays features of "Semitising Greek," while the sayings source displays features of "Hellenised Aramaic."

Third, Bultmann infers *the addition of the so-called eucharistic interpolation* (John 6:51c–58) on the assumption that the Fourth Evangelist was an antisacramentalist, and that the redactor was an ecclesial revisionist. In contrast to other source-critical inferences, these verses display no stylistic differences with the narrator, leading Bultmann to infer that the redactor must have "imitated the style of the evangelist" in this case. Bolstered by the view that John 6:51c–58 required participation in the Eucharist for salvation to be obtained, vv. 53–54 clearly seem at odds with the evangelist's christocentric soteriology. If one has no life and is thus damned apart from participating in cultic instrumentalism, such a requirement is indeed at diametric odds with the evangelist's seeing Christ as the way, the truth, and the life (John 14:6) and worship in spirit and in truth being independent of form and place (4:21–24). Thus, if the redactor added John 21, featuring

21. Anderson, *Christology*, 80.

22. For a thorough analysis of the theological, stylistic, and contextual evidence for Bultmann's operation, see ibid., 70–136.

something like a sacramental meal on the shore, with overtones of futuristic eschatology associated with referencing the death of the Beloved Disciple, Bultmann infers the same redactor's contribution to have involved the adding of this section at the end of the Bread of Life discourse. Therefore, if John 6:51c–58 is ritualistically eucharistic, it is likely to represent a later interpolation.

These theological concerns point to a more direct set of tensions involving a fourth set of issues: *differences of theological Tendenz*, possibly reflecting different religious backgrounds of the signs material and the sayings material in John 6. In Bultmann's view, the miracles in the Fourth Gospel originated from a *Sēmeia* Source reflecting a *Theios Anēr* Christology, which the evangelist sets straight in existential directions. This accounts for the disparaging of signs faith in John 4:48 and 6:26, in tension with affirming those who believe without having seen in 20:29. Further, the agency of the *Logos* and the work of the Revealer in the Johannine Gospel are thought to prefigure the later-more-common Gnostic Redeemer-Myth, bolstering further Bultmann's inference of the evangelist's utilization of disparate sources. Thus, the evangelist's incarnational theology is set in dialectical tension with the high Christology of the sayings material in John, accounting for a number of John's theological riddles as representing dialogues external to the thinking of the evangelist.

A fifth issue—one with which Bultmann and Borgen would agree—involves *the relation of John's tradition to those of the Synoptic Gospels*. Whereas Barrett, and to some degree Streeter before him, inferred John's indebtedness to the Synoptic Gospels, and Mark in particular, Bultmann and Borgen see John's tradition as independent and self-standing.[23] John 6 thus provides the premier case study for determining Johannine-Synoptic relations, as it is in this chapter that the only miracle in all four Gospels—the feeding of the five thousand—is found (Matt 14:13–21; Mark 6:30–44; Luke 9:10–17; John 6:1–15; cf. also the feeding of the four thousand: Matt 15:32–39; Mark 8:1–10). Additional similarities include the sea crossing (Matt 14:22–33; Mark 6:45–52; John 6:16–21), debates over the meaning of the feeding, and the

---

23. Borgen's earlier essay on the subject had questioned views regarding John's dependence on the Synoptics, "John and the Synoptics in the Passion Narrative," *NTS* 5 (1959) 246–59. He later wrote several other essays on the subject, and these are gathered in his collection of essays, *The Gospel of John: More Light from Philo, Paul and Archaeology*, NovTSup 154 (Leiden: Brill, 2014): "Gospel Traditions in Paul and John: Methods and Structures; John and the Synoptics" (67–77); "John and the Synoptics" (121–46); "The Independence of the Gospel of John: Some Observations" (147–64).

confession of Peter shortly thereafter (Matt 16:16; Mark 8:29; Luke 9:20; John 6:68–69). If there were thus one unit within John's narrative wherein similarities and differences with other first-century narratives could be tested—other than the Passion narratives—John 6 would be it.

Therefore, Borgen has chosen well in selecting John 6 as a case study for testing the Fourth Gospel's theological and literary unity and disunity. First, if John 6 follows on John 5, the need for an extensive theory of disordering and reordering is diminished; Borgen shows that John 6 follows logically on the statement of Jesus in 5:46. Second, if the order within John 6 flows coherently as a unity, the narrative makes sense as it stands—focusing on the manna and bread motifs throughout the chapter. Third, Borgen shows how the signs and discourses actually flow together in an apparent traditional unity, and the Jewish-exegetical backdrop of the chapter demonstrates its text-based integrity. Fourth, if verses 51–58 follow the previous discussion without reflecting a theological disruption, the intrusive work of a redactor becomes superfluous. That is precisely what Borgen demonstrates, as these verses are not explicitly or instrumentally eucharistic, but they flow from expansions on the biblical texts associated with Exod 16:4. Fifth, while the similarities between John 6 and parallel passages in the Synoptics are intriguing, so are the differences. Borgen thus demonstrates how the Johannine discourses and dialogues in John 6 actually reflect expansions upon the ministry of Jesus in the earlier part of the chapter, in addition to the midrashic developments that ensue. They are not synoptic-dependent; rather, they stem from Palestinian midrashic debates over the ministry of Jesus and its interpretations, casting light upon earlier and later stages in the Johannine tradition's development.

While Borgen spells out the synchronic implications of his findings more extensively in later works, their basis is already established in the outcomes of his first monograph.[24] In addition to providing a compelling case study for the autonomy and unity of the Johannine tradition, Borgen makes two further contributions that continue to impact Johannine studies to this day. These contributions address the two great Johannine riddles set forth by Ashton, above: John's provenance within the development of early Christianity and the central theological thrust of the Fourth Gospel.

---

24. See especially his essay arguing for the continuity between John 5 and 6 in Peder Borgen, "John 6: Tradition, Interpretation and Composition," in Culpepper, *Critical Readings of John 6*, 95–114; see also "The Unity of the Discourse in John 6," in his *Logos Was the True Light, and Other Essays on the Gospel of John*, Relieff 9 (Trondheim, Norway: Tapir, 1983) 21–22.

Borgen's Advances on the Two Great Johannine Riddles: John's Provenance and Central Thrust

In addition to posing a compelling case for the compositional synchronicity of the Johannine narrative, Borgen also contributes further advances along other lines. In following Dahl's lead, Peder Borgen performs the most extensive comparison-contrast to date between John's tradition and the writings of Philo and the Palestinian midrashim. As parallels are evident between the ways the Fourth Evangelist and roughly contemporary Jewish authors worked with biblical texts interpretively and rhetorically, it is now uncontroversial to see the Fourth Gospel as an essentially Jewish document.[25] While John was finalized in a Hellenistic setting, the thoroughly Jewish character of the Johannine tradition argues for a setting in Palestine as the origin of its tradition, and that likelihood casts light upon the ministry of Jesus and its reception among Jewish leaders in Galilee and Judea as well as its later developments.[26] In providing a text-based analysis of similarities between treatments of Jewish interpretive expansions on biblical texts and the narration of signs, dialogues, and discourses in John 6, Borgen poses a correction to Bultmann's answer to the first of the great Johannine riddles: John's provenance. In the contribution of Borgen, the Johannine narrative has not departed from its Jewish ethos in its engagement with the Hellenistic world; rather, it maintains its Jewishness, even within a diaspora setting. This development poses three weighty implications.

First, Borgen's work makes unprecedented contributions toward understanding *the originative character of the Johannine tradition*, as well as early engagements over its subject, Jesus the Galilean. Borgen's analysis of the Palestinian midrashim shows that Jewish engagements of Scripture in

---

25. This case is argued by C. K. Barrett, *The Gospel of John & Judaism* (London: SPCK, 1975); John Ashton sees John's provenance as being rooted in the apocalyptic worldview of Qumranic Judaism, *Understanding the Fourth Gospel*; Gail Yee sees the Jewish feasts embodied in the Johannine Jesus, *Jewish Feasts and the Gospel of John* (Wilmington: M. Glazier, 1989); Daniel J. Boyarin sees John's Logos theology as essentially Jewish, "The Gospel of the *Memra*: Jewish Binitarianism and the Prologue to John," *HTR* 9 (2001) 243–84; Ben Reynolds sees the Son of Man in John as fulfilling Jewish apocalypticism, *The Apocalyptic Son of Man in the Gospel of John*, WUNT 2.249 (Tübingen: Mohr Siebeck, 2008).

26. Therefore, the debates between Jesus and Jewish leaders as portrayed in John 6 display midrashic exchanges, which could have taken place in Galilee or Judea, if not during the ministry of Jesus, certainly among his later followers and their interlocutors—before the move to a Hellenistic setting—as well as continuing on within later synagogue-Johannine exchanges; cf. Anderson, "Johannine Bread of Life Discourse," 24–58.

John 6 not only reflect the later developments of the Johannine tradition; it also shows how the Jewish leaders of Palestine might have used Scripture rhetorically in their engagements with Jesus of Nazareth.[27] That being the case, in John 6 we have not simply an exegetical development of Exod 16:4 as a proem text by a homiletician; we have echoes of debates with religious leaders in Galilee over Jesus's ministry and its authorization, in which biblical texts are cited, interpreted, and used rhetorically as means of procuring more bread (the crowd and the Jewish leaders) or asserting the authorization of Jesus. That being the case, we have in John 6 an alternative temptation narrative—where compelling Jesus to produce (more) bread, scriptural references are cited by discussants, which Jesus overturns with further scriptural citations—but in a more realistic way than the Q narratives preserved in Matt 4:1–11 and Luke 4:1–13.[28]

A second contribution of Borgen's work is that because it demonstrates clear parallels with how a contemporary Jewish interpreter of Scripture in a diaspora setting might have engaged Mosaic and manna-related texts, it also informs *the evangelist's engagement of audiences in the emerging Johannine situation*. Of course, a multiplicity of midrashic and homiletical patterns abound within ancient Jewish literature, and as Borgen himself shows, manna texts are used in a variety of ways. Whereas midrashic explorations of a proem biblical text such as Exod 16:4 are featured in Rabbah 25:1–8 and elsewhere, references to Scripture in other settings often simply serve primarily the interests of the interpreter.[29] For instance, Philo of Alexandria provides ample parallels for understanding how the manna motif was characteristically used in other socioreligious settings—sometimes exegetically, but most often rhetorically.

A fascinating detail is that when engagements of the manna motif are analyzed in Philo, as well as the Palestinian midrashim, manna is only used as a proem text about 15 percent of the time. Rather, the majority of

27. Of course, these midrashim were finalized much later, but if they convey a *topos*-based approach to Scripture engagement among Jewish leaders in Galilee and Judea, their parallels with John 6 may indeed convey soundings of the sorts of debates that might have ensued within the first level of the Johannine tradition's development. Cf. Anderson, "Johannine Bread of Life Discourse," 11–17.

28. Raymond E. Brown comments on these parallels, noting that we have a parallel temptation narrative in John 6 to that of the Q tradition in the Synoptics (261–64), "Incidents That Are Units in the Synoptic Gospels but Dispersed in John," in his *New Testament Essays* (Garden City, NY: Image, 1965) 246–71. Cf. Anderson, *Christology*, 201–2.

29. Jacob Neusner, *Midrash in Context: Exegesis in Formative Judaism*, Brown Judaic Studies 141 (Atlanta: Scholars, 1988) xvii.

its uses (85 percent) are rather brief references in which manna is used rhetorically as a proof text, bolstering another point.[30] Especially clear are the treatments of manna in *Mut.* 252–263 and *Leg. All. III* 161–178, where one finds (*a*) a main point of argument, (*b*) discussion in dualistic terms, (*c*) references to God's giving manna as a rhetorical support of the main point, (*d*) continued discussion and implications, (*e*) a reiteration of the main theme in the light of the present discussion.[31] Therefore, the main thrust of *Mut.* 252–263 is that while the man of virtue may resort to actions from below (Abraham's resorting to progeny through Hagar), God's provision through Sarah is like the heavenly food—manna—which nourishes abundantly. Further, whereas the main text of *Leg. All. III* 161–178 is Gen 3:14 (not Exod 16:4), God's judging of the serpent in the garden of Eden differentiates the needs of the human body from those of the soul; the nourishment of the latter is the Word of God, like manna descended from heaven. Therefore, whether arguing that the Jewish synagogue schools are superior to the Greek encyclical schools in Alexandria (Philo) or whether the teachings of Jesus are superior to the stances of the synagogue leaders there or elsewhere in the diaspora mission (John), God's giving heavenly manna provides a rhetorical trump card to be played as the last word within these socioreligious situations.[32]

A third contribution is that Borgen argues compellingly the likelihood that there were several phases and sets of audiences within the longitudinal Johannine situation, so *taking seriously the antidocetic thrust of John 6* is just as important as noting its engagements with Jewish audiences. In exploring the parallels with the Ignatian letters, Dahl and Borgen are on solid ground. While the third generation of the Jesus movement clearly remained engaged with Jewish communities in the diaspora, however, it cannot be said that dialogues with members of local synagogues were the only groups to be engaged.[33] Even before the move to an Asia Minor setting (if the traditional view is assumed) the Johannine Jesus movement seems to

---

30. Anderson, *Christology*, 58–61.

31. "Appendix VII: Philo's Use of Manna as a Secondary Text," in ibid., 272–73.

32. Anderson, *Christology*, 194–251; Anderson, "Johannine Bread of Life Discourse," 17–24.

33. This is the greatest weakness of the Martyn hypothesis; in seeking to elucidate the second level of history in the Johannine tradition, he obliterates the first. Cf. Edward W. Klink, "The Overrealized Expulsion in the Gospel of John," in *John, Jesus, and History*, vol. 2, *Aspects of Historicity in the Fourth Gospel*, Early Christianity and Its Literature 2 (Atlanta: SBL, 2009) 175–84.

have been engaging religious leaders in Jerusalem, reflecting north-south debates between Galileans and Judeans. Along these lines, religious authorization was an issue, as centralized religion stood in resistant tension with the charismatic prophetic challenge from the hinterlands. Another set of dialectical engagements involved competition between followers of John the Baptist and Jesus—tensions between the followers of charismatic and prophetic leaders. These engagements within Palestinian Judaism are palpable in the Johannine narrative, reflected in the ways Jesus's reception in Jerusalem is presented and the ways John serves as the primary witness to Jesus's Messiahship. With the move to a Gentile-mission setting, however, engagements with other groups come into play, and Borgen's building on the writings of Ignatius points the way forward.

Within the writings of John and Ignatius, four further dialectical engagements come to the surface. These include engagements with local Jewish leaders and docetizing teachers, within the presence of Roman persecution, to which Ignatius poses a monepiscopal and structural approach to church leadership as a means of addressing these crises. While Ignatius references Judaizers who challenged adherence to Jesus as the Christ (*Magn.* 10), emphasizing Jewish law and customs (*Magn.* 8; *Phila.* 6)—including the keeping of the Jewish Sabbath (*Magn.* 9)—he also warns of false teachers, who include heretics and Docetists (*Eph.* 7, 9, 16). Those called heretics poison the potion of Christ, introduce division and false doctrine, deny the way of the cross, and abstain from the eucharistic commemorating of the suffering and death of Jesus (*Tral.* 6; *Phil.* 2; *Smyrn.* 4, 7). Further, the Docetists (*Eph.* 7, 20; *Tral.* 11) deny the human history of Jesus and his ministry—especially his death on the cross—and against these divisive ministers, Ignatius points to the importance of maintaining unity in the church under a single appointed bishop as the means of countering divisive threats. After all, within Ignatian ecclesiology, unity with the single bishop and his community implies unity with the one Lord, Jesus Christ (*Eph.* 1–6, 20; *Magn.* 2–6, 13; *Tral.* 1–3, 7, 13; *Phil.* 2–4, 7–8; *Smyrn.* 8–9; *Polycarp* 5–6). And, of course, the Roman persecution against Christian leaders and his own impeding martyrdom are acutely on his mind, so he advises believers to be strong against the empire and its demands—exhorting the way of the cross in solidarity with Christ and his communities of faith (*Eph.* 1, 9, 12, 21; *Rom.* 2–10).[34] With these connections being the case, Ignatius's em-

---

34. Cyril Charles Richardson, "Ignatius and John," in *The Christianity of Ignatius of Antioch* (1935; New York: A.M.S., 1967) 68–80; see also his "Evidence for Two Separate

phasis upon receiving "the bread of God" bears with it clear martyrological associations, likely reflecting echoes of John 6 (*Eph.* 5, 20; *Rom.* 4, 7). In elucidating the Palestinian and Hellenistic developments of John's story of Jesus, Borgen's work thus affirms the synchronicity of the Johannine tradition while illuminating the diachronicity of the Johannine situation.

Having addressed the first of the great Johannine riddles by showing the Jewishness and unity of the Johannine tradition while also featuring its place in the development of Hellenistic Christianity, Borgen thus lays the groundwork for addressing the second great Johannine riddle: John's *Leitmotiv* (central thrust). If there were a central motif and guiding theological thrust of the Johannine witness, it would have to feature God's sending of the Son, out of love for the world, that humanity might respond to the divine initiative, in faith, leading to the enjoyment of abundant life, in the here and now as well as in the hereafter.[35] Such themes are sounded in the Johannine Prologue (1:1–18), passages denoting the central structure of John's Christology (3:31–36; 12:44–50), the prayer of Jesus (John 17), and the purpose statement of the evangelist (20:30–31).[36] Along these lines, Borgen establishes a firm basis for a Jewish agency schema rooted in Deut 18:15–22, which addresses several of the other Johannine riddles, as well.

While Borgen develops the Prophet-like-Moses agency schema more fully in his later works,[37] he builds in the present book a case for the agency of the Son as sent by the Father, rooted in the halakhic concept of agency (pp. 158–64). Within this juridical model of sending and representation, the one who is sent is in all ways like the one who sends him, and this similitude relates not only to the mission of the agent but also to his person. Therefore, Jesus's representation of the Father and desire to carry out his will in John 6:38–40 show that Jewish principles of agency are at work in John's presentation of Jesus as the Messiah/Christ. Given that bread from

---

Heresies" as an argument for a Judaizing threat and a Docetizing threat in Ignatius, with implications for the dialectical Johannine situation (81–85). On an analysis of Ignatius's Letters with relation to John 6, see Anderson, *Christology*, 119–27.

35. This set of themes is outlined by William R. G. Loader, "The Central Structure of Johannine Christology," *NTS* 30 (1984) 188–216; Loader, *Jesus in John's Gospel: Structures and Issues in Johannine Christology* (Grand Rapids: Eerdmans, 2017).

36. Anderson, *Christology*, 17–31.

37. See especially Borgen's essay "God's Agent in the Fourth Gospel," in Jacob Neusner (ed.), *Religions in Antiquity: In Memory of E. R. Goodenough* (Leiden: Brill, 1968) 137–48; published also in John Ashton (ed.), *The Interpretation of John*, 2nd ed. (Edinburgh: T. & T. Clark, 1997) 83–95.

heaven is also associated with wisdom, agency, and even the Torah, John's "I am" formulas cohere with the representative agency schema of halakhic mysticism in ways that legitimate his authority. Therefore, rather than seeing Johannine Christology as rooted in the Gnostic Redeemer-Myth, the Mosaic agency schema poses a closer history-of-religions parallel, and its use would have been at home within the Palestinian phase of the Johannine tradition's development as well as its later diaspora phases.

Further Johannine Riddles

In addition to Borgen's demonstrating the Jewishness of John's narrative and its central thrust, he addresses other Johannine riddles as well. First, if a grounded Jewish approach to agency—that of a Prophet-like-Moses typology—is seen as operative within the Johannine narrative, signs and discourses come to be seen as *more unitive in their thrust*. Therefore, the relation between signs, dialogues, and discourses appears more integrated than form-critical analyses have allowed, and the plausibility of John's tradition being a self-standing reflection on the ministry of Jesus, rather than a narrative derivative from the Synoptics or alien sources, is compellingly bolstered. Borgen's later work on Deut 18:15–22 also provides a basis for further developments of the *shaliach* (sending) motif as John's central thrust, providing a key to John's overall literary unity. For instance, if 1 John 1:1–3 reflects an embrace of the Gospel's story of Jesus by Johannine believers, the *Logos* hymn underlying John 1:1–18 can be seen as a cross-cultural expansion upon the Jewish agency motif in Hellenism-friendly ways.[38] This central theme, rendered in developing ways, poses a key to John's literary unity despite its development within an emerging situation.

A second Johannine riddle addressed by the Mosaic agency underlying John's story of Jesus is the Father-Son relationship—one of the great theological puzzles throughout Christian history. Theologically, rather than seeing the Father-Son relationship in John as comprising disparate theologies—one subordinated (the Father is greater than I; I can do nothing except what the Father commands) and the other egalitarian (I and the Father are one; if you have seen me, you have seen the Father)—these are best seen

---

38. Paul N. Anderson, "The Johannine *Logos*-Hymn: A Cross-Cultural Celebration of God's Creative-Redemptive Work," in R. Alan Culpepper and Jan G. van der Watt (eds.), *Creation Stories in Dialogue: The Bible, Science, and Folk Traditions; Radboud Prestige Lecture Series*, BINS 139 (Leiden: Brill, 2016) 219–42.

not as contradictory but entwined. Within a Mosaic agency schema, the Son's words, works, and being are identical with the Father because he does nothing except what the Father instructs. As Borgen develops later, supported by presentations of the agency motif in Merkabah mysticism, the agent is in all ways like the one who sent him.[39] In that sense, the egalitarian and subordinated presentation of the Father-Son relationship in the Fourth Gospel conveys not disparate Christologies; rather, it represents flip sides of the same coin: *the Mosaic agency schema rooted in Deuteronomy 18*.[40] Further, when a more extensive analysis is performed between the Father-Son relationship in John and the septuagintal rendering of Deut 18:15–22, no fewer than twenty-four parallels can be found. Most strikingly, the proof of Jesus's being the prophet predicted by Moses is the fact that his word comes true—the sign of his authenticity.[41]

A third riddle addressed by Borgen's contribution involves historical inquiry. Given that the presentation of Jesus as the Mosaic prophet only appears in the Gospels and speeches of Peter and Stephen elsewhere in the New Testament (Acts 3:22; 7:37) and is absent from theological developments in christological hymns and teaching materials, it is unlikely to represent simply a later theological conviction applied to earlier narratives. It might even reflect *some of the debates surrounding the ministry of Jesus of Nazareth*, as his provocative deeds elicited challenges from religious leaders in Jerusalem, leading to his legitimation of his ministry. For instance, if Jesus's healings on the Sabbath, disturbance in the temple, dining with "sinners" and radical teachings evoked controversy among religious leaders—a certain likelihood—might he have defended his mission on the basis of claiming to represent the Father, as predicted by Moses (Deut 18:15–18)? If Jesus of Nazareth received legal pushback from Jewish leaders regarding his provocative actions based upon the Law of Moses, might he also have responded with a prophetic claim to Mosaic authority, citing Mosaic prophetic agency as a support of God's continuing word for his people? Borgen's work thus provides a grounded way forward in understanding more fully the Jesus of history as well as the Christ of faith—precisely because it offers a plausible basis for understanding Jesus as an eschatological

39. Borgen, "God's Agent."

40. Contra A. C. Sundberg, "*Isos tō Theō* Christology in John 5:17–30," *BR* 15 (1970) 19–31.

41. Paul N. Anderson, "The Having-Sent-Me Father: Aspects of Agency, Encounter, and Irony in the Johannine Father-Son Relationship," Adele Reinhartz (ed.), *Semeia* 85 (1999) 33–57.

prophetic figure, appealing to continuing revelation as a basis for his love-based challenge to religious legalism.[42] Thus, Borgen's work addresses the first level of history, which Martyn's work largely sidesteps.

On the second level of history, however, a fourth Johannine riddle is also addressed, as John's presentation of Jesus as fulfilling the agency typology of Deut 18:15–22 also *casts light upon later engagements in the history of the Johannine situation.* Whether Johannine Christianity flowered in Ephesus, Alexandria, or elsewhere, it is without question that tensions between Jesus adherents and local synagogue leaders in Greco-Roman settings would have arisen, especially over convictions that Jesus was the Messiah/Christ and Son of the Father. Here we see a shift from an emphasis upon Mosaic observance of Sabbath-law to a Mosaic emphasis on monotheism. However the *Birkat ha-Minim* may have originated,[43] it certainly came to function as a means of disciplining perceived ditheism in the name of Jewish monotheism. Ironically, in the leveraging of Mosaic authority on the Shema ("Hear, O Israel: The LORD our God is one LORD" [Deut 6:4 RSV]), the Johannine tradents defended their convictions on the basis that the Scriptures point to Jesus, and that Moses wrote of him (John 5:39, 46). Therefore, in showing multiple times and ways that God's word was fulfilled in Jesus, including the fact that his word came true and thus confirming the Mosaic typology, the Jewish leaders inconceivably refused to believe. Thus, like the chained prisoners in Plato's allegory of the cave, they refuse to embrace the light, for that would expose the reality of their understandings and platforms being based on scaffolding of human origin rather than the divine (John 1:10–13; 3:18–21).[44] The fullest irony comes as the religious leaders who accused Jesus earlier of blasphemy commit the same at the crucifixion: chanting that they have no king but Caesar (John 8:59; 19:15).

---

42. In these ways, John's story of Jesus receives a corroborative impression from the Synoptics. Not only is Jesus presented as the Son who is sent from the Father to do God's bidding in Mark 12:1–12, but the emphasis upon the revelatory work of the Spirit is also clear in Mark 13:11 and Luke 12:12. Thus, Jesus's assertion that all will be "taught by God" in John 6:45 embraces a pneumatic Mosaic tradition sounded in Num 11:29 and in the citing of Isa 54:13. Anderson, *Christology*, 206–7.

43. As an alternative to the Martyn hypothesis, Jonathan Bernier argues that the *Birkat* was early (ca. 30 CE), in Jerusalem, and politically targeted—challenging Galilean messianic movements, not a theological motivation primarily: *Aposynagōgos and the Historical Jesus in John: Rethinking the Historicity of the Johannine Expulsion Passages*, BINS 122 (Leiden: Brill, 2013).

44. Anderson, *Christology*, 197.

Responses to Borgen's *Bread from Heaven* and Further Developments

The responses to Borgen's monograph were strongly favorable from the beginning, albeit with a few questions here and there. Virtually all of the major reviews directly following its publication heralded it as a major contribution in elucidating the Jewish background and operation of the Fourth Gospel.[45] Particular concerns were expressed regarding other Jewish sources that could have been accessed, or studies that might have been engaged more fully,[46] but overall the reviews felt the work was compelling.[47] J. Louis Martyn describes Borgen's work as "breathtakingly ingenious" and believes Borgen's Jewish midrashic case to be well established. Not surprisingly, though, Martyn takes issue with Borgen on whether the admonition on eating and drinking the flesh and blood of Jesus was aimed at a docetic target rather than a Jewish one: "Jews who lodge a demand on orthodox typology."[48] Martyn thus argues for a largely singular focus of engagement in the Johannine situation—leaders of the local Jewish synagogue. According to Barnabas Lindars, "The thorough treatment of the Johannine ideas and the Christological teaching of the discourse makes this a book which no serious student of the Fourth Gospel can afford to neglect."[49]

---

45. Major reviews of Borgen's *Bread from Heaven* include Sverre Aalen, *NTT* 67 (1966) 227-60; B. E. Gärtner, *JBL* 86 (1967) 244-45; Albert Vanhoye, *Biblica* 48 (1967) 469-70; Rudolf Schnackenburg, *BZ* 12 (1968) 143-45; George Dunbar Kilpatrick, *TZ* 23 (1967) 439-41; Barnabas Lindars, *JTS* 18 (1967) 192-94; J. Louis Martyn, *JBL* 12 (1967) 143-45; Marie-Emile Boismard, *RB* 74 (1967) 140-41; Gerhard Delling, *TLZ* 92 (1967) 426.

46. George Kilpatrick (*TZ* 23:6, 1967) mentions alternative bread associations: ambrosia in the writings of Homer, the fruit of the tree of life in the Gilgamesh Epic, and the theme of bread in Joseph and Aseneth; Barnabas Lindars (*JTS* 18:1, 1967) comments on the value of J. W. Bowker's essay for Borgen's study: "The Origin and Purpose of St. John's Gospel," *NTS* 11 (1964) 398-408.

47. Schnackenburg (*BZ* 12 [1968] 143-45) and Boismard (*RB* 74 [1967] 140-41) feel the case is strong, and in the extensive doctoral critique by Jacob Jervell and Sverre Aalen (*NTT* 67 [1966] 227-60), Jervell feels that the establishing of a primary Jewish backdrop of John does not preclude Gnostic influence altogether, and Aalen is not convinced about Borgen's internal-external inferences regarding the opponents.

48. Martyn (*JBL* 12:1, 1967) rejects the linking of 1 John and the Gospel of John, and therefore questions the presence of Docetists in the Johannine situation. On this score, however, Martyn seems invested in consolidating the Johannine adversaries into a monolithic Jewish threat rather than seeing a more realistic diversity of dialectical targets in the evolving Johannine situation.

49. Lindars, review of *Bread from Heaven* (*JTS* 18:1, 1967) 194.

A particularly pointed critique of Borgen's work came from Georg Richter, who asserted (following Bultmann) that John 5:51c–58 was indeed a redactor's insertion, as its eucharistic thrust was at odds with the evangelist's christocentric thrust, highlighted in John 20:31. To this critique, Borgen responded that the theme of "belief" is likewise missing from vv. 41–51b, and that the theme of "life" was present at least five times in vv. 51c–58 as well as in vv. 33–51b. Borgen thus argues that Richter is inconsistent in his defining of what is christological in John and what is not, and his championing the unity of John 6 was affirmed by both Schnackenburg and Dunn.[50] Appreciation for Borgen's work over the years is expressed in the eighteen essays comprising his Festschrift, showing that his work continues to make a difference.[51] Borgen was engaged by several scholars in *Critical Readings of John 6*, and he responds to those and other essays in his preface to the present volume.

In addition to the above works, Peder Borgen has continued to make important contributions to New Testament studies internationally. In terms of Philonic studies, Borgen's work not only illumines the Johannine writings, but it has also proved helpful in understanding the Pauline writings.[52] Borgen has also enlightened understandings of the Jewish character of the Johannine tradition, including its autonomy and relations to the Synoptics.[53] And Borgen has continued to enlighten our understandings of the

---

50. Georg Richter, "Zur Formgeschichte und literarischen Einheit von Joh 6:31–58," *ZNW* 60 (1969) 21–55. See Borgen's response: "*Bread from Heaven*: Aspects of Debates on Expository Method and Form," in his *Logos was the True Light, and Other Essays of the Gospel of John*, Relieff 9 (Trondheim, Norway: Tapir, 1983) 32–46. Concurring with Borgen are Rudolf Schnackenburg, "Zur Rede vom Brot aus dem Himmel: Eine Beobachtung zu Joh 6,52," *BZ* 12 (1968) 248–52, and James D. G. Dunn, "John VI—a Eucharistic Discourse?," *NTS* 17 (1971) 328–38.

51. *Neotestamentica et Philonica: Studies in Honor of Peder Borgen*, David E. Aune, Torrey Seland, and Jarl Henning Ulrichsen, eds., NovTSup 106 (Leiden: Brill, 2002).

52. Peder Borgen, *Philo of Alexandria: An Exegete for His Time*, NovTSup 86 (1997; Atlanta: SBL, 2005); "Two Philonic Prayers and Their Contexts: An Analysis of *Who is the Heir of Divine Things (Her.)* 24–29 and *Against Flaccus (Flac.)* 170–75," *NTS* 45 (1999) 291–309; "Philo's *Against Flaccus* as Interpreted History," in Karl-Johan Illman et al. (eds.), *A Bouquet of Wisdom: Essays in Honour of Professor Karl-Gustav Sandelin* (Turku, Finland: Åbo Akademi University Press, 2000) 41–57; "The Gospel of John and Philo of Alexandria," in J. H. Charlesworth and M. A. Daise (eds.), *Light in a Spotless Mirror: Reflections on Wisdom Traditions in Judaism and Early Christianity* (London: Continuum, 2003) 45–76.

53. Peder Borgen, "Observations on the Targumic Character of the Prologue of John," in *Logos Was the True Light*, 13–20; "Observations on the Midrashic Character

Johannine situation, including the challenges faced by Jewish populations in the Greco-Roman world, living under the Roman Empire in the late first century CE.[54] Along these lines, several movements in scholarship are evident.

First, given that the Jewish character of John's ethos is affirmed by Borgen's work, implications also call for better understandings of the character of what Daniel Boyarin describes as "Hellenistic Judaisms" in the early Christian era. In drawing in the works of Philo and the midrashim, the writings of Paul, John, and Hebrews can be seen as "prima facie evidence for a Hellenistic Jewish cultural koine, undoubtedly varied in many respects but having some common elements throughout the eastern Mediterranean."[55] Just because Hellenistic elements adorn a New Testament text, this does not imply a separation from Judaism. Rather, it reflects developments within first-century CE Judaism itself, "as the Palestinian method of interpreting Scripture."[56] Given the fluidity of interpretation, connections between John 6:31-58 are not simply tied to Exod 16:4, but they appear to have

---

of John 6," in ibid., 23-31; "Some Jewish Exegetical Traditions as Background for Son of Man Sayings in John's Gospel (Jn 3,13-14 and Context)," in Marinus de Jonge (ed.), *L'Évangile de Jean* (Leuven: Leuven University Press) 243-58; "The Use of Tradition in John 12:44-55," NTS 26 (1979) 18-35; "John and the Synoptics: Can Paul Offer Help?," in Gerald F. Hawthorne and Otto Betz (eds.), *Tradition and Interpretation in the New Testament: Essays in Honour of E. Earle Ellis for His 60th Birthday* (Grand Rapids: Eerdmans, 1988) 80-94; "The Independence of the Gospel of John: Some Observations," in F. Van Segbroeck et al. (eds.), *The Four Gospels: Festschrift for Frans Neirynck*, BETL 100 (Leuven: Peeters, 1992) 1815-33; "The Scriptures and the Words and Works of Jesus," in Tom Thatcher (ed.), *What We Have Heard from the Beginning: The Past, Present, and Future of Johannine Studies* (Waco: Baylor University Press, 2007) 39-58.

54. "Creation, Logos and the Son: Observations on John 1:1-18 and 5:17-18," *Ex Auditu* 3 (1987) 88-97; *Early Christianity and Hellenistic Judaism* (1996; 2nd ed., Edinburgh: T. & T. Clark, 1998); "The Gospel of John and Hellenism," in R. Alan Culpepper and Clifton Black (eds.), *Exploring the Gospel of John: In Honor of D. Moody Smith* (Louisville: Westminster John Knox, 1996) 98-123; "Emperor Worship and Persecution in Philo's 'In Flaccum' and 'De Legatione ad Gaium' and the Revelation of John," in Hubert Cancik, Hermann Lichtenberger, and Peter Schäfer (eds.), *Geschichte - Tradition - Reflexion: Festschrift für Martin Hengel zum 70. Geburtstag* (Tübingen: Mohr Siebeck, 1996) 3:493-509.

55. Daniel Boyarin, *A Radical Jew: Paul and the Politics of Identity*, Critical Studies in Jewish Literature, Culture, and Society 1 (Berkeley: University of California Press, 1994) 14.

56. James M. Reese, *Hellenistic Influence on the Book of Wisdom and Its Consequences*, AnBib 41 (Rome: Biblical Institute Press, 1970) 96; Martin Hengel, *Judaism and Hellenism: Studies in Their Encounter in Palestine during the Early Hellenistic Period*, John Bowden, trans. (Minneapolis: Fortress, 1974).

engaged other manna-related texts such as Ps 78:24, perhaps reflecting resorting to memory and loose associations with a biblical theme within ongoing homiletical deliveries.[57] Implications of these analyses also suggest that Johannine Christianity in its diaspora setting was less of a sectarian enclave—despite affinities with Qumran writings—and more reflective of faith communities within a cosmopolitan setting. Thus, John's cultic and religious interests should not be seen as attempts to disengage from the world but as markers of seeking to live faithfully within it.[58]

A second development emerging from and alongside Borgen's analysis is the growing consensus that John 6 should be seen as a textual unity rather than an amalgam of disparate sources. (*a*) Because the unity of the discourse itself shows continuity between the themes of manna, bread, eating, and their interpretations, the discourse itself deserves to be seen as a unity.[59] (*b*) Because Borgen sees verses 51–58 not as eucharistic but as primarily antidocetic, there is no need to infer a redactor's addition to the chapter.[60] This analysis thus lifts the discussion of John 6 beyond sacramental-versus-nonsacramental debates, pointing to the implications of a non-suffering Jesus, cohering also with the costly-discipleship implications of a suffering Jesus. If Jesus suffered and died (the very point of the eyewitness testimony in John 19:34–35), so must his followers be willing to do the same. In that sense, John's call to ingest the flesh and blood of Jesus functions in ways entirely parallel with Jesus's question to James and John in Mark 10:38–39 regarding the willingness to drink his cup and be baptized with his baptism. In both cases the call is to martyr-willingness, bolstered

---

57. Maarten J. J. Menken, *Old Testament Quotations in the Fourth Gospel: Studies in Textual Form*, Contributions to Biblical Exegesis and Theology 15 (Leuven: Peeters, 1996) 50–51; Anderson, *Christology*, 202–4.

58. Arguing this case further is Borgen's doctoral student, Kåre Fugsleth, *Johannine Sectarianism in Perspective: A Sociological, Historical, and Comparative Analysis of Temple and Social Relationships in the Gospel of John, Philo and Qumran*, SupNovT 119 (Leiden: Brill, 2005). See also Bruce J. Malina's monograph on the subject: *Palestinian Manna Tradition: The Manna Tradition in the Palestinian Targums and Its Relationship to the New Testament Writings*, AGSJU 7 (Leiden: Brill, 1968).

59. As Borgen had argued earlier: "The Unity of Discourse in John 6," *ZNW* 50:3–4 (1959) 277–78. So also, R. G. Hamerton-Kelly, *Pre-existence, Wisdom, and the Son of Man: A Study of the Idea of Pre-existence in the New Testament* (Cambridge: Cambridge University Press, 2005) 237; see also Pamela Kinlaw, *The Christ Is Jesus: Metamorphosis, Possession, and Johannine Christology*, Academia Biblica 18 (Leiden: Brill, 2005) 145.

60. Maarten J. J. Menken, "John 6,51c–58: Eucharist or Christology?," *Biblica* 74 (1993) 1–26; cf. also Dunn, "John VI—a Eucharistic Discourse?"

by eucharistic imagery, rather than a cultic requirement as the measure of such.[61] (c) Therefore, in John 6 we have an expansion upon the ministry of Jesus in ways that show a third traditional memory of the feeding in the wilderness, a sea crossing, debates over meanings, and the confession of Peter—alongside the traditions underlying Mark 6 and 8.[62] In that sense, John's traditional unity merits consideration alongside Mark's narrative as an autonomous reflection on the ministry of Jesus in its own right. Thus, here we have not primarily an exegetical expansion upon a biblical text, but a homiletical reflection upon the ministry of Jesus, making use of biblical texts and their interpretations along the way. In J. Louis Martyn's analysis, the point of John 6:31 is not to overcome one exegetical interpretation with another; it represents the overcoming of exegesis with eschatology. It is not Moses who gave, but the Father who gives.[63]

This leads to a third development, which raises questions regarding contributions of the Johannine narrative to understanding more clearly the ministry of Jesus. While going beyond Borgen's inferences here, A. M. Hunter speculates whether the presentation of engagements between Jesus and Palestinian religious leaders might indeed represent the sort of debates that characterized the ministry of the prophet from Nazareth, implying the historical value of John's story of Jesus.[64] As Susan Hylen puts it, "Borgen's extensive analysis of the interpretative traditions around the manna might be used to argue that instead of rejecting these traditions, the author relies on the traditions about manna to say something about the identity and significance of Jesus."[65] Then again, Gail O'Day shows how the Johannine sea-crossing narrative echoes scriptural motifs in ways that could be seen as a narrative embodiment of scriptural motifs.[66] Nonetheless, if John 6 represents an independent memory of Jesus and his ministry, rooted in events and their receptions within the Galilean ministry of Jesus, this would

---

61. Anderson, *Christology*, 110–36, 207–20.

62. R. T. Fortna, *The Gospel of Signs: A Reconstruction of the Narrative Source Underlying the Fourth Gospel*, SNTSMS 11 (Cambridge: Cambridge University Press, 1970).

63. Martyn, *History and Theology* (2003) 123.

64. A. M. Hunter, *According to John* (London: SCM, 1968) 97–98; Craig L. Blomberg, *The Historical Reliability of the Gospels*, 2nd ed. (Downers Grove, IL: InterVarsity, 2014) 235.

65. Susan Hylen, *Allusion and Meaning in John 6*, BZNW 137 (Berlin: de Gruyter, 2005) 31.

66. Gail R. O'Day, "John 6:15–21: Jesus Walking on Water as Narrative Embodiment of Johannine Christology," in Culpepper, *Critical Readings of John 6*, 149–59.

have considerable implications for understanding the Jesus of history as well as the Christ of faith. In Borgen's more recent work, he contributed to the John, Jesus, and History Project regarding Johannine glimpses into a fuller understanding of the ministry of Jesus, especially around the theme of agency. This also has implications for the Son of Man motif in John as well as the Mosaic prophet.[67]

A fourth development resulting from Borgen's work involves his development of the Mosaic agency motif at the center of John's christological thrust. Given that the Father sends the Son in John, that the Son is equal to the Father but also subservient to the Father, and that the Son also sends the Spirit, who commissions Jesus's followers in the world, these themes cohere within the agency motif of Merkabah mysticism. Within that system, the agent is in all ways like the one who sent him, and to respond to the agent is to respond to the sender. Thus, the Father-Son relationship in John reflects not a set of contradictory theologies; the Son is equal to the Father precisely because he does nothing on his own but only that which he has been commissioned to do—an agency motif stemming from Deut 18:15–22. These themes are also accompanied by the Son's judging the world on behalf of the Sender, his reporting back to the Sender, and his later return as a judge of the world. The paradoxical mission of the Son of Man in John thus coheres with Daniel's and Ezekiel's presentation of both a heavenly agent and a humble prophet, and therein lies the origin of several of John's theological tensions. Building upon Borgen's work, Wayne Meeks shows how such a schema is also present within Samaritan traditions, and Jan-A. Bühner shows the centrality of the *shaliach* motif throughout John's narrative.[68] In addition to the many ways in which the outline of Deut 18:15–22 is central to John's presentation of the Father-Son relationship, the Johannine *Logos*-hymn displays the re-crafting of this Jewish biblical motif within a Hellenistic cross-cultural setting.[69]

67. Peder Borgen, "Observations on God's Agent and Agency in John 5–9: Tradition, Exposition, and Glimpses into History," in Paul N. Anderson, Felix Just, and Tom Thatcher (eds.), *John, Jesus, and History*, ECL (Atlanta: SBL, 2016) 3:423–38; published in an alternative form in Peder Borgen, *The Gospel of John: More Light from Philo, Paul and Archaeology*, NovTSup 154 (Leiden: Brill, 2014) 193–218.

68. Meeks, *The Prophet-King*; Jan-A. Bühner, *Die Gesandte und sein Weg im vierten Evangelium: Die kultur- und religionsgeschichtlichen Grundlagen der johanneischen Sendungschristologie sowie ihre traditionsgeschichtliche Entwicklung*, WUNT 2.2 (Tübingen: Mohr Siebeck, 1977); and Borgen, "God's Agent."

69. Paul N. Anderson, "On Guessing Points and Naming Stars: The Epistemological Origins of John's Christological Tensions," in Richard Bauckham and Carl Mosser (eds.),

The Present Volume

As a selection in the Johannine Monograph Series, the renewed availing of Peder Borgen's *Bread from Heaven* to readers in the twenty-first century will undoubtedly continue to inspire creative engagements with multiple features of John's story of Jesus in ways beyond imagination. Borgen's own preface engages several scholars along important lines of interest, and he also explains some of the development in his own thinking along the way. While John's tradition remains autonomous, it is not truncated from those of the Synoptics, and the Jesus traditions underlying Paul's writings might even provide us a clue as to how the Johannine tradition might have developed, as well. The Jewishness of John's narrative, however, continues to grow in its implications for understanding both the character and development of the Johannine situation. In contrast to a singular set of issues elucidated by Martyn's treatment of John 9, Borgen's treatment of John 6 exposes dialogues with a multiplicity of audiences, within the dialectical Johannine situation. In so doing, John's narrative not only casts light upon its subject, Jesus of Nazareth, but it also illumines our understanding of Johannine Christianity as the context in which that memory developed and emerged.

The Gospel of St. John and Christian Theology (Grand Rapids: Eerdmans, 2007) 311-45.

Preface to the New Printing of *Bread From Heaven*

By Peder Borgen

IN THIS PREFACE, GLIMPSES are given from my studies on John in the period after the publication in 1965 of the monograph *Bread from Heaven*.[1] Emphasis is placed on the way in which gospel traditions have been rendered and interpreted, and some central topical questions are also touched upon. My recent book on John and Paul covers several of the points, including some changes in my understanding of such subjects as the relationship between John and the Synoptics and antidocetic motifs in John.[2] In addition, fresh observations from Paul and Philo are contributed to illuminate ways in which traditions and historical events are rendered and interpreted.

One important conclusion is that John's use of gospel traditions is more similar to Paul's use than are the ways they are rendered in the other written Gospels. This and other observations strengthen the understanding that John contains some gospel traditions, which like those in Paul's Letters, are similar but independent of the other written Gospels. The works of other scholars are referred to at various points.

---

1. It would lead too far also to survey research done on Philo of Alexandria in the period after the year 1965.
    Thus, I concentrate on John and refer to Philo in that connection. As for Philo of Alexandria, I may refer to my book, *Philo of Alexandria, an Exegete for His Time,* NovTSup 86 (Leiden: E. J. Brill, 1997). Brief recent presentations are given in D. T. Runia, "The Writings of Philo," in L.H. Feldman, J. L. Kugel, and L. H. Schiffman (eds.), *Outside the Bible; Ancient Writings Related to Scripture.* The Jewish Publication Society (Philadelphia, 2013, Vol. 1) 11-17; and T. Seland (ed.), *Reading Philo; A Handbook to Philo of Alexandria* (Grand Rapids: Eerdmans, 2014).

2. Peder Borgen, *The Gospel of John: More Light from Philo, Paul and Archaeology,* NovTSup 154 (Leiden: E.J. Brill, 2014).

Expositions of a Scriptural Text and of Units of Gospel Tradition

One principle I followed in the analysis of the discourse on the bread from heaven in John 6:31-58 is as follows: "The exegetical paraphrase ... fuses together words and fragments from different traditions into traditional forms and patterns. This method of exegetical paraphrase, then, leads to a dynamic process of new combinations within the framework of tradition."[3] There I demonstrated how this principle was seen to be at work in the exegetical commentary in John 6:32-58 on the text in 6:31, "Bread from heaven I gave them to eat," which refers back to the Old Testament.

Do we find that this principle and similar methods also are at work in the transmission and expository elaborations of gospel traditions? The answer is in the affirmative. A Jesus-logion may serve as a 'text,' as seen in John 12:44-45: "He who believes in me, believes not in me but in him who sent me, and he who sees me sees him who sent me." Then in John 12:46-50 this 'text' receives an expository elaboration.

A main version of this Jesus-logion is rendered in 13:20: "he who receives any one whom I send receives me, and he who receives me receives him who sent me." It is important to note that this Jesus-logion has close parallels in Matt 10:40, Mark 9:37, and Luke 9:48. Furthermore, the case story on Jesus healing the lame man in John 5:2-9 serves as a 'text' that is developed further in the narrative. In the subsequent expository exchange (5:10-18), sentences and words from the 'text' are repeated almost verbatim and then interpreted further. In verses 10-13, the sentence, "take up your pallet, and walk" (ἆρον τὸν κράβαττόν σου καὶ περιπάτει, in v. 8 and also in v. 9) is repeated and paraphrased. In verses 14-16, the words "was healed" (ἐγένετο ὑγιὴς) in v. 9 (cf. v. 6) are repeated and paraphrased. Finally, in verses 17-18, the speaking and acting person in the story, Jesus, is the focal point of the commentary. The term "Sabbath" (σάββατον) in v. 9 is repeated in each of the three parts of the commentary, in vv. 10, 16, and 18.

It is important that, in this connection, a reference to Paul can be made. Thus, already at the time of Paul, the gospel tradition had such authority that words by Jesus could serve as a 'text' to be followed by a subsequent exegetical interpretation. In 1 Cor 7:10-11 the Jesus-logion on divorce is cited: " ... that the wife should not separate from her husband ... and that the husband should not divorce his wife." Here Paul states explicitly that

---

3. Borgen, *Bread from Heaven*, 59.

he is engaging a saying of the Lord. It serves as a 'text,' which in vv. 12-16 receives a subsequent exegetical exposition made by Paul himself. So also the story of the Last Supper is cited in 1 Cor 11:23-26. Paul tells the readers that he has received this tradition, and also that he already had delivered it to the church in Corinth: "For I received from the Lord what I also have delivered to you." In a subsequent exegetical exposition in vv. 27-34 Paul draws out implications ("Therefore,. . ."; ὥστε,. . .) from the institution of the Lord's Supper in the commentary that follows in vv. 27-34.

Thus, in John's Gospel we find in John 6 both an expository elaboration of a text from the Old Testament (John 6:31-58), and that correspondingly an expository elaboration of a unit from gospel traditions is given, as shown in John 12:44-50. It is then to be shown how such observations can also be of help in analyzing the wider context of the unit on the manna: the Bread-from-Heaven discourse in John 6:31-58.

The Context of John 6:31-58

What about the wider context of the exegetical discourse on "bread from heaven" in John 6:31-58? Actually, it is part of a larger series of comments that are tied to another 'text,' the case story of the healing of the lame man in John 5:1-9. The expository comments in 5:10-18 conclude with two points being made in vv. 17 and 18. These two points are in 5:19-8:59 expanded into a series of exchanges. The point formulated in v. 17 reads: "My Father is working still and I am working" (Ὁ πατήρ μου ἕως ἄρτι ἐργάζεται κἀγὼ ἐργάζομαι). Accordingly, the focus on the topic of the Son and the Father is seen in 5:19-47 and 6:1-71.

The next point is stated in John 5:18: "the Jews sought . . . to kill him" (ἐζήτουν αὐτὸν οἱ Ἰουδαῖοι ἀποκτεῖναι). This phrase is not repeated in the remaining part of chapter 5, nor in chapter 6, but in John 7:1 one meets again the words from 5:18, and this phrase and related formulations are repeated and discussed throughout chapters 7-8:

- 7:1, The Jews sought to kill him (ἐζήτουν αὐτὸν οἱ Ἰουδαῖοι ἀποκτεῖναι), discussed in 7:1-13.
- 7:19, "Why do you seek to kill me?" (τί με ζητεῖτε ἀποκτεῖναι;); 7:20, "Who is seeking to kill you?" (τίς σε ζητεῖ ἀποκτεῖναι;), 7:14-24.
- 7:25, "Is not this the man whom they seek to kill?" (Οὐχ οὗτός ἐστιν ὃν ζητοῦσιν ἀποκτεῖναι).

- 7:30, So they sought to arrest him (ἐζήτουν οὖν αὐτὸν πιάσαι), 7:25-31.
- 7:32, In order to arrest him. (ἵνα πιάσωσιν αὐτόν), 7:32-36.
- 7:44, Some of them wanted to arrest him (τινὲς δὲ ἤθελον ἐξ αὐτῶν πιάσαι αὐτόν) 7:37-44.
- 7:4-5, "Why did you not bring him?" (Διὰ τί οὐκ ἠγάγετε αὐτόν?) 7:45-52.
- 8:20, No one arrested him, (οὐδεὶς ἐπίασεν αὐτον), 8:12-20.
- 8:22, "Will he kill himself?" (μήτι ἀποκτενεῖ ἑαυτόν), 8:21-30.
- 8:37, " . . . you seek to kill me . . ." (ζητεῖτέ με ἀποκτεῖναι), 8:31-38.
- 8:40, " . . . now you seek to kill me . . ." (νῦν δὲ ζητεῖτέ με ἀποκτεῖναι), 8:39-47.
- 8:59, So they took up stones to throw at him, (ἦραν οὖν λίθους ἵνα βάλωσιν ἐπ' αὐτόν), 8:48-59.[4]

The understanding that these formulations refer back to John 5:18 receives additional support from the observation that John 7:19-25 refers back to the healing story in John 5:5-9, as seen from Jesus' question in 7:19: "Why do you seek to kill me?" and from the words in v. 23: "on the Sabbath I made a man's whole body well."

In John 9 we find another case story: Jesus' healing of a blind man. Here a judicial exchange is built into the framework of the healing story itself,[5] and the closing question by some of the Pharisees near Jesus presses: "Are we also blind?" A comment by Jesus then follows in 10:1-18, where Jesus tells the story of the sheep and the shepherd. This comment by Jesus then causes a division among 'the Jews' in John 10:1-21. A subsequent exchange about Jesus and his works finally takes place in the Temple precinct (10:22ff.). As was the case in 5:18, Jesus is accused for blasphemy: "because you, being a man, make yourself God." (10:33) The point about the attempt to kill Jesus is explicitly stated in 10:31 (Ἐβάστασαν πάλιν λίθους οἱ Ἰουδαῖοι ἵνα λιθάσωσιν αὐτόν) and again in John 10:39 (Ἐζήτουν [οὖν] πάλιν αὐτὸν πιάσαι), forming a larger thematic unity between John 5-10.

4. On the question of forms of trial, see the studies of my former Ph.D. students, T. Seland, *Establishment Violence in Philo and Luke: A Study of Non-Conformity to the Torah and Jewish Vigilante Reactions*, BIS 15 (Leiden: E. J. Brill, 1995); and P. J. Bekken, *The Lawsuit Motif in John's Gospel from New Perspectives. Jesus Christ, Crucified Criminal and Emperor of the World*, NovTSup 158 (Leiden: E. J. Brill, 2014) 23-175.

5. Note that in a different story in Matt 9:1-8, the exchange is an integral part of the healing story itself.

A Pragmatic Concern in John[6]

In addition to the contextual setting of John 6, what is the pragmatic concern running throughout the Gospel of John? In *Bread from Heaven* (pp. 2–3 and 172–92) I saw an anti-docetic motif at work in John 6. I maintained that one aim of John 6:31–58, as well as of the Gospel in general, was to criticize a docetizing tendency that drew a sharp distinction between the spiritual sphere and the external or physical sphere, playing down the unique role of Jesus Christ in history. This point has been challenged by such Johannine scholars as John Painter and Martin Menken;[7] there Menken rightly stresses that the 'Jews' (Jewish leaders?) of John 6:41 and 52 sharply distinguish the spiritual bread from heaven and the man Jesus, but his identification of these Jews with the Docetists does not seem to be justified. The Johannine Jews deny Jesus's heavenly provenance, while the Docetists deny his humanity that culminates in his death.

I agree with Menken's overall understanding, as the 'Jews' were people who knew Jesus' human family. Therefore, they questioned his claim to be the Son of God and the bread that came down from heaven. In a pointed way, this tension is present in the trial, verdict, and execution of Jesus. The claim is that a criminal, publicly crucified, is the heavenly Son of God the Father. John 20:31 is thus to be read against this background: " . . . these [signs] have been written that you may believe that Jesus is the Christ, the Son of God, and that believing you may have life in his name." It is by believing in the criminal who suffered capital punishment, and who, nevertheless or for just that reason, is the Son of God, that people "have life in his name." That indeed is scandalous!

Comments and Reactions

In my analysis of John 6:31-58 in *Bread from Heaven* (pp. 28-98) and in *The Gospel of John: More Light* (pp. 29-39), I showed that these verses were an

---

6. An important subject, which is not dealt with by me here, is the characterization by some scholars that John reflects a sectarian setting. A broad and significant piece of research challenging this inference is performed by my former Ph.D. student, K. S. Fuglseth, in *Johannine Sectarianism in Perspective. A Sociological, Historical, and Comparative Analysis of Temple and Social Relationship in the Gospel of John, Philo, and Qumran*, NovTSup 119 (Leiden: E. J. Brill, 2005).

7. J. Painter, "Jesus and the Quest for Eternal Life," pages 61-94 in R. A. Culpepper (ed.) *Critical Readings of John 6*, BIN 22 (Leiden: E. J. Brill, 1997) 80; and M. J. J. Menken, "John 6:51-58: Eucharist or Christology," pages 183-204 in Culpepper (ed.), 1997, 198-99. The comment made by Menken (199, n. 61) is to the point in Borgen 1965, 183–92.

exposition of a quotation from the Old Testament. This exposition is characterized by midrashic features found in the writings of Philo of Alexandria and in the Palestinian midrashim. Common here is the feature of the systematic paraphrasing of words from Old Testament quotations, interwoven with fragments from haggadic traditions. This understanding has received general and broad acceptance, as can be seen from leading commentaries on the Gospel of John,[8] and both agreements and disagreements are found in the essay of G. Richter and in the monograph by P. N. Anderson.[9] It should be added that Anderson's emphasis on Christology here is important.

In my work on *Bread from Heaven*, I realized that further studies were needed on the christological applications of the idea of agency. Thus, I have done further studies on Jesus as the one sent by God.[10] In 1999 P. N. Anderson did a parallel study, which rightly placed an emphasis on traditions about Moses as the one sent by God.[11]

Gospel Traditions and Interpretations in Paul and John

The question of the relationship between John and the Synoptic Gospels has been a challenge I have felt since my days as a student at The University of Oslo, when I wrote a paper on the subject. For years I maintained that John is based essentially on an independent tradition with some influence from the Synoptic Gospels. John's differences and distinctives led me to the conclusion that John is independent of the other written Gospels. Further

---

8. Cf. R. E. Brown, *The Gospel According to John*, I-XII (Garden City, NY: Doubleday, 1966) 262-303; C. K. Barrett, *The Gospel According to St. John*, London, 2nd ed. (Louisville: Westminster John Knox, 1978) 279-97; B. Lindars, *The Gospel of John* (London: Oliphants 1972) 250-53; R. Schnackenburg, *Das Johannesevangelium*, 4:1 HTKNT (Freiburg: Herder 1965) 53-58; H. Thyen, *Das Johannesevangelium*, HNT 6 (Tübingen: Mohr/Siebeck, 2005) 252-53.

9. G. Richter, "Zur Formgeschichte und literarische Einheit von John 6:31-58," *ZNW* 60 (1969): 21-55; P. N. Anderson, *The Christology of the Fourth Gospel: Its Unity and Disunity in Light of John 6*, WUNT 2.78 (Tübingen: Mohr/Siebeck, 1996; 3rd printing with a new introduction and epilogue, Eugene: Cascade Books, 2010).

10. One of my studies, "God's Agent in the Fourth Gospel," was published in J. Neusner, (ed.), *Religions in Antiquity: in Memory of E.R. Goodenough*, SHR 14 (Leiden: E. J. Brill, 1968) 137-48; more recent studies are reflected in Borgen, *More Light* (2014) 167-78 and 193-218.

11. P. N. Anderson, "The-Having-Sent-Me Father: Aspects of Agency, Encounter, and Irony in the Johannine Father-Son Relationship," Adele Reinhartz (ed.), *Semeia* 85 (1999): 33-57.

observations of agreements between gospel traditions and their interpretations in Paul's Letters and in the Gospel of John, however, have led me to change my mind somewhat in this respect.

These observations are:

1. As shown above, gospel tradition can be cited and serve as a 'text' in such a way that words from the text are repeated and interpreted by means of paraphrase and interpreted with other words. As seen above on 1 Cor 7:10-11, the Jesus logion on divorce is cited as a saying of the Lord, and in vv. 12-16 it receives a subsequent exegetical exposition made by Paul himself. So also the story of the Last Supper is cited in 1 Cor 11:23-26, and an expository paraphrase follows in vv. 27-34. Examples in John include versions of the logion on agency cited in John 12:44-45, with a subsequent exposition in vv. 46-50. The story of the healing of the lame man is rendered in John 5:1-9, and phrases and words from the story are repeated and interpreted in vv. 10-18. Thus, already at the time of Paul's writing, expository methods were in use, similar to those found in John.

2. At various points other insights from Paul's Letters are gained. Of special importance is the christological statement in Phil 2:5-11, where the person and work of Jesus are interpreted within a cosmic setting. Note also 1 Cor 8:4-6. This cosmic setting of the life of Jesus has a parallel application also in John's Prologue (John 1:1-18). Just as Paul seems to draw on a tradition that existed before it is used by him in Phil 2:5-11, so John seems to operate in ways similar within the Fourth Gospel.

3. Also, it should not be overlooked that both Paul and John fuse together traditions on the Lord's Supper and the manna, in 1 Cor 10:3-4 and in John 6:53-58, respectively. Thus, John 6:53-58 resonates with Paul and gives support for the understanding that John is independent relative to the written Synoptic Gospels. This agreement between Paul and John speaks against regarding the eucharistic tradition in John 6:53-58 to be a late development added by an ecclesiastic editor.

4. Moreover, both in John 6:51-58 and 1 Cor 10:16-21 the story of the institution of the Lord's Supper is presupposed, but not rendered.

5. Paul was commissioned as an 'agent'—an apostle—by the risen Jesus, the Lord, in 1 Cor 9 and 15. Correspondingly, the commissioning was extended to the disciples by the risen Lord according to John 20:21-23.

6. Insights gained from archaeology are also of importance in this connection. In an important essay, U. C. von Wahlde writes, "In the Gospel of John, there are thirteen geographical references not mentioned in the other Gospels. If we include in our list those places about which we learn details not mentioned in the other Gospels, the number increases to twenty."[12]

On the question of archaeology, see further the work of J. H. Charlesworth, who claims that "the Fourth Evangelist is exceptional among the four evangelists for his knowledge of pre-70 religious customs and especially of the topography and architecture of Jerusalem."[13] It should be noted that Martin Hengel in 1999 also recognized that John and archaeology illuminate ancient Judaism especially with regard to historical geography and religious feasts. As also confirmed with archaeology, John contains precise historical details for the period between Herod the Great and to the destruction of Jerusalem in the year 70 C.E.[14]

Historical Events as Interpreted in John and Philo.

Philo not only provides running texts and expositions from the Laws of Moses; he also writes *Against Flaccus* and *On Virtues: On the Embassy to Gaius,* that is, treatises on historical events in his own time in the first century of the Christian era. Correspondingly, the four Gospels deal with Jesus and other persons and events in Palestine at the beginning decades of the Christian era. In different ways all of these documents narrate theologically and judicially interpreted history.

All of these documents narrate tragic events, but they also communicate important positive messages to the communities concerned. In Philo's treatise *On the Embassy*, the words "On the Virtues" are used in the title. This historical narrative shows how the Jews were tested in the pogrom

---

12. U. C. von Wahlde, "The Road Ahead—Three Aspects of Johannine Scholarship," pages 343-53 in T. Thatcher (ed.), *What We Have Heard from the Beginning: The Past, Present, and Future of Johannine Studies* (Waco: Baylor University Press, 2007) 351.

13. J. H. Charlesworth, "Jesus Research and Near Eastern Archaeology: Reflections on Recent Developments," pages 37-70 in D. Aune, T. Seland, and J.H. Ulrichsen (eds.), *Neotestamentica et Philonica*, NovTSup 106 (Leiden: E. J. Brill, 2003) 60.

14. M. Hengel, "Das Johannesevangelium als Quelle für die Geschichte des antiken Judentum," pages 293-334 in M. Hengel et al (eds.), *Judaica, Hellenistica et Christiana; Kleine Schriften II*, WUNT 100 (Tübingen: Mohr/Siebeck 1999) 334.

of AD 38-41, how they nonetheless reacted firmly in accordance with the virtues formulated in the Laws of Moses. The fatal punishment of Flaccus corresponded to his crimes against God's people, and his fate showed that God's help to the nation of Israel was not withdrawn.

Correspondingly, the tragic death of Jesus as a crucified criminal—a blasphemer who made himself equal to God—became in John's Gospel the good news and the joyful message about the Risen Lord and God and his sending out disciples as ambassadors. Corresponding positive developments are also narrated in the interpretations of the crucifixion and resurrection of Jesus in the other three Gospels. God's faithfulness is thereby also attested.

It should also be noted that correspondingly to John, Philo has a cosmological prologue to his historical narrative in the treatise *On the Embassy to Gaius*, which also features *The Virtues*. In different ways, both books deal with the question of the divinity and agency of specific humans. Moreover, as stated above, John refers to several geographical locations not mentioned in the other three Gospels. Archaeological excavations have given more direct information of several of the places. They point to the time before the year 70 AD[15]

The Quest of the Historical Jesus

In my research on John, I have concentrated on Scripture, traditions, and interpretation. The question of the historical Jesus has only been touched. My teacher in New Testament back at the University of Oslo, N. A. Dahl, gives this picture of Jesus based mainly on the Gospels: "Jesus acted as a teacher, prophet, exorcist, and healer, but the role of king and prophet may overlap. He acted as an agent of God, with an authority that did not quite fit any category. Both followers and opponents may have thought of him as a messiah, even though he himself did not claim to be *the* prophet or the Messiah."[16]

Thus the title of an agent, an ambassador, allowed people to associate him with various figures and offices. It made way for officials to accuse him of being a royal pretender and to execute him as the 'king' of the Jews. Moreover, this understanding can explain the combination, on the one hand, of Jesus being a Galilean with a lowly background—a man who acted

---

15. See the excellent collection of essays in J. H. Charlesworth (ed.), *Jesus and Archaeology* (Grand Rapids: Eerdmans, 2006).

16. N. A. Dahl, cited by J. H. Charlesworth, *The Messiah: Developments in Earliest Judaism and Christianity* (Minneapolis: Augsburg Fortress, 1992) 402.

violently in the Temple and broke Sabbath laws, and, on the other hand, one who challenged his surroundings with extraordinary authority. Here it is pertinent to reference Philo's stating that those who do not keep the ordinances of the Sabbath and the feasts will incur the censure of the many, and that charges will be brought against them (*Migr.* 88-99).

While Jesus claims prophetic agency in John, his role as the One who is sent by the Father clearly goes beyond that of his being merely a prophet. John ties it to that of being the son of a father: God's Son is God's, the Father's, ambassador.[17] The question of the dating of the Gospel of John is not taken up in this preface. Thus, further deliberations are needed on this topic.

Conclusion

The Gospel of John contains a good number of gospel traditions and interpretations that are independent of the three other written Gospels. Some of the traditions in John overlap with those in the three other Gospels, just as gospel traditions in Paul are engaged in his Letters, especially in the first Letter to the Corinthians. However, John deals with such parallel Gospel traditions in ways that are closer to Paul's usage than to their renderings in the other written Gospels.

Moreover, several other agreements and parallels between John and Paul have also been listed. Of special importance is the observation that already Paul in his First Letter to the congregation in Corinth fuses together traditions on the Lord's Supper and the manna. This operational agreement between John and Paul speaks against regarding the eucharistic section in John 6:51-58 as a late addition made by an ecclesiastic editor.

In my book *More Light* (2014) a beginning advance is made, drawing Philo's treatises *On Virtues: On the Embassy to Gaius* and *Against Flaccus* into the research on the Gospel of John (and the other Gospels). In various ways, these writings spell out positive messages in stories of tragic events. Likewise, just as the Gospel of John begins with a cosmological Prologue, so also does the treatise *On Virtues–On the Embassy to Gaius.*

---

17. Sverre Aalen in an essay, written in Norwegian, characterizes the Christology of all four Gospels in the following way: Jesus "attributes to himself characteristics and functions which in the Old Testament are the prerogative of God himself." (My translation) S. Aalen, *Gud i Kristus* (Oslo, 1986) 42.

PREFACE

The following work deals with central questions in Johannine and Philonic research: 1) sources and traditions, 2) form and style, and 3) origin and interpretation of ideas. The approach is exegetical in two respects: The study is concentrated around a detailed analysis of a few selected passages, which in turn are expositions on parts of the Old Testament.

Most of the research has been undertaken during the years 1958-62 at the University of Oslo under the favorable auspices of the Norwegian Research Council for Science and the Humanities. The Council has also subsidized the printing. My appreciation goes to its officials for their interest in the project.

The connection with the University of Oslo made it possible for me to continue and benefit from relationships with its outstanding teachers and scholars. Most of all, I am indebted to Professor, Dr. Nils A. Dahl, who kindled my interest in the Gospel of John, and whose eminent knowledge, advice and encouragement have guided and inspired me for many years. Professor Dahl also introduced me to the works and ideas of other Scandinavian scholars like H. Odeberg, A. Fridrichsen, K. Stendahl and B. Noack, who together with him represent an approach to Johannine studies akin to the one here advanced.

Besides Professor N. A. Dahl, other professors have made an impact on me in different ways: in the fields of Bible, Church History and Comparative Religion at the University of Oslo, Professor, Dr. Sigmund Mowinckel; Professor, Dr. Arvid Kapelrud; Professor, Dr. Einar Molland; and Professor, Dr. H. Ludin Jansen. The Royal University Library, Oslo, has provided excellent facilities for my research. Other materials have been found in the Royal Danish Library, Copenhagen, the University Library (The Rosenthal Collection), Amsterdam, and the Institutum Judaicum Delitschianum, Münster in Westfalen.

I am grateful to my parents, Mr. and Mrs. O. E. Borgen, who taught me to consider Scripture central in my life and thought. Others to whom I am indebted are: Bishop Odd Hagen and the late Rev., Dr. Alf Lier, both of whom regarded my research fully in accordance with my call as minister in the Methodist Church.

Scholarships from the World Council of Churches, the Crusade Scholarships of the Methodist Church and the Fulbright Scholarships sponsored my graduate studies during the years 1953-56 at Drew University, Madison, N. J., where Dr. H. J. Cadbury and Dr. H. C. Kee were very important to my development.

Dr. M. W. S. Swan, the United States Information Service, Oslo, Dr. G. Snyder, Bethany Theological Seminary, Chicago, Ill. and Dr. G. W. Buchanan, Wesley Theological Seminary, Washington, D. C., all read the manuscript and suggested improvements for its clarity and literary style. My typist, Miss Reidun Sveen, was both diligent and efficient.

I should like to thank the publishers, represented by Dr. W. C. van Unnik and Dr. B. A. van Proosdij, for undertaking the publication of the book and including it in the series Supplements to Novum Testamentum.

Last but by no means least, my thanks are due to my wife, Inger, whose understanding patience and constant encouragement have made the successful completion of this work possible.

Wesley Theological Seminary
Washington, D. C.

August, 1964.

PEDER BORGEN

PREFACE TO THE SECOND EDITION

In view of the discussion of the present work in reviews, commentaries and on-going research, it would not have been out of place for me to have made some modifications to my terminology, and also to have added some comments on the points which have given rise to discussion.

However, I have found no reason for such substantial changes or additions to be made, so as to necessitate a revised edition. A photomechanical reprint of the work is therefore justified, even though this type of reprint only allows for minor textual corrections.

The lines of research incorporated in the present work have been continued and developed in some of my subsequent publications.

Among my studies on the Fourth Gospel, the following might be listed:

1. "God's Agent in the Fourth Gospel", *Religions in Antiquity*, E. R. Goodenough Memorial Volume, edited by J. Neusner, Leiden 1968, 137-48.
2. "Observations on the Targumic Character of the Prologue of John", *New Testament Studies*, 16, 1970, 288-95.
3. "Logos was the true light". *Novum Testamentum*, 14, 1972, 115-30.
4. "Some Jewish exegetical traditions as background for Son of Man sayings in John's Gospel (3, 13-14 and context)," in M. de Jonge (ed.), *L'Évangile de Jean. Sources, rédaction, théologie*, Gembloux 1977, 243-58.
5. "The place of the Old Testament in the formation of New Testament theology, Response", *New Testament Studies*, 23, 1976, 67-75.
6. "The use of tradition in John 12, 44-50", *New Testament Studies*, 26, 1979, 18-35.
7. Reviews of books on John in *Theologische Zeitschrift*, 29, 1973, 52-3; *Biblica*, 55, 1974, 580-3;
   Theologische Literaturzeitung, 101, 1976, cols 127-30; and 105, 1980, cols 357-9.

Among my studies on Philo of Alexandria, some relevant titles are:

1. "Quaestiones et Solutiones, Some observations on the form of

Philo's exegesis", (co-author: Roald Skarsten), *Studia Philonica*, 4, 1976-7, 1-15.
2. "Observations on the theme "Paul and Philo", in *Die Paulinische Literatur und Theology*, edited by S. Pedersen, Århus and Göttingen 1980, 85-102.
3. "Philo of Alexandria", in *Compendia rerum judaicarum ad Novum Testamentum*, Section II, Vol. 2, edited by M. E. Stone, Assen. (in preparation).

Trondheim, Norway
January 1981

PEDER BORGEN

CHAPTER ONE

THE USE OF A HAGGADIC TRADITION

Thesis

This study is based on the fact that Philo and John [1] both interpret the Old Testament, and that in so doing they both expound the pericope on manna—the bread from heaven.

The investigation leads to the following conclusion: In their expositions, both Philo (Mut. 258-260, Leg. all. III 162.168 and Congr. 170.173-174) and John (6, 31-58) paraphrased words from the Old Testament quotations and interwove them with fragments from the haggadah about manna. The main haggadic traditions upon which Philo drew can be identified with certainty; those on which John is dependent can be identified with a great degree of probability. The Palestinian midrashim [2] also interpret Old Testament quotations by means of haggadic traditions, but they tend more to compile traditional units than to create fresh paraphrases of particular fragments (Ch. I).

The expositions of the Old Testament are, moreover, presented according to a common homiletic pattern, comprising Mut. 253-263, Leg. all. III 162-168 and John 6, 31-58. Philo also employed the same pattern elsewhere in his writings, and it occurs frequently in Palestinian midrashim, but in a later and stereotyped form (Ch. II).

There are clear parallels among Philo, John 6, 31-58, and Palestinian midrashim in such details as exegetical method, patterns and terminology, with John resembling the midrashim more than Philo (Ch. III).

---

[1] In this study "John" signifies both the Fourth Gospel and its author. No assumption is implied regarding the identity of the latter.

[2] The terms "Alexandrian Judaism" and "Palestinian Judaism/midrashim/haggadah", etc. are used as neutral designations for two centers and two groups of traditions. The terms are only used for sake of convenience rather than as rigid definitions of principal nature. Whenever the terms occur, they should be understood within their contexts. They do not imply, for example, that all the midrashim were actually written in Palestine.

In the homily of Mut. 253-263 Philo related the Old Testament and haggadic words about the manna to Greek educational ideas about philosophy and encyclia. But Philo retained the common Jewish belief that wisdom is tied to the laws of Moses. He identified manna with the wisdom, and Mek. Ex. 13, 17, similarly, identified manna with Torah. The etymological interpretation of Israel as the visionary people was tied to the empirical Jewish nation. The actual position of Judaism in Alexandria at the time of Philo is reflected in the homily,—more specifically, the relationship between the heavenly philosophy of the synagogue and the (pagan) encyclical education (Ch. IV).

In the homily of Leg. all. III 162-168 Philo linked the Old Testament and haggadic words about the manna to Stoic ideas about a cosmic law, Platonic thought patterns of heaven and earth, soul and body, Greek physical terms and Greek ideas about equality and justice. These ideas were used, however, to interpret the laws of Moses and the Jewish nation and to throw light upon problems facing the Jews in Alexandria as they pursued a pagan career. In spite of ideas about cosmic order and principles, the Jewish concept of a personal God who should be trusted by men, was retained in the homily of Leg. all. III 162-168 (Ch. V).

In the homily of John 6, 31-58 the Old Testament and haggadic words about manna were brought into a fresh combination with haggadic fragments about the gift of Torah at Sinai, with ideas from the wisdom tradition and with halakhic ideas of agency. Eschatological ideas in Palestinian Judaism and in the different parts of the New Testament are in John re-interpreted to place the main emphasis on their present realization, although the perspective of future and past is still held. The homily criticized and was influenced by a gnosticizing tendency to draw a sharp distinction between the spiritual sphere and the external sphere. Consequently, the manna was interpreted as a polemic against a docetic Christology and an understanding of the vision of God which was so general that it played down the importance not only of the external Torah but also of the unique role of Jesus Christ of history. In this way the actual position of the Johannine Church was reflected in the homily. The theophanic ideas and the spiritualizing tendency suggest that the Jewish background of John largely belongs to the early stages of Merkabah mysticism. The Jewish exegetical traditions throughout the homily were interwoven with gospel tradition, as fragments from the institution of the eucharist, etc. (Ch. VI).

Certain underlying principles for the study are of more general nature. The different groups within Judaism in New Testament times had so many features in common that it is impossible to distinguish sharply between "normative Judaism" and "Hellenistic Judaism".[1] Even Philo reflected many of the common features in his exegesis. At certain points, at least, he depended on the (Palestinian) haggadah, and was partly a side-branch of early Merkabah mysticism. In some cases, therefore, Philo's material helps to date the use of midrashic methods and haggadic traditions.

John did not depend upon Philo, but was a parallel phenomenon.[2] John reflects common Jewish features in his exegesis and drew on haggadic and halakhic traditions, especially from early Merkabah mysticism. The method of paraphrase seems to solve the difficult problem of sources both in Philo and John. Both Philo and John interpreted Jewish traditions under influence of non-Jewish thought-categories and ideas. Philo's writings show a rich variety of influences, whereas John mainly reflects a gnosticizing tendency in accordance with similar tendencies in the development of Merkabah. The environment for Philo's writings was the synagogue, whereas John's environment seems to have been a "school" of a church after the break with the synagogue had become a definite fact.

Before considering relevant texts about bread from heaven, it would be helpful for background purposes to review the present state of research as it relates to the use of sources and traditions in Philo's commentaries and the Gospel of John.

---

[1] See similar viewpoints expressed by D. Daube, *The New Testament and Rabbinic Judaism*, (Jordan Lectures 1952), London 1956, p. ix, and E. M. Sidebottom, *The Christ of the Fourth Gospel in the Light of First-Century Thought*, London 1961, pp. 15-16. G. F. Moore, *Judaism in the First Centuries of the Christian Era. The Age of the Tannaim*, I-III, Cambridge, Mass. 1927-1930, incorrectly drew a sharp distinction between "normative Judaism" and "Hellenistic Judaism". So also does Moore's opponent, E. R. Goodenough, *Jewish Symbols in the Greco-Roman Period*, I, New York 1953, especially pp. 11-21.

[2] See the survey on research about John's relationship to Philo in W. F. Howard, *The Fourth Gospel in Recent Criticism and Interpretation*, 4th edition, revised by C. K. Barrett, London 1955, pp. 146-147, 185-186, 259; E. Haenchen, "Aus der Literatur zum Johannesevangelium. 1929-1956", *ThR* XXIII, 1955, pp. 318-324.

The present stage of the research

Research in Philo and John has in common the fact that the literary criticism has failed to solve the problem of sources. It is true that a number of individual sources have been identified in Philo.[1] Attempts to uncover sources on a larger scale in his commentaries on the Pentateuch have not, however, proved successful. When Bousset analyses Philo's work from the viewpoint of content only, his criterion for literary criticism is quite arbitrary. In contrast to Jewish sources, which were rather secular and open to Hellenistic culture, Bousset thinks that Philo's own contribution to his commentaries was (Jewish and) religious in its emphasis.[2]

There is a certain parallelism between Bousset's theory and Bultmann's analysis of the discourses in John. Bultmann finds that gnostic revelatory discourses ("Offenbarungsreden") are the main source. "The Evangelist" commented upon this source and made glosses, and finally a "Redactor" supplied additions to make the Gospel more acceptable to the Church.[3]

There is, however, a basic difference between Bultmann's approach and that of Bousset. While Bousset puts the main emphasis on differences in content, Bultmann emphasizes criteria of style and linguistic characteristics.[4] As a preliminary study to his analysis of John, Bultmann applied this method to 1 John and found there the revelatory source and the added comments and glosses.[5]

---

[1] P. Wendland, "Eine doxographische Quelle Philo's," *SAB*, Berlin 1897 II, pp. 1074-1079; H. von Arnim, *Quellenstudien zu Philo von Alexandria*, *PhU* XI, Berlin 1888; cf. M. Apelt, *De rationibus quibusdam quae Philoni Alexandrino cum Posidonio intercedunt*, Lipsiae 1907.

[2] W. Bousset, *Jüdisch-Christlicher Schulbetrieb in Alexandria und Rom. Literarische Untersuchungen zu Philo und Clemens von Alexandria, Justin und Irenäus*, FRLANT, N.F. VI, (G.R. XXIII), Göttingen 1915, especially pp. 15, 65, 74, 80-83, 153.

[3] See R. Bultmann, *Das Evangelium des Johannes*, Meyer II, 11th ed., Göttingen 1950; cf. surveys, as in W. F. Howard, *Criticism*, pp. 166 f.; Ph.-H. Menoud, *L'évangile de Jean d'après les recherches récentes*, Cahiers III, 2nd ed., Neuchâtel/Paris 1947, pp. 17 ff.

[4] Cf. R. Bultmann, "Das Johannesevangelium in der neuesten Forschung," *ChrW* XLI, 1927, cols. 502-503; E. Ruckstuhl, *Die literarische Einheit des Johannesevangliums*, SF, N.F. III, Freiburg in der Schweiz, 1951, pp. 20-32.

[5] R. Bultmann, "Analyse des ersten Johannesbriefes," *Festgabe für Adolf Jülicher*, Tübingen 1927, pp. 138-158, where he refers to similar conclusions already reached by E. v. Dobschütz, "Johanneische Studien I," *ZNW* VIII, 1907, pp. 1-8. As in his study of the Gospel, Bultmann also detects interpolations by a Redactor in 1 John: See R. Bultmann, "Die

Bultmann's analyses of John have undergone severe criticism by several scholars. Some attack him primarily for his use of observations on the Johannine style and linguistic characteristics, E. Schweizer and E. Ruckstuhl, for example. These men assert that the stylistic and linguistic uniformity of the Gospel renders it impossible to detect comprehensive bodies of sources within it by stylistic and linguistic methods.[1]

Their position parallels prevailing opinion in Philonic research: The general stylistic and linguistic unity of Philo's commentaries on the Pentateuch makes an over all source analysis impossible.[2]

The stylistic and linguistic unity may seem to discourage any analysis of the material which has been utilized in these works. H. Blauert and S. Schulz have, nevertheless, tried to make the stylistic and linguistic characteristics of John fruitful tools for an analysis of the oral traditions on which the Gospel draws. They think that these stylistic characteristics are due to the author's individual taste. In cases where few such characteristics are present, the reason is that John made use of material from older traditions.[3]

The basic weakness of Blauert's and Schulz's approach is that they take for granted that the stylistic and linguistic characte-

---

kirchliche Redaktion des ersten Johannesbriefes," *In Memoriam E. Lohmeyer*, Stuttgart 1951, pp. 189-201.

[1] E. Schweizer, *EGO EIMI. Die religionsgeschichtliche Herkunft und theologische Bedeutung der johanneischen Bildreden, und Zugleich ein Beitrag zur Quellenfrage des vierten Evangeliums*. FRLANT LVI (N.F. XXXVIII), Göttingen 1939; E. Ruckstuhl, *Einheit*. Cf. Ph.-H. Menoud, *L'évangile de Jean*, pp. 14-16 and W. F. Howard, *Criticism*, pp. 167, n. 1 and 267 ff. See also the more moderate criticism by J. Jeremias, "Johanneische Literarkritik," *ThB* XX, 1941, cols. 33-46. A survey is given by E. Haenchen, *ThR* XXIII, 1955, pp. 305 ff.

[2] Cf. H. Thyen, *Der Stil der Jüdisch-Hellenistischen Homilie*, FRLANT LXV (N.F. XLVII), Göttingen 1955, pp. 8-9.

[3] H. Blauert, *Die Bedeutung der Zeit in der johanneischen Theologie. Eine Untersuchung an Hand von John 1-17 unter besonderer Berücksichtigung des literarischen Problems*, Diss. Tübingen 1954 (typewritten); review in *ThLZ* LXXVIII, 1953, cols. 689-690. S. Schulz, *Untersuchungen zur Menschensohn-Christologie im Johannesevangelium*, Göttingen 1957, pp. 55-59. "Die stilstatistische Methode in ihrer Anwendung auf das Joh-Ev kann sowohl zum Erweis der literarischen Einheit als auch für den Nachweis der Existenz von Überlieferung dienen. Sie ist der stete Trabant—allgemein gesprochen—der überlieferungsgeschichtlichen Analyse und wird damit zu einem unentbehrlichen Hilfsmittel der sachgemässen Unterscheidung von Tradition und Komposition bzw. Interpretation,..." (pp. 58-59). See also S. Schulz, *Komposition und Herkunft der Johanneischen Reden*, BWANT, Fünfte Folge I, (Der ganze Sammlung LXXXI), Stuttgart 1960, p. 9, etc.

ristics they observe are peculiar to the author of the Gospel. Thus Blauert and Schulz fail to discuss the possibility that these characteristics may also themselves be traditional. The relevance of this question was already indicated by Bultmann, however, when he talked about the "homiletic comments" in 1 John and John and admitted that the author of these comments uses many rabbinic phrases.[1]

In his criticism of Bultmann's analysis, B. Noack, on the other hand, argues that the Johannine style belongs to the Johannine tradition. Thus Noack does not draw a distinction between the characteristics of the author and the traditional material which he used. Noack rejects the idea of comprehensive sources behind John, as advanced by Bultmann's analysis. Rather, he thinks in terms of an oral tradition of which the smallest units, the single logia, etc., are basic. Hence, he analyses the structures of these small units from the viewpoint of form.[2]

Two weaknesses with Noack's analysis are apparent. He produces no comparative material showing that the structures of the small units are traditional. And he does not take into account Schulz's suggestion that the traditional material has been reshaped and interpreted to produce John as we know it.

Against this background, then, it becomes important to examine just how units from the tradition actually were used in the time of Philo and John. Fortunately, we are able to demonstrate how a tradition about the manna—common to the Palestinian midrash and Philo—was reduced into fragments, which in turn were built into commentaries on quotations from the Old Testament.

Our first task, then, is to examine the versions of this unit about the manna, and show that it was common to Palestinian midrash and Philo.

---

[1] R. Bultmann, "Analyse," *Festgabe für A. Jülicher*, pp. 142-143 (homiletic comments). With regard to rabbinic phrases, see R. Bultmann, *Evangelium*, p. 29, n. 1; p. 50, nn. 3, 6, 7, etc.; cf. references collected by E. Ruckstuhl, *Einheit*, p. 27, n. 2. On p. 61, n. 4, Ruckstuhl touches this question: "Es wäre natürlich auch noch zu untersuchen, inwieweit die rabbinischen Wendungen einfach exegetische Wendungen sind,...".

[2] B. Noack, *Zur johanneischen Tradition. Beiträge zur Kritik an der literarkritischen Analyse des vierten Evangeliums*, PSSLAa, III, Copenhagen 1954, especially pp. 46, 108-109, 157.

The six relevant texts for the tradition about bread from heaven and earth

Ex. R. 25, 2:

"Another explanation of 'But the Lord, the God of ẓeba'oth' is that He performs His will in the world. When He desires, He brings forth bread from the earth, as it says: 'To bring forth bread out of the earth' (Ps. 104, 14), and brings down water from heaven, as it says, 'And drinketh water as the rain of heaven cometh down' (Deut. 11, 11). Yet when He desired, He brought up water from the earth, for it says: 'Spring up, O well—sing ye unto it' (Num. 21, 17), and made manna [which is bread] come down to Israel from heaven, for it says: 'Behold, I will cause to rain down bread from heaven for you'" (Ex. 16, 4).

Ex. R. 25, 6:

"Among mortals, the water comes from above and the bread from below, but in the case of God we read that the water came from below, namely the well, for it says, 'Spring up, O well', etc. (Num. 21, 17), and the bread came from above, for it days, 'Behold, I will cause to rain bread', etc." (Ex. 16, 4).

Mos. I 201-202:

"Mortals have the deep-soiled plainland given over to them, which they cut into furrows with the plough, and there sow their seed, and perform the other tasks of the husbandman, thus providing the yearly fruits, and through them abundance of the necessaries of life.

But God has subject to Him not one portion of the universe, but the whole world and its parts, to minister as slaves to their master for every service that He wills. So now it has seemed good to Him that the air should bring food instead of water, for the earth too often brings rain. What is the river of Egypt, when every year it overflows and waters the fields with its inroads, but a rain-pour from beneath?"

Mek. Ex. 16, 4:

"Come and see how much beloved the Israelites are by Him by whose word the world came into being. Because they are so much beloved by Him, He made for them a change in the natural order of things. For their sake He made the upper region like the lower and the lower like the upper. In the past the bread came up from the earth and the dew would come down from heaven, as it is said: 'The earth yielding corn and wine; yea, His heavens drop down dew' (Deut. 33, 28). But now things have changed. Bread began to come down from heaven, and the dew came up from the earth, as it is said: 'Behold, I will cause to rain bread from the heaven,' and it says: 'And the layer of dew came up'" (Deut. 33, 14).

Petirat Moses:[1]

"... for thy sake too did I invert the order of heaven and earth, for the order of heaven it is to send down dew and rain, and earth's order is it to produce bread, but thou didst say to Me, 'I do not wish it so, but bid heaven to send down bread, and earth to bring forth water', and I acted accordingly, as it is said: 'I will rain bread from heaven for you' (Ex. 16, 4), and it says: 'Spring up, O well!—Sing to it!'" (Num. 21,17).

Mos. II 267:

"The copy reproduces the original very exactly: for, as God called up His most perfect work, the world, out of not being into being, so He called up plenty in the desert, changing round the elements to meet the pressing need of the occasion, so that instead of the earth the air bore food for their nourishment, and that without labour or travail for those who had no chance of resorting to any deliberate process of providing sustenance."

Versions of the same haggadic tradition

The following four points of agreements between these six units from the Palestinian midrash and the works of Philo show that they are merely different versions of the same haggadic tradition.

a) All six versions tell about bread from heaven and from earth:

Mek. Ex. 16, 4　　הלחם עלה מן הארץ
　　　　　　　　　הלחם יורד מן השמים
Ex. R. 25, 2　　　הוציא לחם מן הארץ
　　　　　　　　　והוריד מן ... מן השמים

---

[1] *Bet ha-Midrasch. Sammlung kleiner Midraschim und vermischter Abhandlungen aus der ältern jüdischen Literatur*, I, 2nd ed., edited by A. Jellinek, Jerusalem 1938, p. 119. The English translation draws upon that of L. Ginzberg, *The Legends of the Jews* III, Philadelphia 1911, p. 428.

Petirat Moses	והארץ להוציא לחם
	השמים יוריד לחם
Ex. R. 25, 6	והלחם מלמטן
	והלחם מלמעלן
Mos. II 267	ἵν' ἀντὶ γῆς ὁ ἀὴρ
	— τροφήν — φέρῃ [1]
Mos. I 201-202	τὸν ἀέρα τροφὴν ἐνεγκεῖν

To be sure, in Mos. I 201-202 only the idea about bread (= food) from heaven (= the air) is listed. This does not mean, however, that the part about bread from earth is absent. The fact is, rather, that this element of the story has been expanded to a broader description of production from earth: "Mortals have the deep-soiled plainland given over to them, which they cut into furrows with the plough, and there sow their seed, and perform the other tasks of the husbandman, thus providing the yearly fruits, and through them abundance of the necessaries of life."

This amplified description of agricultural production is, therefore, but a variant interpretation of the traditional idea about bread from the earth. Our understanding is further supported by Mut. 259, which also uses the traditional parts on bread from heaven and earth, where the idea about bread from the earth is expanded in this way: "The earthly food is produced with the co-operation of husbandmen."[2]

Therefore all six versions contain the element of bread from heaven and from earth.

b) Another agreement among these texts is the fact that all the versions, apart from Mos. II 267, mention water from heaven and from earth:

Mek. Ex. 16, 4	והטל יורד מן השמים
	והטל עולה מן הארץ
Ex. R. 25, 2	והוריד מים מן השמים
	העלה מים מן הארץ
Petirat Moses	שמים להוריד טל ומטר
	והארץ תוציא מים

---

[1] As an isolated fragment, Mos. II 258 has these parts about bread from heaven and from earth: τροφῆς, ἣν γῆ μὲν οὐκ ἤνεγκε —, ὤμβρησε δ' οὐρανὸς — καρπὸν αἰθέριον ("and this food was not produced by the earth, ... but heaven rained down... a celestial fruit....").

[2] See discussion of Mut. 259 on page 106.

Ex. R. 25, 6   המים מלמעלן
                      המים מלמטן

Mos. I 201-202   τὸν ἀέρα — ἐνεγκεῖν — ὕδατος,
ἐπεὶ καὶ γῆ πολλάκις ὑετὸν
ἤνεγκεν, — ὑετός ἐστι κάτωθεν
ἐπινίφων.

As in the case of the bread element, there are certain peculiarities in Mos. I 201-202, due to interpretation of tradition. The lack of rain and the presence of the Nile made it necessary for Philo, who lived in Egypt, to re-interpret the element of rain in the tradition: "So now it has seemed good to Him that the air should bring food instead of water, for the earth too often brings rain. What is the river of Egypt, when every year it overflows and waters the fields with its inroads, but a rainpour from beneath?"

c) All six versions also agree in making heaven and earth interchange their normal functions when the manna came down: Mek. Ex. 16, 4 distinguishes between the past (when the bread came from the earth and the dew from heaven) and now (when just the opposite happens because the upper region became like the lower and the lower like the upper). Mos. II 267 relates how the elements were changed, so that the air, instead of the earth, bore food. Similarly Petirat Moses describes how God inverted the functions of heaven and earth, while Mos. I 201-202 says that the air brought food instead of water. Finally, Ex. R. 25, 6 states that although mortals are bound to the regular functions of heaven and earth, God can turn them up side down, and Ex. R. 25, 2 stresses God's sovereign will in the world to the effect that He can make heaven and earth interchange their functions.

These close agreements at the very core of the six versions show that they all are different manifestations of the very same tradition.

d) This conclusion is further confirmed by the fact that there are additional agreements between Ex. R. 25, 6 and Mos. I 201-202. Both versions employ the term "from below", מלמטן κάτωθεν, meaning "from the earth". And they both exhibit the pattern of contrast between mortals and God:

Ex. R. 25, 6   .... בבשר ודם
                      .... והקדוש ברוך הוא אינו כן אלא

Mos. I 201-202   θνητοῖς μὲν —
θεῷ δ' οὐ — ἀλλ' —

Having thus shown that we have six versions of the same unit of tradition, we shall move on to see that this tradition probably came from Palestine and seems to have been taken over from there by Philo, directly or indirectly.

Certain pecularities in Philo's versions indicate that this tradition did not originate from Egypt but came from Palestine. As we have already noted, to Philo, in Egypt, it was impossible to think of rain from heaven as the common order of nature because Egypt has so little rain. Since, however, the tradition from Palestine gave this usual picture, Philo in Alexandria had either to omit the parts about the rain, as he did in Mos. II 267, or re-interpret them rather awkwardly, as in Mos. I 201-202.

In Mos. I 202 Philo writes: "So now it has seemed good to Him that the air should bring food instead of water, for the earth too often brings rain. What is the river of Egypt, when every year it overflows and waters the fields with its inroads, but a rainpour from beneath?" By underscoring the words referring to the water from earth in four of the other versions, we discover the following: ἐπεὶ καὶ γῆ πολλάκις ὑετὸν ἤνεγκεν. ὁ γὰρ ἐν Αἰγύπτῳ ποταμὸς καθ' ἕκαστον ἐνιαυτὸν ταῖς ἐπιβάσεσι πλημμυρῶν ὅταν ἄρδῃ τὰς ἀρούρας, τί ἕτερον ἢ ὑετός ἐστι κάτωθεν ἐπινίφων; Philo added the word "often" (πολλάκις) to the traditional words about water from the earth, to account for the frequent flooding of the Nile. More important, he interpolates a direct statement about the Nile and connects it with a traditional reference to rain by the interpretative phrase "what is... but", τί ἕτερον ἢ. The reference to the Nile and the lack of rain in Egypt prevent him from talking about rain "from above" (ἄνωθεν, cf. Ex. R 25, 6 מלמעלן), but forces him to write awkwardly of the Nile as rain "from below" (κάτωθεν, cf. Ex. R. 25, 6 מלמטן).

In several places, actually, Philo shows that he is well aware of the differences in climatic conditions between Egypt and other countries. It is of significance to notice that in some of these places he re-interprets haggadic fragments about water from heaven and earth. He then advocates the interpretation that water from the earth refers specifically to Egypt, while the water from heaven refers to the other countries.

In Mos. I 114-115 Philo discusses the fact that Egypt is almost the only country which has no winter. The reason may be that it is

not far from the torrid zone. Then, in § 116-117, he continues:
"Another possible reason is that winter is unneeded in Egypt. For the river, by making a lake of the fields, and thus producing the yearly crops, serve the purpose of rainfall. And, indeed, nature is no wastrel in her work, to provide rain for a land which does not want it. At the same time she rejoices to employ her science in works of manifold variety, and thus out of contrarieties form the harmony of the universe. And therefore she supplies the benefit of water to some from heaven above, to others from the springs and rivers below."

Philo's concluding sentence here is a re-interpretation of a fragment from our tradition about bread from heaven and from earth. By underscoring the words which are parallel to words in this tradition we see the similarity most strikingly: καὶ διὰ τοῦτο τοῖς μὲν ἄνωθεν ἐξ οὐρανοῦ τοῖς δὲ κάτωθεν ἐκ πηγῶν τε καὶ ποταμῶν παρέχει τὴν ἐξ ὕδατος ὠφέλειαν. Ex. R. 25, 2 and Mek. Ex. 16, 4 have the phrase "from heaven", מן השמים, as has also this sentence from Mos. I 117, ἐξ οὐρανοῦ. All the other underscored words have parallels in Ex. R. 25, 6: המים מלמעלן .... המים מלמטן זו הבאר ("the water comes from above ... the water came from below, namely the well, ..."). Thus, to the traditional notion of the springs (cf. Ex. R. 25, 6 "the well"), Philo living in Egypt added "rivers", so that the tradition could be applied to the Nile.

The same re-interpretation of fragments from our tradition is also found in Fug. 180:

ὁ γὰρ χειμῶνος ταῖς ἄλλαις χώραις οὐρανός, τοῦτ' Αἰγύπτῳ θέρους ἀκμάζοντος ὁ Νεῖλός ἐστιν. ὁ μὲν γὰρ ἄνωθεν ἐπὶ γῆν τὸν ὑετὸν ἀποστέλλει, ὁ δὲ κάτωθεν ἄνω, τὸ παραδοξότατον, ὕων ἄρδει τὰς ἀρούρας.

("For what the sky is in winter to other countries, this the Nile is to Egypt in the height of summer: the one sends the rain from above upon the earth, the other, strange to say, rains up from below and waters the fields.") The terms ἄνωθεν — κάτωθεν are the same as מלמעלן .... מלמטן in Ex. R. 25, 6. The other underscored words are close to the version in Petirat Moses: שמים להוריד טל ומטר .... והארץ תועיא מים ("heaven ... to send down dew and rain—and earth to bring forth water").[1]

---

[1] Cf. also the discussion of the Nile in Mos. II 195, a passage which is included in the statements about the Nile collected by S. Sauneron, "Un

The most important conclusion from the study of passages in Philo (Mos. I 201-202 and II 267) and Palestinian midrashim (Ex. R. 25, 2.6; Mek. Ex. 16, 4 and Petirat Moses) has already been stated: all these passages draw on the same haggadic tradition about bread and rain from heaven and earth. Now a minor observation can be added: the haggadic tradition reflects the view that rain from heaven is the common order of nature. To Philo, on the other hand, the common order of nature is rather the difference between Egypt —with the Nile and no rain—and other countries—with rain from heaven. In different ways Philo adjusted the haggadic tradition to his own outlook,—an observation which suggests that at this point Philo is dependent upon Palestinian haggadah. [1]

---

thème littéraire de l'antiquité classique: Le Nil et la pluie," *BIAO* LI, 1952, pp. 41-48.

[1] A survey of the debate on the question of Philo's dependence on Palestinian traditions is found in S. Sandmel, "Philo's Place in Judaism: A Study of Conceptions of Abraham in Jewish Literature," *HUCA* XXV, 1954, pp. 213-234. Cf. the brief summary in P. Borgen, "Bröd fra himmel og fra jord. Om haggada i palestinsk midrasj, hos Philo og i Johannesevangeliet," *NTT* LXI, 1960, p. 218 and the comprehensive surveys of Philonic research in W. Völker, *Fortschritt und Vollendung bei Philo von Alexandrien. Eine Studie zur Geschichte der Frömmigkeit*, *TU*, 4th S., IV, Leipzig 1938, pp. 1-47, and L. H. Feldman, "Scholarship on Philo and Josephus (1937-1959)," *CW* LIV, 1960/1961, pp. 281-291, and LV, 1961/1962, pp. 36-39. See also R. Marcus, "Recent Literature on Philo (1924-1934)," *Jewish Studies in Memory of G. A. Kohut*, New York 1935, pp. 463-491, and *Les oeuvres de Philon d'Alexandrie*, by R. Arnaldez, J. Pouilloux and C. Mondésert, I, Paris 1961, pp. 87-94. The problem is posed in a pointed way by M. M. Kaplan in a discussion of the parallels between Philo and Palestinian haggadah: "But what of those parallels which are genuine and unmistakable? There is no point to the existence of such parallels unless it can be shown that they could not have been arrived at independently. This certainly the author [E. Stein] does not attempt to do, because the evidence is all to the contrary. For in all cases of intrinsic parallelism there is no need of assuming interaction between Palestinian and Alexandrian exegetes after the Bible was translated into Greek." M. M. Kaplan, "Philo and the Midrash," (review of E. Stein, *Philo und der Midrasch. Philos Schwaerung der Gestalten des Pentateuch verglichen mit der des Midrasch*, *ZAW* Beih. LVII, Giessen 1931) in *JQR*, N.S. XXIII, 1932/1933, p. 289. In our analysis of the parallels between Mos. I 201-202 and II 267 and Palestinian midrashim, we have given the evidence which Kaplan asks for and shown that Philo at these and other places draws on the very same tradition as also found in Palestinian haggadah. In the hitherto unresolved debate on this central question in Philonic research, we have thus established a point of certainty. See P. Borgen, *NTT* LXI, 1960, pp. 218-226. It is important that N. A. Dahl, "Manndraperen og hans Far (Joh 8: 44)," *NTT* LXIV, 1963, pp. 140 f. shows Philo to have a tradition about Cain in common with the Palestinian Targum. Cf. also H. Köster, "Die Auslegung der Abraham-Verheissung in

Another significant conclusion can be deduced. Since Ex. R. 25, 2.6; Mek. Ex. 16, 4 and Petirat Moses are versions of the same tradition also known by Philo, the kernel of these versions must go back at least to the time of Philo, that is, to the beginning of the Christian era. And since both in Philo and in the Palestinian midrash versions can be isolated as independent units, they seem to be written manifestations of the same story in oral tradition.

Fragments of the haggadic tradition used in Philo's exegesis

We have seen how versions of a story from tradition have been written down, if necessary with slight omissions and interpretative changes and additions. We also saw that Philo could incorporate fragments of this tradition in new contexts. We shall now observe how Philo, by the exegetical method of paraphrase, weaves fragments from this tradition together with words and phrases from Old Testament quotations. An analysis of John 6, 31-58 will show that there, too, fragments from haggadic units are interwoven with an exegetical paraphrase of the Old Testament quotation. Similar investigations in the Palestinian midrash indicate that this exegetical method was common to Jewish exegesis in general.

For his part, Philo clearly used fragments from the tradition about bread from heaven and from earth in the following three passages:

Mut. 258-260 a:

"Why then need you still wonder that God showers virtue without toil or trouble, needing no controlling hand but perfect and complete from the very first? And if you would have further testimony of this can you find any more trustworthy than Moses, who says that while other men receive their food from earth, the nation of vision alone has it from heaven? The earthly food is produced with the co-operation of husbandmen, but the heavenly is sent like the snow by God the solely self-acting, with none to share his work. And indeed it says 'Behold, I rain upon you bread from heaven' (Ex. 16, 4). Of what food can he rightly say that it is rained from heaven, save of heavenly wisdom which is sent from above on souls which yearn for virtue by Him who sheds the gift of prudence in rich abundance, whose grace waters the universe, and chiefly so in the holy seventh which he calls the Sabbath?"

Hebr. 6," *Studien zur Theologie der Alttestamentlichen Überlieferungen*, Festschrift für G. von Rad, Neukirchen 1961, pp. 95-109.

Congr. 170. 173-174:

170: "'... and He afflicted thee and made thee weak by famine and fed thee with manna...' (Deut. 8, 3).

173: And this is conformed by the words that follow, 'He fed thee with the manna.' He who provided the food that costs no toil or suffering, the food which without the cares and pains of men came not from the earth in the common way, but was sent, a wonder and a marvel from heaven for the benefit of those who should use it—can we rightly speak of Him as the author of famine and affliction? Should we not on the contrary call Him the author of thriving and prosperity and secure and ordered living? 174: But the multitude, the common herd, who have never tasted of wisdom, the one true food of us all, think that those who feed on the divine words live in misery and suffering, and little know that their days are spent in continued well-being and gladness."

Leg. all. III 162.168:

162: "That the food of the soul is not earthly but heavenly, we shall find abundant evidence in the Sacred Word. 'Behold I rain upon you bread out of heaven, and the people shall go out and they shall gather the day's portion for a day, that I may prove them whether they will walk by My law or not' (Ex. 16, 4).

You see that the soul is fed not with things of earth that decay, but with such words as God shall have poured like rain out of that lofty and pure region of life to which the prophet has given the title of 'heaven'. 168: Such men have the privilege of being fed not with earthly things but with the heavenly forms of knowledge."

In all three passages we find the traditional elements of bread from heaven and from earth:

Mut. 258-259

ἀπὸ γῆς — τὰς τροφάς — ἀπ' οὐρανοῦ —
ταῖς — ἀπὸ γῆς — τὰς ἀπ' οὐρανοῦ —.
ἀπ' [οὐρανοῦ] τροφὴν (Mss ἀποτροφήν)[1]. — τὴν οὐράνιον

---

[1] Although Markland's suggested reading ἀπ' οὐρανοῦ τροφὴν better fits the thesis that words from the Old Testament quotation are interwoven with fragments from the haggadah, the reading of the Mss, ἀποτροφήν, does not disturb it, since the employment of such fragments in Mut. 258-260 is still evident. For the readings of Markland and of the Mss, see *Philonis Alexandrini opera quae supersunt*, ed. L. Cohn and P. Wendland, III, Berlin 1898, p. 201.

Congr. 173

— τὴν — τροφὴν — ἐκ γῆς — ἀπ' οὐρανοῦ

Leg. all. III 162 and 168

— γήινοι — οὐράνιοι αἱ — τροφαί —.
— γηίνοις — οὐρανὸν —.
— γηίνοις — ἐπουρανίοις —.

The quotations from Ex. 16, 4 about the manna in Mut. 259 and Leg. all. III 162, and from Deut. 8, 3 in Congr. 170, do not explain why in all these places the bread from earth is closely tied to the idea of manna from heaven. The reason for this correlation is that the elements belong closely together in the tradition of haggadah. They are fragments from the story about bread from heaven and earth.

It is worth noticing that these fragments are in closer agreement with some versions in the Palestinian midrash than with those in Mos. I 201-202 and II 267. While the latter name the correlatives earth and air, these fragments use the words earth and heaven, just as in Ex. R. 25, 2 and Mek. Ex. 16, 4, (cf. Peṭirat Moses). Thus Ex. R. 25, 2 has the same phrasing as the fragments in Mut. 258-259 and Congr. 173: לחם מן הארץ....מן השמים. In Leg. all. III 162 and 168 and Mut. 259 the words have been given the form of adjectives, earthly ... heavenly.

This suggests that in Mut. 258-259, Congr. 173 and Leg. all. III 162-168 Philo did not take the fragments from the written versions of the tradition in De vita Mosis, but drew upon the oral forms which were closer to the versions from Palestine.

It is interesting to note that Mut. 260 also has the term ἄνωθεν which does not occur in Mos. I 201-202 or II 267, but is found in Ex. R. 25, 6 as מלמעלן. As we have seen, Philo also uses this term in the fragments which are incorporated in Mos. I 117 and Fug. 180.[1]

One peculiar agreement between Mut. 258, Congr. 173 and Mos. II 267, is not to be found in the versions rendered in the Palestinian midrashim.

Mut. 258

ἄπονον καὶ ἀταλαίπωρον

---

[1] See p. 12.

Congr. 173

τὴν ἄπονον καὶ ἀταλαίπωρον τροφὴν

Mos. II 267

τροφὴν ἄπονον — καὶ ἀταλαίπωρον
("food ... without labour or travail")

This phrase is hardly an invention of Philo himself, but rather comes from the traditions about the manna. The description of the manna in Wisd. 16, 20 has a similar idea and therefore supports this viewpoint. There it is stated ἕτοιμον ἄρτον ἀπ' οὐρανοῦ — ἀκοπιάτως ("bread ready for use ... from heaven without their toil").[1]

Another similarity between Congr. 174 and Wisd. 16, 25 indicates that there were more traditions about the manna available to Philo than those reproduced in De vita Mosis. In Congr. 174 for instance, Philo qualifies the idea of manna with the uncommon word "all-nurturing", πάντροφος. A different form of the same term is used in Wisd. 16, 25, παντοτρόφος.[2]

So far, then, we have seen 1) that Philo in his exegesis employed fragments from the common tradition about bread from heaven and earth, and 2) that he also used fragments from traditions about the manna apart from this specific tradition as it is written down in the Palestinian midrashim. These other fragments correspond with the passage about the manna in Wisd. 16, 20 ff.

These fragments from the traditions about the manna are interwoven with words and phrases from the Old Testament quotations to form an exegetical paraphrase. This may be seen quite readily by comparing the quotation concerned with parts of its exposition. The fragments from haggadah are indicated by underlining. As

---

[1] Text in *Septuaginta*, ed. A. Rahlfs, II, 4th ed., Stuttgart 1949, p. 370. Translation in R. H. Charles, *The Apocrypha and Pseudepigrapha of the Old Testament in English*, I, Oxford 1913, p. 562. C. L. W. Grimm, *Das Buch der Weisheit*, HAAT VI, Leipzig 1860, p. 268, has seen the correspondence between the phrases in Wisd. 16, 20 and Congr. 173. This correspondence is clear even if ἀκοπιάτως is separated from ἕτοιμον, as Grimm does.

[2] In Wisd. 16, 25 the term seems to refer to the tradition, to which also v. 20 alludes, that the manna could serve as all kinds of food. This tradition is frequent in the Palestinian midrash, as in Ex. R. 25, 3; Yoma 75, etc.; cf. J. Fichtner, *Weisheit Salomos*, HAT, 2nd S. VI, Tübingen 1938, p. 61, and R. H. Charles, *The Apocrypha*, p. 562. Thus, it is probable that the term in Congr. 174 also alludes to this tradition.

can be seen, some words in the fragments are identical with words from the quotations.

Mut. 258-260 quotes Ex. 16, 4: ἰδοὺ ὕω ὑμῖν ἄρτους ἀπ' οὐρανοῦ ("Behold, I rain upon you bread from heaven.") These words (apart from ἰδοὺ and ὑμῖν) are then paraphrased together with the fragments in this way: ἄπονον καὶ ἀταλαίπωρον — ἀπὸ γῆς — τὰς τροφάς, — ἀπ' οὐρανοῦ —. ταῖς — ἀπὸ γῆς — τὰς — ἀπ' οὐρανοῦ —. — ἀπ' [οὐρανοῦ] τροφήν[1] (Mss ἀποτροφήν) — ὕεσθαι — τὴν οὐράνιον — ἄνωθεν —.

Leg. all. III 162 offers a fuller quotation of Ex. 16, 4 of which the relevant parts for our purposes are: ἰδοὺ ἐγὼ ὕω ὑμῖν ἄρτους [ἐκ] τοῦ οὐρανοῦ, καὶ ἐξελεύσεται ὁ λαὸς καὶ συνάξουσι τὸ τῆς ἡμέρας εἰς ἡμέραν, — ("Behold I rain upon you bread out of heaven, and the people shall go out and they shall gather the day's portion for a day.") Most of these words are paraphrased together with the fragments in this way in §§ 162 and 168:

γήινοι — οὐράνιοι αἱ — τροφαί —.
γηίνοις — ἐκ — οὐρανὸν ἐξίτω — ὁ λεὼς —
συναγαγέτω — τὸ τῆς ἡμέρας εἰς ἡμέραν
168: γηίνοις — ἐπουρανίοις.

Finally, in Congr. 170-174 the exegesis is based upon Deut. 8, 3 of which the relevant sentences are: καὶ ἐκάκωσέ σε καὶ ἐλιμαγχόνησέ σε καὶ ἐψώμισέ σε τὸ μάννα ("and He afflicted thee and made thee weak by famine and fed thee with manna ..."). These words are woven together with the fragments in this way:

ἐψώμισέ σε τὸ μάννα. — τὴν ἄπονον καὶ ἀταλαίπωρον
τροφήν — ἐκ γῆς — ἀπ' οὐρανοῦ — λιμοῦ καὶ κακώσεως —;

Thus we have seen how Philo in Mut. 258-260, Leg. all. III 162. 168 and Congr. 170-174 wove fragments from the haggadic tradition about bread from heaven and earth together with words from the Old Testament quotation by means of an exegetical paraphrase.

It now remains to place this conclusions within the framework of Philonic research. Scholars have paid much attention to Philo's exegesis, but mainly from the viewpoint of his allegorical interpretation, which is usually classified as Greek and Hellenistic in

---

[1] The word τροφή is here, as frequently, just a synonym for the word ἄρτος in Ex. 16, 4 and it can therefore to some degree be treated as a word from this Old Testament quotation.

contrast to Palestinian allegory and exegesis. By these men Philo's allegory is then characterized as mystical, abstract, non-Biblical and philosophical.[1]

These scholars have not, however, undertaken any detailed analysis of Philo's exegesis to examine possible influence from the haggadah and to uncover the method of paraphrase. To be sure, E. Stein touched on the first question, when he suggested that the idealization of Biblical persons in the haggadah is transformed into abstract concepts in the allegories of Philo.[2] Stein has not, however, observed the actual use of fragments from haggadah in Philo's exegesis of quotations from the Old Testament.

The question of Philo's exegetical paraphrase has been dealt with by P. Katz. His thesis is that the original text of Philo's works only presupposed the passages in the LXX without quoting them. The actual quotations were added and interpolated into the text at a later stage partly from a "modernized" Greek translation of the Old Testament. Katz attempts, however, to reconstruct Philo's original text of the Old Testament from the exegetical paraphrase of his exposition.[3]

Several objections can be raised to this proposal. As we have seen the exegetical paraphrase allows both a close connection and freedom between the exposition and quotations from the Old Testament. Such a freedom, together with the fact that fragments from the haggadah are interwoven with this paraphrase, makes

---

[1] See L. Treitel, "Ursprung, Begriff und Umfang der allegorischen Schrifterklärung," *MGWJ* LV, (N.F. XIX), 1911, p. 551; I. Heinemann, *Altjüdische Allegoristik*, Leiden 1936, pp. 83 f.; L. Ginzberg, *On Jewish Law and Lore*, Philadelphia 1955, pp. 127, 130-131; R. P. C. Hanson, *Allegory and Event. A Study of the Sources and Significance of Origen's Interpretation of Scripture*, London 1959, pp. 62 ff.; cf. J. Daniélou, *Philon d'Alexandrie (Les Temps et les Destins)*, Paris 1958, pp. 129-142 and J. Pepin, *Mythe et Allégorie. Les Origines Grecques et les Contestations Judeo-Chrétiennes (Philosophie d' l'Esprit)*, Paris 1958, pp. 231-242.

[2] E. Stein, *Philo und der Midrasch*, p. IV, and *Die allegorische Exegese des Philo aus Alexandreia, ZAW Beih.* LI, 1929, p. 15. It is of interest to notice that L. Treitel, *MGWJ* LV (N.F. XIX), 1911, p. 546, has indicated that there is a similarity of structure between Philo's exegesis and the Palestinian midrash.

[3] P. Katz, "Das Problem des Urtextes der Septuaginta," *ThZ* V, 1949, pp. 15 f.; and *Philo's Bible. The Aberrant Text of Bible Quotations in Some Philonic Writings and its Place in the Textual History of the Greek Bible*. Cambridge 1950, pp. 3-4, 103; cf. "Septuagintal studies in the mid-century," in *The Background of the New Testament and its Eschatology*, in honour of C. H. Dodd, Cambridge 1956, pp. 205 f.

impossible any reconstruction of an original Septuagint text on the basis of this paraphrase. In certain cases the exposition nevertheless proves that it presupposes the Old Testament quotation which is cited. P. Wendland has, for instance, shown that in Post. 102 two or more Old Testament passages are quoted together, and the exposition presupposes just this very combination.[1] This shows that the cited quotations and the exposition are knit together, and that Philo treated the texts as an exegete, a fact which Katz has failed to see.[2]

Thus, our examination of the way haggadic fragments were woven together with an exegetical paraphrase of words from Old Testament quotations has given us a fresh insight into Philo's commentaries. The next question is whether this insight can deepen our understanding of John in the New Testament.

Fragments of haggadah used in John's exegesis, John 6, 31-58.

At some points it is quite clear that John worked fragments from the haggadah into the composition of 6, 31-58. First is the fragment about the bread that came down from heaven. It is almost identical with parts of the narratives concerning bread from heaven and earth found in Mek. Ex. 16, 4 and Ex. R. 25, 2:

John 6, 33	ὁ — ἄρτος — ὁ καταβαίνων ἐκ τοῦ οὐρανοῦ
6, 50	ὁ ἄρτος ὁ ἐκ τοῦ οὐρανοῦ καταβαίνων
6, 41	ὁ ἄρτος ὁ καταβὰς ἐκ τοῦ οὐρανοῦ
6, 51	ὁ ἄρτος — ὁ ἐκ τοῦ οὐρανοῦ καταβάς
6, 58	ὁ ἄρτος ὁ ἐξ οὐρανοῦ καταβάς [3]

---

[1] P. Wendland, "Zu Philos Schrift de posteritate Caini (Nebst Bemerkungen zur Rekonstruktion der Septuaginta)," *Philologus* LVII (N.F. XI), 1898, p. 267.—See further on p. 41, n. 5.

[2] P. Katz, *Philo's Bible*, p. 113, has seen that pecularities both in the quotation and the exposition bind these two parts closely together at some places. This observation disturbs his hypothesis severely, and his only way out is to suggest that the interpolator of the quotations from the Old Testament had reshaped the exposition as well. This weakens, indeed, Katz's idea that the interpolator introduced quotations which differ from the exposition.

[3] E. Schweizer, *EGO EIMI*, p. 156, especially n. 95, and "Das johanneische Zeugnis vom Herrenmal," *EvTh* XII, 1952/53, pp. 353-354, finds that ἐξ (against 13 ἐκ τοῦ) οὐρανοῦ in v. 58 is non-Johannine. J. Jeremias, *ThB* XX, 1941, col. 44, agrees with Schweizer on this. Several explanations have been offered on the variation, cf. E. Ruckstuhl, *Einheit*, pp. 265-266. Our understanding of the phrase in John 6, 33.38. etc. as a fragment from haggadah, explains quite well the change from ἐκ τοῦ (v. 33, etc.) to ἀπὸ

6, 38	καταβέβηκα ἀπὸ τοῦ οὐρανοῦ
6, 42	ἐκ τοῦ οὐρανοῦ καταβέβηκα
Mek. Ex. 16, 4	הלחם יורד מן השמים
Ex. R. 25, 2	והוריד מן ... מן השמים

Here John is even closer to the phrases in the Palestinian midrashim than is Philo, since Philo lacks the significant word "to descend" (καταβαίνειν). Thus this fragment in John seems to be taken from the haggadic traditions about the manna. It is quite possible even that it is taken precisely from the tradition about bread from heaven and from earth. John 6, 41 f. may support this identification, since here Jesus as bread from heaven is contrasted to Jesus as the earthly man, the son of Joseph. This combination may reflect the similar combination of bread from heaven and from earth in this unit of the tradition.

The other fragments, that is, those about the fathers who ate manna in the desert and those about such words as "eat and drink", "food" and "drink", have parallels in the phrasing of 1 Cor, 10, 1 ff. So far as content is concerned several parallels can be produced, as exemplified by Spec. II 199 and a passage in Petirat Moses.

John 6,31a	οἱ πατέρες ἡμῶν τὸ μάννα ἔφαγον ἐν τῇ ἐρήμῳ
6, 49	οἱ πατέρες ὑμῶν ἔφαγον ἐν τῇ ἐρήμῳ τὸ μάννα
6, 58	ἔφαγον οἱ πατέρες
6, 53	φάγητε — καὶ πίητε
6, 54.56	(ὁ τρώγων) — καὶ πίνων
6, 55	βρῶσις, καὶ — πόσις
6, 57.58	(ὁ τρώγων)
1 Cor. 10, 1-4	οἱ πατέρες ἡμῶν — βρῶμα ἔφαγον, καὶ — ἔπιον πόμα

τοῦ (v. 38) and ἐξ (v. 58). The variations come from the slight differences in the wordings which occur as the oral tradition is handed down. Thus we find the same variations in Philo's renderings of traditions about the manna: In general he uses ἀπ' οὐρανοῦ (Mut. 258-259, Congr. 173, etc.); more seldom ἐξ οὐρανοῦ (Spec. II 199, and Mos. I 117); occasionally ἐκ and determined article as in Leg. all. III 162b. Similar variations occur in the citation of Ex. 16, 4: ἀπ' οὐρανοῦ in Mut. 259; ἐκ τοῦ οὐρανοῦ in Fug. 137 and [ἐκ not in Mss] τοῦ οὐρανοῦ in Leg. all. III 162a.

1 Cor. 10, 1-4 is a brief summary of events during the Exodus from Egypt:

"I want you to know, brethren, that our fathers were all under the cloud, and all passed through the sea, and all were baptized into Moses in the cloud and in the sea, and all ate the same supernatural food and all drank the same supernatural drink."

Such summaries of the events of the Exodus were obviously a common pattern of the haggadic tradition in Judaism, both in Palestine and in the Diaspora.[1] In addition to this one from 1 Cor. we should also take a look at one from Philo, Spec. II 199, and one from Petirat Moses.[2]

Spec. II 199:
"See, for example, how the many thousands of our forefathers as they traversed the trackless and all-barren desert, were for forty years, the life of a generation, nourished by Him as in a land of richest and most fertile soil; how He opened fountains unknown before to give them abundance of drink for their use; how He rained food from heaven, neither more nor less than what sufficed for each day, that they might consume what they needed ... ."

Petirat Moses:[3]
" ... tell them that through me [Moses] Thou didst cleave the Red Sea, and give the Torah to Israel, that throughout forty years Thou didst cause manna to rain from heaven for Israel and water to rise from the well."

These suggest the strong probability that the fragments listed from John 6, 31.49.53.54.55.56.57.58 are taken from summaries of events at the Exodus. All their details have parallels in the summaries just quoted. The one in 1 Cor. 10, 1-4 is the closest verbal parallel.[4]

---

[1] Cf. B. Gärtner, *John 6 and the Jewish Passover, CN* XVII, Lund 1959, pp. 15-18, who points to the central place such summaries of the events of the Exodus had in the Passover Haggadah.
[2] See also a similar summary in Mek. Ex. 16, 28.
[3] Translation in L. Ginzberg, *Legends* III, p. 427, rendering freely the Hebrew text in *Bet ha-Midrasch*, ed. A. Jellinek, p. 118.
[4] See also pp. 91 f. The strange exchange of τρώγειν for φαγεῖν by John will be discussed at a later point in our investigation. See pp. 92 f. We shall also analyse at a later stage exegetical patterns and terminology in John 6, 31-58, and thus support the isolation of these fragments from their context and our understanding of them as coming from certain units of tradition in the haggadah. See Ch. III.

The belief that haggadic fragments were used in John 6, 31-58, as well as in the exegesis of Philo, is further confirmed by the fact that John, like Philo, has interwoven them into a paraphrase with words from an Old Testament quotation. In this paraphrase words from the quotation often coincide with words from the haggadic fragments.

In the paraphrase quoted, fragments from the haggadah are underscored. First comes the quotation from the Old Testament in John 6, 31b:

ἄρτον ἐκ τοῦ οὐρανοῦ ἔδωκεν αὐτοῖς φαγεῖν

("He gave them bread from heaven to eat"). These words are then paraphrased together with the fragments in this way:

John 6, 31a	οἱ πατέρες ἡμῶν τὸ μάννα ἔφαγον ἐν τῇ ἐρήμῳ
6, 32-35	δέδωκεν — τὸν ἄρτον ἐκ τοῦ οὐρανοῦ — δίδωσιν — τὸν ἄρτον ἐκ τοῦ οὐρανοῦ —. ὁ — ἄρτος — ὁ καταβαίνων ἐκ τοῦ οὐρανοῦ —. — δός — τὸν ἄρτον —. — ὁ ἄρτος
6, 38	καταβέβηκα ἀπὸ τοῦ οὐρανοῦ
6, 41	ὁ ἄρτος ὁ καταβὰς ἐκ τοῦ οὐρανοῦ
6, 42	ἐκ τοῦ οὐρανοῦ καταβέβηκα
6, 48-51	— ὁ ἄρτος —. οἱ πατέρες ὑμῶν ἔφαγον ἐν τῇ ἐρήμῳ τὸ μάννα —. ὁ ἄρτος ὁ ἐκ τοῦ οὐρανοῦ καταβαίνων — φάγῃ —. ὁ ἄρτος — ὁ ἐκ τοῦ οὐρανοῦ καταβάς. φάγῃ — ἄρτου —. ὁ ἄρτος — δώσω —.
6, 52-58	— δοῦναι — φαγεῖν; — φάγητε — καὶ πίητε —. (ὁ τρώγων) — καὶ πίνων —. βρῶσις, καὶ — πόσις. (ὁ τρώγων) — καὶ πίνων —. (ὁ τρώγων) —. ὁ ἄρτος ὁ ἐξ οὐρανοῦ καταβάς — ἔφαγον οἱ πατέρες —. (ὁ τρώγων) — τὸν ἄρτον —.

Thus the words in the quotation from the Old Testament in John 6, 31b are paraphrased together with fragments from haggadic traditions in John 6, 31-58. The exegetical method employed here is, therefore, the same as the one used by Philo in the passages previously examined.[1]

This method of exegesis is not common only to Philo and John but is also found in the Palestinian midrash. The combination of quotations from the Old Testament with haggadic traditions is, of course, basic to the haggadic midrashim. The combination often means that words from the Old Testament are paraphrased by the haggadic exposition. Thus, in Mek. Ex. 16, 4 the tradition about the bread from heaven and earth is connected with the quoted text from Ex. 16, 4, paraphrasing on the words "from heaven" and "bread" in it.

In the following the Old Testament words are underscored. First comes the quotation:

Ex. 16, 4   הנני ממטיר לכם לחם מן השמים

("Behold, I will cause to rain bread from heaven for you.")

Here are the paraphrasing parts of the exposition:

והטל יורד מן השמים

("the dew would come down from heaven")

התחיל הלחם יורד מן השמים

("Bread began to come down from heaven.")

The tradition about bread from heaven and earth serves as exposition of Ex. 16, 4 in Ex. R. 25, 2.6 as well.

There is one difference between Philo and John on the one hand, and these passages discussed in the Palestinian midrash on the other. The latter do not work only fragments from the haggadah into the paraphrase of words from the quotations, as do Philo and John. Instead, in Mek. Ex. 16, 4 and Ex. R. 25, 2.6 the complete versions of the haggadah about bread from heaven and earth are given as an exposition of the quotations from the Old Testament. Thus, we find here a compilation of Old Testament quotation and traditions rather than words from quotation and haggadah closely interwoven in a fresh way.

We reach, neverthless, the significant conclusion that Philo, John and the Palestinian midrash all paraphrase words from an Old Testament quotation by means of haggadic traditions.[2]

---

[1] See further P. Borgen, *NTT* LXI, 1960, pp. 233 f.; and cf. N. A. Dahl, *NTT* LXIV, 1963, pp. 129-162.

[2] Cf. that the method of midrashic paraphrase also was used in the interpretation of the Old Testament in the Qumran sect. See W. H. Brownlee,

The task now is to relate these conclusions to the present state of Johannine research.

The analysis so far cautions against isolating John 6, 51b-58 as an interpolation made by a Church-minded "Redactor" who wanted a reference to the Eucharist at this point. The interpolation theory of Bultmann, who at this point merely is a recent representative of a strong and stereotyped exegetical tradition, is therefore not convincing.[1] As we have seen these verses, like vv. 32-51a, are tied to the Old Testament quotation, cited in v. 31b, by way of a paraphrase. In vv. 51b-58 we find words from the quotation rendered this way:

"Biblical Interpretation among the Sectaries of the Dead Sea Scrolls," *BA* XIV, 1951, pp. 60, 62 ff.; O. Betz, *Offenbarung und Schriftforschung in der Qumransekte*, *WUNT* VI, Tübingen 1960, pp. 166 ff. and 170 ff.; L. H. Silbermann, "Unriddling the Riddle. A Study in the Structure and Language of the Habakkuk Pesher," *RQ* III, 1961/1962, pp. 323-364. (Cf. K. Elliger, *Studien zum Habakkuk-Kommentar vom Toten Meer*, *BhTh* XV, Tübingen 1953, pp. 157-164, rejecting the viewpoint of a midrashic method.)

[1] R. Bultmann, *Evangelium*, pp. 161 f., 174-176; *Theology of the New Testament* I, New York 1951, pp. 147-148 and II, New York 1955, p. 54. Among those maintaining this quite traditional viewpoint are: J. Wellhausen, *Erweiterungen und Änderungen im 4. Evangelium*, Berlin 1907, p. 29; *Das Evangelium Johannis*, Berlin 1908, pp. 32 f.; E. Schwartz, "Aporien im 4. Evangelium," *NAG*, Göttingen 1907, p. 363, n. 2; A. Andersen, "Zu Joh 6, 51b ff.," *ZNW* IX, 1908, pp. 163 f.; F. Spitta, *Das Johannes-Evangelium als Quelle der Geschichte Jesu*, Göttingen 1910, pp. 145-156; W. Bousset, "Johannesevangelium," *RGG* III, Tübingen 1912, col. 616; J. M. Thompson, "The Interpretation of John VI," *Exp.*, Ser. 8, XI, 1916, pp. 344 f.; (cf. A. Loisy, *Le Quatrième Évangile*, 2nd éd., Paris 1921, pp. 49, 233); J. E. Carpenter, *The Johannine Writings. A Study of the Apocalypse and the Fourth Gospel*, London 1927, p. 428 and n. 2; E. von Dobschütz, "Zum Charakter des 4. Evangeliums," *ZNW* XXVIII, 1929, pp. 163, 166; E. Hirsch, *Studien zum vierten Evangelium*, *BhTh* XI, Tübingen 1936, p. 14; E. Schweizer, *EGO EIMI*, p. 155; (cf. M. Dibelius, "Johannesevangelium," *RGG* III, 2nd ed., Tübingen 1929, col. 355); E. Käsemann, "Besprechung von R. Bultmann, Das Evangelium des Johannes," in *Verkündigung und Forschung* III, (Theologischer Jahresbericht 1942/46), München 1947, p. 197; J. Jeremias, *ThB* XX, 1941, col. 44; *The Eucharistic Words of Jesus*, Oxford/ New York 1955, p. 73; K. Schaedel, *Das Johannesevangelium und "die Kinder des Lichtes". Untersuchungen zu den Selbstbezeichnungen Jesu im 4. Evangelium und zur Heilsterminologie der "En Fesha-Sekte"*, Diss. (typewritten) Wien 1953, p. 186; G. Bornkamm, "Die eucharistische Rede im Johannes-Evangelium," *ZNW* XLVII, 1956, pp. 168-169; R. Bultmann, "Johannesevangelium," *RGG* III, 3rd ed., Tübingen 1959, col. 841. See also further discussion on p. 189.

ὁ ἄρτος — δώσω —. — δοῦναι — φαγεῖν; — φάγετε —.
ὁ ἄρτος — ἐξ οὐρανοῦ — ἔφαγον —. — τὸν ἄρτον —.[1]

Thus, these verses continue the midrashic exposition of the quotation and do not break off from the exegetical paraphrase.

Bultmann lists the following verses in the source called the revelatory discourses: John 6, 27a.35.37b.44a.45b.47 f.[2] According to him "the Evangelist" has then added to this source the dialogue and the comments found in John 6, 27-51a. The paraphrase of words from the Old Testament quotation, cited in John 6, 31b, and of fragments from the haggadah is mainly found in those parts which Bultmann ascribes to "the Evangelist." In this connection Bultmann rightly observes that these parts assigned to "the Evangelist" are dependant upon both the Old Testament and Jewish traditions about the manna.[3] He should not ignore, however, the fact that vv. 35.48, which he lists in the revelatory discourse, paraphrases the Old Testament word "bread" from v. 31b. Since John 6, 31-58 has midraschic character, the question then is: Can midrashic patterns and style provide a better solution to the problem of composition than Bultmann's proposed distinction between "the revelatory discourses" and the comments of "the Evangelist"?

Our analysis shows the inadequacy of Noack's study as far as the question of the history of tradition is concerned. He attempts to split up the discourse in John 6 into small single units, logia, which he claims came to the author of the Gospel by the way of the oral tradition.[4] This cannot be the case, since the exegetical paraphrase of the Old Testament quotation integrates John 6, 31-58 to such a degree that it cannot be fragmentized into independent logia. Noack is right, however, to think in terms of traditions, but, as we have seen, John 6, 31-58 does not just reproduce units from tradition, as Noack thinks, but has the tradition in a reshaped form.[5]

---

[1] See also P. Borgen, "The Unity of the Discourse in John 6," *ZNW* L, 1959, pp. 277 f.

[2] See E. Ruckstuhl, *Einheit*, p. 25; R. Bultmann, *Evangelium*, pp. 164, n. 5; 168, n. 1; 172, 171, 170.

[3] R. Bultmann, *Evangelium*, p. 169.

[4] B. Noack, *Tradition*. See index on John 6, 31-58 on pp. 166-167.

[5] At one point, Noack (*Tradition*, p. 69) is quite close to our observations when he writes: "6, 32 steht im Zusammenhang der Rede über das Himmelsbrot und scheint den Einwand in V. 31 οἱ πατέρες ἡμῶν τὸ μάννα ἔφαγον und besonders das Zitat mit seinem ἄρτον ἐκ τοῦ οὐρανοῦ ἔδωκεν vorauszusetzen;

In the many studies of John's use of the Old Testament quotations and allusions have been discussed mainly in their relationship to the Old Testament passages to which they refer.[1] Thus the Old Testament quotation cited in John 6, 31b has been analysed without any simultanious consideration of midrashic exposition of it.

B. Gärtner and A. Guilding have discussed the possibility of the Jewish Passover Haggadah being the background of John 6, but they have limited themselves chiefly to the conclusions that they possess some themes in common.[2] Hence, they did not undertake to discuss the midrashic exposition of the Old Testament quotation in John 6, 31b by means of fragments from haggadah worked into an exegetical paraphrase.

Against this background it is necessary to discuss the larger midrashic compositions which the exegetical paraphrase indicates.

---

der Satz liesse sich aber auch als selbständige Aussage verstehen, wenn angenommen werden darf dass ὁ ἄρτος ὁ ἐκ τοῦ οὐρανοῦ ein geläufiger Terminus war." We have found that v. 32 is, indeed, closely tied to the quotation in v. 31b, as an exposition which has absorbed the phrase ὁ ἄρτος—ὁ καταβαίνων ἐκ τοῦ οὐρανοῦ from the tradition. Cf. below on p. 68.

[1] See A. H. Franke, *Das alte Testament bei Johannes. Ein Beitrag zur Erklärung und Beurtheilung der johanneischen Schriften*, Göttingen, 1885, pp. 255-293; E. Hühn, *Die alttestamentlichen Citate und Reminiscenzen im Neuen Testamente (Die messianischen Weissagungen des israelitisch-jüdischen Volkes bis zu den Targumim historisch-kritisch untersucht und erläutert* II), Tübingen 1900, pp. 70-95; R. Harris, *Testimonies* II, Cambridge 1920, pp. 71-76; C. F. Burney, *The Aramaic Origin of the Fourth Gospel*, Oxford 1922, pp. 114-125; (A. Faure, "Die alttestamentlichen Zitate im 4. Evangelium und die Quellenscheidungshypothese," *ZNW* XXI, 1922, pp. 99-121, has without success tried to use the Old Testament quotations as criteria for source analysis. See the criticism by F. Smend in "Die Behandlung alttestamentlicher Zitate als Ausgangspunkt der Quellenscheidung im '4. Evangelium," *ZNW* XXIV, 1925, pp. 147-150); C. K. Barrett, "The Old Testament in the Fourth Gospel," *JThSt* XLVIII, 1947, pp. 155-169; K. Stendahl, *The School of St. Matthew and its use of the Old Testament*, ASNU XX, Uppsala 1954, pp. 162-163; B. Noack, *Tradition*, pp. 71-89,; B. Lindars *New Testament Apologetic*, London 1961, especially pp. 265-277, and the discussion in commentaries on John. Cf. A. Guilding, *The Fourth Gospel and Jewish Worship. A Study of the relation of St. John's Gospel to the ancient Jewish lectionary system*, Oxford 1960, who thinks that specific Passover lections have influenced John 6 (pp. 58-68). The midrashic use of the quotation from The Old Testament in John 6, 31 is discussed by P. Borgen, *ZNW* L, 1959, pp. 277 f. and "Observations on the Midrashic Character of John 6," *ZNW* LIV, 1963, pp. 232-240.

[2] B. Gärtner, *Passover*; A. Guilding, *Worship*, pp. 58-68.

CHAPTER TWO

A HOMILETIC PATTERN

The state of research. Homilies in translation

The preceding chapter showed the way Philo and John wove together fragments from haggadic traditions and words from Old Testament quotations. This investigation promps a further question: What is the composition of expositions formed from such a method? An examination of this question will show that Mut. 253-263, Leg. all. III 162-168 and John 6, 31-58 all follow the same homiletic pattern.

Before citing these homilies in translation and discussing them, previous investigations in the question of homiletic compositions in Philo and John will be reviewed briefly.

Bousset's thesis is that Philo's exegetical works consist mainly of a Jewish source strongly influenced by secular Hellenistic culture. This source, or rather body of sources, can further be identified as traditions preserved in the form of lectures, dissertations, etc. from a Jewish exegetical school in Alexandria. This scholarly source, however, was reshaped and commented upon by Philo in order to give his works their present form.[1]

Correspondingly Bultmann holds the theory that a main source in John consists of gnostic revelatory discourses ("Offenbarungsreden"). "The Evangelist" then reshaped and commented on the source. This revelatory source is basicly characterized by antithetic parallelism between paired sentences which thus have received poetic form. As parallels to the form used by the revelatory discourse source, Bultmann points to the Odes of Salomon and the Mandean Scriptures.[2]

As an alternative to the theories of Bousset and Bultmann some scholars have suggested that Philo and John contain sermons and homilies from the synagogue and the Church respectively,[3] whereas

---

[1] W. Bousset, *Schulbetrieb*, pp. 43-45, 153-154, etc.
[2] See page 4, n. 3 and Bultmann, *Evangelium*, p. 2 and n. 5. Cf. E. Ruckstuhl, *Einheit*, pp. 24 f., where also other characteristics are listed.
[3] For such criticism of Bousset, see I. Heinemann in *Die Werke Philos von Alexandria in deutscher Übersetzung*, by L. Cohn, I. Heinemann, M.

others have advanced this theory quite apart from any consideration of Bousset and Bultmann.¹

Thus it is surprising that to date no one has made a serious and broad attempt to analyse the structure of such homilies as these. As far as Philo is concerned, H. Thyen has gone so far as to state that it is impossible to identify and single out individual homilies, since Philo so completely worked the traditions together into a unified whole.² As for John, the attempt of J. Schneider to analyse the structure of the sermonic meditation in John 6, 27-58 is not convincing. One basic weakness is the lack of comparative material for his study.³ Thus the question is open for a detailed investigation.

The method of exegetical paraphrase found in Philo and John 6, 31-58 can guide this new investigation. As a starting point the following principle will be followed: The unit which belongs to a quotation from the Old Testament may be traced by examining the extent to which the paraphrase of that quotation goes.

The employment of this principle uncovers the following units: Leg. all. III 162-168; Mut. 253-263 and John 6, 31-58. For convenience in investigation the cited and paraphrased words of the Old Testament quotations (and their immediate Old Testament context) are italicized in the following translation of the three passages:⁴

Leg. all. III 162-168:

a) 162: "That the *food* of the soul is not earthly but *heavenly*, we shall find abundant evidence in the Sacred Word:

Adler and W. Theiler, III, (*SJHLD*), Breslau 1919, p. 6, n. 1. For such criticism of Bultmann, see J. Schneider, "Zur Frage der Komposition von Joh. 6, 27-58 (59)," *In Memoriam E. Lohmeyer*, Stuttgart 1951, pp. 132-142, cf. "Zur Komposition von Joh. 10," *CN* XI, Lund 1947, pp. 220-225 and "Zur Komposition von Joh. 7," *ZNW* XLV, 1954, pp. 108-119.

¹ About Philo, see the survey in H. Thyen, *Der Stil*, pp. 7-11, with references to scholars as H. Ewald, J. Freudenthal, Z. Frankel, L. Cohn, I. Heinemann, H. Leisegang, W. Völker, L. Goppelt and M. Adler. We can add to this list L. H. Feldman, *CW* LIV, 1960/1961, p. 287. The list of Johannine scholars holding this view is less numerous but includes such names as C. K. Barrett, *The Gospel According to St. John. An Introduction with Commentary and Notes on the Greek Text*, London 1958, pp. 17, 20 f., 113 f. and K. Stendahl, *The School*, pp. 162 f.

² H. Thyen, *Der Stil*, pp. 8-9: "Philo hat fast alle von ihm aufgenommenen Traditionen sehr stark überarbeitet und einheitlich stilisiert, sodass es nicht mehr möglich ist, durch literarkritische Analyse einzelne ganze Homilien in seinen Traktaten aufzufinden."

³ See above p. 28, n. 3 for reference to Schneider's work.

⁴ Concerning Congr. 170-174, see p. 42, n. 1.

a) *'Behold I rain upon you bread out of heaven,*
b) *and the people shall go out and they shall gather the day's portion for a day,*
c) *that I may prove them whether they will walk by My law or not.'* (Ex. 16, 4).

You see that the soul is fed not with things of earth that decay, but with such words as God shall have poured like rain *out of* that lofty and pure region of life to which the prophet has given the title of *'heaven'*.

b) (1) 163: To proceed. *The people*, and all that goes to make the soul, is *to go out and gather* and make a beginning of knowledge, not all at once but *'the days portion for a day.'*

For to begin with it will be unable to contain all at once the abundant wealth of the gracious gifts of God, but will be overwhelmed by them as by the rush of a torrent. In the second place it is better, when we have received the good things sufficient of themselves as duly *measured out* to us, to think of God as Dispenser of those that still remain.

164: He that would fain have all at once earns for himself lack of hope and trust, as well as great lack of sense. He lacks hope, if he expects that now only but not in the future also will God shower on him good things; he lacks faith, if he has no belief that both in the present and always the good gifts of God are lavishly bestowed on those worthy of them; he lacks sense, if he imagines that he will be, though God will it not, a sufficient guardian of what he has *gathered together*; for the mind that vaingloriously ascribes to itself sureness and security has many a time been rendered by a slight turn of the scale a feeble and insecure guardian of all that it looked on as in its safe-keeping.

(2) 165: *Gather together*, therefore, O soul, what is adequate of itself and *suitable*, and neither *more* than sufficient so as to be excessive, nor on the other hand *less* so as to fall short, that dealing in right *measures* thou mayest do no wrong. For thou art required also, when making thy study to cross over from the passions and when sacrificing the Passover, to take the forward step, whose symbol is the lamb, not without *measure*, for he says:

'each man shall reckon what suffices for him as a lamb' (Ex. 12, 4).

166: Both in the case of *manna* then and in the case of every boon which God confers upon our race, it is good to take what is fixed by strict *measure* and *reckoning* and not that which is above and beyond us; for to do this is to be over-reaching.

(3) Let the soul, then, *gather the day's portion for a day*, that it may declare not itself but the bountiful God guardian of the good things.

167: And the reason for the injunction we are considering seems to me to be this.

The day is a symbol of light, and the light of the soul is training. Many, then, have acquired the lights in the soul for night and darkness, not for *day* and light; all elementary lessons for example, and what is called school-learning and philosophy itself when pursued with no motive higher than parading their superiority, or from desire of an office under our rulers. But the man of worthy aims sets himself to acquire *day* for the sake of *day*, light for the sake of light, the beautiful for the sake of the beautiful alone, not for the sake of something else.

c) And this is why he goes on with the words: '*that I may prove them whether they will walk in My law or not*'; for this is the divine *law*, to value exellence for its own sake. 168: The right principle, therefore, tests all aspirants as one does a coin, to see whether they have been debased in that they refer the soul's good to something external, or whether, as tried and approved men, they distinguish and guard this treasure as belonging to thought and mind alone.

Such men have the privilege of being fed not with earthly things but with the *heavenly* forms of knowledge.

Mut. 253-263

253: "He said to him, we read,

a) 'Yes, b) Sarah thy wife shall bear a son' (Gen. 17, 19).

a) How significant is that answer '*Yes*', fraught as it is with inner meaning. For what can be more befitting to God than to grant and promise His blessings in a moment (§ 254:) and with a sign of assent? Yet those who receive a sign of assent from God are refused assent by every fool.

Thus the oracles represent Leah as hated and for this reason She received such a name. For by interpretation it means 'rejected and weary', because we all turn away from virtue and think her wearisome, so little to our taste are the commands she often lays upon us. 255: But from the Ruler of all she was awarded such acceptance that her womb which He opened received the seed of divine impregnation, (Gen. 29, 31) whence should come the birth of noble practices and deeds.

b) (1) Learn then, soul of man, that *Sarah* also, that is virtue, *shall bear thee a son*, as well as Hagar, the lower instruction. For Hagar's offspring is the creature of teaching, but Sarah's learns from none other at all than itself.

256: And wonder not that God, who brings about all good things, has brought into being this kind also, and though there be few such upon earth, in Heaven vast is their number. You may learn this truth from the other elements, out of which man is constituted. Have the eyes been taught to see, do the nostrils learn to smell, do the hands touch or the feet advance in obedience to the orders or exhortations of instructors? 257: As for our impulses and mental pictures, which are the primal conditions of the soul, according as it is in notion or at rest, are they made what they are by teaching? Does our mind attend the school of the professor of wisdom and there learn to think and to apprehend? All these exempt from teaching make use of self-worked independent nature for their respective activities.

258: Why then need you still wonder that God showers virtue without toil or trouble, needing no controlling hand but perfect and complete from the very first? And if you would have further testimony of this can you find any more trustworthy than Moses, who says that while other men receive their food from earth, the nation of vision alone has it from heaven? 259: The earthly food is produced with the co-operation of husbandmen, but the heavenly is sent like the snow by God the solely self-acting, with none to share his work.

And indeed it says

'Behold I rain upon you bread from heaven' (Ex. 16, 4).

Of what food can he rightly say that it is rained from heaven, save of heavenly wisdom (260:) which is sent from above on souls which yearn for virtue by Him who sheds the gift of prudence in rich abundance, whose grace waters the universe, and chiefly so in the holy seventh which he calls the Sabbath? For then he says there will be a plentiful supply of good things spontaneous and self-grown, which even all the art in the world could never raise, but springing up and bearing their proper fruit through self-originated, self-consummated nature.

(2) 261: Virtue, then *shall bear thee a* true-born, male *child*, one free from all womanish feelings, *and thou shalt call his name* by the feeling which he raises in thee, which feeling is most surely joy. And therefore thou shalt give him a *name* significant of joy, even laughter. 262: Just as fear and grief have their own special ejaculations, which the overpowering force of emotion coins, so moods of happy planning or of gladness compel us to break out into natural utterances, as aptly and exactly expressing our meaning as any which an adept in the study of names could devise.

263: Therefore he says:

'*I have blessed him, I will increase and multiply him*: *he shall beget twelve nations* (that is, the whole round and train of the earthly branches of the professional schools), *but my covenant will I establish with Isaac*' (Gen. 17, 20 f.).

Thus both forms of virtue, one where the teacher is another, one where teacher and learner are the same, will be open to human kind. And where man is weak he will claim the former, where he is strong the latter which comes ready to his hands."

John 6, 31-58

[31] "Our fathers *ate* the manna in the wilderness; as it is written,

a) '*He gave them bread from heaven*   b) *to eat.*'

a)   [32] Jesus then said to them, 'Truly, truly I say to you, not Moses gave you the *bread from heaven*; but my Father *gives* you the true *bread from heaven*.[1] [33] For the *bread* of God is that which comes down *from heaven*, and gives life to the world.'

[34] They said to him, 'Lord *give* us this *bread* always.' [35] Jesus said to them, 'I am the *bread* of life; he who comes to me shall not hunger, and he who believes in me shall never thirst. [36] But I said to you that you have seen me and yet do not believe. [37] All that the Father gives me will come to me; and him who comes to me I will not cast out. [38] For I have come down *from heaven*, not to do my own will, but the will of him who sent me, [39] and this is the will of him who sent me, that I should lose nothing of all that he has given me,

---
[1] Translation mine.

but raise it up at the last day. ⁴⁰ For this is the will of my Father, that every one who sees the Son and believes in him should have eternal life; and I will raise him up at the last day.' ⁴¹ The Jews then *murmured* at him, because he said, 'I am *the bread* which came down *from heaven.*' ⁴² They said, 'Is not this Jesus, the son of Joseph, whose father and mother we know? How does he now say, 'I have come down *from heaven*'?' ⁴³ Jesus answered them, 'Do not *murmur* among yourselves. ⁴⁴ No one can come to me unless the Father who sent me draws him; and I will raise him up at the last day. ⁴⁵ It is written in the prophets,

'And they shall all be taught by God.'

Every one who has heard and learned from the Father comes to me. ⁴⁶ Not that any one has seen the Father except him who is from God; he has seen the Father. ⁴⁷ Truly, truly, I say to you, he who believes has eternal life. ⁴⁸ I am the *bread* of life.

b) ⁴⁹ Your fathers *ate* the manna in the wilderness, and they died. ⁵⁰ This is the *bread* which comes down *from heaven*, that a man may *eat* of it and not die. ⁵¹ I am the living *bread* which came down *from heaven*; if any one *eats* of this *bread*, he will live for ever; and the *bread which* I *shall give* for the life of the world is my flesh.'

⁵² The Jews then disputed among themselves, saying, 'How can this man *give* us his flesh *to eat*?' ⁵³ So Jesus said to them, 'Truly, truly, I say you, unless you *eat* the flesh of the Son of man and drink his blood, you have no life in you; ⁵⁴ he who eats my flesh and drinks my blood has eternal life, and I will raise him up at the last day. ⁵⁵ For my flesh is food indeed, and my blood is drink indeed. ⁵⁶ He who eats my flesh and drinks my blood abides in me, and I in him. ⁵⁷ As the living Father sent me, and I live because of the Father, so he who eats me will live because of me.

⁵⁸ This is the *bread* which came down *from heaven*, not such as the fathers *ate* and died; he who eats this *bread* will live for ever.' "

The exegetical paraphrase. The similarity between opening and closing

The italicizing shows clearly the main quotations from the Old Testament and the manner in which words from them are paraphrased throughout the respective paragraphs. The systematizing work of the exegetes is also evident: They divide the quotation as they deal with it in the exposition, discussing one part after the other in a successive sequence.

Thus in Leg. all. III 162-168 the first phrase of the quotation, (a), "Behold I rain upon you bread out of heaven", is paraphrased and discussed in § 162. The second phrase, (b), "and the people shall go out and they shall gather the day's portion for a day", follows in the paraphrase and discussion of §§ 163-167b. The paraphrase of this part is repeated three times, dividing the exposition into three subdivisions (1) §§ 163-164, (2) §§ 165-166a and (3) §§ 166b-167a. Finally, the third phrase, (c), "that I may prove them whether they will walk by My law or not" is repeated verbatim in connection with the exposition in §§ 167b-168.

This effort at systematization is also present in Mut. 253-263. There the very first word, (a), "Yes" is singled out and is repeated in the first part of the exposition, §§ 253b-255a. Then follows the main phrase, (b), "Sarah thy wife shall bear a son", §§ 255b-263. This phrase is paraphrased twice, dividing the exposition into two parts, (1) §§ 255b-260 and (2) §§ 261-263.

The same method of systematization is employed in John 6 as well. The first part (a) of the quotation cited in v. 31, "He gave them bread from heaven" is paraphrased and discussed in vv. 32-48. The last word, (b), "to eat" is then paraphrased and interpreted in vv. 49-58. The paraphrase of the part (a) of the Old Testament quotation is, however, also continued into the paraphrase of this word "to eat".

Again there is an argument against the theory that vv. 51b-58 is a later interpolation. It has already been observed that words from the quotation in v. 31b are paraphrased in this section as in the preceding verses. Now it is possible to add one further point. In vv. 51b-58 the discussion of the eating is at the center. This fact ties the section closely to the exposition from v. 49 onwards, where the word "to eat" is the main subject for the exegesis.[1]

A closer examination of Leg. all. III 162-168, Mut. 253-263 and John 6, 31-58 points up, furthermore, that their closing statements both refer back to the main statement at the beginning and at the same time sum up points from the homily as a whole.

The opening statement in Leg. all. III 162 runs, "Ὅτι δὲ οὐ γήινοι ἀλλ' οὐράνιοι αἱ ψυχῆς τροφαί, κτλ. — (Ex. 16, 4 cited).

ὁρᾷς ὅτι οὐ γηίνοις καὶ φθαρτοῖς τρέφεται ἡ ψυχή, ἀλλ' οἷς ἂν ὁ

---

[1] See p. 189, n. 3. Also P. Borgen, *ZNW* L, 1959, pp. 277 f.

θεὸς ὀμβρήσῃ λόγοις ἐκ τῆς μεταρσίου καὶ καθαρᾶς φύσεως, ἣν <u>οὐρανὸν</u> κέκληκεν.

("That the food of the soul is *not earthly but heavenly*, etc. (Ex. 16, 4 cited).

You see, that the soul *is fed not* with things *of earth* that decay, *but* with such words as God shall have poured like rain out of that lofty and pure region of life to which the prophet has given the title of *'heaven'*.")

The closing statement in Leg. all. III 168 runs, τούτοις συμβέβηκε <u>μὴ</u> τοῖς <u>γηίνοις</u> ἀλλὰ ταῖς <u>ἐπουρανίοις ἐπιστήμαις τρέφεσθαι</u>.

("Such men have the privilege of *being fed not* with *earthly things but* with the heavenly forms of knowledge.")

The underlining or italicizing point up the fact that the opening and closing statements have several words in common. Furthermore, both statements are a paraphrase of the first part (a) of the quotation from the Old Testament, "Behold I rain upon you bread out of heaven." At the same time the closing statement is a concluding remark to the homily as a whole, since it refers to the men who receive knowledge, and this has been the theme also of § 163-168a.

In Mut. 253-263 the main statement at the beginning does not come right after the quotation from the Old Testament in § 253b. There is, rather, a preface before the statement comes in § 255b:

μάθε οὖν, ὦ ψυχή, ὅτι καὶ "Σαρρα", ἡ ἀρετή, "τέξεταί σοι υἱόν," οὐ μόνον Ἄγαρ, ἡ μέση παιδεία· ἐκείνης μὲν γὰρ τὸ ἔγγονον <u>διδακτόν</u>, ταύτης δὲ πάντως <u>αὐτομαθές ἐστι</u>.

("Learn then, soul of man, that Sarah also, that is *virtue*, shall bear thee a son, as well as Hagar, the lower instruction. For Hagar's offspring is the creature *of teaching*, but Sarah's *learns from none other* at all *than itself*.")

The closing statement is in Mut. 263:

— ἵν' ἑκατέρας ἀρετῆς τὸ ἀνθρώπων μεταποιῆται γένος, <u>διδακτῆς</u> τε καὶ <u>αὐτομαθοῦς</u>, τὸ μὲν ἀσθενέστερον διδασκομένης, ἑτοίμης δὲ τὸ ἐρρωμένον.

("Thus both forms of *virtue*, one where the *teacher is another*, one where *teacher and learner are the same*, will be open to human kind. And where man is weak he will claim the former, where he is strong the latter which comes ready to his hands.")

Here again the opening and closing statements have central terms in common, as is indicated by the underlining. But whereas the opening statement paraphrases words from the Old Testament quotation, the closing statement does not repeat them. This closing statement is at the same time, however, a concluding remark on the discussion of the whole homily, which deals just with religious intuition versus man-made efforts.

John 6, 31-58 follows this same pattern closely. The opening statement is given in vv. 31-33.

οἱ πατέρες ἡμῶν τὸ μάννα ἔφαγον ἐν τῇ ἐρήμῳ, καθώς ἐστιν γεγραμμένον· ἄρτον ἐκ τοῦ οὐρανοῦ ἔδωκεν αὐτοῖς φαγεῖν. Εἶπεν οὖν αὐτοῖς ὁ Ἰησοῦς· ἀμὴν ἀμὴν λέγω ὑμῖν· οὐ Μωϋσῆς δέδωκεν ὑμῖν τὸν ἄρτον ἐκ τοῦ οὐρανοῦ, ἀλλ' ὁ πατήρ μου δίδωσιν ὑμῖν τὸν ἄρτον ἐκ τοῦ οὐρανοῦ τὸν ἀληθινόν· ὁ γὰρ ἄρτος τοῦ θεοῦ ἐστιν ὁ καταβαίνων ἐκ τοῦ οὐρανοῦ καὶ ζωὴν διδοὺς τῷ κόσμῳ.

("Our *fathers ate* the manna in the wilderness; as it is written, 'He gave them *bread from heaven to eat.*' Jesus then said to them, 'Truly, truly, I say to you, it was not Moses who gave you *the bread from heaven*; my Father gives you the true *bread from heaven*. For *the bread* of God is that *which comes down from heaven*, and gives *life* to the world.'")

The closing statement is given in John 6, 58:

οὗτός ἐστιν ὁ ἄρτος ὁ ἐξ οὐρανοῦ καταβάς, οὐ καθὼς ἔφαγον οἱ πατέρες καὶ ἀπέθανον. ὁ τρώγων τοῦτον τὸν ἄρτον ζήσει εἰς τὸν αἰῶνα.

("This is *the bread which came down from heaven*, not such as *the fathers ate* and died; he who eats this *bread* will *live* for ever.")

Again the opening and closing statements contain many words in common, as seen from the underlining and italicizing. And, corresponding to Leg. all. III 162 and 168, both have a paraphrase of words from the Old Testament quotation cited in John 6, 31b, "He gave them bread from heaven to eat". At the same time John 6, 58 sums up the whole homily, and so refers also to dying in the desert, as said in vv. 49 ff., and uses the word τρώγειν, to eat, which occurs in vv. 54 ff.

Bultmann noticed that John 6, 58 has the function of a closing and concluding statement: "V. 58 endlich schliesst die Rede und damit das Ganze ab, indem die Einheit des Ganzen durch Wiederaufnahme von Begriffen und Wendungen des joh. Textes hergestellt wird. Deshalb wird jetzt der Begriff des 'von Himmel gekommenen Brotes' aus V. 51a bzw V. 33 und 50 wieder aufgenommen, und durch das οὗτός ἐστιν wird versichert, dass jenes wunderbare Himmelsbrot eben das Sakrament des Herrenmahles sei. Und der letzte Satz, der abschliessend dem Teilnehmer am Sakrament das ewige Leben verheisst, nimmt aus V. 31 f. 49 das Motiv des Gegensatzes des Lebensbrotes zum Manna wieder auf." Bultmann's analysis is excellent, apart from the idea that v. 58 is added by a Redactor.[1] Verse 58 is, namely, an integral part of the whole homily in John 6, 31-58, and the parallel patterns in Philo give support to this claim that the opening and closing statements here in John were composed together from the beginning.

Subordinate quotations from the Old Testament

So far it is clear that the pattern of a homily has the following characteristics: A quotation from the Old Testament is followed by an exegetical paraphrase which determines its exposition; this exposition can further be identified as a united whole by the similarity between the opening and concluding statements.

Still another characteristic is now to be added. All three homilies under consideration contain subordinate quotations from the Old Testament in addition to the main quotation, the text, at the beginning. Leg. all. III 162-168 quotes Ex. 16, 4 as the text in § 162. Then in § 165 the subordinate quotation follows from Ex. 12, 4. In Mut. 253-263 the text is quoted in § 253 and is taken from Gen. 17, 19. Then in § 259, Ex. 16, 4 is given as the subordinate quotation from the Old Testament. In addition to this quotation, Gen. 17, 20 f. is quoted in § 263.

John 6, 31-58 has this same characteristic. The main Old Testament quotation (the text) is given in v. 31b: "as it is written, 'He gave them bread from heaven to eat.'" Then in v. 45 there follows the subordinate quotation from Is. 54, 13: "It is written in the prophets, 'And they shall all be taught by God.'"

In addition to the main quotation, the text, at the beginning of the homily, these homilies thus also draw upon other quotations from the Old Testament. It is worth noticing that in Philo's homilies the subordinate quotations are also drawn from the Pentateuch,

---

[1] R. Bultmann, *Evangelium*, p. 176. Cf. also C. K. Barrett, *St. John*, p. 248. Bultmann's interpretation of the ideas expressed in John 6, 51b-58 is hardly correct. See below on pp. 189 f.

but in the Johannine homily the subordinate quotation comes from another division of the Old Testament, the Prophets.

The subordinate quotation from Gen. 17, 20 f. incorporated into Mut. 263 raises the question if these homilies often drew upon larger Old Testament pericopes. The quotation continues, namely, the text which is taken from Gen. 17, 19 (§ 253). On the basis of both homilies of Philo discussed, the question must be answered positively. Thus in addition to the quotation from Gen. 17, 20 f. in Mut. 263, § 261 contains the phrase which follows the text quotation in Gen. 17, 19: "and thou shalt call his name . . . ". The text and its Old Testament context is then recorded in the following fashion in the homily of Mut. 253-263:

Gen 17, 19 aα: the text, in quotation and paraphrase
Gen 17, 19 aβ: in the paraphrase
Gen 17, 20. 21: as subordinate quotation.[1]

In Leg. all. III 162-168, the Old Testament context of the text, Ex. 16, 4, is also reflected in the exegesis. Thus Ex. 16, 16 ff. is paraphrased together with Ex. 16, 4 in §§ 163.165-166: [2]

Ex. 16, 4 cited in Leg. all. III 162: καὶ συνάξουσι[3] τὸ τῆς ἡμέρας εἰς ἡμέραν. LXX 16, 16: Συναγάγετε ἀπ' αὐτοῦ ἕκαστος εἰς τοὺς καθήκοντας, γομορ κατὰ κεφαλὴν κατὰ ἀριθμὸν καὶ μετρήσαντες τῷ γομορ οὐκ ἐπλεόνασεν ὁ τὸ πολύ καὶ ὁ τὸ ἔλαττον οὐκ ἠλαττόνησεν.	Leg. all. III 163.165-166: μεμετρημένα —. σύναγε — τὰ — καθήκοντα καὶ μήτε πλείω — μήτε ἐλάττω — μέτροις —. — ἀμέτρως —. — ἐνάριθμον καὶ μεμετρημένον —. τὸ τῆς ἡμέρας οὖν εἰς ἡμέραν συναγαγέτω —.

Ex. 16, 4 and its Old Testament context are then used in this way in the homily of Leg. all. III 162-168:

Ex. 16, 4: the text, in quotation and paraphrase.

Ex. 16, 16 ff.: in the paraphrase, partly interwoven with the paraphrase of the text.

---

[1] The reference to Hagar in Mut. 255 could also be mentioned in this connection. There is, however, no paraphrasing of words from the passage about her in Gen. 16, and she occurs regularly together with Sarah in Philo's discussions. See pp. 108 ff.

[2] Cf. the quotation and paraphrase of Ex. 16, 16.18 in Heres 191.

[3] Philo's reading in Ex. 16, 4, συνάξουσι may even have been influenced by Ex. 16, 16. In LXX Ex. 16, 4 reads συλλέξουσιν.

At this point an analysis of the homily in John 6, 31-58 is difficult, because the exact source of the Old Testament quotation in v. 31b is uncertain. Barrett suggests that John may here have combined parts of Ps. 78(77),24; Neh 9, 15 and Ex. 16, 15.[1] There are three reasons which point to Ex. 16 as the source.

First, John would in this instance fit well into the strong homiletic tradition that a text from the Pentateuch is followed by a subordinate quotation from the Prophets or the Writings (Is. 54, 13 in John 6, 45).[2] Second, Ex. 16, 15 provides a good basis for the philological exegesis of the text (John 6, 31b) in vv. 32-33.[3] Third, only Ex. 16 provides a context which includes both the words about the bread in John 6, 31b. 32-33.51, and the word about the murmur, John 6, 41.43:

(A) Ex. 16, 4   לחם מן השמים
     Ex. 16, 4 LXX   ἄρτους ἐκ τοῦ οὐρανοῦ
     John 6, 31b   ἄρτον ἐκ τοῦ οὐρανοῦ

(B) Ex. 16, 15   הלחם אשר נתן יהוה לכם לאכלה
     Ex. 16, 15 LXX   ὁ ἄρτος, ὃν ἔδωκεν κύριος ὑμῖν φαγεῖν
     John 6, 31   ἄρτον — ἔδωκεν αὐτοῖς φαγεῖν
     John 6, 32   δέδωκεν ὑμῖν τὸν ἄρτον —,
                          ὁ πατήρ μου δίδωσιν ὑμῖν τὸν ἄρτον
     Joh 6, 33   ὁ — ἄρτος τοῦ θεοῦ —
     John 6, 51   ὁ ἄρτος — ὃν — δώσω —

(C) Ex. 16, 2   וילינו כל־עדת בני־ישראל על־משה
     Ex. 16, 2 LXX   διεγόγγυζεν πᾶσα συναγωγή
                          υἱῶν Ισραηλ ἐπὶ Μωυσῆν
     John 6, 41   Ἐγόγγυζον οὖν οἱ Ιουδαῖοι περὶ αὐτοῦ
     John 6, 43   μὴ γογγύζετε μετ' ἀλλήλων

(A) By rendering singular ἄρτον, John 6, 31 is nearer to the MT Ex. 16, 4 (לחם) than is the LXX plural ἄρτους[4]. This means that John also is closer to the MT than Philo is, since Philo in this respect follows the LXX when he quotes Ex. 16, 4 in Leg. all. III 162 and Mut. 259. And John's ἐκ τοῦ οὐρανοῦ follows Ex. 16, 4 מן השמים/LXX

---

[1] C. K. Barrett, *St. John*, p. 240. For other possible references, cf. P. Borgen, *NTT* LXI, 1960, p. 235, n. 26; K. Schaedel, *Das Johannesevangelium und "die Kinder des Lichts,"* p. 187 and S. Schulz, *Komposition*, p. 94.
[2] See pp. 51 f.
[3] See pp. 65 f.
[4] See C. F. Burney, *The Aramaic Origin*, p. 117.

ἐκ τοῦ οὐρανοῦ rather than the parallel expressions in Neh. 9, 15 ולחם משמים/LXX ἐξ οὐρανοῦ, in Ps. 78(77), 24 ודגן־שמים/LXX ἄρτον οὐρανοῦ and Ps. 105(104), 40 ולחם שמים/LXX ἄρτον οὐρανοῦ.[1]

(B) There are, however, two differences between Ex. 16, 15 and John 6, 31. John lacks יהוה/LXX κύριος and has third person plural αὐτοῖς instead of the second person plural לכם/LXX ὑμῖν in Ex. 16, 15. In this respect John is closer to Ps. 78(77), 24 נתן למו/ LXX ἔδωκεν αὐτοῖς. The first difference is not decisive, however, since ὁ πατήρ μου in John 6, 32 and θεοῦ in v. 33 are probably an exegetical interpretation of יהוה/LXX κύριος in Ex. 16, 15.[2] And with regard to the second difference, John 6, 32 has the second person plural ὑμῖν as does Ex. 16, 15.

In connection with the last point it is worth noticing that in exegesis the pronouns of the Old Testament quotations are often changed. Thus Philo in Leg. all. III 169 renders Ex. 16, 15 by the first person plural, ἡμῖν, and in Fug. 139 by the third person plural, ἔδωκε κύριος αὐτοῖς φαγεῖν, as John 6, 31 does.[3] The same practise of varying the pronouns in exegetical exposition was also employed in the Qumran literature and in Matthew, and probably also in the Palestinian midrash.[4]

Since the reference to the murmuring (C) in John 6, 41.43 seems to be a paraphrase of Ex. 16, 2, the conclusion must be: John 6, 31-33.41.43.51 draws upon Ex. 16 in the following way:

Ex. 16, 4 ⎫ In the text and in the paraphrase [5]
Ex. 16, 15 ⎭
Ex. 16, 2   In the paraphrase.

---

[1] K. Schaedel and S. Schulz have overlooked this agreement between Joh 6, 31b and Ex. 16, 4 in contrast to all the other parallels to which they refer. See the references on p. 40, n. 1.

[2] So also K. Schaedel, *Das Johannesevangelium und "die Kinder des Lichts"*, p. 187 and S. Schulz, *Komposition*, p. 95.—See further the analysis on pp. 65 ff.

[3] It is of interest to notice that in Fug. 137-139 Philo duscusses Ex. 16, 4 together with Ex. 16, 15, as we believe that John 6, 31 f. also does.

[4] About the Qumran literature and Matthew, see K. Stendahl, *The School*, pp. 186, 199; cf. W. H. Brownlee, *BA* XIV, 1951, pp. 60 ff., 66; concerning the Palestinian midrash, V. Aptowitzer, "Das Schriftwort in der rabbinischen Literatur," *SAW* CLIII, 6, Wien 1906, p. 28 (Deut. 11, 4: אהריכם – אהריהם) and p. 30 (Is. 56, 5: לו – להם); M. R. Lehmann, "Talmudic Material Relating to the Dead Sea Scrolls," *RQ* I, 1958/1959, p. 402 (Is. 43, 9: בכם – בהם).

[5] There is an exegetical method to be traced as the reason for this combination of Ex. 16, 4 and 15. The wording of the quotation cited in John

It is apparent, then, that the homily in John 6 reflects a pericope rather than a single verse from the Old Testament, just as the homilies in Leg. all. III 162-168 and Mut. 253-263 reflect the pericopes from which the Old Testament texts are taken.

So far the following characteristics have been detected in the homiletic pattern employed in Leg. all. III 162-168, Mut. 253-263 and John 6, 31-58: [1] In a systematic way the words from the main Old Testament quotation, the text, are paraphrased and repeated throughout the homily. The closing statement of the homily refers back to the main statement at the beginning and at the same time sums up points from the entire homily. Besides the main quotation from the Old Testament (the text), there are subordinate quotations; in Philo they come from other parts of the Pentateuch, but in John

---

6, 31b corresponds to and is determined by the midrashic exposition in John 6, 32-58. The first part, vv. 32-48, interprets the phrase ἄρτον ἐκ τοῦ οὐρανοῦ ἔδωκεν αὐτοῖς in v. 31b, while the second half, vv. 49-58, puts the word φαγεῖν, v. 31b, in the center of the discussion. The exposition has therefore caused the combination of Ex. 16, 4 and 15. See further P. Borgen, *NTT* LXI, 1960, p. 235, n. 26. Philo can in the same way combine phrases from different Old Testament quotations due to the exegetical interest in the exposition. This is the case in Post. 102, where Deut. 28, 14 is combined with a phrase which probably comes from Deut 4, 2. P. Wendland has observed: "§ 102 weicht das Citat Deut. 28, 14 stark von der LXX ab, ist aber gegen die Annahme einer Interpolation durch die folgende Paraphrase geschützt. Die Erscheinung lässt sich zum Teil aus einer Einwirkung anderer Bibelstellen erklären. ἀπὸ τοῦ ῥήματος konnte etwa Reminiscenz aus Deut. 4, 2; 6, 6 ... sein." (*Philologus* LVII (N.F. XI), 1898, p. 267). Cf. the method of combining two abbreviated Old Testament quotations in rabbinic traditions; see V. Aptowitzer, "Das Schriftwort," *SAW* CLIII, 6, 1906, pp. 22, 24-25. C. K. Barrett, *St. John*, p. 240 and *JThSt* XLVIII, 1947, pp. 155-169, has seen that in other places John also combines different passages from the Old Testament in his quotations. Barrett has not, however, realized that this may be due to a conscious exegetical effort. This exegetical effort found in John 6, 31-58 speaks against C. F. Burney's attempt to characterize the use of the Old Testament as free reminiscence or recollection. Cf. his *The Aramaic Origin*, pp. 116-117, and B. Noack, *Tradition*, pp. 73-74.

The conscious exegetical effort in John is indicated by K. Stendahl, *The School*, p. 163; N. A. Dahl, "Kristus, jödene og verden etter Johannesevangeliet," *NTT* LX, 1959, pp. 193 f.; "The Johannine Church and History," *Current Issues in New Testament Interpretation*, ed. W. Klassen and G. F. Snyder, New York 1962, p. 141, and P. Borgen, *ZNW* L, 1959, pp. 277 f.; *NTT* LXI, 1960, pp. 233-236.

[1] Congr. 170-174 has been omitted from this discussion, since it follows a different pattern and has only one characteristic in common with this homiletic pattern, i.e. the paraphrase and repetition of words from the Old Testament quotation. An analysis of the pattern in Congr. 170-174 has therefore not been undertaken, since it would only sidetrack the principal investigation.

6, 31-58, from the Prophets. These homilies seem to draw upon parts of the pericopes to which the texts belong in the Old Testament. Thus, they may presuppose the reading of pericopes from the Old Testament.[1]

The homilies and their literary contexts

Having analysed a homiletic pattern which occurs in Philo and John, it is important to consider the literary contexts of the homilies concerned. Two questions will direct this enterprise: Is the separation of these homilies from their contexts natural? How are the homilies incorporated into these contexts?

The beginning of the homily in Mut. 253-263 clearly has been reshaped literarily to fit it into the composition of the book. Mut. 253 cites Gen. 17, 19. The exposition of Gen. 17, 18 began already in § 201. Mut. 252-253a makes the literary connection between Gen 17, 19 in § 253b and the preceding sections in the following way:

a) "These and similar ways of analysing and distinguishing things become familiar to the man of virtue through breeding and practise,

b) and does it not therefore seem natural that he should pray that Ishmael may live, if he cannot as yet be the parent of Isaac?

c) What then does God in His kindness do? Abraham had asked for one thing, God gives him two. He had prayed for the less, God grants him the greater."

Point a) refers to the preceding interpretation of the sin offerings, etc., in the digression of § 233-251. Point b) refers to the account of Ishmael in Gen. 17, 18 and the exposition of it in §§ 201-232. This point also forecasts the subsequent exposition of Gen. 17, 19, to which point c) is the direct bridge. Thus the quotation from Gen. 17, 19 in § 253 clearly marks a new beginning from the preceding sections of the book.

The analysis has shown that the verses of Gen. 17, 19aβ. 20.21 were integrated into the homily in Mut. 263 without any independent exposition to interpret them. The homily in §§ 253-263 is, however, followed by the exposition of Gen. 17, 21b in §§ 264 ff. This exposition makes a fresh start on a new theme, and no paraphrase of

---

[1] See further discussion on pp. 51 ff.

Gen. 17, 19, the text of the homily, is given. Thus, the homily of Mut. 253-263 delimits itself in a very natural way.

The homily in Leg. all. III 162-168 is incorporated into the exposition of Gen. 3, 14c, which runs from § 161 to § 181, whereas § 182 moves on to a commentary on Gen. 3, 15a.[1] All the different parts of this broad exposition have as a common theme a discussion of the idea of food.[2]

The homily in Leg. all. III 162-168 is a unit clearly independent from §§ 169 ff., although the subject of manna does continue. The independence is seen from the fact that §§ 162-168 paraphrases Ex. 16, 4, while §§ 169 ff. paraphrases Ex. 16,13-15 without referring to Ex. 16, 4 at all.

The homily is connected with the preceding section by the transition in Leg. all. III 162a: "That the food of the soul is not earthly but heavenly, we shall find abundant evidence in the Sacred Word, etc." (Ex. 16, 4 cited). This statement includes fragments from the tradition about bread from heaven and earth. They are probably brought into this literary "bridge" from § 162b, where they also occur.[3]

The most significant observation for this analysis, however, is that the quotation about the serpent in § 161, (taken from Gen. 3, 14) is not paraphrased from § 162 and onwards, where Ex. 16, 4 is introduced. Thus the connection between the homily in §§ 162-168 and the preceding section does not speak against the independence of the homily, although the idea of earthly and heavenly bread is the connecting link.[4]

To many scholars a basic distinction in the source analysis of John 6 has been the division between the narratives and the discourse.[5] Thus Bultmann distinguishes between John 6, 1-26 (where "the Evangelist" builds on a source of narratives, "die σημεῖα-Quelle") and John 6, 27 ff. (where according to Bultmann "the Evangelist" reshapes and amplifies the revelatory source).[6]

---

[1] Cf. M. Adler, *Studien zu Philon von Alexandreia*, Breslau, 1929, p. 17.
[2] See *Philo*. With an English Translation by F. H. Colson and G. H. Whitaker, I, (*Loeb*), London/New York 1929, p. 298.
[3] See pp. 15 f.
[4] It is even possible that Leg. all. III 161 reflects the tradition about bread from heaven and earth: τροφὰς ἃς ἀναδίδωσιν ἡ γῆ—αἰθερίους καὶ θείας ("food... which earth yields,... ethereal and divine food").
[5] Cf. surveys of theories in J. Jeremias, *ThB* XX, 1941, cols. 34 ff.
[6] R. Bultmann, *Evangelium*, p. 155 and pp. 161-163.

An analysis like that of Bultmann ignores, however, the striking parallel points between John 6 and a cycle of traditions in the Synoptics. These agreements have been pointed out by N. A. Dahl, B. Gärtner, J. Jeremias and R. E. Brown.[1]

Brown writes:[2] "The multiplication of the loaves in Jn 6 is the occasion of a long discourse on the bread of life of which the Synoptic Gospels know nothing. Yet if we make allowance for the fact that Jn like Lk has only one multiplication, we find an interesting sequence which is not unlike Mk's. Thus (the Vulgate enumeration of verses for the end of Jn 6 is followed):

Multiplication for 5000:	Jn 6,1-15	Mk 6, 31-44
Walking on the sea:	16-24	45-54
(then skipping to after Mk's second multiplication in 8, 1-10)		
Request for a sign:	25-34	Mk 8,11-13
Discourse on bread:	35-60	14-21
Confession of Peter:	61-70	27-30
Passion theme; denial:	71-72	31-33"

Although details in Brown's divisions need further discussion, his analysis is as a whole quite convincing. The task of this study, however, is not to discuss whether John is dependent upon the Synoptics, but only to establish that John 6 follows a traditional scheme in its structure.[3] Within the scheme the homily in John 6,31-58 has been given the place of the discourse on bread. In this way it has been linked to the traditional idea of the request for a sign, v. 30. The traditional request for a sign thus clearly identifies the subsequent homily as an independent unit relative to the preceding context.

Just as the theme of bread (food) was common to the different parts of Leg. all. III 161-181, it is also a theme common to the homily of John 6,31-58 and the preceding context, John 6,1-30.

---

[1] N. A. Dahl, *Matteusevangeliet*, Oslo 1949 (typewritten), p. 205; B. Gärtner, *Passover*, pp. 6-12; J. Jeremias, *ThB* XX, 1941, cols. 42-43; R. E. Brown, "Incidents that are Units in the Synoptic Gospels but Dispersed in St. John," *CBQ* XXIII, 1961, pp. 155-156. Both Jeremias and Brown find rightly that the parallelism between John 6 and the Synoptics speaks strongly against Bultmann's analysis of sources and displacement in John.

[2] R. E. Brown, *CBQ* XXIII, 1961, p. 156.

[3] On the question of John and the Synoptics, see P. Borgen, "John and the Synoptics in the Passion Narrative," *NTSt* V, 1959, pp. 246-259.

The verses 26-29(30) form the transition from the narratives to the homily. Thus vv. 26-27a refer back to the multiplication of the bread, while v. 27b ff. point forward to the homily on the bread from heaven. The words ἐφάγετε ἐκ τῶν ἄρτων in v. 26 are hardly meant to be a paraphrase of the Old Testament quotation in v. 31b, since they so directly refer back to the story on the multiplication of the bread. The words ὑμῖν δώσει [δίδωσιν ὑμῖν] in v. 27 may, however, be an allusion forward to the Old Testament quotation and the homily. Similar allusions also exist in the transitional sections which introduced the homilies in Leg. all. III 162-168 and Mut. 253-263.

The homily closes with John 6, 58, as the remark in v. 59 confirms: "This he said in the synagogue, as he taught at Capernaum." Accordingly there is no paraphrase in vv. 60 ff. of the Old Testament text of the homily (cited in v. 31b).

Brown includes the whole remaining part of the chapter in the confession of Peter and the denial. It seems better to call vv. 60-65 a transitional section, binding the homily and the following confession of Peter together. The connection between the homily, John 6,31-58(59), and the following transitional section, vv. 60-65, agrees with the traditional pattern of public discourse and private conversation.[1]

Thus, the analysis of the contexts of the homilies in Mut. 253-263, Leg. all. III 162-168 and John 6,31-58 confirms the belief that they are independent paragraphs. No paraphrase of the Old Testament texts is found outside the homilies, apart from certain traces in the transitional sections which introduce them. The homilies in Leg. all. III 162-168 and Mut. 253-263 are incorporated into the framework of comprehensive, running commentaries on parts of Genesis, and the homily in John 6, 31-58 is incorporated into the framework of a fixed sequence of traditions which also occurs in the Synoptics.

Parallels elsewhere in Philo and in Paul

The analysis of two homilies in Philo and one in John needs to be tested. Then one question becomes urgent. Is it possible to identify this homiletic pattern elsewhere in Philo and in the New Testament?

---

[1] Cf. the public teaching of Jesus in Matt. 13, 1-9 and private conversation from v. 10 ff. See also D. Daube, *The New Testament and Rabbinic Judaism*, pp. 141 ff. in which one special type of this pattern is discussed in the New Testament and rabbinic sources: "Public Retort and Private Explanation."

The three main characteristics of the pattern will guide the investigation at this point: 1) There is a correspondence between the opening and closing parts of the homily. At the same time the closing statement sums up points from the homily; but for the present purposes it would lead too far to analyse this particular characteristic in every case. 2) In addition to the main quotation from the Old Testament, the text, there is at least one subordinate quotation, also from the Old Testament. 3) Words from the text are paraphrased or quoted in the homily.

It is fortunate that there are other examples of this homiletic pattern: Leg. all. III 65-75a; III 169-173; Sacr. 76-87; Gal. 3, 6-29, Rom. 4, 1-22 and probably also Somn. II 17-30.[1] The opening and closing statements in these homilies will receive first attention.

The homily of Leg. all. III 169-173 can be compared with Leg. all. III 162-168 and John 6, 31-58. The closing statement of Leg. all. III 168 paraphrases parts of the text in § 162. The same is the case in the closing and opening statements of the homily in John 6, 31-58. The homily in Leg. all III 169-173 goes one step further at this point: The closing statement in § 173 clearly repeats parts of the main quotation from Ex. 16, 13-15 cited in § 169. (The italicizing shows the close agreements in the wording between the opening and closing statements):

Opening (§ 169): "And *Moses* said unto them, *'This bread which* the Lord *hath given us to eat, is this word*, which the Lord hath prescribed' " (Ex. 16, 15b).

Close (§ 173): "But it is taught by the hierophant and prophet *Moses*: he will tell it, *This bread* is the food *which* God *hath given* to the soul, for it to feed on His own *utterance* and His own word; for *this bread, which* He *hath given us to eat, is 'this word.*' "

The closing statement of the homily in Rom. 4, 1-22 similarly quotes verbatim one part of the text cited at the beginning.

Opening (v. 3): "For what does the scripture say? 'Abraham believed God, and it *was reckoned to him as righteousness*' " (Gen. 15, 6).

Close (v. 22): "That is why his faith *'was reckoned to him as righteousness.*' "

In the other homilies, the opening and closing statements are more independent of the main quotations from the Old Testament

---

[1] Although Somn. II 17-30 shows the characteristics of the homiletic pattern, its separation from the literary context is less apparent.

at the beginning. Again the agreements in the wording between the two statements are italicized.

First come the opening and closing statements of the homily in Leg. all. III 65-75a:[1]

Opening (§ 65): "And the Lord God said to *the serpent*, 'Because thou hast done this, *cursed* art thou ...' (Gen. 3, 14). For what reason does He *curse the serpent without giving it the opportunity to defend itself* ...?"

Close (§ 75a): "Thou seest that God both *curses the serpent* without *allowing him to defend himself*—for he is pleasure—and slays Er without bringing an open charge against him; for he is the body."[2]

The function of summarizing is especially evident in this example when the closing statement mentions Er, who is discussed in the homily, §§ 69 ff. The same function is also quite developed in the next homily, Sacr. 76-87.

Opening (§ 76): "Wherefore, 'if *you bring an offering of first-fruits*' make such division as Holy Writ prescribes. First *the new*, then *the roasted*, then *the sliced* and last *the ground*" (Lev. 2, 14).

Close (§ 87a): "When then you acknowledge as God wills these four things, *the 'new'*, that is the blossom or vigour; *the 'roasted'*, that is the fire-tested and invincible reason; *the 'sliced'*, that is the division of things into their classes; *the 'pounded,'* that is the persistent practice and exercise in what the mind has grasped, *you will bring* an *offering of the first-fruits*, even the first and best offspring of the soul."

The closing statement of the homily in Gal. 3, 6-29 both refers to the opening and sums up a central point in the homily:

Opening (v. 7): "So you see that it is men of faith who are *the sons of Abraham*."

Close (v. 29): "And if you are Christ's, then you are *Abraham's offspring*, heirs according to promise."

Of special interest for the analysis of the homily in Mut. 253-263 is the homily in Somn. II 17-30. In Mut. 253-263 there was a brief expository preface between the text in § 253 and the opening statement in § 255b. This preface interpreted the very first word

---

[1] It is beyond the scope of this study to analyse the appendix which follows right after the closing statements in Leg. all. III 75b-76; Rom. 4, 23-25; Sacr. 87b; cf. also below, p. 49, n. 1 and p. 53, n. 2.

[2] The homily is divided into two parts with a preliminary conclusion about the case of the serpent in § 68.

from the quotation of Gen. 17, 19, "yes". Exactly the same outline is used in Somn II 17-30. In § 17, Gen. 37, 7 is quoted. Then, the interpretation of the first word, "methought", is given as a preface in §§ 17-20, being followed by the opening statement in § 21.

Opening (§ 17) " '*Methought,*' says he, 'that we were *binding sheaves*' (Gen. 37, 7) ... (§ 21): Now, when I listen to him who is telling the dreams I marvel at his deeming that they were *tying up sheaves, not reaping* them. The former is the work of unskilled underlings, the latter the business of masters and of those thoroughly well versed in farm work."

Close (§ 30): "But in fact the man who has never learned the mysteries of *reaping* vaunts him saying, '*Methought* I was in company with others *binding sheaves* which I had *not reaped*' (Gen. 37, 7), and failed, as I pointed out a little while ago, to take into account that this is a service performed by unskilled slaves."

Thus there is a series of homilies in Philo and Paul having the same characteristic correspondence between the opening and closing statements as had the homilies in Leg. all. III 162-168, Mut. 253-263 and John 6, 31-58. All these homilies also possess the second homiletic characteristic, that is, they have subordinate quotations from the Old Testament besides the main quotation, "the text".

In Leg. all. III 169-173 the text is taken from Ex. 16, 13-15, while Ex. 15, 8 supplies the subordinate quotation.

In Rom 4, 1-22 the text is taken from Gen. 15, 6, while the subordinate quotations are Ps. 32, 1-2, Gen. 17, 5 and 15, 5.

In Leg. all. III 65-75a the text is Gen. 3, 14-15, and the subordinate quotations are Deut. 19, 17; Gen. 3, 13; 38, 6-7.

In Sacr. 76-87 the text is Lev. 2, 14, and the subordinate quotations are Lev. 19, 32; Num. 11, 16; Lev. 26, 10; Lev. 1, 6.[1]

In Gal. 3, 6-29 the text is Gen. 15, 6, and the subordinate quotations are Gen. 12, 3/18, 18; Deut. 27, 26; 21, 23. Probably Hab. 2, 4, Lev. 18, 5 and Gen. 12, 7 also are meant to be subordinate quotations.

Finally, in Somn. II 17-30 the text is Gen. 37, 7, and the subordinate quotations are Gen. 28, 12; 31, 10-11; Lev. 19, 9; Deut 1, 17; (Num. 31, 28).

The discussion of the second identifying characteristic, in which

---

[1] In the appendix, § 87, Ex. 6, 7 and Lev. 26, 12 are quoted.

the text of the homilies is followed by subordinate quotations from the Old Testament, is to be followed by an analysis of the third characteristic: Words from the principal quotation, the text, are paraphrased or quoted in the homily.

The paraphrase of words from Lev. 2, 14 is very evident and systematic in Sacr. 76-87. The word "new" is paraphrased and interpreted in §§ 76-79, the words "roasted" in §§ 80-81, "slicing" in §§ 82-85 and "grounding" in § 86.

In the homily of Leg. all. III 169-174 the paraphrase of words from the text in Ex. 16, 13-15 is also highly developed and systematic. Most of the words and phrases are paraphrased, and in the same sequence as they are given in the quotation.

Likewise, in Rom. 4, 1-22 the main words in the text are paraphrased. Here the text is Gen. 15, 6. The paraphrase does not, however, follow the sequence in which the words occur in the quotation. Rather the words are drawn upon as they can throw light on the problem which is discussed.

Such concentration on specific subject matter has caused the paraphrase to be less well developed in the homilies of Somn. II 17-30, Leg. all. III 65-75a and Gal. 3, 6-29. The reason is that the exposition is focused upon the specific problem, which is linked to the text, but not to every word or phrase in it.

In Somn. II 17-30 the paraphrase is still quite systematic, since the first word in the text, "methought" (Gen. 37, 7), is paraphrased in §§ 17b ff. Then the paraphrase of two later words in the text, "binding sheaves", follows at the point at which the problem of the homily is raised in § 21: "Now, when I listen to him who is telling the dreams I marvel at his deeming that they were tying up sheaves, not reaping them." The main body of the homily then discusses the allegorical meaning of "the reaping" (judgement and cleansing by the guidance of God), which in the closing statement is related again to the words "tying up sheaves", etc., from the text.

In the homily in Leg. all. III 65-75a Philo discusses the problem of pleasure and body. The paraphrase therefore works only on the two words in the text, Gen. 3, 14-15, which are relevant to the question of pleasure: "the serpent" and "cursed". This paraphrase, in which the serpent means pleasure, continues down to § 68, while from § 69 and onwards the connected problem of "the body" is discussed on the basis of Gen. 38, 7. The closing remark in § 75a then turns back to the paraphrase of "the serpent" and "cursed".

The paraphrase in Gal. 3, 6-29 follows a corresponding method. It works only on the words "Abraham", "believed" and "righteousness" in the text from Gen. 15, 6, because these words are relevant to the problem which is developed in the homily.

The thesis that a certain homiletic pattern was represented in Leg. all. III 162-168, Mut. 253-263 and John 6, 31-58 has in this way received a clear confirmation, since other homilies of the same kind are found elsewhere in Philo and also in Paul. They all have in common the three characteristics of the pattern that the opening and closing statements correspond, that the text is supplemented by subordinate quotations from the Old Testament and, finally, that words from the text are paraphrased in the homily.

The same pattern in Palestinian midrash

Is the pattern discovered only of a Jewish-Hellenistic homily, or is there also evidence for the existence of similar homilies in Palestinian midrash? This pattern seems to be present also in Palestinian midrash. If so, then a homiletic pattern is defined that is common to Judaism within and outside Palestine at the time of the New Testament and Philo.

There is a striking similarity between the pattern discussed and the pattern which S. Maybaum finds to be typical to Palestinian midrash. He lists the main points of the Palestinian pattern in this way: [1]

A. The text. The first verse(s) of a pericope from the Pentateuch.
B. The connecting formula between the text and the second text cited in the proem.
C. The second text, the proemial text, (from the Prophets or the Writings) followed by an exposition.
D. The connecting formula between the exposition and the close.
E. The text from the pericope is repeated, as the closing point of the pattern.

This outline immediately reveals the similarity with two of the characteristics which were discovered in the homiletic pattern discussed above. One is that the opening and closing statements correspond. This agrees with the points A and D + E on May-

---

[1] S. Maybaum, *Die ältesten Phasen in der Entwicklung der jüdischen Predigt. Neunzehnter Bericht über die Lehranstalt für die Wissenschaft des Judentums in Berlin*, Berlin 1901, pp. 15 ff.

baum's outline, in which the close repeats the text at the opening. The pattern showed more variation in Philo, John and Paul, but there also the close could repeat the text cited at the opening, as in the homilies of Leg. all. III 169-173 and Rom 4, 1-22, cf. Leg. all. III 162-168 and John 6, 31-58. This characteristic of a correspondence between the opening and the close, then, has in Palestinian midrash developed into a stereotyped repetition.

A second characteristic of the homilies in Philo, John and Paul was that the text from the Old Testament was supplemented by subordinate quotations also taken from the Old Testament. This agrees with points B + C on Maybaum's outline, in which a subordinate quotation from the Prophets or the Writings supplements the text from the Pentateuch. John 6, 31-58 and Rom. 4, 1-22 (and Gal. 3, 6-29) are in this respect closer to Palestinian midrash than Philo is, since they also cite subordinate quotations from the Prophets and the Writings, whereas the homilies discussed in Philo cite the Pentateuch.

Again there is a tendency to stereotype in the Palestinian midrash, since one of such subordinate quotations is promoted to "a second text", a so-called proemial text. W. Bacher has already realized that this proemial text was developed from the earlier practise of supplementing a text from the Pentateuch with subordinate quotations from the other parts of the Old Testament.[1]

The question now arises whether the third characteristic, the paraphrase of the text, is also present in the homily of the Palestinian midrash. In point C Maybaum indicates that the proemial text is followed by an exposition. Later in his study he makes it clear that this exposition may be an exegesis of either the proemial text or the pericopal text itself. He thinks that in the earlier stage of development the proem only introduced the exegesis of the pericopal text, while later the proem was turned into an independent sermon based on the proemial text.[2] Such an earlier stage, then, would be close to the homiletic pattern which was analysed above. Maybaum's later stage would then follow as a consequence

---

[1] W. Bacher, *Die Proömien der alten jüdischen Homilie. Beitrag zur Geschichte der jüdischen Schriftauslegung und Homiletik*, BWA(N)T XII, Leipzig 1913, pp. 14-26. H. Thyen, *Der Stil*, p. 75, has overlooked this earlier stage from which the proem has developed. So his observation that no such developed proems are found in the Jewish Hellenistic homily has no relevance whatsoever.

[2] S. Maybaum, *Predigt*, pp. 41-42.

of the tendency that one subordinate quotation was promoted into serving as "a second text", a proemial text.

Against this background it is important to examine a few homilies in Ex. R. 25. They belong to the section of Ex. R. 15-52, which is a collection of homilies.[1] The homilies in Ex. R. 25 follow Maybaum's outline, although sometimes the pericopal text is omitted at the opening or the close, since series of homilies on the same texts are given in sequences.[2]

In the homily of Ex. R. 25, 1 the text is Ex. 16, 4 "Behold, I will, cause to rain bread from heaven for you". The proemial text (= subordinate quotation) is Ps. 135, 6, "Whatsoever the Lord pleased, that hath He done, in heaven and in earth". The proemial text is followed by a brief paraphrase of its words "in heaven and earth", but throughout the remaining part of the homily the words "from heaven" in the pericopal text are paraphrased. Thus, this homily conforms to the pattern under discussion.

In the homily of Ex. R. 25, 2 the pericopal text is also Ex 16, 4, while the proemial text is Hos. 12, 6 "But the Lord, the God of Hosts, the Lord is His name." Here the Hebrew word for Hosts (הצבאות) is interpreted and paraphrased throughout the homily, whereas only the final section paraphrases words from Ex. 16, 4 by rendering the tradition about bread from heaven and from earth. The case is similar in Ex. R. 25, 6 in which another version of the same tradition is given.[3]

The exegetical paraphrase, then, may be based either on the main pericopal text or the subordinate quotation, raised to a proemial text. In general, however, the paraphrase is less developed and does not weave the homily together into a closely knit unity.

---

[1] See S. M. Lehrman's introduction in *Midrash Rabbah*, Translated into English under the Editorship of H. Freedman and M. Simon, III (Exodus), London 1939, p. VII: "The first fourteen chapters form a running commentary on each verse of Exodus I-XI, keeping, at the same time, the continuity of the narrative steadily in view. The rest of the book (XV-LII) cites only selected verses,—as a rule, the first verse in the section of the weekly *Sidra*. The result is a medley of heterogenous homilies with the first verse only as their text."

[2] Ex. R. 25, 3 has a brief appendix attached to the close, to be compared with the appendixes mentioned above on p. 48, n. 1. Such appendixes are discussed by E. Stein, "Die homiletische Peroratio im Midrasch," *HUCA* VIII-IX, 1931-32, pp. 353-371.

[3] See above, p. 24. Cf. that Ph. Bloch, "Studien zur Aggadah," *MGWJ* XXXIV, 1885, pp. 221 f. classifies one group of homilies in the Palestinian midrash as paraphrasing homilies.

Thus the whole version of the tradition about bread from heaven and earth is rendered in the exegesis of Ex. 16, 4 in Ex. R. 25, 2, but in the homilies of Leg. all. III 162-168 and Mut. 253-263 and probably also in John 6, 31-58 only fragments of this tradition are woven into the paraphrase of Ex. 16, 4. Here, too, the tendency to stereotype is evident in Palestinian midrash. In this way the fresh and creative paraphrase of words from the text and fragments from the haggadah has developed into a rather mechanical compilation of units from the haggadah, so that only traces of the paraphrase are left.[1]

One observation made in Leg. all. III 162-168, Mut. 253-263 and also John 6, 31-58 gives an additional indication supporting the theory that they represent an early stage of this homiletic pattern of which the material in Palestinian midrash provides examples from a later stage. These homilies in Philo and also John 6, 31-58 reflect the context of the texts from the Old Testament. Thus they seem to be based on a pericope from the Old Testament, just as the homilies in the Palestinian midrash presuppose a pericope of which one or a few verses are quoted.[2]

It is reasonable, in the light of the evidence given, to conclude that the same homiletic pattern is found in Philo, John, Paul and Palestinian midrash. The material produced from the Palestinian midrashim was written down later than the time of Philo, John and Paul, but the homiletic pattern here must also go back to that period. Since it cannot have been brought into the Palestinian midrash from Philo, John or Paul, the only reasonable deduction is that this homiletic pattern was commonly used in Judaism and the early Church both within and outside Palestine in the first century of the Christian era.

There remains but to place this conclusion within the present state of research. In his analysis of the Jewish Hellenistic homily H. Thyen abstains from making a comparison with the Palestinian homily.[3] Against Thyen it must now be said that such a comparison is of great importance, and it will lead to the conclusion that there

---

[1] Cf. K.-G. Eckart, *Untersuchungen zur Traditionsgeschichte der Mechiltha*, (Diss.), Berlin 1959, pp. 103-109, who emphasizes the changes of form and content taking place in the historical development of rabbinic traditions.

[2] See S. Maybaum, *Predigt*, p. 17; *Midrash Rabbah* (ed. Freedman and Simon) III, (Exodus), p. VII; Ph. Bloch, *MGWJ* XXXIV, 1885, pp. 215-217.

[3] H. Thyen, *Der Stil*, p. 5.

are homiletic patterns which both have in common. Thus the distinction between the terms "Jewish Hellenistic" and "Palestinian" homilies is artifical and misleading as far as homiletic patterns are concerned.[1]

Thyen supposes that the texts of both the Jewish Hellenistic and the Palestinian homilies are based on the readings of pericopes from the Pentateuch (the Parashah).[2] We have discovered reflections of such pericopes at certain points in Philo and John, and they supply further support for Thyen's contention. Thus Frankel's assumption is hardly valid, namely, that there was no reading of such pericopes in Alexandria, but only citations of the homiletic texts.[3]

The present analysis has also given support to one point of the thesis of A. Guilding that John 6 is to be related to the pericopal reading of the Old Testament.[4] At this point it is possible to be even more specific than Guilding is. Instead of just collecting allusions to the readings of the Old Testament, this study has demonstrated in John 6, 31-58 midrashic exegesis within the framework of a homiletic pattern common to Judaism and the early Church.

Against the background of the reading of pericopes from the Old Testament one word must be said about the "Sitz im Leben" of this homiletic pattern. It was originally used for lecturing (preaching) in the synagogue. Just as reading the Old Testament

---

[1] Cf. that the diatribe, which Thyen finds in the Jewish Hellenistic homily can also be traced in the Palestinian midrash. See A. Marmorstein, "The Background of the Haggadah," *HUCA* VI, 1929, pp. 141-204; E. Stein, *HUCA* VIII-IX, 1931-32, pp. 370 f.

[2] H. Thyen, *Der Stil*, p. 74.

[3] Z. Frankel, *Vorstudien zu der Septuaginta. Historisch-kritische Studien zu der Septuaginta*, I, 1, Leipzig 1841, p. 55.—A liturgical pecularity in Alexandria seems, rather, to be indicated by Philo's neglect of the Prophets and the Writings. Such an explanation is more plausible than the theory of W. L. Knox ("A Note on Philo's Use of the Old Testament," *JThSt* XLI, 1940, pp. 30-34) that Philo knew only the Pentateuch, apart from "testimonies" of a few passages from other Old Testament books, or the theory of F. H. Colson, ("Philo's Quotations from the Old Testament," *JThSt* XLI, 1940, pp. 237-251) that Philo concentrated on the exegesis of the Pentateuch because of its higher authority and because of his personal predilections.

[4] A. Guilding, *Worship*, pp. 1-5, et passim. Cf. E. Haenchen's review in *ThLZ* LXXXVI, 1961, cols. 670-672, who in spite of sharp criticism admits the relevance of John 6, 25-59 for her thesis.—Our study of Philo and John makes no further comment possible on her theory that the cyclic reading of the Pentateuch was used already at New Testament times.

and lecturing were commonly done both inside and outside Palestine, so also was this homiletic pattern widespread. This "Sitz im Leben" is stated right after the close of the homily in John 6, 31-58: "This he said in the synagogue, as he taught at Capernaum" (v. 59). Philo, who uses this homiletic pattern, at several places testifies to exegetical lecturing in the synagogue.[1]

From the investigation made it is clear that the method of form criticism can be applied to the composition of John. Hence, this method is not inadequate for the analysis of John, as Schulz maintains in his discussions of similar analyses made by Dibelius and Windisch. These scholars have, unfortunately, overlooked Philo and the Palestinian midrash as parallel material to John.[2]

The conclusion thus reached can also clarify certain questions of research in the Palestinian midrash. Bacher defends the position that the homiletic midrashim contain hardly any homilies. They are, rather, a collection of proems to homilies.[3] Others, like Bloch and Baeck, think homilies are preserved in these midrashim.[4]

---

[1] Hypoth. 7, 12-15; Probus 80 ff.; Cont. 30-31; Spec. II 61-62; Mos. II 215; Somn. II 127; cf. Legat. 312. See Z. Frankel, *Vorstudien*, pp. 52-56; E. Schürer, *Geschichte des jüdischen Volkes im Zeitalter Jesu Christi*, 4th ed., II, Leipzig 1907, pp. 527 f.; W. Bousset, *Die Religion des Judentums im späthellenischen Zeitalter*, 3rd ed. by H. Gressmann, *HNT* XXI, Tübingen 1926, pp. 173-174; P. Wendland, *Die Therapeuten und die philonische Schrift vom beschaulichen Leben*, *JclPh*, Supplementband XXII, Leipzig 1896, pp. 744 ff.; G. F. Moore, *Judaism*, I, pp. 305 f.; cf. Zunz, *Die gottesdienstlichen Vorträge der Juden, historisch entwickelt. Ein Beitrag zur Alterthumskunde und biblischen Kritik, zur Literatur- und Religionsgeschichte*, Berlin 1832, pp. 328-360; I. Elbogen, *Der jüdische Gottesdienst in seiner geschichtlichen Entwicklung*, (*Grundriss der Gesamtwissenschaft des Judentums*), Leipzig 1913, pp. 195 f., 250. See also below on pp. 112 f.

[2] S. Schulz, *Menschensohn - Christologie*, pp. 75-76, with references to M. Dibelius, "Joh 15, 13. Eine Studie zum Traditionsproblem des Johannes-Evangeliums," in *Festgabe für A. Deissmann*, Tübingen 1927, pp. 168-186; H. Windisch, "Die fünf johanneische Parakletsprüche," in *Festgabe für A. Jülicher*, Tübingen 1927, pp. 112 f.

[3] W. Bacher, *Die Proömien*, pp. 1-4, (with reference to S. Maybaum who has a similar viewpoint).

[4] Ph. Bloch, *MGWJ* XXXIV, pp. 174-184, 210-224, 257-264. L. Baeck, *Aus drei Jahrtausenden. Wissenschaftliche Untersuchungen und Abhandlungen zur Geschichte des jüdischen Glaubens*, Tübingen 1958, pp. 158 f.; cf. J. Mann, *The Bible as Read and Preached in the Old Synagogue. A Study in the Cycles of the Readings from Torah and Prophets, as well as from Psalms, and in the Structure of the Midrashic Homilies*, I, Cincinnati 1940 (cf. also M. Smith, *Tannaitic Parallels to the Gospels*, *JBL Monograph Series* VI, Philadelphia 1951, pp. 101-109).

Our analyses have shown that both these viewpoints are inadequate. On comparing Ex. R. 25,2.6 with homilies such as Leg. all. III 162-168; Mut. 253-263 and John 6, 31-58, it is evident that although Ex. R. 25, 2.6 has kept the same homiletic pattern, nevertheless, different units from tradition (haggadah, etc.) have been compiled in a rather mechanical way within it. So, although authentic sermons are not preserved here, the homiletic pattern has been the collecting basin for material of different kinds from the tradition.[1] Already John 6, 31-58 reflects this use of the homiletic pattern, since the passage represents the Church's understanding of Jesus' teaching rather than it being a homily directly from Jesus himself.

With regard to the history of exegesis several theories have been suggested. For instance, Freudenthal distinguished between the earlier period of exegetical homily which later developed into thematic sermons.[2] Bacher pictures the development as from philological, simple and literal exegesis into the authoritative body of exegetical traditions in the midrashim.[3] The same viewpoint is also expressed in the Jewish Encyclopedia: "the simple exposition of Scripture is more and more lost in the wide stream of free interpretation." [4]

Our analyses have shown that one significant aspect of this developmental process is that a fresh, creative paraphrase of words from the Old Testament text together with fragments from the tradition has changed into a text being followed by compilations of fixed units from the tradition. The homilies in Leg.all. III 162-168, Mut. 253-263 and John 6, 31-58, etc., represent the earlier stage of this development.

The analysis made in the present chapter shows that the pattern

---

[1] Cf. the similar viewpoint of Zunz, *Vorträge*, pp. 359 f., expecially p. 359: "Wir besitzen daher in vielen Fällen mehr die Materialen der Rede als die Rede selber; aber jede Ausarbeitung der Art in Vajikra rabba, Pesikta, Tanchuma, Midr. Thren. u.s.w. repräsentiert in der Form wirkliche Vorträge und besteht meistentheils aus Fragmenten derselben."

[2] J. Freudenthal, *Die Flavius Josephus beigelegte Schrift über die Herrschaft der Vernunft (IV. Makkabäerbuch), eine Predigt aus dem ersten nachchristlichen Jahrhundert*, Breslau 1869, pp. 4-10; cf. a similar viewpoint in I. Elbogen, *Der jüdische Gottesdienst*, pp. 195-196.

[3] W. Bacher, *Die Jüdische Bibelexegese vom Anfange des zehnten bis zum Ende des fünfzehnten Jahrhunderts*, 1892, p. 1.

[4] J. Theodor, "Midrash Haggadah," *JE* VIII, New York/London 1904, p. 554.

of a homily explains the whole composition of these passages in Philo and John much more cogently than Bousset's theory on Philo and Bultmann's theory on John.

The next task is to discover the way this midrashic and homiletic understanding of the passages can account even for details in the structure. In turning to that undertaking special attention will be given to John, the document in which analytic research has been most detailed and thorough.

CHAPTER THREE

MIDRASHIC METHOD, PATTERNS AND TERMINOLOGY

Approach

The two preceding chapters have pointed out several midrashic features which are common to parts of Philo, John and the Palestinian midrash: the systematic paraphrase of words from Old Testament quotations and fragments from haggadic traditions, and the use of a widespread homiletic pattern.

This chapter will show in detail the way midrashic method, patterns and terminology are employed in such homilies. In undertaking this task it is necessary to draw a distinction between the history of tradition in terms of content, on the one hand, and of form criticism, on the other hand. The exegetical paraphrase makes such a distinction necessary, since it fuses together words and fragments from different traditions into traditional forms and patterns. This method of exegetical paraphrase, then, leads to a dynamic process of new combinations within the framework of tradition.

Ignoring, therefore, the question of content as much as possible, concentration will be directed to a discussion of the characteristics of form. As basis for the analysis the homily in John 6, 31-58 will be used. There are two reasons for this choice: First, this section has been the object of very thorough stylistic and linguistic analysis by several scholars. Second, it lends itself very well to a comparison both with the Palestinian midrash and Philo, since it has close parallels with the midrash; but at the same time it was written in Greek, as were the works of Philo.

Although John 6, 31-58 is chosen as a basis for the investigation, the approach employed will also throw light upon the question as to whether Philo uses midrashic method, patterns and terminology or not. Scholars have differed very much on this question. One group has maintained that Philo uses rabbinic methods and patterns of interpretation, although Greek philosophy did make a deep impact upon the content. This group includes scholars like Frankel,

Siegfried, Treitel and R. M. Grant.[1] On the other hand, there are those who analyse Philo from the viewpoint of Greek exegetical method and style. According to them Philo's allegorical method has Greek roots and is strongly influenced by the style of diatribe. Proponents of this theory include Heinisch, Stählin, Heinemann, Pepin, Stein, Daniélou, Wendland and Thyen.[2]

These two different points of view should not, however, be considered as mutually exclusive. Some of the scholars mentioned above have adopted intermediary positions. For instance Siegfried and Grant find in Philo influences from the Stoic method of allegorical interpretation as well as the rabbinic one.[3] And even I. Heinemann observes that Philo's methods of exegesis and the rabbinic coincide at certain points.[4] Finally, Stein relates Philo's allegory to the haggadah.[5]

This contrast is also weakened by some studies which demonstrate close points of agreements between the Greek and rabbinic style and method of exegesis.[6] Therefore, it is possible to analyse Greek

---

[1] Z. Frankel, *Vorstudien*, pp. 185 ff.; *Ueber den Einfluss der palästinischen Exegese auf die alexandrinische Hermeneutik*, Leipzig 1851, pp. 190-200, and "Ueber palästinische und alexandrinische Schriftforschung," *Programm zur Eröffnung des jüdisch-theologischen Seminars zu Breslau*, Breslau 1854, pp. 1-42; C. Siegfried, *Philo von Alexandria als Ausleger des Alten Testaments an sich selbst und nach seinem geschichtlichen Einfluss betrachtet. Nebst Untersuchungen über die Graecitaet Philo's*, Jena 1875, pp. 168 ff.; R. M. Grant, *The Letter and the Spirit*, London 1957, pp. 35 f.; L. Treitel, *Gesamte Theologie und Philosophie Philo's von Alexandria*, Berlin 1923, pp. 60 ff., and *MGWJ* LV (N.F. XIX), 1911, p. 546.

[2] P. Heinisch, *Der Einfluss Philos auf die älteste christliche Exegese*, (*Barnabas, Justin und Clemens von Alexandria*). *Ein Beitrag zur Geschichte der allegorisch-mystischen Schriftauslegung im christlichen Altertum*, ATA I/II, Münster i.W. 1908, pp. 123-125; W. Schmid and O. Stählin, *Geschichte der Griechischen Litteratur*, HklAW VII; 2, 1, 6th ed., München 1920, pp. 654 f.; I. Heinemann, "Philons Lehre vom Heiligen Geist und der intuitiven Erkenntnis," *MGWJ* LXIV (N.F. XXVIII), 1920, p. 121, n. 1; cf. *Altjüdische Allegoristik*, pp. 13,83 f.; J. Pepin, *Mythe et Allégorie*, pp. 234 ff.; E. Stein, *Die allegorische Exegese*, pp. 1-6; J. Daniélou, *Philon*, pp. 129-142; P. Wendland, *Philo und die kynisch-stoische Diatribe*, BGgrPhR, Berlin 1895; H. Thyen, *Der Stil*, especially pp. 62 f. and 79 ff.

[3] C. Siegfried, *Philo von Alexandria*, pp. 165 ff.; R. M. Grant, *The Letter and the Spirit*, pp. 34 f.

[4] See *Die Werke Philos* (Cohn, Heinemann, Adler, Theiler) III, pp. 7 f.

[5] See the reference on p. 19, n. 2.

[6] With regard to style, cf. A. Marmorstein, *HUCA* VI, 1929, pp. 183-204 and E. Stein, *HUCA* VIII-IX, 1931-32, pp. 370-371, who trace the diatribe in Palestinian sources. Concerning Greek and rabbinic exegetical method, see S. Lieberman, *Hellenism in Jewish Palestine. Studies in the Literary Transmis-*

elements both in the Palestinian midrash and in Philo. The more limited undertaking to investigate the midrashic method in John 6, 31-58 and draw upon Palestinian midrash and Philo for comparative material, therefore, does not exclude the possibility of an influence from Greek exegetical method.

John 6, 31-33

v. 31a "*Our fathers ate the manna in the wilderness*;
v. 31b as it is written,
   '*He gave them bread from heaven to eat.*'
v. 32 Jesus then said to them,
   'Truly, truly, I say to you,
   not Moses *gave* you *the bread from heaven*;
   but my Father *gives* you the true *bread from heaven*.[1]
v. 33 For *the bread* of God is that *which comes down from heaven* and gives life to the world.'"

The italicizing indicates the quotation from the Old Testament cited in John 6, 31b, the paraphrasing of words from this quotation and the uncovered fragments from haggadah.

John 6, 31b is the text of the homily. The Old Testament quotation is linked to the fragment from the haggadah in v. 31a.[2] The closest parallel is the frequent custom of the Palestinian midrash to connect an Old Testament quotation to a sentence from the haggadah. The versions of the tradition about bread from heaven and earth in Ex. R. 25, 2.6 and Mek. Ex. 16, 4 are examples of this custom. One sentence and the following Old Testament quotation in Ex. R. 25, 2 runs as follows:

"...and made manna [which is bread] come down to Israel from heaven, for it says:

---

sion, Beliefs and Manners of Palestine in the I Century B.C.E.-IV Century, C.E., TStJThS XVIII, New York 1950, pp. 47-82; and D. Daube, "Rabbinic Methods of Interpretation and Hellenistic Rhetoric," HUCA XXII, 1949, pp. 239-264; "Alexandrian Methods of Interpretation and the Rabbis," *Festschrift Hans Lewald*, Basel 1953, pp. 27-44, and A. Kaminka,"Bibel VII, Bibelexegese," EJ IV, Berlin 1929, col. 622; M. Hadas, "Plato in Hellenistic Fusion," JHI XIX, 1958, pp. 11-12.

[1] Translation mine.
[2] Note that the formula in v. 31 καθώς ἐστιν γεγραμμένον (also John 12, 14) corresponds to the Hebrew formula כאשר כתוב, which occurs in the Qumran literature. See J. A. Fitzmyer, "The Use of Explicit Old Testament Quotations in Qumran Literature and in the New Testament," NTSt VII, 1960-61, p. 300.

'Behold, I will cause to rain down bread from heaven for you' "
(Ex. 16, 4).¹

Philo also makes quotations from Ex. 16, 4 follow after haggadic statements, as in Leg. all. III 162a and Mut. 259. The parallel in Leg. all. III 162a is quite close to John 6, 31, though it may have been written by Philo as a literary transition.² The haggadic elements are italicized: "That *the food* of the soul is not *earthly* but *heavenly*, we shall find abundant evidence in the Sacred Word. 'Behold I rain', etc." (Ex. 16, 4).

Thus it is logical to conclude that the text of the homily, John 6, 31, is introduced together with a preceding haggadic fragment. The closest parallel is the midrashic custom of letting a sentence from the haggadah be followed by an Old Testament quotation. Philo indicates an awareness of the same custom.

Even more striking is the use of a midrashic method and pattern in John 6, 32-33, which is an exposition of the Old Testament quotation cited in v. 31b. This exposition is given by a pattern of contrast (v. 32 οὐ — ἀλλ') followed by a sentence introduced by "for", (γάρ v. 33).

Two patterns of contrast occur frequently in connection with Old Testament quotations as they are cited in the Palestinian midrash. The one gives a philological correction of the Old Testament text, using the formula אל תקרי — אלא — (do not read ... but ...) or similar formulas.³ Philo also uses this pattern of contrast when correcting the text. The other pattern confirms the reading of the Old Testament quotation in contrast to a different one. Here the usual formula is — אין כתיב כאן אלא (it is not written here ..., but ...).⁴ Both Philo and Paul also use this pattern.

---

¹ Cf. CD 3, 7 which probably is an explicit quotation of Deut. 9, 23 attached to a survey of the fidelity of the Patriarchs, etc. See J. A. Fitzmyer, *NTSt* VII, 1960-61, p. 308.

² See p. 44.

³ A. Rosenzweig, "Die Al-tikri-Deutungen. Ein Beitrag zur talmudischen Schriftdeutung." *Festschrift zu I. Lewy's siebzigsten Geburtstag*, Breslau 1911, pp. 204-253; H. Torczyner, "Al Tikre," *EJ* II, Berlin 1928, cols. 74-87; W. Bacher, *Die exegetische Terminologie der jüdischen Traditionsliteratur*, I (*Die Bibelexegetische Terminologie der Tannaiten*), Leipzig 1899, pp. 175-177; J. Bonsirven, *Exégèse rabbinique et exégèse Paulinienne*, (Bibliothèque de théologie historique), Paris 1939, p. 120.

⁴ W. Bacher, *Die exegetische Terminologie* I, pp. 88-89 and II (*Die Bibel- und Traditionsexegetische Terminologie der Amoräer*), Leipzig 1905, p. 92; B. M. Metzger, "Formulas Introducing Quotations of Scripture in the NT and the Mishnah," *JBL* LXX, 1951, p. 299.

Two examples of the pattern of correction are Mek. Ex. 16, 15 and Deter. 47-48, (Again the Old Testament quotations and the words from them in the exposition are italicized). In both places the pattern of contrast is followed by an added explicative statement.

Mek. Ex. 16, 15:

" '*Man did eat the bread of strong horses*' (Ps. 78, 25).
Do not read (אל תקרי) '*of strong horses*' (אבירים),
but (אלא) '*of the limbs*' (איברים),
that is, *bread* that is absorbed by the *limbs*."

Deter. 47-48:[1]

" '...*Cain rose up against Abel his brother and slew him* (αὐτὸν)' (Gen. 4, 8) ...
It must be read in this way (ὥσθ' οὕτως ἀναγνωστέον·),
'*Cain rose up and slew himself* (ἑαυτόν),'
not (ἀλλ' οὐχ) someone else.
And this is just what we should expect to befall him. For the soul that has extirpated from *itself* (αὐτῆς) the principle of the love of virtue and the love of God, has died to the life of virtue..."

The exegetical pattern of contrast in John 6, 31-33 is clearly the same as this pattern in the Palestinian midrash and Philo, as the agreements between them show: 1) In all the three cases the Old Testament quotation is followed by an exegetical pattern of contrast using the terms אל – אלא (Mek.), ἀλλ' οὐχ (Philo) and οὐ — ἀλλ' (John). 2) To this pattern of contrast an explicative statement can be added, as is done in these examples from Palestinian midrash and Philo, and as is also the case in John 6, 33. 3) The determining agreement is, however, that John 6, 32 gives a different reading of the Old Testament quotation cited in v. 31b, in accordance with this midrashic pattern for correcting the Hebrew text.

This third point becomes clear as soon as the verbs in John 6, 31-32 are translated back into Hebrew:

(31b) "He gave (ἔδωκεν / נתן) them bread from heaven to eat."
(32) Truly, truly, I say to you,
    not ... gave (δέδωκεν [ἔδωκεν] / נָתַן)
    but ... gives (δίδωσιν / נוֹתֵן) [2]

---

[1] C. Siegfried, *Philo von Alexandria*, p. 176, has observed that Philo at this place uses the method of אל תקרי.

[2] Translation mine.

Thus v. 32 shows that the understanding of the Old Testament quotation in v. 31b is not based upon the vocalization for perfect tense, נָתַן, but upon the vocalization for the participle, נֹתֵן, which in the Greek of v. 32 is rendered by the present tense. This participle may also be rendered in the future tense, as is supposed in v. 51, δώσω.

This philological exegesis is not an isolated phenomenon in John. Burney and Dahl have shown that John's rendering of Is. 6, 10 in John 12, 40 is based upon a vocalization of the Hebrew text different from that of the MT.[1] And it is commonly accepted by scholars since Burney and Odeberg that Gen. 28, 12 is interpreted in John 1, 57 on the basis of rabbinic exegesis of בו in the Hebrew text.[2]

While Mek. Ex. 16, 15 and Deter. 47-48 suggest a different reading, a correction, John 6, 32 gives the interpretation as an authoritative statement by Jesus: "Truly, truly I say to you, ..." This peculiarity in John emphasizes the fact that the exegesis by Jesus is not to be regarded just as one correction to the text among other readings. It is the correct and authoritative rendering of the Old Testament quotation in contrast to the wrong rendering of it. So the distinction between the two exegetical patterns of contrast, the philological correction and the philological confirmation of the text, is blotted out in John. A few examples of the pattern of philological confirmation are as follows:

Mek. Ex. 15, 11:

"'Doing (עושה) wonders' (Ex. 15, 11).
It is not written here (אין כתיב כאן): 'Who did (עשה) wonders', but (אלא) 'who does (עושה) wonders,' that is, in the future."

Migr. 1 and 43:

"'into the land which I shall shew (δείξω) thee' (Gen. 12, 1).
He says not (εἰπὼν οὐχ) 'which I am shewing (δείκνυμι)'
but (ἀλλ') 'which I will shew (δείξω) thee'.
Thus he testifies to the trust, etc."

This pattern can be developed into a paraphrasing exegesis of the Old Testament quotation, examples of which can be found both in Palestinian midrash (Mek. Ex. 17, 9), Paul (Gal. 3, 16) and in Philo, as in Leg. All. I 67:

---

[1] C. F. Burney, *The Aramaic Origin*, pp. 120-21; N. A. Dahl, *NTT* LX, 1959, p. 193.
[2] C. F. Burney, *The Aramaic Origin*, p. 115; H. Odeberg, *The Fourth Gospel. Interpreted in its Relation to Contemporaneous Religious Currents in Palestine and the Hellenistic-Oriental World*, Uppsala 1929, p. 35.

"And the words, *'there where* (or *'whose'*) (οὗ) *the gold is*' (Gen. 2.11) are not (οὐ ἔστι) a mere piece of local information, *there* where (ὅπου) *the gold is,* but (ἀλλ') *there* (*is He*) *whose* (οὗ) *is* the treasure, even prudence gleaming like gold, tried by the fire, and precious."

There are also striking agreements between this exegetical pattern and that of John 6, 31-32: 1) The Old Testament quotation is followed by a pattern of contrast with parallel terms, אין – אלא (Mek.), οὐχ — ἀλλ' and οὐκ — ἀλλ' (Philo) and οὐ — ἀλλ' (John). 2) As in Leg. all. I 67, it can be developed into an amplifying paraphrase of the Old Testament quotation, provided that the point of philological interest in the text remains clear. Thus John 6, 32 has incorporated such words as "Moses", "my Father" and "the true" in the pattern, although they are not directly used in the quotation cited in v. 31b. 3) Mek. Ex. 15, 11 gives an exegesis of the verb that is identical to the treatment of the verb in John 6, 32. In both cases the rendering of the participle (John נותן, Mek. עושה) is given as a contrast to the perfect tense (John נתן, Mek. עשה). Even more significantly, in Mek. Ex. 15, 11 the participle is related to the eschatological time (לעתיד לבא). Thus John, too, probably refers by the presupposed participial form, נותן, to the eschatological time.

Having established evidence for such a midrashic pattern of contrast in John 6, 31b-33, it is necessary to examine some of the details. The contrast between the tenses of the verbs in v. 32 has been shown. The next step will be to examine the contrast between the subjects. Since there is a pattern of philological exegesis employed in v. 32, the meaning of this contrast must be: "Moses" is not the subject of the verb "to give" (נתן) in the Old Testament text, rather "my Father" is the subject. This interpretation fits very well into the suggestion that the quotation cited in v. 31b refers back to Ex. 16, 4 and 15. Ex. 16, 15b runs, "And Moses said to them, 'It is the bread which the Lord has given (נתן) you to eat.'" Here it is clear that Moses is not the subject of the verb "give" (נתן), but the Lord (יהוה) is the subject.

Thus in v. 32 the phrase "my Father" (ὁ πατήρ μου) and in v. 33 the word "God's" (τοῦ θεοῦ) render the word "the Lord" (MT יהוה / LXX ὁ κύριος) in Ex. 16, 15.[1] This interpretation is supported

---

[1] S. Schulz, *Komposition*, p. 95, who regards Ex. 16, 15 as the closest background of v. 33: "so hat die johanneische Bezeichnung des Brotes als ἄρτος τοῦ θεοῦ (6, 33) ihre grösste Entsprechung in Ex. 16, 15." See also K. Schaedel, *Das Johannesevangelium und "Die Kinder des Lichts"*, p. 187.

by the fact that John elsewhere alternates between the word "God" and the word "Father".[1] And Philo testifies even that "the Lord" in Ex. 16, 15 could be rendered as "God", when he cites in Leg. all. III 173 οὗτός ἐστιν ὁ ἄρτος, ἡ τροφή, ἣν δέδωκεν ὁ θεος, κτλ. ("This bread is the food which God hath given", etc.).

The previous chapter has shown the way John and Philo can render the second person plural "to you" (MT לכם, LXX ὑμῖν) in Ex. 16, 15 by pronouns for other persons. For example John 6, 31b and Fug. 139 have the third person plural (αὐτοῖς), while Leg. all. III 169 and John 6, 34 use the first person plural (ἡμῖν). The paraphrase of the text in the saying of Jesus in v. 32, however, keeps the second person plural (ὑμῖν) in exact correspondance with Ex. 16, 15. In this saying, Jesus addresses himself to his listeners, indicating that even the pronouns in the formulas of dialogue interpret this word in the text, as the underlining shows: Jesus then said *to them* (αὐτοῖς), "Truly, truly, I say *to you* (ὑμῖν), it was not Moses who gave *you* (ὑμῖν) the bread from heaven ... ." John 6, 32 ff. therefore applies the Old Testament quotation cited in v. 31b to the listeners of Jesus.

In John 6, 32b the word "the bread" (τὸν ἄρτον) is supplemented by a qualifying adjective, "the true" (τὸν ἀληθινόν). Because supplemental qualifications of different kinds are quite common in the exegetical paraphrase, there are also some others in the homily of John 6, 31-58, such as, "the bread *of God*" (ὁ — ἄρτος τοῦ θεοῦ, probably based on Ex. 16, 15) in v. 33, the bread *of life* (ὁ ἄρτος τῆς ζωῆς) in vv. 35.48, and "the *living* bread" (ὁ ἄρτος ὁ ζῶν) in v. 51. Correspondingly, in the exegetical paraphrase of Leg. all. III 162 is "the food *of the soul*" (αἱ ψυχῆς τροφαί), and in the paraphrase about the manna in Sacr. 86, "with the *divine* food" (τροφῇ θείᾳ). The italicizing and underscoring show the supplemental qualifications given to the words for manna in the exegetical paraphrase. In v. 33 even a supplemental clause is incorporated in the paraphrase of words taken from the Old Testament quotation and the haggadic fragment, i.e., "and gives life to the world."

One final word about v. 33 should be said. A fragment from the

---

[1] Compare e.g. John 1, 18 Θεὸν οὐδεὶς ἑώρακεν πώποτε with 6, 46 οὐχ ὅτι τὸν πατέρα ἑώρακέν τις. And the quotation of Is. 54, 13 in John 6, 45a has "God" (ὁ θεός) while the exposition of it in John 6, 45b-46 alternates between "Father" (ὁ πατήρ) and "God" (ὁ θεός). See also pp. 40 f.

haggadah has been woven into the exegetical paraphrase of the Old Testament quotation: "the bread...is that which comes down from heaven." [1] Since this is an interpretation of the Old Testament quotation in v. 31b, it is evident that the verb "to give" is here defined as "to come down" (καταβαίνειν).

The analysis, then, leads to the conclusion that midrashic method, patterns and terminology are all evident in John 6, 31-33. The text of the homily in v. 31 is introduced together with a preceding haggadic fragment. The closest parallel is the midrashic custom of letting a sentence from the haggadah be followed by an Old Testament quotation.

In the exposition, vv. 32-33, there are close agreements with the midrashic patterns of contrast, where the Old Testament text is corrected or confirmed over against a different reading. Frequently such patterns of contrast are connected with an explicative statement, as v. 33 is connected with v. 32 in John 6.

The midrashic pattern of contrast makes clear the significance of the tenses of the verbs in v. 32, referring back to a different vocalization of the verb in the Hebrew text (not נָתַן, but נֹתֵן). Parallels in the midrash indicate that the preferred vocalization of a participle (נֹתֵן, in Greek present tense δίδωσιν) makes the verb refer to eschatological time.

The pattern also points up the contrast between "Moses" and "my Father" in v. 32 which is based upon a philological discussion of the subject for the verb "to give". This discussion probably refers back to the text in Ex. 16, 15.

Corresponding exegetical patterns of contrast are also present in Philo and Paul.

Three other exegetical methods are also employed in John 6, 31-33(34). First a pronoun from the Old Testament quotation varies the person according to the exegetical interest (v. 31 αὐτοῖς, v. 32 ὑμῖν, etc.). Second, the words from the Old Testament quotation and the haggadah were supplemented in the paraphrase with other words (v. 32 τὸν ἀληθινόν, v. 33 τοῦ θεοῦ, vv. 35.48 τῆς ζωῆς, v. 51 ὁ ζῶν) and brief clauses (v. 33 καὶ ζωὴν διδοὺς τῷ κόσμῳ). This method of supplementing is also frequently used in Philo. Finally, a word from the haggadah (ὁ καταβαίνων in v. 33) can define and replace a word in the Old Testament quotation (v. 31b ἔδωκεν, v. 32 δέδωκεν — δίδωσιν).

---
[1] See pp. 20 f.

It is necessary to place these conclusions within the framework of present research. Bultmann takes vv. 30-33 together and refers these verses to the dialogue which "the Evangelist" has added to the revelatory source. As he re-arranges the discourse, Bultmann makes this section follow after v. 35 and precede v. 47.[1]

E. Schweizer admits that the order of the discourse seems corrupted. Although he hesitates to accept Bultmann's analysis, he has no alternative suggestion concerning the question of tradition and composition; so he only points out the difficulties in the text without offering any solutions.[2] The approach of Ruckstuhl is still less satisfactory, since he even tries to explain away the existence of the difficulties which Bultmann found.[3]

Noack comes quite close to an alternative to Bultmann's analysis, when he proposes that the discourse is a composition of single logia from the Johannine tradition.[4] His theory breaks down, however, because the midrashic paraphrase binds John 6, 31-58 together as unity. Actually, even Noack himself had difficulties in separating v. 32 from v. 31 as an independent logion.[5]

In his analysis of the discourse in John 6, Schulz modifies Bultmann's viewpoints. He takes, as did Bultmann, the starting point in the statement of "Ego eimi" in v. 35. But instead of thinking in terms of a revelatory source expanded and commented upon by "the Evangelist", he regards v. 35 as the central element from the tradition to which the Evangelist added other elements from the tradition.[6] "The Evangelist's" own reshaping characteristics can also be traced, according to Schulz. He regards then v. 31b as a quotation of Ps. 78, 24,[7] v. 32 as an independent logion from the tradition,[8] and v. 33 as a statement of definition by "the Evangelist", reflecting Ex. 16, 15.[9] Schulz ignores, however, the facts that

---

[1] R. Bultmann, *Evangelium*, p. 163. See also H. Becker, *Die Reden des Johannesevangeliums und der Stil der gnostischen Offenbarungsrede*, FRLANT LXVIII (N.F. L), Göttingen 1956, pp. 67 f.
[2] E. Schweizer, *EGO EIMI*, pp. 151 ff.
[3] E. Ruckstuhl, *Einheit*, pp. 120 ff. Cf. the similar tendency in X. Léon-Dufour, "Le mystère du Pain de Vie (Jean VI)," *RSR* XLVI, 1958, pp. 496 ff.
[4] Cf. B. Noack, *Tradition*, p. 151.
[5] See p. 26, n. 5.
[6] S. Schulz, *Komposition*, pp. 72 ff.
[7] *ibid.*, p. 94.
[8] *ibid.*, p. 73.
[9] *ibid.*, p. 73 and p. 95.

John 6, 32-33 is an exposition of the Old Testament quotation cited in v. 31b, and that this section has the form of a midrashic pattern of contrast commonly used in connection with philological exegesis both in Philo, Paul, and Palestinian midrash.

The criticism of Schulz is equally applicable to Bultmann's analysis, which also ignores the fact that vv. 32-33 is an exposition of v. 31b. By taking vv. 30-33 together, he overlooks the point that the request for a sign in v. 30 belongs to that cycle of traditions also used by the Synoptics [1] and must therefore be separated from v. 31 where the homily begins.

John 6, 34-40

    v. 34 "They said to him,
        'Lord, *give us this bread* always.'

(a) v. 35 Jesus said to them,
        'I am *the bread* of life;
        he who comes to me shall not hunger,
        and he who believes in me shall never thirst.

(b) v. 36 But I said *'you'*, because *you* have seen me and yet do not believe.[2]
    v. 37 All that the Father gives me will come to me; and him who comes to me I will not cast out.

(c) v. 38 For *I have come down from heaven*,
        not to do my own will,
        but the will of him who sent me;
    v. 39 and this is the will of him who sent me, that I should lose nothing of all that he has given me,
        but raise it up at the last day.
    v. 40 For this is the will of my Father, that every one who sees the Son and believes in him
        should have eternal life;
        and I will raise him up at the last day.'"

V. 34 has a parallel in John 4, 15: "The woman said to him, 'Sir, give me this water...'". In the context of the homily of John 6, 31-58, however, v. 34 paraphrases words from the Old Testament quotation cited in v. 31b.[3] Furthermore, v. 34 has the function of introducing the following exposition in vv. 35-40.

---
[1] See pp. 45 f.
[2] The translation is adjusted to the exegesis given below.   [3] See p. 23.

It is quite appropriate to the structure of the homily in John 6, 31-58 that the philological and explicative clarification of the text in vv. 31b-33 is followed by v. 34 which serves as a bridge to the exposition of some of the words in the text.

Analysing the section of John 6, 35 ff., it is evident that points (a) and (b) have the same structure, i.e. a paraphrase of words from the Old Testament quotation (1) followed by a participial (relative) statement (2). Here and in the following parallels the words from the Old Testament quotations are underscored.

(a) v. 35 (1) ἐγώ εἰμι ὁ ἄρτος τῆς ζωῆς·
(2) ὁ ἐρχόμενος πρὸς ἐμὲ οὐ μὴ πεινάσῃ,
καὶ ὁ πιστεύων εἰς ἐμὲ οὐ μὴ διψήσει πώποτε.

(b) v. 36 (1) Ἀλλ' εἶπον ὑμῖν[1] ὅτι καὶ ἑωράκατέ [με] καὶ οὐ πιστεύετε.
v. 37 (2) πᾶν ὃ δίδωσίν μοι ὁ πατὴρ πρὸς ἐμὲ ἥξει,
καὶ τὸν ἐρχόμενον πρός με οὐ μὴ ἐκβάλω ἔξω

John 6, 45 has a similar pattern where an Old Testament quotation is followed by a participial statement:

v. 45 (1) καὶ ἔσονται πάντες διδακτοὶ θεοῦ (Is. 54, 13).
(2) πᾶς ὁ ἀκούσας παρὰ τοῦ πατρὸς καὶ μαθὼν ἔρχεται πρὸς ἐμέ.

Of several examples of this pattern in the Palestinian midrash where an Old Testament phrase is interpreted by a general participial statement, Mek. Ex. 15, 26 and Mek. Ex. 22, 5 are given as illustrations.

Mek. Ex. 15, 26:

(1) " 'And he said: If Thou wilt diligently hearken' (Ex. 15,26) . . .
(2) If a man *hearkens* (שמע אדם) to one commandment he is given the opportunity to *hearken* to many commandments."

Mek. Ex. 22, 5:

(1) " 'And shall let his beast loose' (Ex. 22, 5) . . .
(2) If he turned over (מסר) his sheep to his son, his servant or his agent, he is not liable. But if he turned them over to a deaf and dumb person, to an insane person or to a minor, he is liable."

Occasionally Philo, too, lets an Old Testament quotation be followed by a participial statement. This is the case in connection with a paraphrasing exposition of Gen. 17, 1 in Mut. 47. Again the words from the Old Testament quotation are italicized:

---

[1] See pp. 74 f.

(1) "After saying *'Be well pleasing before Me'* He adds further *'and become blameless'* (Gen. 17, 1).

This is in close sequence to the preceding.

'Best it is,' He means, 'to set your hand to excellence and thus be *well pleasing*, but failing this at least abstain from sins and thus escape *blame*.'

(2) For positively right conduct (ὁ μὲν γὰρ κατορθῶν) brings praise to the doer, but abstantion from iniquity (ὁ δὲ μὴ ἀδικῶν) saves him from censure."

Thus John 6, 35; 6, 36-37 and 6, 45 agree with the midrashic pattern where words from an Old Testament quotation (1) are interpreted by a succeeding participial (or relative) statement (2).

Point (c), John 6, 38 ff., is introduced by a fragment from the haggadah about the bread coming down from heaven, given as a paraphrase of the Old Testament quotation cited in v. 31b. This paraphrase is supplemented by a ἵνα clause. The fragment from the haggadah is italicized.

"For *I have come down from heaven,*
not to (οὐχ ἵνα) do my own will,
but (ἀλλά) the will of him who sent me."

John 6, 38 provides an example of the common midrashic method of interpreting an Old Testament phrase by adding a final clause to it. Philo uses ἵνα as John does, and the Hebrew equivalent in the midrash is the preposition לְ followed by an infinitive. In the examples given the words from the Old Testament quotation are italicized.

Mek. Ex. 19, 7:

" *'The Lord came from Sinai'* (Deut. 33, 2).
Do not read thus, but read: *'The Lord came to Sinai,'* to give (לִיתֵּן) the Torah to Israel."

Leg. all. III 166:

"*Let the soul, then, gather the day's portion for a day* (Ex. 16, 4). that (ἵνα μή) it may declare not itself but (ἀλλά) the bountiful God guardian of the good things."

Both John and Philo combine the ἵνα clause with the contrast of οὐχ/μή — ἀλλά.

So far it is apparent that points (a), John 6, 35, and (b), v. 36-37 follow the midrashic pattern of explaining a paraphrase of or a quotation from an Old Testament passage by means of general participial statements. Point (c), v. 38, has another midrashic pattern, in which the paraphrase is supplemented by a final clause to indicate its meaning. At this juncture it is necessary to discuss some details under each point of John 6, 34-40.

Much attention has been paid to the saying introduced by ἐγώ εἰμι in point (a), v. 35a,[1] but as yet it has not been related to John's midrashic treatment of the Old Testament and fragments from the haggadah. The significance of this becomes evident as the parallel statements in vv. 41 and 51 are placed together with the one in v. 35a and the identical parallel in v. 48: (For convenience the words from the Old Testament quotation in v. 31b and the fragment from the haggadah are underscored).

vv. 35.48 ἐγώ εἰμι ὁ ἄρτος τῆς ζωῆς
v. 41 ἐγώ εἰμι ὁ ἄρτος ὁ καταβὰς ἐκ τοῦ οὐρανοῦ
v. 51 ἐγώ εἰμι ὁ ἄρτος ὁ ζῶν ὁ ἐκ τοῦ οὐρανοῦ καταβάς

It is obvious that the phrase "Ego eimi" is a formula to be used when a word from the Old Testament is to be identified with a person or a figure in first person singular.

The most obvious parallel in John is the word of the Baptist in 1, 23, in which he identifies Is. 40, 3 with himself: ἐγώ φωνὴ βοῶντος ἐν τῇ ἐρήμῳ, κτλ. ("I am *the voice of one crying in the wilderness, etc.*")[2]

John uses also a corresponding formula referring to the Baptist in third person singular, John 5, 35: ἐκεῖνος ἦν ὁ λύχνος, κτλ. ("he was *the lamp*"), where the underscored is taken from Ps. 131, 16b-17.[3]

---

[1] See E Schweizer, *EGO EIMI*; R. Bultmann, *Evangelium*, p. 167, n. 2; C. H. Dodd, *The Interpretation of the Fourth Gospel*, Cambridge 1953, pp. 93-96, 349 f.; K. Kundsin, *Charakter und Ursprung der johanneischen Reden*, AUL I, 4, Riga 1939, pp. 209-268; H. Becker, *Die Reden des Johannesevangeliums*, especiall the survey on pp. 7-11; K. Schaedel, *Das Johannesevangelium und "die Kinder des Lichts"*, pp. 5 ff.; S. Schulz, *Komposition*, pp. 70-131.

[2] Because scholars have overlooked the possibility that ἐγώ εἰμι may be a midrashic formula, they have ignored John 1, 23 as a relevant parallel. Cf. a similar use of the formula in Rev. 2, 23: ἐγώ εἰμι ὁ ἐρευνῶν νεφροὺς καὶ καρδίας, probably interpreting Ps 7, 10, and also in Philo, Somn. II 222: ἐγὼ γάρ εἰμι ὁ ἐξαγαγὼν ἐκ πέτρας ἀκροτόμου πηγὴν ὕδατος, interpreting Deut. 8, 15. See also Rev. 22, 16: ἐγώ εἰμι ἡ ῥίζα κτλ,, interpreting Is. 11, 10.

[3] F. Neugebauer, "Miszelle zu Joh 5, 35," *ZNW* LII, 1961, p. 130, shows that John 5, 35 is based upon LXX Ps. 131, 16b-17. The translation of John 5, 35 in *The Holy Bible. Revised Standard Version*, New York 1953 has ignored the determined use of ὁ λύχνος and translated "a-lamp".

An objection could be raised against the use of John 1, 23 as a parallel. Since it lacks the copula, εἰμι, the fuller formula of ἐγώ εἰμι may seem to be something other than a formula of identifying Old Testament words with a person. The use of the equivalent formula אנא הוא in Lam. R. I, 16 § 45 to Lam. 1, 16 serves as a warning against stressing this point. There it is told that the Emperor Trajan came to kill the Jews at the feast of Hanukkah:
"On his arrival he found the Jews occupied with this verse:

'The Lord will bring a nation against thee from far, from the end of the earth, as the vulture (הַנֶּשֶׁר) swoopeth down.' (Deut. 28, 49). He said to them:
'I am *the vulture* (אנא הוא נשרא)
who planned to come in ten days, but the wind brought me in five.' "

Although the date of this story is uncertain,[1] it exemplifies the phrase "Ego eimi" as a midrashic formula for identifying Old Testament words with a person in first person singular, a formula which can thus be used to refer to John the Baptist and Trajan as well as to Jesus Christ.

It would be distracting to discuss all the occurrences of "Ego eimi" in John from this point of view.[2] In other contexts it may have a different background. The illustrations given suffice, however, to show that from viewpoint of form, the phrase "Ego eimi" in John 6, 35.41.48.51 is a formula by which the words of "bread, etc." from the Old Testament quotation cited in v. 31b can be identified with Jesus in the first person singular.

The supplement "of life" which in the paraphrase is attached to the word "the bread" in v. 35,[3] is probably a new and fresh exegetical combination and is hardly due to the adaption of a fixed and traditional phrase "the bread of life" to the word "bread" in the Old Testament quotation cited in v. 31b. The lack of relevant parallels to such a phrase outside John supports this interpretation.[4]

---

[1] See further the broader discussion of this tradition by R. Loewe, "A Jewish Counterpart to the Acts of the Alexandrians," *JJSt* XII, 1961, pp. 105-122.

[2] K. Schaedel, *Das Johannesevangelium und "Die Kinder des Lichts,"* approaches this view. He classifies "Ego eimi" as a formula of identification, where well known eschatological terms and metaphors are being connected with Jesus. See especially p. 15 and pp. 232-246.

[3] See pp. 66 f.

[4] See further p. 149. Concerning the lack of parallels, see H. L. Strack and P. Billerbeck, *Kommentar zum Neuen Testament aus Talmud und Midrasch,* II, München 1924, pp. 482 f.; K. Schaedel, *Das Johannesevangelium und "Die*

Attention will be given to some details in John 6, 36, point (b). At first, this verse, 'Αλλ' εἶπον ὑμῖν ὅτι καὶ ἑωράκατέ [με] καὶ οὐ πιστεύετε, seems to refer to another word which is now repeated here. Scholars had difficulties, however, in finding the word to which it refers.¹

New light is thrown upon this problem with the realization that v. 36 also paraphrases the Old Testament quotation cited in v. 31b. In v. 32 Jesus gives the authoritative meaning of this quotation, when he renders "them" (αὐτοῖς) in v. 31b as "you" (ὑμῖν). Thus v. 36 refers back to this interpretation by Jesus in v. 32 and repeats "you" (ὑμῖν). This reference is of the same kind as those in John 10, 36 and 1, 15:

John 6,36 'Αλλ' εἶπον "ὑμῖν" ὅτι κτλ
     10, 36   εἶπον "υἱὸς τοῦ θεοῦ εἰμι"
     1, 15   εἶπον "ὁ ὀπίσω μου κτλ"

Thus there is no ὅτι *recitativum* in John 6, 36, but a ὅτι which introduces a motivating causal proposition. And the verse is to be translated in this way: "But I said *"you"*, because *you* have seen me and yet do not believe."

Again Philo's exegesis offers a parallel: his interpretation of Gen. 2, 6 in Leg. all. I 28. The words from the Old Testament quotation are italicized.

Kinder des Lichts," p. 188, and S. Schulz, *Komposition*, pp. 95 f.,97. G. D. Kilpatrick, "The Last Supper (Living Issues)," *ET* LXIV, 1952/1953, pp. 4-8 and K. G. Kuhn, "The Lord's Supper and the Communal Meal at Qumran," in *The Scrolls and the New Testament*, (ed. by K. Stendahl), New York 1957, pp. 74 ff. have drawn the attention to the phrase "the bread of life" in the Egyptian-Jewish legend Joseph and Aseneth. If this isolated parallel indicates that "the bread of life" was a traditional phrase, then it means only that this fixed dictum has been incorporated into the midrashic exegesis in John 6. E. Schweizer, "Das Herrenmahl im Neuen Testament. Ein Forschungsbericht," *ThLZ* LXXIX, 1954, col. 583, warns, however, rightly against reading this legend, for which the earliest evidence must be dated to the 4th or 5th centuries, back to New Testament times. Cf. also J. Jeremias' doubts in his reply to Kilpatrick in *ET* LXIV, 1952/1953, pp. 91 f.

¹ It is generally regarded as an allusion to John 6, 26. See W. Bauer, *Das Johannesevangelium, HNT* VI, 2nd ed., Tübingen 1925, p. 93; C. K. Barrett, *St. John*, p. 243; R. Bultmann, *Evangelium*, p. 173, n. 4; B. Noack, *Tradition*, pp. 147-148, correctly stresses the inadequacy of this reference to John 6, 26, and suggests, therefore, that it quotes a word from oral tradition.—See further pp. 175 f.

" 'And a spring (πηγὴ) went up out of the earth (ἐκ τῆς γῆς) and watered all the face (τὸ πρόσωπον) of the earth' (Gen. 2, 6).

He calls (εἴρηκε) the mind 'a spring of the earth' (γῆς πηγήν), and the senses its 'face' (πρόσωπον) because (ὅτι) Nature... assigned this place to them... etc."

Here, as in John 6, 36, the exposition refers to (and repeats) words from the Old Testament quotation, and a causal proposition introduced with ὅτι is added as a motivation.

Having dealt with some exegetical and stylistic details in John 6, 35, point (a), and 6, 36-37, point (b), the next step will be to look at some details in 6, 38-40, point (c). Since the exegetical paraphrase and the supplementary final proposition in v. 38 have already been discussed, only the remaining verses 39-40 need to be analysed.

These verses consist of two parallel statements which have an interesting structure. The principal proposition begins with the demonstrative pronoun, then follow the copula and a definite noun. Next comes a subordinate proposition, introduced by "that", the ἵνα — *epexegeticum*. The stylistic pattern is, thus, as follows: οὗτός (αὕτη, τοῦτό) ἐστιν definite noun, ἵνα —. The pattern occurs in John 6, 29.39.40.50; 15, 12; 17, 3; 1 John 3, 11.23; 5, 3 and 2 John 6.[1] In all these cases the definite noun refers to or repeats a preceding term, which it defines.

In John 6, 39.40 the statements of definition refer back to the term "the will of him who sent me" in v. 38:

v. 38   "For I have come down from heaven,
        not to do my own will,
        but the will of him who sent me (τὸ
        θέλημα τοῦ πέμψαντός με).
v. 39   and this is the will of him who sent me (τὸ
        θέλημα τοῦ πέμψαντός με), that ...
v. 40   For this is the will of my Father (τὸ
        θέλημα τοῦ πατρός μου), that ..."

It is significant that the same commenting style of definition is present in I QS 4, 2 f. where "their ways" is discussed. (The occurence of this term is italicized).

---

[1] See also R. Bultmann, "Analyse," *Festgabe für A. Jülicher*, p. 142; E. Schweizer, *EGO EIMI*, p. 89; K. Kundsin, *Charakter*, pp. 206 f.

(4, 2) "Now these (ואלה) are *their ways* (דרכיהן) in the world:
to enlighten (להאיר) the heart of man,
and to make straight (ולישר) before him all
   the ways of true righteousnes,
and to make (ולפחד) his heart tremble with
   the judgments of (3) God."[1]

As in John 6, 39.40 etc., I QS 4, 2-3 begins with the demonstrative pronoun (ואלה), goes on with a definite noun (דרכיהן), and has then a subordinate clause introduced by the Hebrew lamedh—which here has the function of ἵνα—*epexegeticum*. Moreover, the determined noun (דרכיהן) repeats a preceding word in 3, 26 which in this way receives an explicative definition.[2]

It is also interesting that an exegetical statement in the homily of Leg. all. III 162-168 seems to be a variant of the same style, when it says: " 'that I may prove them whether they will walk in My *law* (τῷ νόμῳ) or not' (Ex. 16, 4); for this is the divine *law*, to value excellence for its own sake" (νόμος γὰρ θεῖος οὗτος, τὴν ἀρετὴν δι' ἑαυτὴν τιμᾶν), (§§ 167-168).

Also here a noun is repeated (νόμος) and it receives a definition by means of a demonstrative pronoun (οὗτος) pointing forward to the explicative proposition, which in this case has the infinitive τιμᾶν as verb.

Since a clear parallel is found in the Qumran literature and a similar style also occurs in Philo, the stylistic pattern of an explicative definition is not a phenomenon limited to the Johannine literature. Once again John is seen to belong within the framework of Jewish tradition.[3]

---

[1] The *Dead Sea Manual of Discipline. Translation and Notes*, by W. H. Brownlee, *BASOR Suppl. Studies* X-XI, New Haven, Conn. 1951, p. 14. (From 4, 3 and onwards the different style of "a catalogue of virtues" follows). Brownley's unnecessary addition "[The way of the Spirit of truth is]" in 4, 2 is not rendered. Hebrew text in *Megilloth Midbar Yehuda. The Scrolls from the Judean Desert*, ed. by A. M. Habermann, Israel 1959, p. 63.

[2] This stylistic parallel between the Johannine literature and I QS 3 and 4 is hardly an accident, since John 4, 34 also has a similar parallel. Here the same stylistic pattern occurs, but the demonstrative pronoun is lacking: ἐμὸν βρῶμά (cf. v. 32) ἐστιν, ἵνα —. Correspondingly I QS 4, 6 f. has ופקודת כול הולכי בה, למרפא (from 3, 18) ("and the visitation of all who walk by it consists in healing ...." See *The Dead Sea Manual of Discipline* (W. H. Brownlee), p. 14 and n. 12. Hebrew text in *Megilloth Midbar Yehuda* (A. M. Habermann), p. 63. Also I QS 4, 12 f. has this variant of the pattern.

[3] Against E. Schweizer, *EGO EIMI*, p. 89 and E. Ruckstuhl *Einheit*, p. 203, who list this stylistic pattern among the characteristics of the individual style of the author of John.

A participial (relative) clause is incorporated in each of the two statements of definition in John 6, 39.40. Almost as an addition, the same sentence follows in each case: I will raise him up at the last day. There are only slight variations between v. 39 and v. 40 in the wording of the sentence; so too is the case in v. 44 and v. 54 where it also occurs. The pattern where a participial statement has an explicative appendix to its principal clause is not without parallels in the Jewish literature. As an example Ex. R. 38, 3 is quoted together with John 6, 39.40.44.54.

Ex. R. 38, 3: (1) "a priest who eats (כל כהן שהוא אוכל) terumah, but who is ignorant of the Torah, (2) will not (אינו) serve as a priest in the Time to come, (3) but (אלא) will suffer a threefold rejection."

John 6, 39: ... (1) "of all that he has given me (πᾶν ὃ δέδωκέν μοι) (2) I should lose nothing (μὴ ἀπολέσω ἐξ αὐτοῦ) (3) but (ἀλλά) raise it up at the last day."

John 6, 40: ... (1) "every one who sees (πᾶς ὁ θεωρῶν) the Son and believes in him (2) should have (ἔχῃ) eternal life, (3) and (καί) I will raise him up at the last day."

John 6, 54: (1) "he who eats (ὁ τρώγων) my flesh and drinks my blood (2) has (ἔχει) eternal life, (3) and I (κἀγώ) will raise him up at the last day."

John 6, 44: (2) "No one can come (Οὐδεὶς δύναται ἐλθεῖν) to me (1) unless (ἐὰν μή) the Father who sent me draws him; (3) and I (κἀγώ) will raise him up at the last days."

This pattern, common to Ex. R. 38, 3 and John 6, 39.40.54, consists of the following points: (1) One (or two) participial or relative clauses. (2) The principal clause. (3) An explicative clause added to the principal clause, point (2). Ex. R. 38, 3 is especially a close parallel to John 6, 39, because both construct points (2) and (3) as antithetic statements.[1]

John 6, 44 is a variation of the same pattern, since point (1) has conditional style, and the sequence of the clauses differ from that of the other examples.

It is evident, then, that John 6, 34 serves as an introduction to the section 6, 35-40, which develops an exposition of some of the words in the text, cited in v. 31b. Points (a), 6, 35, and (b), 6, 36-37,

---

[1] Philo seems to use the same pattern in Immut. 100: (1) "Those, too, who perform (τοὺς — πράττοντας) any other right action without the assent of their judgement or will, but by doing violence to their inclination, (2) do not achieve righteousness (μὴ κατορθοῦν) (3) but (ἀλλά) are wounded and chased by their inward feelings."

have the same structure, that is to say, that phrases from the Old Testament quotation are followed by general statements of participial (and relative) nature. Both the Palestinian midrash and Philo exhibit parallels to this pattern. The beginning of point (c), 6, 38, has a different pattern, however. In it a paraphrase of words from the Old Testament is interpreted by means of the addition of a final clause. Similar patterns occur both in Philo and the Palestinian midrash.

As for details in the section, it is significant to notice that so far as form is concerned, the formula "Ego eimi" in 6, 35 (and 6, 41.51) is a midrashic formula by which words from the Old Testament (and the tradition) are identified with persons as Jesus, John the Baptist and Trajan, in the first person singular. The phrase "bread of life" in v. 35 is probably a new and fresh exegetical combination in this context, a position supported by the lack of relevant parallels outside John.

John 6, 36 is not quoting an unknown statement by Jesus, but refers back to the pronoun ὑμῖν in v. 32, which interprets the pronoun αὐτοῖς in v. 31b. The reference in v. 36 is followed by a causal motivation (ὅτι) to which Philo supplies a parallel.

The stylistic pattern of "οὗτός (αὕτη, τοῦτό) ἐστιν —definite noun, ἵνα — *epexegeticum*" in 6, 39.40.50 is not peculiar to the style of John, since I QS 4, 2 f. has a corresponding construction. Also in this respect, therefore, John can be placed within the framework of Jewish tradition. The reference to "the last day" in a clause added to the principal clause and a participial statement (6, 39.40. 54. cf. 44) is not completely exceptional either, since Ex. R. 38, 3 has a similar pattern.

It is necessary to examine the conclusions reached in the light of present research. Bultmann reconstructs the order according to "the Evangelist" as follows: vv. 34.35.30-33.47-51a.41-46.36-40. The basis for his reconstruction is not, however, criteria of form, but of logical development of thought. Thus Bultmann says that the request in v. 34 cannot follow vv. 30-33, since it presupposes a more superficial understanding of the bread than this section gives. Therefore v. 34 must precede vv. 30-33, and be followed by the words "I am the bread of life," v. 35, which introduce the thought which is elaborated in vv. 30-33.[1]

---

[1] R. Bultmann, *Evangelium*, p. 163.

An analysis of forms, on the other hand, runs counter to Bultmann's attempt. It was quite appropriate to the structure of the homily for the philological and explicative clarification of the text in vv. 31b-33 to be followed by a "bridge" in v. 34, which in turn leads into a systematic exposition of some words from the text. This midrashic pattern of John 6, 34-40 also runs contrary to Bultmann's suggestion to place vv. 36-40 after v. 46.

Bultmann, who isolates 6, 35 as a word from the revelatory source, is followed by Becker.[1] Other scholars, as Blauert, Noack and Schulz classify it as an independent logion from the Johannine tradition.[2] Several objections can be raised against this suggestion. V. 35 (and v. 48) is a paraphrasing exposition of the word "bread" from the text in v. 31b. In the parallels of vv. 41.51 also other words from the text and the haggadah are utilized.[3] The formula "Ego eimi" is a formula by which Old Testament words are identified with a person in first person singular. The participial statement in v. 35b may have been an independent saying which was connected with this paraphrase in v. 35a of the word "bread" from the Old Testament. More probably, though, different elements from tradition also were fused together in v. 35b.[4]

The last point made about the participial statement in v. 35b is also relevant to v. 37, which Becker refers to the same source, whereas Bultmann includes only v. 37b in his revelatory source.[5] Schulz classifies v. 37 as an independent logion.[6] But v. 37 together with v. 36 follows the same midrashic pattern as v. 35.

Noack completely ignores 6, 34.40.[7] As for the problem of the apparent quotation of a word by Jesus in v. 36, Noack suggests that it refers to an oral logion not included in the Gospel.[8] The fact is, of course, that it refers to and expounds the pronoun in the text (v. 31b) as interpreted by Jesus in v. 32. As a parallel to v. 38

---

[1] *ibid.*, p. 168, n. 1; H. Becker, *Die Reden des Johannesevangeliums*, p. 69.
[2] H. Blauert, *Die Bedeutung der Zeit*, pp. 90 ff.; B. Noack, *Tradition*, p. 51; S. Schulz, *Komposition*, pp. 72-74.
[3] Cf. that S. Schulz, *Komposition*, p. 97, admits that even as a pre-Johannine logion John 6, 35 must have referred to the Old Testament words about the manna.
[4] See further the analysis on p. 166, n. 2.
[5] R. Bultmann, *Evangelium*, p. 172; H. Becker, *Die Reden des Johannesevangeliums*, p. 69.
[6] S. Schulz, *Komposition*, p. 73; cf. B. Noack, *Tradition*, p, 38.
[7] See the index, B. Noack, *Tradition*, p. 166.
[8] *ibid.*, pp. 147-148.

Noack draws attention to the statements of the type "I have come to...etc." to explain the mission of Jesus in the Synoptics and elsewhere in John.[1] This observation of his is correct. Here the midrashic pattern of an Old Testament phrase interpreted by a final clause coincides with the structure of such statements of "self predications".

John 6, 41-48

(2) v. 41: "The Jews then murmured at him, because he said (εἶπεν),
'I am the bread which came down from heaven.'
(3) v. 42: They said (καὶ ἔλεγον),
'Is not this (οὐχ οὗτός ἐστιν) Jesus, the Son of Joseph, whose father and mother we know?
(4) How does he now say (πῶς νῦν λέγει ὅτι)
'I have come down from heaven?' '
(5) v. 43: Jesus answered them (ἀπεκρίθη Ἰησοῦς καὶ εἶπεν αὐτοῖς),
'Do not murmur among yourselves.
v. 44: No one can come to me unless the Father who sent me draws him;
and I will raise him up at the last day.
v. 45: It is written in the prophets,
'And they shall all be taught by God.'
Every one who has heard and learned from the Father comes to me.
v. 46: Not that any one has seen the Father
except him who is from God;
he has seen the Father.
v. 47: Truly, truly, I say to you,
he who believes has eternal life.
v. 48: I am *the bread* of life.' "

So far, it is evident that the text of the homily in John 6, 31b was followed by a midrashic pattern of a philological contrast in vv. 32-33. Then vv. 34-40 gave a systematic exposition of parts of the text, which were introduced by the heading in v. 34. The next section runs from vv. 41-48, and follows a usual pattern of exegetical debate in the Palestinian midrash and in Philo.

Mek. Ex. 12, 2 provides a typical example of this pattern. As in

---

[1] *ibid.*, pp. 50-51.

the citation of John 6, 41-48 the corresponding words in points 2, 4 and 5 are italicized.

(1) " 'This new moon shall be unto you' (Ex. 12, 2).
(3) R. Simon the son of Yohai says (רבי שמעון בן יוחאי אומר): Is it not a fact that (והלא) all the words which He spoke to Moses He spoke only in the daytime;
(2) the *new moon*, of course, He *showed him at nighttime.*
(4) How then (כיצד) could He, while speaking with him at daytime, *show him the new moon ,at nighttime?*
(5) R. Eliezer says (רבי אליעזר אומר): He spoke with him at daytime near nightfall, and then *showed him the new moon right after nightfall.*"

Here is an example from Philo Mut. 141a. 142b-144, where Gen. 17, 16 is interpreted:

(1) 141a): "So much for the phrase 'I will give to thee'. We must now explain 'from her' (Gen. 17, 16).
(2) 142b): There is a third class (τρίτοι δέ εἰσιν) who say (λέγοντες) that virtue is *the mother* of any good that has come into being, receiving the seeds of that being from nothing that is mortal.
(3) 143: Some ask, however,[1] whether (πρὸς δὲ τοὺς ζητοῦντας, εἰ) the barren can bear children, since the oracles (οἱ χρησμοί) earlier describe Sarah as barren.
(4) and now admit that (νῦν ὅτι — ὁμολογοῦσι) she will become *a mother.*
(5) Our answer to this must be that (λεκτέον ἐκεῖνο, ὅτι) it is not in the nature of a barren woman to bear, any more than of the blind to see or of the deaf to hear.
But as for the soul which is sterilized to wickedness and unfruitful of the endless host of passions and vices, scarce any prosper in childbirth as she.
For she bears offspring worthy of love, even the number seven according to the hymn of Hannah, that is, grace, who says, 'The barren hath borne seven, but she that is much in children hath languished' (1. Sam. 2, 5). 144: She applies the word 'much' to the mind which is a medley of mixed and confused thoughts, which, because of the multitude of riots and turmoils that surround it, brings forth evils past all remedy. But the word 'barren' she applies to the mind which refuses to accept any mortal sowing as fruitful, the mind which makes away with and brings to abortion all the intimacies and the matings of the wicked, but holds fast to the 'seventh' and the supreme peace which it gives. This peace she would fain bear in her womb and be called its *mother.*"

---

[1] The English translation in *Philo* (Colson and Whitaker) V, p. 215 is altered to bring forth the midrashic pattern which Philo is using.

These three passages follow the same exegetical pattern, which consists of the following five points: Point (1) has a quotation from the Old Testament. In the Johannine example, as we have seen, the quotation is cited in John 6, 31b. Point (2) gives the interpretation of the quotation. In John 6, 41 this interpretation paraphrases words from the Old Testament quotation together with a fragment from the haggadah. In this way it also combines elements from the exposition in John 6, 35 and 38.¹ In Mek. Ex. 12, 2 only one word from the Old Testament quotation is paraphrased, "the new moon" (החדש). No words from the Old Testament quotation, however, are paraphrased in Mut. 142b, but the central term "mother" clearly refers to the phrase "from her" in the quotation cited in § 141a.

Point (3), then, introduces the objection against the interpretation. In Mek. Ex. 12, 2 this point precedes point (2). Point (4) refers to and repeats the interpretation in point (2), which has been questioned. In all three examples this repetition is very free and fragmentary.

Finally, point (5) gives the answer to the objection and the solution of the problem. In all three cases the conclusion of this point refers back to point (2), the interpretation, by paraphrasing parts of it. In John 6, 41-48, the conclusion (vv. 47:48) also refers back to the exposition in v. 35, indicating that this pattern of exegetical debate has hardly had an independent existence, but is, rather, an integral part of the homily.²

The exegetical and stylistic terminology in these passages show close similarities, as can be expected within the same pattern. The table on the next page makes evident the terminological similarities.

This pattern occurs also elsewhere.³ No further evidence, however, is needed to establish the fact that John 6, 41-48 utilizes this midrashic pattern of debate, which also exists in Palestinian midrash and in Philo.

It is necessary to examine some details of John 6, 43-48, point (5). The pattern of v. 44 as a whole, has been dealt with above on page 77. The first half of it, however, needs more attention. It

---

¹ See X. Léon-Dufour, *RSR* XLVI, 1958, p. 499.
² Both John and Philo incorporate a subordinate Old Testament quotation into the discussion under point 5. In John this Old Testament quotation (Is. 54, 13) coincides with the subordinate Old Testament quotation of the homily as a whole. See p. 38.
³ See Mek. Ex. 12, 1; 15, 5, etc.

The passage	John 6, 31b.41-48	Mek. Ex. 12, 2	Mut. 141a.142b-144
1	Old Testament quotation	Old Testament quotation	Old Testament quotation
2	εἶπεν	רבי שמעון בן יוחאי אוסר [1]	τρίτοι δέ εἰσιν οἱ — λέγοντες
3	καὶ ἔλεγον οὐχ οὗτός ἐστιν	והלא	πρὸς δὲ τοὺς ζητοῦντας, εἰ
4	πῶς νῦν λέγει ὅτι	כיצד	οἱ χρησμοὶ νῦν ὅτι — ὁμολογοῦσι
5	ἀπεκρίθη Ἰησοῦς καὶ εἶπεν αὐτοῖς	רבי אליעזר אומר	λεκτέον ἐκεῖνο, ὅτι

has the structure of a negated clause, followed by a conditional clause. The same structure of form is also present in the words of 6, 65 and 3, 2. A similar construction is found in some statements of the Mishnah. From the viewpoint of content they could be classified as conditioned prohibitions. An example is Bikkurim I, 5. In Spec. I 242 Philo has a parallel, which he adjusts to Greek style.

John 6, 44:

"No one (Οὐδείς) can come to me unless (ἐὰν μή) the Father who sent me draws him."

Bikkurim I, 5:

"A woman who is an offspring of proselytes may not (לא) marry into the priesthood unless (עד שתהא) her mother was an Israelite." [2]

---

[1] This phrase introduces both point (2) and point (3), which appear in the reverse sequence of the one given here in this tabular form. See the analysis above.

[2] See *Mishnayoth*, text and translation by Ph. Blackmann, I, London 1951, p. 469. This pattern of conditioned prohibition is frequent in the Mishnah. Another example is found in *ibid.*, p. 68, Berakot 8, 8 "One must not (ואין) respond with Amen after a Samaritan who recites a Blessing unless (עד-ש) he has heard the whole blessing." Cf. I QS 5, 13: "...they will not (לוא) be cleansed unless (כי אם) they have turned from their wickedness." (*The Dead Sea Manual of Discipline* (W. H. Brownlee), p. 20; Hebrew text in *Megilloth Midbar Yehuda* (A. M. Habermann), p. 65).

Spec. I 242:

"none (οὐδενὶ) of the priests is permitted to perform the rites, if he is not (ὃς ἂν μὴ) wholly sound."

John 6, 44 thus seems to take its structure from the Jewish judicial traditions, here represented by the halakah of the Mishnah and Philo's books on the laws.

The Old Testament quotation from Is. 54, 13 cited in John 6, 45a rates a brief exposition in vv. 45b-46. As in the Old Testament text cited in 6, 31, so also here only the parts which are relevant to the exposition are quoted.[1] As often in the Palestinian midrash the passage cited from the Old Testament is interpreted by a general statement of participial nature (πᾶς ὁ ἀκούσας, κτλ., see above on page 70). Then follows a statement of reservation in v. 46:

"Not that (οὐχ ὅτι) any one has seen the Father except (εἰ μὴ) him who is from God; he has seen the Father."

This reservation clears away any possible misunderstanding of the Old Testament passage and the interpretation in v. 45. A similar pattern occurs in John 7, 22 (οὐχ ὅτι — ἀλλ' —), but here without any explicit quotation from the Old Testament.

Again the style of exegesis is clear, and Philo can produce a good parallel in *Opif.* 149:

"So Moses says that God brought all the animals to Adam, wishing to see what appellations he would assign to them severally (paraphrase of Gen. 2, 19). Not that (οὐχ ὅτι) he was in any doubt... but because (ἀλλ' ὅτι) he knew that He had formed in mortal man the natural ability to reason of his own motion..."

---

[1] The quotation is based upon the MT since Is. 54, 13 is rendered as an independent sentence, while in LXX it is formulated together with Is. 54, 12. The use of θεοῦ in place of κυρίου (MT יהוה) may be due to LXX influence. See C. F. Burney, *The Aramaic Origin*, pp. 117-118, Burney's conclusion is, however, weakened by the fact that the word "God" and not "the Lord" is frequently used where the phrase "those taught by God", etc. occurs. See I Thess. 4, 9; CD, 20, 4; Barnabas 21, 6. Cf. B. Noack, *Tradition*, p. 76, especially nn. 185 and 186.

With regard to the introductory formula of the quotation, cf. the Hebrew equivalent indicated by A. Schlatter, *Der Evangelist Johannes. Wie er spricht, denkt und glaubt. Ein Kommentar zum vierten Evangelium*, Stuttgart 1930, p. 176. B. Noack, *Tradition*, p. 75, is wrong when he thinks that the general reference to "the prophets" indicates a free quotation from memory. The general reference is rather due to the fact that it was in accordance with the rather fixed wording of a formula of citation.

A further parallel is to be found in Mut. 270:

" 'the Lord went up from Abraham,' says Moses (Gen. 17, 22). He does not mean (οὐχ ὅτι) that Abraham was parted from him,... but (ἀλλά) he wished to shew the independence of the learner."

In Palestinian midrash the terms לא - אלא can be used in a similar way, as is seen from Mek. Ex. 13, 21:

"It is not (לא) that I have no one to take the torch and light the way for my sons. It is merely (אלא) to show you how dear my sons are to me....".[1]

This stylistic pattern of reservation is shown to use a similar terminology in John, Philo and Palestinian midrash: John 6, 46 οὐχ ὅτι — εἰ μή, 7, 22 οὐχ ὅτι — ἀλλ', Opif. 149 οὐχ ὅτι — ἀλλ' ὅτι, Mut. 270 οὐχ ὅτι — ἀλλά, Mek. Ex. 13, 21 אלא - לא.

The analysis of forms in John 6, 41-48 leads to the conclusion that the midrashic background is quite evident. This section follows a pattern of exegetical debate to which Palestinian midrash and Philo exhibit several parallels. The pattern consists of the following points: (1) The Old Testament quotation. (2) The interpretation. (3) The objection to the interpretation. (4) Point (2), the interpretation, freely repeated and questioned. (5) The answer which can conclude with a reference to point (2), the interpretation.

This pattern, together with the pattern of philological contrast in John 6, 31-33, is decisive proofs for the thesis that the discourse in John 6 is to be placed within the midrashic traditions.

With regard to details, it is thus apparent that the structure of v. 44a has parallels in the "conditioned prohibitions" in Mishnah and Philo. The midrashic pattern is evident in the exposition of the Old Testament quotation from Is. 54, 13 as given in John 6, 45-46: The quotation is followed by a general statement of participial style, and then by a statement of reservation to which Philo and the Palestinian midrash also supply parallels.

These points will now be linked to the present state of research. In the discussion of John 6, 31-40 the structure was seen to be very similar to midrashic patterns, and required no reconstruction of a hypothetical order like that of Bultmann. The same is the case in 6, 41-48. Bultmann makes vv. 41-46 to follow after v. 51a.[2]

---

[1] See A. Schlatter, *Der Evangelist Johannes* p. 195.
[2] R. Bultmann, *Evangelium*, p. 163.

Such a rearrangement is quite unnecessary for it is fitting that the exposition of parts of the text in vv. 34-40 should be followed in vv. 41-48 by a pattern of exegetical debate which discusses certain aspects of this exposition. Furthermore, Bultmann's separation of vv. 47-48 from v. 46 is impossible, since vv. 47-48 are the natural conclusion of this pattern of exegetical debate.

Bultmann, Becker, Blauert and Schulz agree that 6, 44a.45b and 47-48 belong to the tradition, though Blauert and Schulz think in terms of different logia, while the others refer them to a written source.[1] From the standpoint of form analysis, however, there is no reason for giving these parts a special classification different from the other segments which also have traditional style and structure. They may have existed as independent logia which have been integrated into the midrashic exposition, or they may fuse together fragments from different traditions. The clear paraphrase in vv. 41.42.48 of words from the Old Testament text (v. 31b) and of a haggadic fragment supports the last suggestion.[2]

Noack observes correctly that the quotations of the word by Jesus in v. 41 and v. 42b do not repeat the exact wording of any previous saying. To Noack this is an indication of the inaccuracy which characterizes oral tradition generally, especially since v. 41 even seems to refer forward to v. 51![3] It is, however, possible to be more specific in locating the background of this pecularity. John 6, 41 sums up parts of the previous exposition in one statement which is to be tested within the framework of a pattern for exegetical debate. In this pattern a fragmentary and free repetition of such a statement is quite common, just as it happens in v. 42b and v. 48.

The midrashic treatment of the quotation from Is. 54, 13 in John 6, 45 runs counter to Noack's idea that the author only cites from free recollection. The quotation and the following exposition point rather to conscious scholarly effort.

John 6,49-58:

(A) v. 49 " 'Your fathers ate the manna in the wilderness, and they died.

---

[1] *ibid.*, pp. 170-172. H. Becker, *Die Reden des Johannesevangeliums*, p. 69; H. Blauert, *Die Bedeutung der Zeit*, pp. 90-92; S. Schulz, *Komposition*, p. 73.

[2] This point is also overlooked by B. Noack, *Tradition*, pp. 135,145,52.

[3] *ibid.*, p. 145.

>   v. 50 This is *the bread which comes down from heaven*, that a man may *eat* of it and not die.
>   v. 51 I am the living *bread which came down from heaven*; if any one *eats* of *this bread*, he will live for ever; and the *bread* which I *shall give* for the life of the world is my flesh.'
>
> (B) v. 52 The Jews then disputed among themselves, saying, 'How can this man *give us* his flesh *to eat?*'
>   v. 53 So Jesus said to them: 'Truly, truly I say to you, unless you *eat* the flesh of the Son of man *and drink* his blood, you have no life in you;
>   v. 54 he who eats my flesh *and drinks* my blood has eternal life,
>   and I will raise him up at the last day.
>   v. 55 For my flesh is *food* indeed, and my blood is *drink* indeed.
>   v. 56 He who eats my flesh *and drinks* my blood abides in me, and I in him.
>   v. 57 As the living Father sent me, and I live because of the Father,
>   so he who eats me will live because of me.
>   v. 58 This is *the bread which came down from heaven*, not such as *the fathers ate* and died;
>   he who eats *this bread* will live for ever.' "

Verse 49 marks a new beginning by repeating—with slight differences and a supplement (καὶ ἀπέθανον)—the haggadic fragment at the beginning of the homily in v. 31a. A part of this fragment is also included in the closing statement of the homily in v. 58. In this way it plays a central function in the structure of the whole homily, by marking out the beginning, the middle and the close.

In v. 49 this haggadic fragment introduces the word φαγεῖν, to eat, into the exposition; so the systematic exegesis of the homily proceeds to place this word from the text in the center of the exposition from v. 49 to the end.[1]

The structure of this exposition runs as follows: In (A), vv. 49-51a, the word φαγεῖν is interpreted by connecting it to the interpretation of the other words of the text (v. 31b) given in vv. 32-48. Then in (B), vv. 52-57, it is given a more independent

---
[1] See p. 35.

discussion, while the concluding statement of v. 58 again places it within the exposition of the whole text. Verse 51b serves as a bridge between the two parts in which the exposition of φαγεῖν is divided in this way.

In the first part (A), vv. 50-51 appear as a contrast to the statement from the haggadah in v. 49 (v. 49 ἀπέθανον, v. 50 μὴ ἀποθάνῃ and v. 51 ζήσει). The first contrast (v. 50) takes the form of a statement of explicative definition.[1] The phrase to be qualified is "the bread which comes down from heaven," and it repeats, freely, the haggadic paraphrase of the text given in v. 33. Then the proposition introduced by ἵνα—*epexegeticum* in v. 50 adds also the word φαγεῖν from the text.

Verse 51a freely repeats the same haggadic paraphrase of the text. Here, however, it is combined with the formula "Ego eimi" and supplemented with the qualification ὁ ζῶν, referring back to the exposition in vv. 35.38.41.42.48. The succeeding clause of the conditional style adds φαγεῖν to these elements also found in the first half of the homily.

Previously cited parallels from the midrash and Philo illustrate the way an Old Testament quotation can be interpreted by a general participial statement.[2] In such cases, however, the conditional clause also can be used as in John 6, 51a, Mek. Ex. 22, 3 and Leg. all. III 71. (The italicizing indicates the Old Testament quotation, in John rendered by a haggadic fragment).

John 6, 51a:

"I am the living *bread which came down from heaven;*
If (ἐάν) any one eats of this bread,
he will live for ever."

Mek. Ex. 22, 3:

" '*If the sun be risen upon him*' (Ex. 22, 3)....
If (אם) it is known that this burglar had peaceful intention toward the owner and yet the later kills him, he is guilty of murder."

Leg. all. III 71:

" '*Er was wicked in the sight of the Lord*' (Gen.38, 7).
For when (ὅταν) the mind soars aloft and is being initiated in the mysteries of the Lord, it judges the body to be wicked and hostile.

---

[1] See pp. 75 f
[2] See pp. 70f

But when (ὅταν) it has abandoned the investigation of things divine, it deems it friendly to itself, its kinsman and brother."

Thus Joh. 6, 31-58, Mekilta to Exodus and Philo can alternate between participial and conditional style in the interpretation of Old Testament quotations, a feature well known in the judicial traditions of the Old Testament and Judaism.[1]

The second part (B) of the exposition of φαγεῖν, vv. 52-57, falls into four points: First v. 52 raises a question. Then three points make comments to this question, v. 53, taking the conditional style and vv. 54.56, the participial style. Both the last two verses develop the exposition into subordinate explications (v. 55 and v. 57 respectively). Finally, v. 58 is the concluding part of the whole homily.[2]

The next step will show the way words from the Old Testament quotation (v. 31b) are paraphrased and interpreted in vv. 52-57. But, first it is necessary to examine one aspect of "the bridge" in v. 51b. This is an exegetical remark of the pattern "A is B", parallels to which are found in Leg. all. II 86 and CD 6, 4. The words from the Old Testament quotations are underscored or italicized:

John 6, 51   καὶ ὁ ἄρτος δὲ ὃν ἐγὼ δώσω
                  ἡ σάρξ μού ἐστιν
Leg. all. II 86 ἡ γὰρ ἀκρότομος πέτρα (Deut. 8, 16)
                    ἡ σοφία τοῦ θεοῦ ἐστιν
                    (For *the flinty rock* is the wisdom of God.")
CD 6, 4[3]   הבאר (Num. 21, 18) הוא התרה
                    (*The Well* is the Law).

By the help of this pattern "A is B", it is said that a word or a phrase from the Old Testament is identical with another word or phrase.

In John 6, 52, the Jews questioned the interpretation that identifies "the bread which I shall give" with "my flesh". They tested it by putting the words "flesh" and "this one" into the

---

[1] Cf. W. Nauck, *Die Tradition und der Charakter des ersten Johannesbriefes*, WUNT III, Tübingen 1957, pp. 29 f. has pointed to the same variation of participial and conditional style in 1 John. As background, he refers to the style of Hebrew judicial tradition and also parallels in the Qumran literature (*ibid.*, p. 32, n. 10).

[2] See pp. 37 f.

[3] Text and translation in *The Zadokite Documents*, edited with a translation and notes by Ch. Rabin, Oxford 1954, pp. 22-23.

wording of the Old Testament quotation cited in v. 31b. Philo also used a corresponding method by replacing one or more words in the Old Testament quotation with other words, as for instance in the homily of Mut. 259:
(The words from the Old Testament are underlined).

John 6, 31b   ἄρτον — ἔδωκεν αὐτοῖς φαγεῖν (Ex. 16, 4.15)
6, 52   οὗτος ἡμῖν δοῦναι τὴν σάρκα φαγεῖν
Mut. 259   ἄρτους ἀπ' οὐρανοῦ (Ex. 16, 4)
259   τὴν οὐράνιον σοφίαν

The example cited shows the way John 6, 52 replaces the Old Testament word ἄρτον with τὴν σάρκα and Philo ἄρτους with τὴν — σοφίαν.

At the same time v. 52 questions Jesus' interpretation that he himself (v. 51b ἐγώ, v. 52 οὗτος) is the subject of the Old Testament text in v. 31b, which has God as subject according to vv. 32-33. This part of the question in v. 52 is answered in v. 57 by a reference to the correspondance between the Father and the Son.

It is, therefore, obvious that v. 52 is a paraphrase of parts from the Old Testament text cited in v. 31b. This clear exegetical discussion in John 6, 52 ties the whole section of vv. 51b ff. closely to the Old Testament quotation in v. 31b, and weighs heavily against a theory of interpolation.[1]

The paraphrase of the Old Testament quotation (v. 31b) in 6, 52 is followed by statements of a participial and conditional nature. Again the same midrashic pattern occurs as in vv. 35, in vv. 36-37, in v. 45 and v. 51: 1. A paraphrase or a quotation of words from the Old Testament. 2. An exposition of participial or conditional nature. While vv. 45 and v. 51 each has a single statement of participial or conditional style, v. 35 and vv. 36-37 have double statements, vv. 52-57 have three such statements.

The exposition of the text in vv. 51b-57 (58) is developed by the help of fragments from eucharistic traditions which are fused together with haggadic fragments about the manna.

It is very fortunate that Paul in 1 Cor. 11, 23 ff. both quotes the tradition about the eucharist and uses fragments of it in comments of a participial (relative) and imperative nature. Here are a few of these comments and the words from the tradition italicized:

---

[1] See pp. 25 f.

1 *Cor.* 11, 27-29:

v. 27 "Whoever (ὅς ἄν), therefore, *eats the bread* or *drinks the cup of the Lord* in an unworthy manner will be guilty of profaning *the body* and *blood of the Lord*.
v. 28 Let a man examine himself,
and so *eat* of *the bread* and *drink* of *the cup*.
v. 29 For any one who *eats* and *drinks*
(ὁ γὰρ ἐσθίων καὶ πίνων)
without discerning *the body*
eats and *drinks* judgment upon himself."

There are three significant observations to be made from I Cor. 11, 27-29. First, it shows that fragments from a tradition can be paraphrased in a fresh way within the framework of the traditional participial style. This fact also supports the thesis about the corresponding use of haggadic tradition in John 6, 31-58. Second, Paul uses the participial style together with imperative applications to the readers; hence this style does not occur in independent and pure form. This observation weighs against isolating statements of a participial and conditional nature from the commenting glosses in John 6, 31-58. Third, Paul shows the way a tradition about the eucharist can be reduced to fragments and used in a paraphrasing exposition.

Paul's eucharistic comments suggest that fragments from the eucharistic traditions may have been paraphrased in a similar way in John 6, 51-58. The agreements between John and the eucharistic sections of the New Testament can serve as guide. At the same time there are indications that the section also draws upon traditions similar to the haggadah about the manna in I Cor. 10, 1-4.[1] Here are the words of John 6, 51-58 which have parallels in the eucharistic traditions in the Synoptics and in I Cor. 11:

John 6, 51 ὁ ἄρτος — δώσω ἡ σάρξ μού ἐστιν ὑπέρ
    Cf. Luke 22, 19 ἄρτον — ἔδωκεν — ἐστιν τὸ σῶμά μου τὸ ὑπέρ
    I Cor. 11, 23-24 ἄρτον — μού ἐστιν τὸ σῶμα τὸ ὑπέρ
John 6, 52 δοῦναι τὴν σάρκα φαγεῖν
    Cf. Matt. 26, 26 δοὺς — φάγετε — τὸ σῶμά
    Luke 22, 19 ἔδωκεν — τὸ σῶμά
John 6, 53 φάγητε τὴν σάρκα — πίητε — τὸ αἷμα vv. 54.56
    ὁ τρώγων μου τὴν σάρκα καὶ πίνων μου τὸ αἷμα
    v. 55 ἡ — σάρξ μου — τὸ αἷμά μου

---
[1] See pp. 21 f.

Cf. the words quoted above from Matt., Luke and 1 Cor. and
Matt. 26, 27-28 πίετε — τὸ αἷμά μου
Mark. 14, 23-24 ἔπιον — τὸ αἷμά μου
1 Cor. 11, 27 ἐσθίῃ — πίνῃ — τοῦ σώματος καὶ τοῦ αἵματος
John 6, 57-58 ὁ τρώγων — ὁ τρώγων — τὸν ἄρτον
Cf. Matt. 26, 26 ἄρτον — φάγετε
1 Cor. 11, 27 ἐσθίῃ τὸν ἄρτον

The corresponding points between John 6, 51-58 and the eucharistic traditions indicate clearly that John draws upon traditions in the same way that 1 Cor. 11, 27 ff. uses fragments from the institution of the eucharist in 1 Cor. 11, 23 ff. The corresponding points between John and the haggadah of 1 Cor. 10, 1-4 (φάγητε — πίητε — πίνων / ἔφαγον — ἔπιον. βρῶσις — πόσις / βρῶμα — πόμα) indicate that fragments from a haggadic story about the manna and the well are also used in this section of John. These fragments about the eucharist and the manna coincide to some degree, thus making the interweaving process more natural. Moreover, as the underscoring shows, these fragments are at the same time partly interwoven with words from the Old Testament text, John 6, 31b, which they interpret.

The theory that John draws from these two traditions in his paraphrase is strongly supported by John 6, 55, where the "flesh" and "blood" from the eucharistic tradition are qualified in an emphatic way as "food" and "drink" from the tradition about the manna by a variant of the midrashic pattern of "A is B", which also was used in v. 51b:

A (Eucharist)	is	B (Manna, etc.)
ἡ γὰρ σάρξ μου	ἀληθῶς ἐστιν[1]	βρῶσις
καὶ τὸ αἷμά μου	ἀληθῶς ἐστιν[1]	πόσις

There are a few details to be expanded further in this connection. It is strange that in vv. 54.56.57.58 the word τρώγειν is used as the

---

[1] The Mss ℵ D Θ Ω it vg sin cur pesh have this reading, while the Mss B W have ἀληθής. It seems most probable that the latter reading could develop when v. 55 was not any longer understood as an exegetical pattern of the form "A is B". Note that John uses ἀληθῶς in the similar pattern of "this is indeed" (οὗτός ἐστιν ἀληθῶς) 4, 42; 6, 14; 7, 40. See C. K. Barrett, *St. John*, p. 247.

present substitute for φαγεῖν instead of the usual ἐσθίειν. John's vocabulary has, however, parallels in Hellenistic Greek usage.[1] The word τρώγειν is also used in the quotation of Ps. 41, 10 as a translation of the Hebrew אוכל in John 13, 18.[2] There are even agreements in wording between this quotation and John 6, 58.

John 6, 58   ὁ τρώγειν τοῦτον τὸν ἄρτον
John 13, 18 ὁ τρώγειν μου τὸν ἄρτον   (Ps. 41, 10)

These agreements and the fact that the word τρώγειν occurs only in the two eucharistic passages in John indicate that it comes from the eucharistic traditions, probably as a peculiar translation of Ps. 41, 10. In any case, the presence of τρώγειν in John 13, 18 and the parallels in Hellenistic Greek texts show that no special theological significance should be attached to the use of the word in 6, 54.56.57.58.[3]

Another problem is found in John 6, 51b, in which the sentence is quite awkwardly formulated. The reasons seems to be that it is a compromise between the exegetical gloss of the pattern "A is B" and a eucharistic formula:

The exegetical gloss, John 6, 51:
    καὶ ὁ ἄρτος δὲ ὃν ἐγὼ δώσω
    ἡ σάρξ μού ἐστιν
The eucharistic formula, in 1 Cor. 11, 24:
    τοῦτο μού ἐστιν τὸ σῶμα τὸ ὑπὲρ ὑμῶν
The compromise of John 6, 51:
    καὶ ὁ ἄρτος δὲ ὃν ἐγὼ δώσω
    ἡ σάρξ μού ἐστιν ὑπὲρ (τῆς τοῦ κόσμου ζωῆς).

In John 6, 51 the preposition ὑπέρ follows ἡ σάρξ corresponding to the eucharistic formula of 1 Cor. 11, 24.[4] John has kept the preposition at this traditional place although it does not any longer

---

[1] See J. H. Moulton and G. H. Milligan, *The Vocabulary of the Greek Testament; illustrated from the papyri and other non-literary sources*, London 1952 and H. G. Liddell and R. Scott, *A Greek-English Lexicon*, 9th ed. (by H. Stuart Jones, etc.), Oxford 1958 on the word τρώγειν. See also H. Schürmann, "Joh 6, 51c — ein Schlüssel zur grossen johanneischen Brotrede", *BZ* N.F. II, 1958, p. 247, n. 16.

[2] LXX translates ὁ ἐσθίων.

[3] Against R. Bultmann, *Evangelium*, p. 176; G. Bornkamm, *ZNW* XLVII, 1956, p. 162, etc.

[4] Concerning the Johannine ἡ σάρξ where the Synoptics and Paul use τὸ σῶμα, cf. pp. 181, 185-192.

qualify the noun, ἡ σάρξ, but the verb, δώσω. The definitive article preceding ὑπέρ in the formula had to be left out, so the run of the sentence became clumsy.[1]

Finally in the analysis of John 6, (51) 52-57(58) attention will be turned to vv. 57-58. Both verses continue the participial statement, ὁ τρώγων κτλ., but in addition both have statements of different style connected to them. Thus in v. 57 the participial statement is incorporated in the pattern of a comparison, "as — so" (καθώς — καί). Contrary to the views of E. Schweizer,[2] this terminology is not a characteristic peculiar to the author of John, but is rather a traditional pattern. It has the same function as the term כ - כך, which occurs in the midrash. Thus in Ex. R. 3, 17 the relationship between God and Moses is compared to the relationship between Moses and Aaron, and in John 6, 57 the relationship between the Father and His Son is compared with the relationship between the Son and the person "who eats" him:

Ex. R. 3, 17 "Just as (כ) My fear is upon thee,
so (כך) will thy fear be upon him."
John 6, 57 "As (καθώς) the living Father sent me, and I live because of the Father,
so (καί) he who eats me will live because of me."

On this basis it is reasonable to conclude that where the Palestinian midrash can use the terms כ - כך, the Johannine tradition used the terminology of καθώς — καί. The same terminology is also used by most MSS in Luke 6, 31; cf. also 1 Cor 15, 49. The similar terms ὡς — καί occurs in Matt. 6, 10; Acts 7,51 and Gal. 1, 9.

The participial statement (ὁ τρώγων κτλ) in John 6, 58 is preceded by two brief clauses, introduced by the phrase "this is" (οὗτός ἐστιν), — a phrase which refers back to what precedes in the homily and indicates that the conclusion follows. Dealing with the patriarchs Abraham, Isaac, Jacob and Jacob's twelve sons, Philo uses the same concluding phrase in Praem. 65, summing up the preceding paragraphs and referring back to § 57. Thus he says in

---

[1] Note that the variant readings of John 6, 51 attempt to improve the run of the sentence by connecting ὑπέρ with δώσω. See the discussion in C. K. Barrett, *St. John*, p. 246.
[2] See E. Schweizer, *EGO EIMI*, p. 91; *EvTh* XII, 1952/53, p. 354 and E. Ruckstuhl, *Einheit*, p. 204.

§ 65: "This is (οὗτός ἐστιν) the household (§ 57), which kept safe from harm, perfect and united both in the literal history and in the allegorical interpretation, received for its reward, as I have said (§ 57), the chieftaincy of the tribes of the nation."

This concludes the analysis of the form of John 6, 49-57 (58) where the word φαγεῖν from the text (v. 31b) is interpreted. It occurs in the haggadic fragment about the manna in the desert, v. 49, and in vv. 50 and 51a, it is connected with the haggadic fragment about the bread which comes down from heaven. This fragment paraphrases parts of the text, v. 31b, and sums up here the main point of the exposition in vv. 32-48.

In vv. 52-58 the word φαγεῖν is connected with fragments from the eucharistic traditions. So the method of using fragments is the same in 6, 52-58 as was the use of the haggadic traditions in the previous part of the homily. Certain elements from the haggadic tradition about the manna and the well also seem to have been interwoven with eucharistic traditions and words from the text. Paul uses the same method in 1 Cor. 11, 27 ff., where he paraphrases fragments from the previous tradition about the eucharist.

With regard to style and patterns, the section John 6, 49-58 follows the preceding part of the homily. The main pattern consists of (1) a paraphrase of the text, (v. 51a and 52), followed by one or more statements of (2) a conditional (vv. 51a and 53) or participial nature (vv. 54.56.57b.58b). The background of this pattern and style is clearly midrashic.

V. 50 has the style of an explicative definition (οὗτός ἐστιν —, ἵνα), as also vv. 39.40. Verse 51b and v. 55 are variants of the common exegetical pattern "A is B", of which parallels are to be found in Philo and the Qumran literature. In the paraphrase of words from the text (v. 31b) verse 52 has used the exegetical method of replacing one word (ἄρτον) with another (τὴν σάρκα). The homilies of Philo provide examples of the same method. Verse 57 has expanded the participial statement (ὁ τρώγων κτλ.) into a comparison by using the terms καθώς — καί, which belong to the terminology of the Johannine tradition, since they have the same function as the terms כ – כן have in the midrash. Thus they do not come from the individual stylistic taste of the Evangelist. Verse 58 is introduced by a concluding "this is", οὗτός ἐστιν,[1] which in a

---

[1] Cf. R. Bultmann, *Evangelium*, p. 176, and n. 8.

natural way brings the homily to a close. Philo uses the same concluding phrase in Praem. 65.

These conclusions will next be placed against the background of the present state of research. Bultmann joins those scholars who regard John 6, 51-58 as an interpolation.[1] Although he maintains this view, he must, nevertheless, admit that John 6, 51 ff. has the same style as that of "the Evangelist".[2] And Ruckstuhl, Schweizer, Jeremias and Schulz stress that the Johannine characteristics are also present in this section, although they find some non-Johannine pecularities as well.[3]

Two more observations favour the theory that John 6, 51-58 is an integral part of the homily of John 6, 31-58. First the use of tradition here is the same as in vv. 31-51a: Fragments from the traditions are woven together. Second, the midrashic style is the same, where conditional and participial styles interchange and exegetical glosses occur.

Most of the scholars, whether or not they favour a theory of interpolation, find that John 6, 51 ff. draws upon the eucharistic tradition.[4] J. Jeremias and a few others have classified this tradition as a eucharistic homily.[5] It is now evident, however, that John

---

[1] See pp. 25 f. [2] R. Bultmann, *Evangelium*, p. 174.

[3] J. Jeremias, *ThB* XX 1941, col. 44, defended the interpolation theory by referring to the so called non-Johannine pecularities in 6, 51b-58, but not convincingly. The main pecularities are: 1) φαγεῖν, πίνειν c. acc. instead of ἐκ. Both constructions, however, also occur elsewhere in the Gospel (6, 23.31.49; 18, 11 accusative, and 6, 26.51; 4, 12-14 with ἐκ). Paul also varies between accusative and ἐκ in his commentary on the eucharistic tradition, 1 Cor. 11, 27-28. 2) ἐξ (in stead of ἐκ τοῦ) οὐρανοῦ. See above on p. 20, n. 3. 3) οἱ πατέρες without ὑμῶν or ἡμῶν as in 6, 31.49. Ruckstuhl and Schweizer have made the right observation that v. 58 repeats previous phrases in an abbreviated form. This point of view is supported by our realization that v. 58 is the closing statement of the homily, 6, 31-58. 4) ἀληθής instead of ἀληθινός. This point is irrelevant when the reading ἀληθῶς is correct, see above on p. 92, n. 1.

To this analysis, see E. Ruckstuhl, *Einheit*, pp. 220-267; E. Schweizer, *EvTh* XII, 1952/53, pp. 353 f.; J. Jeremias, "Joh. 6, 51c-58—redaktionell?," *ZNW* XLIV, 1952/53, pp. 256 f.; H. Blauert, *Die Bedeutung der Zeit*, pp. 88-97; S. Schulz, *Menschensohn-Christologie*, pp. 115 f. J. Jeremias and E. Schweizer have in the later studies moved away from their former inclination towards a theory of interpolation.

[4] See the list of those in favour of the theory of interpolation on p. 25, n. 1. See also below on p. 97, n. 1. H. Odeberg, *The Fourth Gospel*, pp. 260-261 denies any reference to the eucharist in John 6, 51-58.

[5] J. Jeremias, *ZNW* XLIV, 1952/53, pp. 256 f.; Cf. E. Schweizer, *EvTh* XII, 1952/53, p. 362, n. 82 (referring to O. Michel) and S. Schulz, *Menschensohn-Christologie*, p. 116.

6, 31-58 is in itself a homily, and that vv. 51b ff., as an integral part of it, probably employ fragments of traditions about the institution of the eucharist.[1]

Noack's discussion of John 6, 51-58 is incomplete in that his index lacks any reference to vv. 52.54.57,[2] and he offers only occasional remarks about vv. 55.56.58.[3] Only v. 53, which Noack classifies as an independent logion, receives a fuller analysis.[4]

The paraphrase of the word φαγεῖν (v. 53, φάγετε) from the text (v. 31b) together with fragments from traditions about the eucharist (and the manna) makes Noack's theory of logia improbable. This objection is supported by the parallel use of eucharistic traditions in 1 Cor. 11, 27 ff. which do not consist of independent and fixed logia from the tradition.

From this discussion of John 6, 51b-58 attention is turned to 6, 49-51a. Bultmann assigns vv. 49-50 to "the Evangelist",[5] but makes no clear statement about the background of v. 51a. Becker includes v. 51a in the revelatory source,[6] whereas Blauert and Noack classify v. 51a as a logion. Schulz regards it as a variation of the "Ego eimi" logion in v. 35.[7]

The weakness of these suggestions becomes apparent with the realization that v. 51a, as also v. 50, is closely connected to the Old Testament quotation cited in v. 31b, since both paraphrase its words together with a haggadic fragment. This makes it impossible to separate v. 51a from v. 50 and v. 31b and to place it in a literary source or classify it as an independent logion. So it is also impossible to make "the Evangelist" responsible for vv. 49-50 and not for v. 51a.

Noack's analysis of 6, 49-50 is rather inadequate. His theory that the statement of "Ego eimi" is followed by a statement

---

[1] Note that W. Bauer, *Das Johannesevangelium*, pp. 95 f. finds the whole terminology of the eucharist in John 6; (cf. also C. H. Dodd, *The Interpretation*, p. 338). Others maintaining that the section draws on a tradition about the institution are: H. Windisch, *Johannes und die Synoptiker, UNT* XII, Leipzig 1926, p. 78; J. H. Bernard, *A Critical and Exegetical Commentary on the Gospel according to St. John*, I, ICC, Edinburgh 1928, pp. CLXVII ff.; R. H. Strachan, *The Fourth Gospel. Its Significance and Environment*, 3rd ed., London 1958, pp. 189 ff.; H. Schürmann, *BZ* N.F. II, 1958, pp. 245 ff., etc.
[2] B. Noack, *Tradition*, p. 167.   [3] *Ibid.*, pp. 49,32,48.
[4] *Ibid.*, pp. 66,69.   [5] R. Bultmann, *Evangelium*, p. 170, n. 2.
[6] H. Becker, *Die Reden des Johannesevangeliums*, p. 69.
[7] H. Blauert, *Die Bedeutung der Zeit*, p. 92; B. Noack, *Tradition*, p. 52; S. Schulz, *Komposition*, pp. 72,74.

expressing the condition for salvation, makes him connect v. 48 with v. 50.[1] Without any justification he merely ignores v. 49. And we have seen that the haggadic fragment in v. 49 begins the interpretation of the word φαγεῖν from the text in v. 31b, while v. 50 continues this interpretation and can therefore not be separated from v. 49, as Noack does.

Although the attention has been focused upon the midrashic features in the homily of John 6, 31-58, the analysis in this chapter is of central interest also to Philonic research, and it supports those scholars who have suggested that Philo uses midrashic methods and patterns of interpretation. Some of the references to Philo are to homilies which were discussed in the preceding chapter. Thus in the homily of Leg. all. III 65-75a Philo made an Old Testament quotation be interpreted by statements of conditional nature (§ 71). In the homily of Leg. all. III 162-168 Philo used the midrashic method of interpreting Old Testament quotations by an attached ἵνα clause (§ 166). And the exegetical method of replacing words from the Old Testament quotation with interpretative words or of supplementing such words is also found in the homilies of Leg. all. III 162-168 and Mut. 253-263.

Several midrashic features have been observed scattered elsewhere in Philo's commentaries. Some of the main points are these: The pattern of correcting a reading of an Old Testament quotation (Deter. 47-48), of confirming the given reading (Leg. all. I 67 and elsewhere), and the midrashic pattern of exegetical debate, referred to in connection with the analysis of John 6, 41-48 (Mut. 141a. 142b-144).

These main points substantiate the assertion that Philo uses midrashic methods and patterns. Several other details are referred to in the body of this chapter.

The investigation so far has dealt with the use of haggadic traditions by Philo and John and with questions regarding the form of homiletic and other midrashic patterns, and with midrashic method and terminology. Philo and John 6, 31-58 join with the Palestinian midrash in this respect. The next task will be to discuss the content of the homilies in Mut. 253-263, Leg. all. III 162-168 and John 6, 31-58. Because the homilies deal with different subjects, they must be considered separately.

---

[1] B. Noack, *Tradition*, p. 52.

CHAPTER FOUR

THE HEAVENLY PHILOSOPHY OF THE SYNAGOGUE AND THE ENCYCLIA

MUT. 253-263

The analysis of different homilies, a relevant approach to the ideas of Philo

In the preceding chapters it was shown that there were close similarities among Mut. 253-263, Leg. all. III 162-168 and John 6, 31-58 in the matter of exegetical method and patterns: They employed the same method in using traditions and in paraphrasing words from a cited Old Testament quotation; and they all had the same form of a homiletic pattern. Even in details there were similarities in exegetical method, patterns and terminology, although on this point parts of Philo's commentaries other than the two homilies mentioned above provided much of the material parallel to the homily in John 6. On all the main points there were also striking similarities between these homilies and parts of the Palestinian midrash, which on the basis of this comparison seem to represent a later and more stereotyped stage of the same exegetical method and patterns.

In spite of similarities also in the ideas expressed in the homily of John 6 and the homilies of Philo, in a discussion of their content they must be dealt with separately, because they differ much as to subject matter. The difference in subject matter and focal points have provided one significant key to the commonly recognised differences and inconsistences in Philo.[1] L. J. Feldman has suggested a similar solution to all the inconsistencies of Philo in his criticism of H. A. Wolfson's attempt to iron them out: "W. is obviously more orderly than P.; one wonders whether perhaps he has put P. into a neat procrustean bed. Is it not more likely that one

---

[1] See the survey in W. Völker, *Fortschritt*, pp. 7-8; cf. especially A. J. Festugière, *La Révélation d'Hermès Trismégiste* II (*Le Dieu Cosmique*), Paris 1949, pp. 519-585, who argues vehemently that Philo has no system at all. Philo's writings are rather to be regarded as a manual of Hellenistic commonplaces.

reading P. without preconceived notions would conclude that we have merely a collection of sermons that draw heavily on popular philosophy, much as sermons today often do?" [1]

Feldman's viewpoint is not, however, quite adequate as a solution, since he has ignored the fact that Philos exegetical interest in the Pentateuch both gives his commentaries a common point of orientation, the Scripture, and at the same time makes possible a wide range of variations in the actual interpretations. In this way Philo defends the belief that the Holy Scripture is the source of all wisdom. The recent study of J. Jervell stresses this point also observed by some earlier scholars.[2]

An adequate approach to Philo's ideas, then, must be based on his exegesis of the Old Testament which presents itself in different passages and patterns. Mut. 253-263 and Leg. all. III 162-168 will be examined along these lines, drawing upon other parts of Philo's works only insofar they can throw light upon aspects of these homilies.

Since Philo develops in both homilies an exegetical paraphrase of words from Old Testament quotations interwoven with fragments from the haggadah, his method can serve as a good point of departure. Usually he supplements this paraphrase with other terms and phrases. The task, therefore, is to analyse these terms, define their background and discuss their combinations and modifications within the context of the homilies.

Such an analysis will reveal that in the homily of Mut. 253-263 Philo connects Old Testament quotations and fragments from the haggadah with Greek educational ideas.

The encyclical education and philosophy

In the preceding chapter it was shown that words from an Old Testament quotation could be replaced by other terms in the

---

[1] L. H. Feldman, *CW* LIV 1960/1961, p. 287; cf. that he modifies his own viewpoint in *CW* LV, 1961/1962, p. 47.

[2] J. Jervell, *Imago Dei. Gen.* 1, 26 f. *im Spätjudentum, in der Gnosis und in den paulinischen Briefen*, FRLANT, N.F. LVIII (G.R. LXXVI), Göttingen 1960, p. 52: "Methodisch hat man ja eigentlich nicht viel geleistet, wenn man die verschiedenen von ihm verwandten Begriffe und Vorstellungen auf ihren Ursprung hin zurückführen kann. Man muss auch seinen 'Synkretismus' mit seiner Schriftauslegung verbinden: Das Gedankengut der griechischen Philosophie ist schon in der Schrift da." Cf. W. Völker, *Fortschritt*, p. 9; R. Reitzenstein, *Das iranische Erlösungsmysterium. Religionsgeschichtliche Untersuchungen*, Bonn a. Rh. 1921, p. 110, n. 1; L. Treitel, *MGWJ* LV (N.F. XIX), 1911, pp. 544 f.

exposition. This method was used in John 6, 52, and paralleled in Mut. 259. Here the word for manna in Ex. 16, 4, ἄρτους, was replaced by the term wisdom, τὴν — σοφίαν.[1]

Philo also applied the same method to fragments of the haggadah, where he replaced a word from the tradition by another word. A comparison between a traditional part of Mos. II 267 and the fragment in Mut. 258 demonstrates this point.[2]

Mos. II 267   τροφὴν ἄπονον — καὶ ἀταλαίπωρον
            ("food ... without labour or travail")
Mut. 258   ἀρετὴν ἄπονον καὶ ἀταλαίπωρον
            ("virtue without toil or trouble")

In Mut. 258 the word virtue (ἀρετή) has obviously replaced a word for the manna (τροφή). Hence in Mut. 258-260 Philo interprets the manna as "virtue" and "wisdom".

What is the background for these terms here? The homily as a whole indicates clearly that they are ideas which characterize philosophy in contrast to the encyclical education. The use of the term "virtue" in §§ 255, 258 and 263 makes this evident. In § 255 this concept is contrasted with "the lower instruction", ἡ μέση παιδεία, a synonym term for "the encyclical training", ἡ ἐγκύκλιος παιδεία. These terms occur often in Philo's works, and their use, e.g. in Congr. 12.14.20.22, etc., shows that they designate the same education.

A third and more elaborate term for encyclical education is found in Mut. 263: "the whole round and train of the early branches of the professional schools".[3] This expression is also contrasted with the "virtue" of philosophy here in § 263.

The contrast between "virtue" and "authority" or "dominion", ἐπιστασία, in Mut. 258 reflects also the difference between philosophy and encyclical training. The context mentions teacher and teaching (§ 257), so that "dominion" must refer to the teacher's "controlling hand".[4] The word ἐπιστασία has the same meaning in Heres 125, where it also is connected with the idea of education.

---

[1] See p. 90.
[2] See pp. 16-17.
[3] τὸν κύκλον καὶ τὸν χορὸν ἅπαντα τῶν σοφιστικῶν προπαιδευμάτων. Concerning the different expressions for the encyclical education, see C. Siegfried, *Philo von Alexandria*, p. 260.
[4] The translation of F. H. Colson in *Philo* (Colson and Whitaker) V, p. 275.

At other places, however, the term can refer to other forms of dominion, as that of the parents, the king, etc.[1]

Thus, by replacing words for manna with the terms "virtue" and "wisdom", Philo has interpreted Ex. 16, 4 and fragments from the haggadah on bread from heaven and earth within the context of the conflict between philosophy and encyclical education.

This conflict was a burning issue in the Hellenistic schools of philosophy. Cynics and Epicureans repudiated the encyclical education. Stoics differed in their attitudes.[2]

In his *Ad Lucilium Epistulae Morales*, epistle LXXXVIII, Seneca defends a position which shows many similarities to that of Philo in Mut. 253-263.[3] Like Philo, Seneca also closely associates the terms, "virtue" (virtus) and "wisdom" (sapientia), with philosophy in contrast to encyclical education (artes liberales). Although Seneca admits that this education can prepare the soul for the reception of the philosophical virtue, he attacks it rather sharply, because, in his opinion, it contributes nothing at all so far as "virtue" itself is concerned.[4]

Philo shows a somewhat more moderate attitude, since in Mut. 263 he allows the encyclical education to be characterized by the term "virtue", although its "virtue" is of a lower quality than that of philosophy.[5] At other places Philo draws the same distinction

---

[1] See Deter. 145 and Ebr. 91.

[2] See F. H. Colson, "Philo on Education," *JThSt* XVIII, 1917, p. 153; W. Richter, *Lucius Annaeus Seneca. Das Problem der Bildung in seiner Philosophie*. Diss. Lengerich, Westf. 1939, pp. 14-31; H. von Arnim, *Leben und Werke des Dio von Prusa. Mit einer Einleitung: Sophistik, Rhetorik, Philosophie in ihrem Kampf um die Jugendbildung*, Berlin 1898, pp. 73, 77, 91 ff.; H. J. Mette, "ΕΓΚΥΚΛΙΟΣ ΠΑΙΔΕΙΑ," *Gymnasium* LXVII, 1960, p. 304; H. A. Wolfson, *Philo* I, Cambridge, Mass. 1948, p. 145.

[3] *Seneca, ad Lucilium Epistulae Morales*, translated by R. M. Gummere, II, (*Loeb*), London/New York 1920, pp. 348-377.

[4] See especially *ibid.*, pp. 360 f. (§ 20). For a discussion of Seneca's critical viewpoints, see W. Richter, *Das Problem der Bildung*, pp. 32 ff., 37, 50, 52 ff.; M. Lechner, *Erziehung und Bildung in der griechisch-römischen Antike*, München 1933, pp. 210 f.; F. H. Colson, *JThSt* XVIII, 1917, p. 153; Seneca links his discussion to the viewpoints of Poseidonios, who regarded the encyclical subjects as auxiliary to philosophy. See especially Seneca, *Ad Lucilium Epistulae* (Gummere) II, pp. 362-367 (Epistle LXXXVIII, 21-28). Cf. H. J. Mette, *Gymnasium* LXVII, 1960, p. 304; M. Apelt, *De rationibus*, pp. 118 ff.; M. Pohlenz, *Philon von Alexandreia*, *NAG*, Göttingen 1942, pp. 429 ff.

[5] For a broader discussion of Philo's ideas on education against the background of Stoic ideas, see the works by Colson, Wolfson, Apelt and Pohlenz in the notes 2 and 4 above. See also *Die Werke Philos* (Cohn, Heinemann,

between two "virtues" of entirely different kinds. Thus in Sacr. 78 the "self-taught wisdom" (— αὐτομαθοῦς σοφίας) and "perfect virtue" are contrasted with "civic virtue" which makes it profitable to pay attention to the great literature of the past.

Teaching and the selftaught by nature

There is, however, a basic difference between the ideas of Philo's homily and the ideas of Seneca. While Seneca discusses two different kinds of teaching, that of the schools of philosophy in contrast to that of the schools of the liberal arts, Philo associates the idea of the selftaught by nature with the philosopher and teaching with the student of the encyclia.

The terms which Philo uses to make this distinction are διδακτόν and αὐτομαθές, Mut. 255(263). These two words and their equivalents occur frequently in the triad which distinguishes among "teaching", "selfteaching" (or "nature") and "practice." Philo associates this triad with the patriarchs, Abraham, Isaac and Jacob.[1]

At this point Philo draws upon a broad Greek tradition about education, in which this triad is discussed in its relationship to virtue.[2] And Plutarch can even associate the triad with Pythagoras, Socrates and Plato in a way similar to Philo's association of them with the three patriarchs.[3]

In the homily of Mut. 253-263, however, the use of the terms "the taught" and "the selftaught" differs to some degree from the

---

Adler, Theiler) V, p. 24, n. 5 and VI, p. 42, n. 5; W. Bousset, *Schulbetrieb*, pp. 98 ff. and 107 ff.; E. Bréhier, *Les Idées philosophiques et religieuses de Philon d'Alexandrie*,. Paris 1908, pp. 287 ff.; C. Siegfried, *Philo von Alexandria*, pp. 260 ff.; W. Völker, *Fortschritt*, pp. 171 ff.; E. Norden, *Das Antike Kunstprosa vom VI. Jahrhundert v. Chr. bis in die Zeit der Renaissance*, II, Leipzig 1898, pp. 670-687.

[1] Mos. I 76; Abr. 52; Jos. 1; Somn. I 167-168; II 10; Congr. 34-36; Mut. 88; Praem. 27, etc.

[2] See *Die Werke Philos* (Cohn, Heinemann, Adler, Theiler) III, p. 216, n. 3 (with numerous references); H. Leisegang, *Der Heilige Geist*, I, 1. *Die vorchristlichen Anschauungen und Lehren vom* πνεῦμα *und der mystisch-intuitiven Erkenntnis*, Berlin 1919, pp. 147 ff.; W. Völker, *Fortschritt*, pp. 154 ff.; E. Bréhier, *Les Idées*, p. 272 ff.; F. H. Colson, *JThSt* XVIII, 1917, pp. 160 f.; S. Sandmel, *HUCA* XXVI, 1955, pp. 263 f.; C. Siegfried, *Philo von Alexandria*, pp. 256 ff.; *Philo* (Colson and Whitaker) II, p. 488, and V, p. 586; H. A. Wolfson, *Philo* II, pp. 196-198.

[3] P. Hadot, "Être, Vie, Pensée chez Plotin et avant Plotin," *Les Sources de Plotin, Entretiens* V, Vandoeuvres-Genève, 1960, pp. 125-126. See Plutarch's De liberis educandis, 2A-C.

customary use of this triad. The first difference is that only two terms, and not all three, are used. The second one is that the idea of "teaching" is not, as is usual in Philo, connected with Abraham, but with Hagar and Ishmael.

The isolation of the two terms "the taught" and "the selftaught" also has parallels in Greek educational traditions, where they can be associated both with men and animals.[1] So although Plutarch's Moralia 991E ff. and 973E discuss the contrast between "nature" and "teaching" as regards animals, the same passages show, nevertheless, striking parallels to the ideas of Philo in the homily of Mut. 253-263.

Both Philo and Plutarch refer to nature (φύσις) as the source of the selftaught in contrast to teacher and instruction. They both insist that the selftaught talent of nature is sufficient and perfect,[2] and is therefore also characterised as strength and not weakness.[3] So there is no need for teaching by instructors.[4] Plutarch clearly states that the selfteaching by nature ranks higher than the learning from others.[5] The same point of view is implicitly present in Philo's

---

[1] See *Hermetica. The Ancient Greek and Latin Writings which contain Religious or Philosophic Teachings ascribed to Hermes Trismegistus*, ed. W. Scott, III, Oxford 1926, pp. 354 f.; H. Lewy, *Sobria Ebrietas. Untersuchungen zur Geschichte der Antiken Mystik, ZNW Beih.* IX, Giessen 1929, p. 59, n. 2.

[2] Plutarch's Bruta animalia ratione uti, sive Gryllus (991Eff.) and Terrestriane an aquatilia animalia sint callidora (973E). For the citations of text and translation in this and the following notes, see *Plutarch's Moralia*, with an English translation by H. Cherniss and W. C. Helmbold, XII, (Loeb), London/New York 1957, ad loc. Moralia 992A: ἀπροσδεής.—τελειότητι τῆς κατὰ φύσιν ἀρετῆς ("self-sufficient"...."because of...completeness of its native virtue"). Mut. 258: ἐξ ἀρχῆς ὁλόκληρον καὶ παντελῆ ("perfect and complete from the very first"). H. Hegermann, *Die Vorstellung vom Schöpfungsmittler im hellenistischen Judentum und Urchristentum*, TU LXXXII, Berlin 1961, pp. 16 f., has ignored the background of Greek educational ideas, and therefore interprets wrongly this phrase in Mut. 258 about the creation in general.

[3] Moralia 992A: οὐ δι' ἀσθένειαν ἀλλὰ ῥώμῃ ("not for lack of strength... just because of health"). Mut. 263: τὸ μὲν ἀσθενέστερον in contrast to τὸ ἐρρωμένον.

[4] Moralia 992A: χαίρειν ἐῶσα τὸν παρ' ἑτέρων διὰ μαθήσεως τοῦ φρονεῖν συνερανισμόν ("it is indifferent to the contribution to its intelligence supplied by the lore of others"). Mut. 258: μηδεμιᾶς δεομένην ἐπιστασίας ("needing no controlling hand").

[5] Moralia 973E: τῆς εὐμαθείας λογικωτέραν εἶναι τὴν αὐτομάθειαν ἐν αὐτοῖς ("...self-instruction implies more reason in animals than does readiness to learn from others"). The same idea is applied to men by Pindar, The Olympian Odes IX 100 ff.: "That which cometh of Nature is ever best, but many men have striven to win their fame by means of merit that cometh

homily and is explicitly stated by him in Leg. all. III 135.[1]

The parallels between Philo and Plutarch's Moralia 991E ff. and 973E show that in Mut. 253-263 Philo develops Greek educational ideas concerning the contrast between intuitive talents by nature and progress by teaching. Philo, however, characterizes philosophy by the talents from nature in contrast to the encyclical education with its progress by teaching.

The concept of manna in Mut. 255-263 has then been interpreted within this context of Greek educational ideas. Manna itself is interpreted as the "virtue" and "wisdom" of philosophy in contrast to encyclical education. This "manna" of philosophy is sufficient and perfect, because it is associated with the selftaught by nature. In this context the "toil" and "trouble" without which the manna came, according to the tradition, are applied to the teaching effort in the encyclical training (§ 258).

Some scholars, W. Völker for instance, have drawn attention to the inconsistencies which are present in Philo's educational ideas. One problem is that (as in Abr. 53) Philo makes "nature" join with teaching and practice while in other places (as here in Mut. 253-263) he develops this idea of nature, in contrast to training and progress, as being perfect from the very first.[2] It is not necessary to discuss all the different passages about education in Philo's works, but only to call attention to the fact that this idea of the perfection of nature is very fitting in Mut. 253-263, since, as in Plutarch, it is associated with the idea of the "selftaught" in contrast to education. In the same way also the other passages where such educational ideas occur must be examined primarily as independent contexts of their own.

Agriculture and self-grown fruits

In the homily of Mut. 253-263 Philo combines the ideas of the encyclical teaching and the selftaught nature of philosophy with

---

from mere training." (*The Odes of Pindar*, with an English Translation by J. Sandys, *(Loeb)*, London/New York 1919, p. 105).

[1] "For, as toiling itself falls short of the toilless achievement and is inferior to it, so does the imperfect fall short of the perfect, and that which learns of that which is self-taught."

[2] See W. Völker, *Fortschritt*, pp. 155-156; E. Bréhier, *Les Idées*, pp. 273-279; C. G. Montefiore, "Florilegium Philonis," *JQR* VII, 1894, pp. 518 f.; cf. H. A. Wolfson, *Philo* II, p. 197 and F. H. Colson, *JThSt* XVIII, 1917, pp. 160 f. who only indicate the problems.

the idea of the cultivation of the earth and the self-grown fruits of the Sabbatical year.

As early as in § 257 a phrase about the Sabbatical year occurs: "self-worked independent nature" (ἀπαυτοματιζούσῃ φύσει). Similar characterizations of the Sabbatical year are used in Fug. 171, Spec. II 105.107 and Virt. 97. In Mut. 257 it is given as a contrast to the teaching at school. This interpretation of automatic growth is further developed in § 260, where the term is changed into "the selftaught good things" of the Sabbatical year.

Mangey has corrected this reading τῶν αὐτομαθῶν ἀγαθῶν into τῶν αὐτομάτων ἀγαθῶν, because he ignored the fact that the context discusses the question of "selftaught" and "the taught one".[1] Unfortunately, P. Wendland and F. H. Colson have accepted Mangey's error at this point.[2] The defence of the reading of the MSS is also supported by Fug. 170 where the "selftaught" (τὸ αὐτομαθές) and the "automatic" (τὸ αὐτόματον) are used interchangeably as descriptions of the Sabbatical year.

In contrast to these "selftaught good things" of the Sabbatical year is, then, the cultivation of the earth by technical means. Technical cultivation, to which Mut. 260 refers, represents, in this context, teaching in the encyclical education. In Mut. 259 the part about bread from earth in the haggadic tradition about bread from heaven and earth is developed into a picture of cultivation to illustrate this teaching: "*The food from earth* is produced with the cooperation of husbandmen" (§ 259).[3]

Philo also compares education with agriculture in other places, e.g. Agr. 9.13 ff. 17 ff., etc. In this respect he reflects an educational illustration widely used in the Greek world, e.g., in the writings of Plutarch, Cicero and others.[4] In Mut. 253-263 he links this edu-

---

[1] See the textual apparatus in *Philonis Alexandrini opera* (ed. Cohn and Wendland) III, p. 201, where the reading of the MSS and Mangey's correction is given.

[2] See Wendland's reading in *ibid.*, and F. H. Colson's text in *Philo* (Colson and Whitaker) V, pp. 274-275.

[3] F. H. Colson's translation "The earthly food..." is less exact. See *Philo* (Colson and Whitaker) V, p. 275. The italicizing shows the haggadic fragment.

[4] Plutarch's De liberis educandis, 2B; Cicero, Tusculanae Disputationes, II, 5. This and other parallels are collected in *Plutarchi Chaeronensis Moralia*, ed. D. Wyttenbach, VI, 1, Oxonii 1810, p. 75. See the broader discussions in Th. Gomperz, *Griechische Denker. Eine Geschichte der antiken Philosophie*, I, 2nd ed., Leipzig 1903, p, 329, especially the note on p. 459, and W. Jaeger,

cational illustration to the Jewish ideas of a Sabbatical year and in this way makes it serve the contrast between him who is taught and him who is selftaught by nature.

If this educational application of the ideas about the Sabbatical year in Mut. 253-263 is compared with the use of the same ideas in Fug. 170 ff. there is an inconsistency similar to that which we discussed in the previous paragraph. In Mut. 253-263 the ideas illustrate the selftaught by nature in contrast to the encyclical education. In Fuga 170 ff., however, "nature", the "selftaught" and the ideas of the Sabbatical year are the foundation upon which education builds. Philo seems to distinguish between two different kinds of education, one which is not based upon the "selftaught" by "nature" and another which has "nature" as its basis in this way.

Before considering the way in which the position of Judaism is expressed in the homily, a summary of the use of Greek educational ideas in it will be given. Philo has combined the polemic of the schools of philosophy against the schools of encyclia with the Greek idea of the selftaught by nature in contrast to training by teachers. He characterizes philosophy in a Greek manner by the terms "virtue" and "wisdom", which replace words for manna in Ex. 16, 4 and in the fragments from the haggadah. The description of manna as "without toil or trouble" is applied to the selftaught virtue of the philosopher versus toil in the encyclical education.

The widely used Greek picture of education as agriculture influenced Philo's treatment of Jewish ideas. Thus, he develops the contrast between encyclia and philosophy by the picture of the production of bread from earth in contrast to the selfgrown fruits of the Sabbatical year. His picture of the production of bread from earth is based on a fragment from the haggadic tradition about bread from heaven and earth.

Encyclia and philosophy are not, however, necessarily mutually exclusive. They operate rather on entirely different levels and so represent two different forms of apprehension, since encyclia brings knowledge by the help of teachers while philosophy, according to this homily of Philo, brings intuitive wisdom, selftaught by nature. The conclusion of the homily in Mut. 253-263 is, therefore, logical when it distinguishes between two different "virtues", the one of the encyclia and the other of philosophy (§ 263).

Paideia: the Ideals of Greek Culture I, (translated by G. Highet), 2nd ed., New York 1945, pp. 312 f.

Encyclia on the borderline between Judaism and paganism

The preceding analysis has uncovered certain inconsistencies between the ideas of the homily in Mut. 253-263 and other parts of Philo's commentaries. One difference was that the homily restricted the idea of teaching to the encyclia and Hagar and Ishmael, while at other places the teaching is associated closely with Abraham. Philo's interpretation of Abraham's relationship to Sarah and Isaac on the one hand and to Hagar and Ishmael on the other hand is therefore to be examined further.

Philonic scholars know that when Philo interprets Abraham's relationships on the basis of educational ideas, he is dependent upon the allegorical interpretation of the figure of Penelope in Homer. For example Plutarch tells that those who, being unable to win philosophy, wear themselves out in the encyclical disciplines are like the suitors of Penelope, who when they could not win the mistress contented themselves with her maids.[1] Correspondingly, when Abraham did not, at first, conceive a child with Sarah, he took the maid, Hagar, in her place.

The transformation of Penelope and her maids into Sarah and Hagar means, however, that Philo claims this allegory for Judaism to interpret its point of view as to encyclical education. In his introduction to De Congressu Heinemann has seen that the position of Judaism is reflected in this allegory. He says that in this writing Philo follows the form and method of the interpreters of Homer, and at the same time bases his discussion on the feeling of the superiority of the schools of philosophy over against the encyclia. The favoring of philosophy was of special significance in Alexandria, where mathematics and philology had higher priority than philosophy. Heinemann then stresses that Philo made all these ideas serve the Jewish apologetics.[2]

Accordingly, Abraham's double relationship, both to Hagar and Sarah, reflects the dual aspects of Judaism in Alexandria, that is its outward and inward relations. This is the reason why Philo often emphasizes the notion that Hagar was an Egyptian woman (Qu. in Gen. III 19.21; Abr. 251 and especially Congr. 20 ff.) Hence,

---

[1] Plutarch's De liberis educandis, 7D. Other versions of this allegory are referred to in *Stoicorum veterum fragmenta*, coll. H. von Arnim, I, Leipzig 1905, 350 (p. 78). See F. H. Colson, *JThSt* XVIII, 1917, pp. 153-154; *Die Werke Philos* (Cohn, Heinemann, Adler, Theiler) V, p. 24, n. 7 and VI, p. 7, n. 2; H. A. Wolfsen, *Philo* I, pp. 145 f.

[2] *Die Werke Philos* (Cohn, Heinemann, Adler, Theiler) VI, p. 4.

the offspring of Abraham and Hagar, Ishmael, is logically enough characterized as a bastard, Sobr. 8. Sarah, on the other hand, represents the inward aspect of Judaism, and is therefore called the mother of the Jews, "the most populous of nations", Congr. 2-3.[1]

Accordingly, Abraham, representing the Jewish nation, receives education from two schools: the encyclical education is the bastard school which the Jews have in common with the pagan surroundings; the other school is the genuine, Jewish philosophy. Philo expresses this situation clearly in his interpretation of Abraham, Sarah and Hagar in Congr. 35: "... the virtue that comes through teaching, which Abraham pursues, needs the fruits of several studies, both those born in wedlock, which deal with wisdom, and the base-born, those of the preliminary lore of the schools."

Philo thus places encyclical education on the borderline between Judaism and paganism, as an adiaforon which in itself is neither good nor bad. It is in harmony with this view of the encyclia that Philo describes it as the "well 'between Kadesh and Bered' ", that is, "on the borderland (μεθόριος) between the holy and the profane", Fug. 212-213.[2] The term ἡ μέση παιδεία, which Philo used in Mut. 255, etc., expresses the same evaluation of the encyclia and means therefore "education on the borderland" or "neutral education".[3]

The main point of the homily in Mut. 253-263 acquires a sharper focus against this background. The homily deals with the relationship between Judaism and the neutral encyclia. Therefore, the term for teaching, τὸ — διδακτόν, is here associated with encyclical education which is represented by Hagar and Ishmael and not, as is usual, with Abraham. Thus, Sarah and Isaac represent the characteristics of Judaism which are defined as the selftaught virtue and wisdom.

In this way Philo clarifies the basic difference between the principle on which Jewish philosophy is built and the principle of the encyclia. Moreover, he further defines selftaught virtue and

---

[1] See *ibid.*, p. 4, n. 3, for this understanding of the passage.

[2] See C. Siegfried, *Philo von Alexandria*, p. 261, who ignores the background of Judaism versus paganism in the passage.

[3] F. H. Colson, *JThSt* XVIII, 1917, p. 153, n. 1 and *Philo* (Colson and Whitaker) I, p. XVII, n. a., refers rightly to the Stoic use of μέσα = ἀδιάφορα, but cannot explain Philo's use, because he has overlooked the fact that it has its place within the context of the relationship between Judaism and paganism.

wisdom as gifts from God. In twentieth century terminology Philo's viewpoint would be expressed by drawing a distinction between the human knowledge communicated by teachers and the knowledge which comes by revelation. In other contexts where the focus is different, Philo does, of course, use these educational terms differently.

In Mut. 253-263, then, Philo not only interprets Ex. 16, 4 and fragments from the haggadah about the manna by means of Greek educational ideas; he also transforms these ideas to explain the position of Judaism regarding the encyclia. At the same time, his adaptation of the Greek ideas also meant a re-interpretation of Judaism itself in the light of Greek educational traditions.

Then, too, papyri show that the encyclia and the gymnasium were a burning issue to the Jews in Alexandria.[1]

Palestinian literature has no such technical and comprehensive discussion of encyclical education as Philo. There are, nevertheless, passages which discuss disciplines that may have come from the encyclia as well as other passages which, in a general way, refer to Greek wisdom. Thus Pirqe Aboth 3, 18 discusses the relationship of wisdom to the disciplines of astronomy and geometry in a way similar to that of Philo:[2] "Astronomy and geometry are but the aftercourses of wisdom".[3] The question of Judaism and paganism, however, is not explicitly dealt with in this passage.

Many of the sources express a negative evaluation of "Greek wisdom", because a study of it leads to the neglect of the study of the Torah, though there are examples which show that at least some of the Jews in Palestine received a Greek education. The sources reflect, however, a more negative attitude than that of Philo in Alexandria, and they do not show clearly whether or not "Greek wisdom" refers to encyclical education in the technical sense.[4]

---

[1] See pp. 125 f. and especially *Corpus Papyrorum Judaicarum*, ed. by V. A. Tcherikover and A. Fuks, I, Cambridge, Mass. 1957, pp. 37-41.

[2] Text in *Mishnayoth* (Blackman) IV, p. 515. The English translation of Ph. Blackman is followed with only slight adjustments.

[3] Astronomy and geometry are listed among the disciplines of the encyclia in Congr. 11.

[4] See S. Lieberman, *Hellenism in Jewish Palestine*, pp. 100-114 and *Greek in Jewish Palestine. Studies in the Life and Manners of Jewish Palestine in the II-IV Centuries C.E.*, New York 1942, pp. 1-2; cf. S. Marcus, *Die Pädagogik des israelitischen Volkes von der Patriarchenzeit bis auf den Talmud*, Wien 1877, pp. 30-34; R. Meyer, *Hellenistisches in der rabbinischen Anthro-*

In general scholars have been reluctant to consider Philo's discussion of the encyclia against the background of the relationship between Judaism and paganism. Ignoring the concrete case of Philo and the other Jews in Alexandria, such scholars as Siegfried, Zeller, Bréhier and Völker interpret the encyclia as a preliminary stage in the moral and religious progress of individuals, although their interpretations give very different emphases to details.[1] Goodenough considers the encyclia a preliminary stage in the ascent towards the vision of the mystery.[2] Finally, Wolfson discusses the relationship among the encyclia, philosophy and Scripture from the viewpoint of the philosophical question of cognition, and concludes that Philo regards Scripture to be superior to the others.[3]

Because a detailed analysis of the homily in Mut. 253-263 has shown that the actual position of Judaism is reflected in it, the contention of these scholars is inadequate. The correct understanding of Philo's ideas in this respect is set forth by I. Heineman, as mentioned above, and by Pohlenz who has also seen that the issue of Judaism and paganism is involved in Philo's evaluation of the encyclia.[4] The homily also has other characteristics which reflect the position of the Jews in Alexandria.

Manna, wisdom and the Sabbath

The reference to the Sabbath in Mut. 259-260 is another feature which interprets the life of the Jews. Colson translates it this way: "... heavenly wisdom which is sent from above on souls which yearn for virtue by Him who sheds the gift of prudence in rich abundance, whose grace waters the universe, and chiefly so in the holy seventh (year) which he calls the Sabbath?"

At this point Wendland refers to the mention of the Sabbath in the passage about the manna in Ex. 16, 23 ff.[5] Colson raises the objection to Wendland that this passage tells that the manna did

---

pologie, BWANT, 4th Ser. XXII, (Der ganzen Sammlung LXXIV), Stuttgart 1937, pp. 135-144.

[1] C. Siegfried, *Philo von Alexandria*, pp. 260-262; E. Zeller, *Die Philosophie der Griechen in ihrer geschichtlichen Entwicklung*, III, 2, (*Die nacharistotelische Philosophie*), 4th ed., Leipzig 1903, pp. 457 f., 460 f.; E. Bréhier, *Les Idées*, pp. 279-295; W. Völker, *Fortschritt*, pp. 158-198.

[2] E. Goodenough, *By Light, Light. The Mystic Gospel of Hellenistic Judaism*, New Haven, Conn., 1935.

[3] H. A. Wolfson, *Philo* I, pp. 145-151.

[4] M. Pohlenz, *Philon, NAG*, Göttingen 1942, pp. 428 ff.

[5] *Philonis Alexandrini opera* (Cohn and Wendland) III, p. 201.

not fall on the Sabbath, while according to Mut. 259-260 it chiefly falls on the Sabbath. Therefore Colson proposes as a better reference Lev. 25, 4 f. where the Sabbatical year is designated by the word Sabbath.[1] Theiler has been convinced by Colson's suggestion.[2]

Colson's interpretation is hardly right. He himself admits that no noun but ἡμέρα can be presupposed by the phrase ἐν ἱερᾷ ἑβδόμῃ.[3] Another weakness in his argument is that he, as well as Wendland, looks only for the biblical background without taking into consideration the exegesis which Philo develops in this passage. Finally, Colson cites no references to traditions where the manna is associated with the Sabbatical year as such. Rightly enough, Philo discusses the Sabbatical year at several places, but a main lesson to be learned from this description is that he does not draw such a sharp distinction between the Sabbath and the Sabbatical year, as Colson does. Rather, Philo includes the Sabbatical year among the Jewish feasts for which the day of the Sabbath is made superior, so that it serves as a heading for his account of them.[4]

It is necessary, then, to examine anew the reference to the Sabbath in Mut. 259-260, remembering that Philo is an exegete. Philo here has replaced the word for manna in Ex. 16, 4 with the word "wisdom", ἡ σοφία, and Philo frequently associates the wisdom of philosophy in a special way with the Sabbath day.

There are even close similarities between the phraseology in Mut. 260 and the various statements about the study of philosophy on the Sabbath. Thus Mos. II 215 says: "for it was customary... preeminently on the seventh day...to pursue the study of wisdom" (προηγουμένως δὲ ταῖς ἑβδόμαις — φιλοσοφεῖν) and the description of the studies of the Essenes in Probus 81 is similar: "In these (the laws of their fathers) they are instructed at all other times, but particularly on the seventh days" (ἐν δὲ ταῖς ἑβδόμαις διαφερόντως). Mut. 259-260 also fits well into this picture when it says: "... wisdom which is sent...and chiefly so on the holy seventh, which he calls the Sabbath" (καὶ μάλιστα ἐν ἱερᾷ ἑβδόμῃ, ἥν σάββατον καλεῖ).

Because in several places Philo says that the manna did not fall

---

[1] *Philo* (Colson and Whitaker) V, p. 274, n.a. Cf. that Colson has added in bracket "year" in his translation, (p. 275).

[2] *Die Werke Philos* (Cohn, Heinemann, Adler, Theiler) VI, p. 160, n. 2.

[3] See supra, note 1; cf. I. Heinemann, *Philons griechische und jüdische Bildung. Kulturvergleichende Untersuchungen zu Philons Darstellung der jüdischen Gesetze*, Breslau 1932, p. 141 and n. 3.

[4] See Decal. 158-164; Spec. II 39-222 and Hypoth. 7, 10-19.

on the Sabbath (Mos. I 205; II 263-264), but in Mut. 259-260 seems to say that it is sent chiefly on the Sabbath, the explanation must be that here the manna is understood to be the wisdom of the Jewish philosophy which has its primary place just on this day in the assemblies of the synagogues.[1] And just as the Sabbath and the Sabbatical year ideologically were closely related to each other, so they are combined in Mut. 259-260 to interpret aspects of the Jewish philosophy found in the laws of Moses. In this way, however, the homily also characterizes its own place and function: It is an expression of this very manna given by God, as the heavenly "wisdom" on the Sabbath.

It is possible to go one step further and say that this homily discusses the relationship between encyclical education and the education in the Jewish synagogues which Philo often calls schools.[2] The basic differences between these two schools, according to this homily, is that the encyclia uses teaching as its basis, whereas the philosophy of the laws of Moses studied in the synagogues has its basis in selftaught wisdom brought forth by nature itself. Both kinds of schools have their virtues, though on entirely different levels (Mut. 263).

In other contexts, where this basic difference between the encyclia and the philosophy of the synagogues is not discussed, Philo makes teaching and practice go together with the selftaught wisdom of this philosophy. For example in Praem. 65-66, he describes the patriarchs with the triad "nature" ("selftaught"), "learning" and "practice" and concludes by saying: "From this household, increased in the course of time to a great multitude, were founded flourishing and orderly cities, schools of wisdom, justice and religion, where also the rest of virtue and how to acquire it is the sublime subject of their research."

In Abr. 52-53 Philo explicitly says that teaching (Abraham) and practice (Jacob) must go together with the selftaught by nature (Isaac): "But indeed we must not fail to note that each possesses the three qualities, but gets his name from that which chiefly predominates in him; for teaching cannot be consummated without nature or practice, nor is nature capable of reaching its zenith

---

[1] Cf. J. S. Boughton, *The Idea of Progress in Philo Judaeus*, New York 1932, pp. 46-50, who thinks that Philo substitutes synagogue instruction by the teaching of Greek philosophy and Hellenistic mystery cults.

[2] See Mos. II 216; Spec. II 62; Praem. 66; cf. Decal. 40.

without learning and practising, nor practice either unless the foundation of nature and teaching has first been laid."

The Torah is often identified with bread in Palestinian traditions, and there are also a few traces of an identification of the manna with the wisdom of the Torah, as Philo has done in the homily of Mut. 253-263.¹ Odeberg has drawn attention to Mek. Ex. 13, 17 which makes the same identification: "... I will 'lead them about' in the desert for forty years that they may eat the manna and drink the water of the well and (thereby) the Torā will be united (assimilated) with their body."²

Philo's interpretation of manna as that wisdom which comes especially on the Sabbath at the reading and expounding of the laws of Moses is paralleled most closely in John 6, where the manna is associated with the eucharistic meal of the Church.

Among Philonic scholars, C. H. Dodd has pointed out this identification of the manna with the wisdom of the Torah: "In rabbinic tradition bread is a standing symbol of the Torah. ... I do not find evidence that this identification was in rabbinic exposition extended to the manna, but the equation of manna with σοφία in Philo almost necessarily implies that in some circles it was taken to be a symbol of Torah."³

Pascher, on the other hand, thinks that Philo knew a sacred meal similar to those in the mystery religions, on the basis of which Philo said that men of vision see the Divine being through the partaking of the Light—Logos—Pneuma—Manna.⁴ Goodenough seems to spiritualize the idea of manna when he includes manna among the "showers of refreshing" of which the mystic is aware during his period of struggle.⁵

---

¹ See especially C. H. Dodd, *The Interpretation*, p. 336. For the understanding of Torah as bread, see *Str.-B.* II, pp. 483 f.

² H. Odeberg, *The Fourth Gospel*, p. 243. See also Ex. R. 25, 7, which identifies manna with the wisdom of Torah. See below on p. 156.

³ See the reference supra, n. 1; also H. A. Wolfsen, *Philo* I, pp. 147 ff. where the identification of wisdom and the Torah is made clear. Wolfson refers, however, to the manna only in the discussion of the essence of God, *ibid.* II, pp. 109-110.

⁴ J. Pascher, *Der Königsweg zu Wiedergeburt und Vergottung bei Philon von Alexandreia*, StGKA XVII, 3-4, Paderborn 1931, p. 186 with reference to Mut. 258 ff. in n. 3. See also the conclusion on p. 191: "Philon kennt ein heiliges Mahl, in dem durch den Genuss von Licht-Logos-Pneuma-Manna der "Seiende" geschaut wird." Cf. the same viewpoint in modified form in H. Hegermann, *Die Vorstellung vom Schöpfungsmittler*, p. 38.

⁵ E. Goodenough, *Light*, pp. 207-208; see also *Jewish Symbols* VIII, New

These viewpoints of Pascher and Goodenough do not represent a sufficiently adequate understanding of the homily in Mut. 253-263, where the manna and Greek educational ideas are used to interpret Judaism and the laws of Moses in their relationship to the encyclia on the borderline of the pagan world.

The nation of vision

The homily of Mut. 253-263 even has a direct reference to Israel by the designation "the seeing one", ὁ ὁρατικός in § 258. Colson is right when he translates "the nation of vision", since this word and other words of the same root are frequently used by Philo as an etymological interpretation of Israel.[1] Immut. 144 serves as an example: "Thus those who are members of that race endowed with vision (- τοῖς τοῦ ὁρατικοῦ γένους), which is called Israel,...find their way contested by Edom...."[2] The etymology is based upon Hebrew philology and is then translated into Greek.[3] This philological operation is thus parallel to the interpretation of the Hebrew vocalization in John 6, 31-32 to which the Greek language did not give any basis either.[4] Although this Hebrew etymology of Israel is frequent in Philo, it is very scarce in Palestinian traditions; it occurs, however, quite clearly in Christian literature, where the Jewish source is still partly evident.[5]

This etymological interpretation in Mut. 258 seems to be caused by the occurrence of the word Israel in the haggadic tradition

---

York 1958, p. 230 where Goodenough combines the spiritual idea of manna with a sacramental meal.

[1] Philo (Colson and Whitaker) V, p. 275.

[2] For other occurrences of the term, see Conf. 91; cf. Mos. II 195-196; Migr. 53 f.; Fuga 139 f. Other variants of the etymology in Post. 63; Conf. 92, etc. A fuller list of references is found in H. Leisegang, *Der Heilige Geist*, I, 1, p. 223, n. 4 and p. 224, n. 3.

[3] L. Ginzberg, *Legends* V, p. 307, n. 253 (איש ראה אל); E. Stein, *Die allegorische Exegese*, p. 59 (שור אל). See also the discussion of the etymology by W. Michaelis, ὁράω, *Theologisches Wörterbuch zum Neuen Testament*, ed G. Kittel, V, Stuttgart 1954(?), p. 337, n. 113.

[4] See pp. 62-65.

[5] For a Hebrew example of the etymology, see *Seder Eliahu rabba und Seder Eliahu zuta*, (*Tanna d'be Eliahu*), ed. M. Friedmann, Wien 1902, 27, (pp. 138-139), interpreting Hos. 9, 10: אל תיקרי ישראל אלא איש ראה אל. For other Jewish writings in Greek, cf. E. Stein, "Zur apokryphen Schrift "Gebet Josepho"," *MGWJ* LXXXI (N.F. XLV), 1937, pp. 280 ff., where also Philo's lack of the noun ἀνήρ in the Greek translation of the etymology is discussed. See also N. A. Dahl, *Das Volk Gottes. Eine Untersuchung zum Kirchenbewusstsein des Urchristentums*, SkrNVA 1941 II, Oslo 1941, pp. 114 f., where also Hieronymus' *De nominibus hebraicis* is referred to.

about bread from heaven and earth, fragments of which are used in the homily. The variant in Ex. R. 25, 2 is of special interest because the phrase, "to Israel from heaven" (לישראל מן השמים) occurs. Since the term ὁ ὁρατικός means Israel, Philo has the same phrase: "to the nation of vision (= Israel) from heaven" (ἀπ' οὐρανοῦ τῷ ὁρατικῷ).[1] This similarity between Mut. 258 and the tradition about bread from heaven and earth in Ex. R. 25, 2 gives additional support to the analysis in Ch. I.

Does Philo by this etymology refer to the Jewish race in the concrete sense or does he develop it allegorically as a spiritualized concept only? Goodenough expresses the latter viewpoint: "This race has got the name of Israel, that is 'Seeing God,' and is distinguished by the fact that it has the vision of God at the end of the mystic Road, the highest possible achievement, to which vision God draws the soul up the Road by the action of the divine Powers. This is not a reference to the race of Israel, but first to the Patriarchs, and then to those who got the vision, whether Jew or Gentile, and only to those."[2]

Goodenough represents a point of view strongly held among the exegetes of Philo. Pascher is very close to Goodenough, while Reitzenstein, Leisegang and Jonas think that Philo's understanding of "he who sees God" is determined by the gnostic idea of the pneumatikoi.[3]

On the other hand, there are scholars who defend the position that Philo refers to the concrete nation of the Jews in his etymology. Strangely enough, Goodenough is also a typical representative of this point of view in his comments upon Legat. 1-7: "This race is, of course, the Jews, and Philo begins, strangely, to plunge the reader into the Mystery. The Jews are Israel, which means, he says,

---

[1] The translation in *Philo* (Colson and Whitaker) V, p. 275 is slightly changed.
[2] E. Goodenough, *Light*, p. 136.
[3] J. Pascher, *Der Königsweg*, pp. 11, 28, 35-36, etc.; R. Reitzenstein, *Die hellenistischen Mysterienreligionen*, 3rd ed., Leipzig/Berlin 1927, pp. 145 f.; H. Leisegang, *Der Heilige Geist* I, 1, pp. 223 ff.; H. Jonas, *Gnosis und spätantiker Geist*, II, 1, (*Von der Mythologie zur mystischen Philosophie*), *FRLANT* LXIII (N.F. XLV), Göttingen 1954, pp. 38 (n. 1), 70, etc. See also similar viewpoints in P. Volz, *Der Geist Gottes und die verwandten Erscheinungen im Alten Testament und im anschliessenden Judentum*, Tübingen 1910, pp. 132 f.; J. Drummond, *Philo Judaeus, or the Jewish-Alexandrian philosophy in its developement and completion*, II, London 1888, pp. 9 f.; W. Gutbrod, Ἰσραήλ, *ThWb* III, p. 373.

'seeing God.' The mystic vision given to Jews, vision of that Deity which is beyond all categories, even the categories of virtue, is hidden from other men ... " [1] It is, indeed, surprising that Goodenough has not discovered that his two contradicting presentations of Philo's etymological interpretation of Israel shake the very foundation of his own understanding of Philo! He should at least have connected them and discussed then together.

Scholars like Wolfson, Stein and Völker link "the nation of vision" to the Jews in order to characterize the aspects of their prophecy, interpretation of the Scripture and mystical vision of God.[2]

Dahl has made an attempt to mediate between these two conflicting views of "the nation of vision", and to place both within a pattern of ascent from earth to heaven. Thus, the concept of Israel in Philo moves from the empirical Jewish nation, through other grades as the invisible "church" of universal character, to the abstract vision of God and, finally, to Logos as the one who has the vision.[3] Philo has, therefore, both the perspective of nationalism and universalism, but on different levels, according to Dahl.

Messel criticizes Dahl's understanding at this point, maintaining that Philo takes his philosophical and mystical ideas from the surroundings of Judaism, transforms them, and employs them to show the unique and superior position of the Jewish nation.[4] On the basis of Messel's position Goodenough's comments upon the concept of Israel in Legat. 1-7 are to be extended to characterize Philo's understanding in general.

The corresponding viewpoints of Goodenough, Messel, Wolfson, Stein and Völker cover the meaning of "the nation of vision" in the homily of Mut. 253-263. The preceding discussion of the encyclia and of the Sabbath demonstrates the fact that the concept of the vision of God is used by Philo as a distinctive characteristic of the

---

[1] E. Goodenough, *The Politics of Philo Judaeus. Practice and Theory*, New Haven, 1938, p. 12.
[2] H. A. Wolfson, *Philo* II, pp. 51 f.; E. Stein, *Die allegorische Exegese*, p. 37; W. Völker, *Fortschritt*, pp. 283 ff.; cf. N. Bentwich, *Philo-Judaeus of Alexandria*, Philadelphia 1910, pp. 50, 133.
[3] N. A. Dahl, *Das Volk Gottes*, pp. 108 ff., 113.
[4] N. Messel, " "Guds folk" som uttrykk for urkristendommens kirkebevissthet. Innlegg ved cand. theol. Nils Alstrup Dahls disputas for doktorgraden i teologi 12. sept. 1941," III, *NTT* XLII, 1941, pp. 229-237. Cf. the similar viewpoint of M. Pohlenz, *Philon*, *NAG*, Göttingen 1942, p. 428.

Jewish nation to place the neutral encyclia on a lower level altogether.

The idea of the vision in Mut. 253-263 is, then, determined both by Greek educational ideas and the actual study of the Jewish philosophy in the synagogues on the Sabbath. Thus the nation of vision is the people that is selftaught by nature, even the Jews, especially as they study the laws of Moses on the Sabbath.

There are points of contacts between Philo and Palestinian literature. The Palestinian midrash sometimes stresses that the ability of vision (of God) distinguishes man, i.e., in Israel, from the animals, Gen. R. 8, 11; 14, 3. And Israel saw the image of God at Sinai, Lev. R. 20, 10; Ex. R. 41, 3.[1] The idea of seeing God and the Shekinah occurs frequently in connection with the study and prayers in the synagogues, Deut. R. 7, 2; Midrash Ps. 105 § 1.[2]

Heaven and earth

The starting point of this analysis of the ideas in the homily of Mut. 253-263 was that the Greek educational concepts of "virtue" and "wisdom" were substituted for manna in Ex. 16, 4 and in haggadic fragments. In this way manna was given a fresh interpretation. This new combination means that the Greek educational ideas at the same time also are understood in a new way. The fragments of the tradition about bread from heaven and earth place these Greek educational ideas within the perspective of heaven and earth.

The contrast between heaven and earth determines the other contrasts in the homily. Thus, the concept of heaven goes with "virtue" and "wisdom" of philosophy, "selftaught" ability, "selfgrown" fruits and the life of the Jews centered around the Sabbaths. Earth, on the other hand, is linked to the encyclia, "teaching" by school masters, agriculture and the borderline between Judaism and paganism.

The contrast between heaven and earth does not mean that Philo develops a cosmic and anthropological dualism in this homily. He does not, as he does in the homily of Leg. all. 162-168, use the

---

[1] See J. Jervell, *Imago Dei*, pp. 86-87 and 115, who also mentions the parallelism between Palestinian traditions and Philo at this point. Cf. also N. A. Dahl, *NTT* LX, 1959, p. 196, and n. 5 with reference to Mek. Ex. 19, 11.

[2] See *Str.-B.* I, pp. 206 f.

dualistic pattern of "not earthly, but heavenly." Although the homily of Mut. 253-263 makes a clear distinction between heaven and earth, the philosophy for the souls and encyclia, it concludes by assigning a positive "virtue" to each, although earth and encyclia represent, of course, a weaker one.

This collision between the Greek educational tradition and Jewish traditions about manna caused a transformation of Greek ideas of "virtue" and "wisdom" of philosophy. They received the new context of being given by God from heaven in contrast to the earthly cultivation of man in the encyclia: "God showers virtue" (§ 258); "Of what food can he rightly say that it is rained from heaven, save of heavenly wisdom ...?" (§ 259).

This transformation explains why Philo has given "virtue" and "wisdom" of philosophy the further qualification that they are selftaught by nature. Here, as often, he understands by nature God and his activity, so that the "selftaught" by "nature" means the one who is the object of divine grace.[1] At this point Philo's interpretation of the Greek concept is not wholly new, since the concepts of "nature" and "selftaught" were already understood as divine inspiration in Greek traditions, but Philo is radical in his stress on it as solely the action of the grace of God.[2]

The reference to bread from earth in the haggadic fragment was interpreted by Philo against the background of the common picture of education as agriculture. He also applied this picture of agriculture to the activity of God by distinguishing between two forms of farming. The one form is expressed by the qualification of God as αὐτουργός[3], a farmer who works his land himself and not by slaves; the other form by contrast was farming done by labourers, γεωπόνοι (§ 259):[4] "The earthly food is produced with the co-operation of husbandmen, but the heavenly is sent like the

---

[1] See E. Goodenough, *Light*, pp. 50 ff.; H. Lewy, *Sobria Ebrietas*, pp. 59 ff.; H. A. Wolfson, *Philo* II, pp. 197 f.

[2] Cf. H. Lewy, *Sobria Ebrietas*, pp. 59 ff.; H. A. Wolfson, *Philo* II, pp. 197 f.

[3] Philo has a rhetorical play on words with αὐτο—in this homily: αὐτομαθές (§ 255), ἀπαυτοματιζούσῃ (§ 257), αὐτουργός (§ 259), αὐτομαθῶν, αὐτογενεῖ καὶ αὐτοτελεῖ (§ 260), αὐτομαθοῦς (§ 263).

[4] For the meaning of αὐτουργός ("one who works his land himself") and γεωπόνος ("labourer"), see H. G. Liddell and R. Scott, *A Greek-English Lexicon*, ad nom. (A parallel contrast between a self producer and a farmer who has labourers, is found in Agr. 5 f.).

snow by God the solely self producer,[1] with none to share his work."

Hence the teaching of the encyclia is compared to farming by the help of teachers as laborers, while the "virtue" and "wisdom" of philosophy are the "selftaught" products brought forth from heaven where God himself is the producer.[2] Against this background the Jewish tradition about the manna sent by God was very fitting as a picture of the distinctive features of the revealed philosophy of the Jews in contrast to the encyclia, which has its place on the borderland of paganism and has as its basis human effort.

Several scholars who have discussed Mut. 258 ff. have misinterpreted the contrast between heaven and earth and used it to support the idea of a cosmic and anthropological dualism in Philo's works. Windisch thinks that a Platonic and Pythagorean dualism is central to Philo and within this framework Philo's ideas of the manna from heaven shows that he is against synergism.[3] Though in different ways, both Pascher and Goodenough place the manna from God on the mystic road away from the flesh to the vision of God, referring also to Mut. 259 f.[4] According to Leisegang, Mut. 259 expresses the sharp dualistic tendency in Philo's works.[5] Jonas stresses that in Philo the Greek concept of virtue is hollowed out by Jewish and crypto-gnostic motives. This transformation is seen by the non-Greek idea that virtue (= manna) comes from above, without co-operation by men (Mut. 258, etc.), leaving the soul to have no καλόν of her own.[6]

All these scholars, however, have ignored the context of Mut. 258-260, which shows that there is no such dualism between heaven and earth, soul and body in this homily. Jonas is right when he thinks that the Greek concept of virtue is transformed, but this

---

[1] Colson, *Philo* (Colson and Witaker) V, p. 275, translates "self-acting".

[2] Philo also develops this idea of God as the solely self-acting in other contexts than this one, which, as we have seen, deals with the relationship between philosophy and the encyclia. See for example Opif. 72.

[3] H. Windisch, *Die Frömmigkeit Philos und ihre Bedeutung für das Christentum. Eine religionsgeschichtliche Studie*, Leipzig 1909, (pp. 4 ff., 86 f. and) p. 33.

[4] J. Pascher, *Der Königsweg*, (p. 11 and) pp. 185 ff.; E. Goodenough, *Light*, pp. 207-208; cf. *An Introduction to Philo Judaeus*, New Haven 1940, p. 16.

[5] H. Leisegang, *Der Heilige Geist*, I, 1, p. 54 and n. 1.

[6] H. Jonas, *Gnosis* II, 1, p. 38, and n. 1; Jonas' understanding is accepted by H. Thyen, "Die Probleme der neueren Philo-Forschung," *ThR* XXIII, 1955, pp. 243 f. Cf. a similar understanding of the concept of "nature" by H. Lewy, *Sobria Ebrietas*, pp. 59 ff.

transformation is caused by a collision between Greek educational ideas on the one hand, Ex. 16, 4 and fragments from haggadah on the other. This collision reflects moreover the actual position of Judaism in Alexandria, where the relationship between the Jewish philosophy and the encyclia was a burning question. Jonas is positively wrong when he cites Mut. 258 to show that Philo does not leave any καλόν to man. In the homily of Mut. 253-263 Philo clearly says that the earthly and human aspect also has its virtue, although of a different kind from the heavenly one.

The homily under consideration is addressed to Jews. In Mut. 254 the lecturer joins with his audience and says "we", and regrets the failure to realize virtue. The intention of the homily is therefore to encourage Jews to place the divine virtue of the Jewish philosophy in the center, without rejecting the encyclia.[1]

---

[1] Cf. H. Hegermann, *Die Vorstellung vom Schöpfungsmittler*, p. 18, who rightly stresses the parenetic intention of Mut. 255-260.

CHAPTER FIVE

THE HEAVENLY ORDER OF THE JEWS AND PAGAN CAREER
LEG. ALL. III 162-168

Stoic thoughts

In the homily of Mut. 253-263, Ex. 16, 4 served only as a subordinate quotation, while in Leg. all. III 162-168 it is the text of the homily. There is also another difference between these two homilies. In Mut. 259 only one phrase of Ex. 16, 4 was cited, while Leg. all. III 162 renders almost the whole verse, which then is divided into smaller parts in the systematic exposition in the homily. It is preferable to start the analysis with the last phrase of the quotation from Ex. 16, 4.

The exposition renders this phrase verbatim in Leg. all. III 167: "that I may prove them whether they will walk in My law (τῷ νόμῳ μου) or not." Philo's interpretation of the term "My law" in this quotation has a form which is similar to that of the explicative definitions in John 6, 39.40.50:[1] "for this is the divine law (νόμος — θεῖος), to value excellence for its own sake (τὴν ἀρετὴν δι' ἑαυτὴν τιμᾶν)". Philo defines "the law" here in Ex. 16, 4 by a maxim which was central to the Stoics, although it also occurs in Greek philosophy in general.[2] The background is that virtue has a value of its own, although the practice of it may not be rewarded by various kinds of external goods.[3]

Philo also employs another basic Stoic term in his elaboration on this theme, "the law," in Leg. all. III 168, namely, "right reason" (ὁ ὀρθὸς λόγος). In Stoicism right reason meant both the cosmic law and man's criterion for distinguishing between right and wrong.[4]

---

[1] See pp. 75 ff.
[2] See the discussion of Leg. all. III 167 in H. A. Wolfson, *Philo* II, p. 295. Concerning the use of the maxim in Greek philosophy, see *ibid.*, pp. 285 f. The Stoic rendering, "virtue is worthy of choice for its own sake" (ἀυτὴν δι' αὐτὴν εἶναι αἱρετήν), is given in Diogenes Laertius, VII, 89. cf. 127, quoted in *StVF* (Arnim) III, pp. 11.
[3] See H. A. Wolfson, *Philo* II, pp. 285 f.
[4] See H. Leisegang, "Logos," *Pauly-W.* XIII, cols. 1058 f.; 1072 f.; M. Pohlenz, *Die Stoa. Geschichte einer geistigen Bewegung*, I, Göttingen 1948,

In accordance with Stoic ideas, therefore, Philo employs "right reason" to distinguish between the external and the internal qualities, and he associates "virtue" not with the external goods, but only with the internal aspects of man.[1] Philo follows the Stoics also when in Leg. all. III 167 he indicates certain concrete points related to external items, luxury and political office.[2]

But these externals are described as the wrong objectives for *education*: "Many, then, have acquired the lights in the soul for night and darkness, not for day and light; all elementary lessons for example, and what is called school-learning and philosophy itself when pursued with no motive higher than luxurious living, or from desire of an office under our rulers."[3]

In this way the homily of Leg. all. III 162-168 deals with the question of education, as the homily of Mut. 253-263 did. The focal points in the two homilies differ, however: whereas Mut. 253-263 discusses the basic difference between Jewish philosophy and the encyclia, Leg. all. III 162-168 criticizes the misuse of education, philosophy included.

The homily of Leg. all. III 162-168 draws, nevertheless, on the educational ideas of the Greek philosophical schools, which also sharply criticize the misuse of education. From the standpoint of the philosophers this misuse of education was championed by the sophists, who made political and commercial career the main objectives and not truth and virtue. This conflict between the philosophers and the sophists dominated the Greek educational life from the time of Plato and Isocrates on.[4] In the Roman period

---

pp. 61-62; *Die Werke Philos* (Cohn, Heinemann, Adler, Theiler) I, p. 78, n. 1; III, p. 31, n. 3; H. A. Wolfson, *Philo* II, pp. 176 ff.; E. Goodenough, *Light*, pp. 54 ff.; E. Bréhier, *Les Idées*, pp. 92 ff.

[1] See *StVF* (Arnim) III, pp. II f.

[2] See P. Wendland, *Philo und die kynisch-stoische Diatribe*; I. Heinemann, *Bildung*, pp. 431-433 makes the correct observation that this criticism of luxury had a much broader support than only the Stoic traditions.

[3] Leg. all. III 167a is an exposition of the word "day" in Ex. 16, 4, introduced by the paraphrase of a part of the quotation in Leg. all. III 166. In § 167, then, the interpretation moves from "day" to "light" and to "education" as "light". The misuse of education, therefore, brings "night" and "darkness".

With regard to the translation given, see *Philo* (Colson and Whitaker) I, p. 413, n.a.

[4] See R. Meister, "Die Entstehung der höheren Allgemeinbildung in der Antike," *WSt* LXIX, 1956, pp. 261 ff.; H. von Arnim, *Dio von Prusa*, pp. 18 ff., 72.

Cicero and Quintilian were worthy representatives of the viewpoints of the sophists, maintaining that all education, both encyclical and philosophical, should serve practical aims in man's life. But at the same time they stressed the need for good discipline and knowledge of ethics.[1]

In the homily of Leg. all. III 162-168 Philo sides with the philosophical schools by insisting that political and social career is not the objective of education. The objective is rather "virtue" which is to be cherished for its own sake. "Right reason" is then the ethical criterion for making a distinction between the external and internal things in life.[2]

Philo's criticism does not go to such an extreme, however, as to reject education, not even the encyclia. When serving the right objectives, education is "light" and "day"; only misuse turns it into "night" and "darkness", (§ 167). Thus the criterion of "right reason" (§ 168) guides men to use their education correctly. Accordingly, Philo in Ebr. 33 encourages men to have "right reason" as father and the encyclia as mother. And the homily of Mut. 253-263 allows the encyclia to play a role, although a lower one than that of philosophy.

The situation in Alexandria

The homily of Leg. all. III 162-168 does not only draw on the Greek educational traditions; it also reflects the actual situation at the time of Philo. At several places he describes the luxurious living surrounding the political rulers in Alexandria. These accounts throw more light upon the situation, which is reflected in the homily.

Of special interest to this question is Flac. 130-145. In §§ 130-134 Philo tells about the gymnasiarch Lampo, who had a high office under the rulers, and he criticizes him for injustice and unreasonable money making. Then in § 135 ff. Philo describes a central figure in the social life of the city, Isidorus, "a mob courter, popularity hunter, practised in producing disturbance and confusion", etc. The feast ruler in most of the clubs, he was known for luxurious

---

[1] See H. von Arnim, *Dio von Prusa*, pp. 97 ff. about the educational ideals of Cicero; and F. H. Colson, *JThSt* XVIII, 1917, p. 152 about Quintilian.

[2] At several places Philo develops the contrast between "right reason" and a luxurious living: Leg. all. III 148; Sacr. 49 ff.; Mos. II 184, etc.

living and political intrigues. Also outside Alexandria the upper social and political class had the same weaknesses for luxurious living and political intrigues, according to Philo.[1]

It is not surprising, then, that Philo (Leg. all. III 167-168) should reject such external things as luxurious living and political office as the proper goal of education.

Philo's stress on education in this context also reflects the actual conditions of his time, since (only) those who had the gymnasium education, the encyclia, could obtain civic rights and enter into the political and social elite in Alexandria, the epheboi.[2]

But Philo's interest is not limited simply to describing right and wrong attitudes and objectives of the epheboi in general. He is rather concerned with the motives which stimulated Jews to receive the necessary education and try to make a political and social career in the pagan environment.[3]

There are many indications that this question was a burning issue in Philo's Jewish surroundings. His own brother, Alexander, was a wealthy banker serving as a high official in Egypt.[4] Alexander's son, Tiberius Alexander, even became a renegade from Judaism and achieved an exceptional public career, finally attaining the highest post of a Roman official in Egypt, that of prefect.[5]

Philo seems to allude to this and similar cases in Mos. I 30-31 which describes prosperous Jews who look down on their relatives and friends and set at naught the laws under which they were born and bred, by adopting different modes of life.[6]

The papyri confirm these glimpses about the position of the Jews

---

[1] Cf. Spec. II 92; IV 172 and the more general description in IV 86-91. Although Philo paints a one-sided picture, his viewpoints are confirmed by the papyri: See I. Heinemann, *Bildung*, p. 431, with references in nn. 3 and 4.

[2] See H. I. Bell, *Egypt from Alexander the Great to the Arab Conquest*, Oxford 1948, pp. 71 f.; cf. *Philo* (Colson and Whitaker) IX, p. 535, note on § 130; *CPJ* (Tcherikover and Fuks) I, pp. 38 f.; 64 f.; V. Tcherikover, *Hellenistic Civilization and the Jews*, Philadelphia 1959, pp. 311 ff.

[3] Cf. that Philo refers to the Jews as "our race" in Leg. all. III 166.

[4] See Josephus, Antiquitates Judaicae XVIII 159 f.; XX 100; XVIII 259; *CPJ* (Tcherikover and Fuks) I, pp. 49,53,67,75; E. Goodenough, *Introduction*, pp. 2 f.; *The Politics*, pp. 64 f.

[5] *CPJ* (Tcherikover and Fuks) I, pp. 53,75,78,79; E. Goodenough, *The Politics*, p. 65; A. Lepape, "Tiberius Julius Alexander, Préfet d'Alexandrie et d'Egypte," *BSAA*, N.S. VIII, 1934, pp. 331-341.

[6] See Die *Werke Philos* (Cohn, Heinemann, Adler, Theiler) I, p. 229, n. 2; and I. Heinemann, *Bildung*, p. 456; Cf. Praem. 152 which has a remark on the punishment of Jewish renegades.

as reported by Philo. They reflect the struggle for emancipation for which the Alexandrian Jews fought, and which the Alexandrian Greeks violently opposed, especially the endeavours of the Jews to enrol their sons among the epheboi.[1] Finally in 41 A.D. the question of the civic rights of the Jews in Alexandria was settled by a letter from Claudius. He ordered the Jews not to aim at the acquisition of new rights. The participation of Jews in gymnastic contests were prohibited, and he also deprived them of gymnasium education; as a result no more Jews could acquire the gymnasium education prerequisite to citizenship or as a help to entering Greek society.[2]

The homily of Leg. all. III 162-168, therefore, presupposes a period when the Jews with the help of formal education could enter the leading social and political circles in Alexandria. And the point of the homily is not to prohibit the Jews from taking leading political positions, but to make certain that they do not regard a successful career as the aim of their education.

The picture of Moses in Mos. I 21-32 expresses Philo's ideals at this point. Moses mastered all kinds of education, reached the very pinnacle of human prosperity, and was even called the young king. He was, nevertheless, zealous for the discipline and culture of his kinsmen and ancestors, the Jews. In Mos. I 35 Philo even comes out explicitly in favour of Jewish emancipation into full citizenship.[3]

Philo thus adjusts Stoic ideas to the prevailing situation of the Jews, saying that also as political and social leaders they are "to value virtue for its own sake" and have "right reason" as an ethical criterion. Although he uses these Stoic ideas to interpret the word "law" in Ex. 16, 4, he still refers to Jewish law.

The maxim "to value virtue for its own sake," by which Philo characterizes the Jewish laws, has interesting parallels in Palestinian traditions, as e.g. the saying in Siphre on Deut. 32,2:[4] "if

---

[1] See H. I. Bell, *Juden und Griechen im römischen Alexandreia, AO Beih.* IX, Leipzig 1926, pp. 12,17; *CPJ* (Tcherikover and Fuks) I, pp. 38 ff., 64 ff. (Only a few scholars maintain that the Alexandrian Jews enjoyed full civic rights, *ibid.*, p. 39, n. 100).

[2] See *CPJ* (Tcherikover and Fuks) I, pp. 69-74; V. Tcherikover, *Hellenistic Civilization*, pp. 311-314.

[3] The same interpretation of Mos. I 35 is given by Tcherikover in *CPJ* (Tcherikover and Fuks) I, p. 63 and n. 32; Cf. similar points of view expressed in F. Geiger, *Philon von Alexandreia als sozialer Denker, TBA* XIV, Stuttgart 1932, p. 29.

[4] Text in *Sifré debé Rab, der älteste halachische und hagadische Midrasch zu Numeri und Deuteronomium*, ed. M. Friedmann, I, Wien 1864, 306 (131b end).

thou hast done the words of the Law for their own sake will they be life unto thee."[1] Although Philo obviously takes the maxim from Greek philosophy, he brings it close to the Palestinian viewpoint by applying it to the Jewish law.

Hardly any scholar has discussed the reference to the misuse of education for social and political aims in Leg. all. III 167. I. Heinemann, being one exception, regards the remark as an additional reference to the luxurious living among the scholars at the court of the Ptolemees (sic!).[2] Goodenough isolates the ideas of day and light and sees in them the mystical illumination.[3] In this way scholars miss the actual focal point of Philo's use of the Stoic ideas "the right reason" and "to value virtue for its own sake," in terms of the dangers facing the Jews entering the leading social and political life. This focal point gives a clue to the situation to which the whole homily of Leg. all. III 162-168 addresses itself.

Platonic thought patterns

Philo (Leg. all. III 167-168) interpreted the word "law" in Ex. 16, 4 on the basis of Stoic terms and ideas and applied them to the actual situation of the Jews in Alexandria to guide their conduct.

The homily, however, regards this situation and the ethical problems involved within a cosmic and religious context, as the Stoic idea of "right reason" also suggests. On this level, though, Philo moves away from the Stoic ideas of a cosmic immanence into Platonic thought patterns.

This shift of thought is evident in Philo's use of the haggadic fragments about the manna in Leg. all. III 168. (The fragments are italicized and underlined). "Such men have the privilege of being fed not with *earthly things* (μὴ τοῖς γηίνοις) but with *the heavenly forms* of knowledge (ταῖς ἐπουρανίοις ἐπιστήμαις)." A comparison with § 162 shows that the word "knowledge" (ἐπιστήμαις) replaces a word for manna in the haggadic fragment: "the food...is heavenly" (οὐράνιοι αἱ — τροφαί, § 162). Thus in Leg. all. III 168 Philo uses the same exegetical method as he employed in Mut. 258-259, to replace a

---

[1] English translation in H. A. Wolfson, *Philo* II, p. 287; See *ibid.*, n. 31 for other references (Taanith 7a, etc.); See also G. F. Moore, *Judaism* II, pp. 96-97.
[2] *Die Werke Philos* (Cohn, Heinemann, Adler, Theiler) III, p. 138, n. 3.
[3] E. Goodenough, *Light*, p. 208.

word from an Old Testament quotation or the haggadah with another term.[1]

This "knowledge" (ἐπιστήμη) belongs to the ethical terminology of the Stoics, as do "right reason" and "virtue", meaning the accurate comprehension of good and evil.[2] Philo says that those who value virtue for its own sake and, in accordance with the criterion of "right reason," do not regard external success as the objectives of education,—those men have the adequate ethical comprehensions.[3]

The association of ethical knowledge with manna, however, means a transformation of the idea into a heavenly quality, in contrast to the earthly ones. The reason is that Philo places the haggadic fragments about bread from heaven and earth within the dualistic pattern of "not — but" (μὴ — ἀλλὰ). In this way Philo identifies the ethical dualism between external and internal things from Stoicism with a cosmic dualism between heaven and earth, a dualism which has a Platonic stamp. The haggadah about the bread from heaven and earth, however, provided the actual words which are developed into a Platonic dualism.

Since § 168 is the closing statement of the homily, it points back to the opening in § 162. Therefore, it is not surprising that at the beginning there occurs the same dualism between heaven and earth: "That *the food* of the soul is not *earthly* (γήινοι) but *heavenly* (οὐράνιοι), we shall find abundant evidence in the Sacred Word" (Ex. 16, 4 quoted).

In this case, however, Philo has not used the exegetical method of replacing one word with an interpretative term, but he has used the method of supplementing the tradition with the qualifying word "soul":[4] οὐράνιοι αἱ ψυχῆς τροφαί (As above, so also here the haggadic fragment is underscored). The manna is then the heavenly food of the soul. Philo obviously presupposes that the soul and heaven belong together.

In Timaeus 90A-C Plato characterizes man as a plant rooted in heaven (φυτὸν οὐράνιον) due to the soul (ἡ ψυχή) which distinguishes

---

[1] See pp. 90, 100 f., and for the use of the same method in John 6, 52, see p. 90.
[2] See M. Pohlenz, *Die Stoa* II, pp. 71 f. (Note on p. 126).
[3] Cf. Th. H. Billings, *The Platonism of Philo Judaeus*, Chicago 1919, p. 33.
[4] See p. 66.

him from the animals.¹ A widespread Greek tradition follows Plato's anthropological pattern and understands man as a being between heaven and earth, between the divine sphere and the animals, etc.² In different ways Philo quite frequently understands man as a being between heaven and earth.³ So he does also in Leg. all III 162-168.

The main point of Leg. all. III 162.168, however, is not identifying the soul directly with heaven, but developing the idea that the soul feeds on heavenly nourishment, manna. Again Philo is influenced by Platonic thought in his interpretation of manna as heavenly food for the soul, for Plato mentions the nourishment of the soul at several places (Phaedrus 247 CD; 248 BC; 246 DE; Protagoras 313 C; Phaedo 84 AB).⁴

According to Leg. all. III 167-168 those men have adequate ethical comprehensions who "value virtue for its own sake" and, following "right reason", do not regard external success as the objectives of their education. Then in §§ 162.168 Philo transforms these Stoic ideas on the basis of a Platonic anthropology: the adequate ethical comprehension is of heavenly quality and nourishes the soul. It follows, then, that "right reason" and "virtue" also belong to the heavenly sphere and not to earthly things.

The Palestinian traditions offer interesting parallels to Philo's anthropology, since there, too, the place of man is between heaven and earth, usually represented by the angels and the animals.⁵ This

---

¹ *Plato*, with an English Translation by R. G. Bury, VII, (*Loeb*), London/New York 1929, pp. 244-247. Philo uses the Platonic phrase φυτὸν οὐράνιον in Deter. 85 and Plant. 17; cf. Th. H. Billings, *The Platonism of Philo Judaeus*, p. 40, and *Philo* (Colson and Whitaker) II, pp. 494 f., note on §§ 84 f.

² See N. A. Dahl, "Imago Dei. Opposisjonsinnlegg ved Jacob Jervells disputas 10.12. 1959," *NTT* LXI 1960, pp. 88 f.; W. Jaeger, *Nemesios von Emesa. Quellenforschung zum Neuplatonismus und seinen Anfängen bei Poseidonios*, Berlin 1914, pp. 98 ff.; E. Skard, "Nemesiosstudien," *SO* XV-XVI, 1936, pp. 23-43; M. Pohlenz, *Die Stoa* I, pp. 83 ff., 227-229; II, p. 114; K. Reinhardt, "Poseidonios" 3), *Pauly-W*. XXII, 1, 1951, cols. 719-725,773-778; W. Kranz, *Kosmos*, *AB* II, 1, Bonn 1955, p. 78; cf. *Hermetica* (Scott) I, pp. 234-237 (Libellus XII, 20a); II, pp. 366-367.

³ Leg. all. III 161; Opif. 135; Deter. 84-85; Conf. 176 ff.; Heres 283; Decal. 134; Plant. 14.20-22; Somn. I 146, etc. Cf. H. Schmidt, *Die Anthropologie Philons von Alexandreia*, (Diss.) Würzburg 1933, pp. 19-21; R. Meyer, *Hellenistisches in der rabbinischen Anthropologie*, pp. 28-29; cf. p. 78, n. 1.

⁴ See Th. H. Billings, *The Platonism of Philo Judaeus*, p. 100, and H. Leisegang, *Der Heilige Geist*, I, 1, p. 54, n. 5, who both refer to this Platonic idea in connection with the manna in Philo's works.

⁵ See the survey of texts for this anthropology in J. Jervell, *Imago Dei*,

idea of man in Judaism is probably due to a Platonic influence, although the dualism between soul and body generally is radically modified by belief in God as the creator of both, and the Jewish Torah has replaced the Greek idea of reason.[1]

To the idea of nourishing the soul there are less striking points of contact between Philo and Palestinian traditions. The closest idea is the rabbinic understanding of the Torah as bread and manna.[2] The Palestinian traditions tell, of course, about the Israelites eating the manna, the heavenly food, so that they therefore were divine beings in the desert.[3] This eating was not limited to the soul, however, but effected the body as well.

Terms from natural science

Philo elaborates this Stoic-Platonic interpretation of manna in terms which belong to the physical speculations of his days. Consider the relevant parts of Leg. all. III 162, in which are italicized words from Ex. 16, 4 and the haggadah about bread from heaven and earth:

"the soul is fed not with *things of earth* that decay (φθαρτοῖς), but with such words as God shall have poured like rain *out of* that lofty and pure region of life (τῆς μεταρσίου καὶ καθαρᾶς φύσεως), to which the prophet has given the title of *'heaven.'* "

Using the exegetical method of supplementing the Old Testament quotation and the haggadah with interpretative words, Philo here characterizes the earth by the word decaying (φθαρτοῖς) and heaven by the words lofty and pure (τῆς μεταρσίου καὶ καθαρᾶς).

The word μετάρσιος, lofty, on high, had a central place in the natural science of Hellenistic times. It usually designated the *sublunar* sphere, the air, and not heaven. Philo uses the word in this exact and scientific way in Plant. 127 and Cher. 4.[4] More frequently, however, he associates it with the *supralunar* sphere, the ethereal heaven with the sun, the moon and the stars.[5] Many

---

pp. 86 ff.: Aboth de Rabbi Nathan 37; Hagigah 16a; Pesiqta Rabbati 43, (179b); Tanhuma B, Bereshith 17; Siphre on Deut. 32,2; Gen. R. 8, 11; 12, 8; 14, 3; 21, 5; Ex. R. 30, 16; Eccl. R. VII, 29 § 1, etc.

[1] See R. Meyer, *Hellenistisches in der rabbinischen Anthropologie*, pp. 25-32; N. A. Dahl, *NTT* LXI, 1960, pp. 88 f.

[2] See p. 114 and nn. 1 and 2.

[3] Num. R. 7, 4, etc. See N. A. Dahl, *NTT* LX, 1959, pp. 196 f.; L. Ginzberg, *Legends* III, p. 44.

[4] See *Philo* (Colson and Whitaker) II, p. 10, n. a.

[5] See Leg. all. III 104; I 43; Gig. 62; Spec. III 1 ff., etc.

Hellenistic writers show the same lack of consistency in the terminological usage, even in more scientific discussions.[1]

In Leg. all. III 162, μετάρσιος qualifies heaven and is used in a homiletic presentation of Philo's anthropological and ethical ideals. It is, therefore, understandable that the more detailed scientific distinctions here are of less interest.

The other attribute of heaven, καθαρός, pure, also has its background in the philosophy of physics, where the ethereal sphere was regarded as the purest element. The Stoics based this viewpoint on the definition of ether as fire, the purest element. Aristotle and the Peripatetics classified ether as an element of its own, the fifth one in addition to the usual four and also on this basis heaven sometimes was called pure.[2]

Philo reflects both of these viewpoints when he describes heaven in his works, and he associates the quality of purity with ether in both cases.[3] Thus either one, or both, may give the background of the notion of the pure heaven in Leg. all. III 162.[4]

The term φθαρτός, perishable, decaying, played a central role in the philosophical debate in the Hellenistic-Roman time. This term and the contrasting term ἄφθαρτος were frequently used in considering whether or not the cosmos had a beginning and whether

---

[1] For the history of this term and the term μετέωρος see especially W. Capelle, Πεδάρσιος — μετάρσιος, *Philologus* LXXI, (N.F. XXV), 1912, pp. 449-456; "Zur Geschichte der meterologischen Litteratur," *Hermes* XLVIII, 1913, pp. 321-358; See also Μετέωρος — μετεωρολογία, *Philologus* LXXI, (N.F. XXV), 1912, pp. 414-448.

The lack of scientific consistency is also seen by the interchange of μετάρσιος and μετέωρος in Migr. 178; Gig. 62; Mut. 66 ff.

[2] About the viewpoints of the Stoics, see *StVF* (Arnim) II, p. 194; M. Pohlenz, *Die Stoa* I, p. 81.

Cicero, Tusculanae disputationes I 41 associates purity with the fifth element of Aristotle, in a context which also draws on Stoic and other ideas.

[3] The Stoic point of view is found in Somn. I 21; and probably also in Heres 86 f.; Opif. 27.114; Plant. 14. See *Die Werke Philos* (Cohn, Heinemann, Adler, Theiler) I, p. 36, n. 1. and VI, p. 177, n. 2; P. Wendland, *Quelle Philo's*, *SAB*, 1897, p. 1075. The idea of purity is based on Aristotle's fifth element in Qu. in Gen. IV 8; and combined with Stoic ideas in Heres 283. Cf. also L. Alfonsi, "Un nuovo frammento del ΠΕΡΙ ΘΙΛΟΣΟΘΙΑΣ Aristotelico," *Hermes* LXXXI, 1953, pp. 45-49.

[4] Note that the idea of purity is associated with ether as such in Josephus, Bellum Judaicum VI 47 (said by Titus). See A. Schlatter, *Die Theologie des Judentums nach dem Bericht des Josefus*, BFchrTh 2nd Ser., XXVI, Gütersloh 1932, p. 13.

or not it was perishable.[1] Philo took part in this debate in his treatise De aeternitate mundi, in which the adjective φθαρτός alternates with the noun φθορά, destruction.[2] This debate is also reflected elsewhere in Philo's works, associated with the term φθαρτός.[3]

There was in Hellenistic time another context for the use of φθαρτός, namely the dualism between heaven and earth. The framework for this dualism was created by the basic distinction, already drawn by Aristotle, between the supralunar ethereal heaven and the sublunar air and earth. By the help of Platonic ideas this distinction was developed into a dualism between the changing, perishable, imperfect and even evil sphere of earth and air and the divine and imperishable supralunar world.[4]

This dualism made a new context in which φθαρτός became a term to describe the world of air and earth in contrast to the ethereal heaven. So, in Philo's works the word also describes the physical elements of earth, water and air, and matter as such.[5] This background of speculative physics is reflected in Leg. all. III 162, since here the earth is described as perishable (φθαρτός) in contrast to the lofty, pure heaven.

It is evident, then, that by the exegetical method of supplementing words from Scripture and haggadah with other terms, in Leg. all. III 162 Philo developed an interpretation within the framework of Platonic thought pattern and speculative physics. The distinct physical associations, however, are to some degree

---

[1] Concerning this debate in general, see the brief summary by W. Kranz, *Kosmos*, *AB* II, 1, p. 62.

[2] See Aet. 7-9 et passim. About the use of φθαρτός see further Aristotle, Analytica Posteriora 75b 24; 85b 18; Metaphysica 992b 17; Plutarch's Moralia, 106 D, etc.

[3] See Spec. II 166; Ebr. 73. 208; Plant. 53, etc.

[4] See M. P. Nilsson, *Geschichte der griechischen Religion* II, *HklAW* V, 2, 2, München 1950, p. 674. See also M. Pohlenz, *Die Stoa* I, p. 322 (Seneca); p. 350 (Plutarch and Marc Aurel); W. Capelle, *Die Schrift von der Welt. Ein Beitrag zur Geschichte der griechischen Popularphilosophie*, *NJklA* VIII, 1905, pp. 536,537 and n. 2 with references: Cicero, De natura deorum II 17.56; De re publica VI 17 (end); Tusculanae disputationes I 42 ff., 60; Seneca, De ira III 6, 1; Ad Lucilium epistulae morales XLIX 16, etc.; cf. Hermetica (Scott) I, p. 209, (Libellus XI (i), 4a). J. Kroll, *Die Lehren des Hermes Trismegistos*, *BGPhM* XII, 2-4, Münster i. W. 1914, pp. 174-176, especially p. 175, nn. 1-5.

[5] Conf. 154; Leg. all. I 88; Post. 115. 163. 165; Plant. 22, etc. Sometimes Philo thinks that not only heaven, but also the air is imperishable, as in Deter 85.

stripped off, since the context is dominated by an anthropological and ethical interest.[1]

The ideas of Greek physics are also found in the Palestinian traditions, both in cosmological and anthropological contexts. Num. R. 14, 12 (end) distributes the four elements of nature from earth to heaven placing, as Philo often does, fire in heaven.[2] And man was made out of the combination of these elements, according to other traditions, Tanhuma, Pequde 3 (end).[3] These ideas from Greek physics are not so predominant in the Palestinian traditions as in Philo. And the anthropological interpretation of man as a being between heaven and earth, is, in the Palestinian midrash, connected with the idea of the heavenly beings rather than with the heavenly physics, as is the case in Leg. all. III 162.

The heavenly quality of the Jewish nation

The Stoic ideas of "right reason", "virtue" and ethical "comprehensions" are elevated to heavenly qualities by the help of a Platonic dualism between heaven and earth. This dualism is influenced by physical terminology, so that heaven is characterized as being of a "lofty (meteoric) and pure nature," while the earth is of a "decaying" nature. The soul is the part of man to which these heavenly qualities and ethical ideas belong.

This interpretation of the meaning of the homily seems to fit into a system of individualistic ethics. The analysis of Leg. all. III 167 indicated, however, that the homily refers to problems connected with the Jewish struggle for emancipation. In this way the conflict between Judaism and paganism provides the context of the interpretation, although Leg. all. 162.168 deals with the

---

[1] This anthropological and ethical interest in Leg. all. III 163 provides no basis for discussing the question whether or not the soul is material, in spite of the physical terminology. At some other places, however, Philo clearly rejects this Stoic viewpoint, although he sometimes uses the Stoic terminology. Cf. H. A. Wolfson, *Philo* I, pp. 394 f. See also H. Leisegang, *Der Heilige Geist* I, 1, pp. 57-58.

[2] For other references, See J. Freudenthal, *Hellenistische Studien I. Alexander Polihistor und die von ihm erhaltene Reste jüdische und samaritanischer Geschichtswerke*, JFS, Breslau 1874/1875, pp. 69-72; H. Diels, *Elementum. Eine Vorarbeit zum griechischen und lateinischen Thesaurus*, Leipzig 1899, p. 46, n. 1; cf. G. F. Moore, *Judaism* I, pp. 381 f.; About the four elements in Josephus' writings, see A. Schlatter, *Die Theologie des Judentums*, pp. 12 f.

[3] See L. Ginzberg, *Legends* V, p. 72 for other references.

dualism of heaven and earth, soul and body. How can this seeming dichotomy be explained?[1]

The solution is that "the soul" does not have primarily an individualistic sense, but refers to the Jewish nation collectively as it is explicitly said in § 163: "The people, and all the organization of the soul ...." Again Philo has used the exegetical method of supplementing words from the Old Testament quotation with other terms, as seen by underscoring the words from the quotation: ὁ λεὼς καὶ πᾶν τὸ τῆς ψυχῆς σύστημα καὶ συναγαγέτω —. We see that the word "the people" (ὁ λεὼς) is explicated by "all the organization of the soul" (πᾶν τὸ τῆς ψυχῆς σύστημα).

Both F. H. Colson and I. Heinemann have spiritualized this phrase completely and removed it from any concrete idea of the Jewish people. Colson's translation is "all that goes to make the soul"; Heinemann renders it as "die Seele in ihrer ganzen Zusammensetzung."[2]

Philo gives the word σύστημα, system, organization, association, different meanings,[3] but in Mut. 150 the term interprets a word similar to the "the nation" (ὁ λεὼς) in Leg. all. III 163, namely ἔθνη, "nations" (Gen. 17, 16). These "nations" are defined as "large and comprehensive combinations both of living creatures and of actions and ideas" (ζῴων ὁμοῦ καὶ πραγμάτων μεγάλα καὶ ἀθρόα συστήματα). If this definition were applied to Leg. all. III 163, this paraphrase would result: all the organization (or combination) of living creatures and of actions and ideas belonging to the soul.

It is even possible to give a more precise definition of this phrase in Leg. all. III 163. Philo's use of the similar phrase "the whole people of the soul" (τὸν λεὼν ἅπαντα τῆς ψυχῆς) in Ebr. 37 gives support to the suggestion that Leg. all. III 163 is an interpretation of the Jewish people:[4] "He (Moses) in his wisdom was recalling the whole people of the soul to piety and to honouring God and was teaching them the commandments and holy laws." Thus, "the soul" is associated with piety, the honouring of God, the commandments

---

[1] Note that H. Windisch, *Die Frömmigkeit Philos*, pp. 62 ff. refers to Philo's anthropology as proof for his individualistic thinking and piety.

[2] *Philo* (Colson and Whitaker) V, p. 411; *Die Werke Philos* (Cohn, Heinemann, Adler, Theiler) III, p. 137; See also N. A. Dahl, *Das Volk Gottes*, p. 112.

[3] See Opif. 48 and Spec. I 342 (music); Leg. all. I 2 (astronomy and calender); Aet. 4 (the cosmos); Migr. 104 (a choir); Cont. 72 (association), etc.

[4] See also the use of the same phrase in Agr. 44.88; Migr. 14.

and holy laws—in short the precise characteristics the of Jewish people in contrast to "a city or commonwealth peopled by a promiscuous horde, who swing to and fro as their idle opinions carry them" (Ebr. 36). In this case, however, the German translator spiritualizes the meaning completely: "Bildhaft wird die Seele vorgestellt als bevölkert oder bewohnt von guten Gefühlen und Strebungen." [1]

The result of such an extreme spiritualizing interpretation of Philo is that a glimpse of factual life, such as the reference in Leg. all. III 167 to the aspirations for social and political success, becomes a mere disturbing element in the context. Thus, Heinemann is inclined to regard this sentence as an addition.[2] In point of fact this reference in Leg. all. III 167 is a convincing argument in favour of § 163 as a spiritual description of the actual, empirical Jewish people.

Plato, Aristotle and others use the word σύστημα in the sense of a political system, organized government, constitution.[3] And at several places Jews have used the word to designate the Jewish community.[4] The Stoics gave a wide cosmic perspective to the term in their philosophy of the state, where the world was seen as a great Polis, a system (σύστημα) of men and gods.[5]

Philo obviously applied this Stoic usage to his own Jewish people and also modified it by the Platonic thought pattern: the Jewish people is the organization (system) in which the heavenly quality, "the soul," is realized. The corresponding idea that "the true men" are realized in the Jewish nation is explicitly stated in other words in Spec. I 303:[6] "Yet out of the whole human race He chose as of special merit and judged worthy of pre-eminence over all, those who are in a true sense men, (τοὺς πρὸς ἀλήθειαν ἀνθρώπους), and

---

[1] M. Adler in *Die Werke Philos* (Cohn, Heinemann, Adler, Theiler) V, p. 21. n. 1. Cf. N. A. Dahl, *Das Volk Gottes*, p. 112.
[2] *Die Werke Philos* (Cohn, Heinemann, Adler, Theiler) III, p. 138, n. 3.
[3] Plato, Laws III 686B; Aristotle, Ethica Nicomachea, 1168b 32, etc.
[4] 2 Maccabees 15, 12; 3 Maccabees 3, 9; Josephus, Contra Apionem I 32; See N. A. Dahl, *Das Volk Gottes*, p. 96.
[5] M. Pohlenz, *Die Stoa* II, p. 112.
[6] F. H. Colson, *Philo* (Colson and Whitaker) VII, p. 275, n. c, is unable to fit this passage into the spiritual and individualistic philosophy of Philo, according to Colson: "The selection of Israel in [Deut. 10] v. 15 is here interpreted as the selection of the worthiest. The meaning thus given to οἱ πρὸς ἀλήθειαν ἄνθρωποι is unusual. Generally 'the true man' is the reasonable mind or conscience in the individual man."

called them to the service of Himself, the perennial fountain of things excellent, from which He sends the shower of the other virtues gushing forth to give drink, delicious and most beneficial, and conferring immortality as much as or more than nectar."

Philo (Leg. all. III 162-163) expressed in Platonic and Stoic terminology an idea which in a different way was present also in Palestine; thus Pirqe Aboth 3, 14 presents the viewpoint that man, created in the image of God, is realized in Israel because she has the Torah, the instrument of creation. As a matter of fact, this point of view is central to the Palestinian understanding of the relationship between Israel and creation.[1] It is even more significant that the anthropological idea of man as a being between the heavenly beings (the angels) and the animals, is applied in the Palestinian midrash to Israel only, so that also here the Jews are the people of heavenly quality, corresponding to Philo's idea.[2]

Heavenly principles embodied in the Jewish laws.

Since the heavenly qualities discussed in Leg. all. III 162-163. 167-168 are not primarily the property of the soul of the individual, but of the spiritual—and empirical—Jewish nation, they must include both the abstract cosmic aspect and the concrete laws and practices of the Jews.

Both of these aspects are present in Philo's use of the Stoic term "right reason" (ὁ ὀρθὸς λόγος) which in Leg. all. III 167-168 is associated with the word "law" (νόμος) in Ex. 16, 4. A few examples in which Philo explicitly uses the term to refer to Jewish laws and practices will next be given.

In Post. 142 and Cher. 128 "right reason" means the Scripture, or rather "the law", in citation formulas introducing quotations from the Pentateuch. In Sobr. 33 and Agr. 130 the term means the right principle for interpreting the Scripture. Virt. 127 refers to the Jewish laws when it says that he whose life would conform to Moses' most holy commonwealth is captained by nature's right reason.[3] Of great interest is also Probus 43-47,

---

[1] See J. Jervell, *Imago Dei*, pp. 78-84.
[2] See *ibid.*, pp. 86 f., especially p. 86, n. 65. About the anthropological viewpoints in the Palestinian midrash, see above on p. 129 and n. 5; p. 130 and n. 1.
[3] Cf. E. Goodenough, *The Politics*, pp. 30 f. where he discusses Somn. II 135 ff. and finds that "right reason" here refers to the Jewish law. In this book, ch. II, Goodenough analyses Philo's politics "in code". Unfortunately in his other book *By Light, Light*, G. has almost forgotten this exegetical

because in § 47 Philo says that those who defend the laws of Athens and Sparta deny right reason, while §§ 43-46 connect right reason with the legislator of the Jews. "In code" Philo indicates that those defending the laws outside Judaism should recognize the Jewish law and its source in right reason.[1]

This brief survey of Philo's use of the term "right reason" shows that at this point Leg. all. III 168 must read: The right reason as expressed in the laws of the Jews.

The same combination of the abstract cosmic aspect and the concrete laws and practices of the Jews is seen in the term λόγοι, words, principles, which in Leg. all. III 162 replaces a word for the manna. The exegetical method used becomes evident when the words from Ex. 16, 4 and the fragment from haggadah are underscored:

Ex. 16, 4: ἄρτους [ἐκ] τοῦ οὐρανοῦ
Exegesis: λόγοις ἐκ τῆς — φύσεως, ἥν
οὐρανὸν κέκληκεν·

Hence, in Leg. all. III 162 a word for manna is replaced by the word λόγοι, just as Philo in § 168 replaces a word for manna by the word ἐπιστῆμαι, ethical comprehensions. The question then arises: What is the meaning of λόγοι, and what is the relationship between the two terms?

Because the plural term λόγοι has many different shades of meanings in Philo's works, in each case it must be defined according to the individual context in which it occurs. The context in Leg. all. III 162-168 is the organization of the soul, the Jewish nation as it is determined by the heavenly quality of right reason as expressed in Jewish laws. Those fail in the test of "right reason" who have external things as the objective of their lives and therefore misuse their education to gain success in pagan social and political life.

Within this context, logoi also must refer to the Jewish laws in one way or another. Spec. II 13 and Decal. 13 clarify the investi-

---

principle and spiritualizes Philo's thoughts away from the concrete situations reflected in his works. Thus in *Light*, p. 389, n. 112 he refers to Somn. II 135 as "right reason" of the individual.

[1] Cf. E. Goodenough, *The Politics*, p. 79.—(In principle "right reason" is the source of all positive laws, Jos. 31, but the peoples did not, however, recognize this source).

gation, since there the laws and ordinances of the Jews are interpreted as divine words:

Spec. II 13: "Justice and every virtue are commanded by the law of our ancestors and by a statute established of old, and what else are laws and statutes (νόμοι δὲ καὶ θεσμοί) but the sacred words of Nature (φύσεως ἱεροὶ λόγοι)...?" Decal. 13: "Naturally therefore he first led them away from the highly mischievous associations of cities into the desert, to clear the sins out of their souls, and then began to set the nourishment (τροφάς) before their minds—and what should this nourishment be but laws and words of God (νόμοι καὶ λόγοι θεῖοι)?"[1]

In these passages the Jewish laws and statutes are interpreted by the terms φύσεως ἱεροὶ λόγοι and λόγοι θεῖοι. Both of these terms betray their Stoic background. As parallel Stoic phrases are cited ὁ κοινὸς τῆς φύσεως λόγος and τὸν — λόγον, τὸν θεόν.[2]

The influence of the mystery language is also discernable in Spec. II 13. The parallel in the mysteries is ἱερὸς λόγος, which also occurs frequently in Philo's works.[3]

Because Philo adjusted these terms to his own Jewish religion, he did not identify logos with God himself, as the Stoics did.[4] Furthermore, the Jewish law with its plurality of statutes and ordinances was so significant to him that he had to use the plural, logoi, as well as the usual singular form (e.g., ὁ ὀρθὸς λόγος).

One point in Decal. 13 connects the term λόγοι θεῖοι directly with the God-given logoi in Leg. all. III 162. Since Decal. 13 describes laws and words of God as food for the minds (ταῖς διανοίαις) in the desert, both passages associate the logoi and the laws with the manna. Moreover, Decal. 17 describes the laws and the ordinances (νόμων καὶ διαταγμάτων) as manna for the souls just as the external manna was food for the bodily life of the Jews in the desert.

This interpretation by Philo of the Jewish laws and statutes implies that they are in harmony with the cosmic laws and prin-

---

[1] See also Qu. in Gen. IV 140: "...the sacred scriptures are not monuments of knowledge and vision but are the divine commands and the divine words." See the comment by R. Marcus, *Philo, Supplement* (R. Marcus) I, p. 422, n.a.

[2] *StVF* (Arnim) II, pp. 269, 111; I, p. 24. See H. Kleinknecht, λέγω B, *ThWb* IV, pp. 83,84,87; E. Schwartz, *Aporien*, NAG, 1908, p. 555, n. 1.

[3] See H. Kleinknecht, λέγω, *ThWb* IV, pp. 84-85.

[4] Rightly noticed in *ibid.*, p. 87, where some modifications also are mentioned.

ciples; thus both concrete and abstract cosmic aspects are included in this usage of the term logoi. The meaning of logoi in Leg. all. III 162 is, therefore, heavenly principles which are present in that nation where the heavenly quality of the soul is realized. These principles are then embodied in the laws and statutes of the Jewish nation.

The relationship between the two words for manna, λόγοι in Leg. all. III 162 and ἐπιστῆμαι in § 168 is now clear: λόγοι refers to the heavenly principles embodied in the Jewish laws and ἐπιστῆμαι means the actual perceptions of these principles. The term ὁ ὀρθὸς λόγος (§ 168) describes another aspect of the same thought. It means the heavenly criterion which tests men, to see if their practices in life are in accordance with the laws and heavenly principles on which they are based.

This analysis now must be placed within the framework of Philonic research. Both Schwartz and Wolfson identify Philo's logos with the wisdom of the Torah. Schwartz, however, holds that Philo always keeps the Jewish idea of the spoken word of God, whereas Wolfson systematizes Philo's use of logos and logoi from the philosophical viewpoints of God's transcendence and immanence and the question of the laws of nature and the Torah. As Wolfson sees it, the plural logoi belongs to the sphere of the immanent laws in nature. These laws, however, are revealed in the Torah of the Jews.[1]

L. Cohn, on the other hand, finds that Stoic and Platonic thoughts are basic in Philo's use of these terms. So, according to Cohn, Philo has combined in these terms the Stoic law of nature and Platonic ideas, in order to bridge the gap between the transcendent God an the immanent world.[2] To an even greater degree Billings and Dodd insist that logos to Philo is the Platonic world of ideas.[3]

The Stoic background of the term of logos is given prominence by Pohlenz, although he realizes that Philo has transformed Stoic terminology to serve his Platonizing Jewish understanding of God

---

[1] E. Schwartz, *Aporien*, NAG, 1908, pp. 548-556; H. A. Wolfson, *Philo* I, pp. 184,226-260,325-347; II 189 and 190, n. 163. Cf. the criticism of Wolfson's system in K. Bormann, *Die Ideen - und Logoslehre Philons von Alexandrien. Eine Auseinandersetzung mit H. A. Wolfson.* (Diss.), Köln 1955.

[2] L. Cohn, "Zur Lehre vom Logos bei Philo," *Judaica. Festschrift zu Hermann Cohens siebzigstem Geburtstage*, Berlin 1912, pp. 303-331.

[3] Th. H. Billings, *The Platonism of Philo*, pp. 28-30; C. H. Dodd, *The Interpretation*, p. 68.

and his dependence upon the Scripture. Pohlenz agrees with Schwartz that the Palestinian term "the words of God" has influenced Philo's use of the plural logoi. Philo's dependence on Stoic ideas is also claimed by F. Geiger, who realizes that Philo, nevertheless, regarded the law of Moses as written formulations of the law of nature, the logos. [1] In addition to these Stoic and Platonic sources, Bréhier draws the attention to Egyptian Stoicism and mystery religions. [2]

The influence of mystery religions has been particularly championed by another group of scholars. Among these, Pasher understands logos as a stage on the royal road of the mystical ascent, and Goodenough sees it basically as the Light-Stream coming down into matter. [3] Leisegang interprets the logos primarily as the transformation of a Greek philosophical (especially Stoic) concept into the message of a mystery. [4]

Closely related to them are scholars who place Philo's thoughts within the gnostic outlook of the world, and so stress the oriental elements in it. Lewy makes the Philonic logos play a significant role within the development to mystical gnosis of Jewish speculations regarding wisdom. [5] Stressing the radical transcendence and the unintelligibility of God, Jonas thinks that Philo's logos represents the attempt to bridge the gap between God and the world, resulting in logos as "a second God". [6] According to Staerk and Hegermann oriental mythology has moulded Philo's concept of wisdom, σοφία, to such an extent as to penetrate also his understanding of logos. [7]

---

[1] M. Pohlenz, *Philon*, NAG, 1942, pp. 445-450; *Die Stoa* I, p. 373; F. Geiger, *Philon als sozialer Denker*, pp. 18, n. 81; 111; cf. the similar conclusion reached by R. Arnaldez in *Les Oevres de Philon* (Arnaldez, Pouilloux and Mondésert) I, pp. 27,30.

[2] E. Bréhier, *Les Idées*, pp. 83-111.

[3] J. Pascher, *Der Königsweg*, pp. 115 ff.; and E. Goodenough, *Light*, p. 58.

[4] H. Leisegang, "Philon," *Pauly-W.* XX, cols. 41-42; *Der Heilige Geist*, I, 1, pp. 66 ff., 209-230; cf. "Logos," *Pauly-W.* XIII, cols. 1072-1077.

[5] H. Lewy, *Sobria Ebrietas*, pp. 15,17 ff.; Cf. H. Ringgren, *Word and Wisdom. Studies in the Hypostatization of Divine Qualities and Functions in the Near East*, Lund 1947, pp. 124 f., who suggests that Philo's logos, although a philosophical concept, is influenced by the Biblical idea of wisdom.

[6] H. Jonas, *Gnosis* II, 1, pp. 74 f.

[7] W. Staerk, *Die Erlösererwartung in den östlichen Religionen*, Stuttgart/Berlin 1938, pp. 71-85 and pp. 105-125; H. Hegermann, *Die Vorstellungen vom Schöpfungsmittler*, pp. 70 f.; J. Jervell, *Imago Dei*, pp. 56 ff. (Logos influenced by gnostic speculations about Anthropos).

The views of Pohlenz and Geiger come closest to the use of the terms ὁ ὀρθὸς λόγος and λόγοι in the homily of Leg. all. III 162-168. These terms have a clear Stoic background, and they have been transformed by Philo on the basis of the Scripture and a Platonic treatment of the haggadah. The cosmic understanding of the Jewish laws and the actual situation of the Jews in Alexandria have also influenced Philo' use of these terms.

The use of ὁ ὀρθὸς λόγος and λόγοι in Leg. all. III 162-168 is not to be harmonized with other usages of the same terms and the parallel term, σοφία, in Philo's works. A detailed analysis of different contexts may explain to some degree the many inconsistencies of Philo on this point. Thus the different terminology of the homily of Mut. 253-263 (σοφία, etc.) and the homily of Leg. all. III 162-168 (ὁ ὀρθὸς λόγος, etc.) is quite appropriate to the different subject matter and the different focal points.

The heavenly measures

The heavenly principles (logoi) which are embodied in Jewish laws make the cosmic and the human order consist of fixed measures to which men are to conform. This is the way Philo understands the portions and the measures of manna in his paraphrase of Ex. 16, 4 (τὸ τῆς ἡμέρας εἰς ἡμέραν) and 16, 16.18 (μετρήσαντες, etc.) in Leg. all. III 163.165.166.

Philo says that going beyond these measures is "overreaching", "covetousness", πλεονεξία, Leg. all. III 166, which destroys the heavenly order. This conflict is described pointedly in Philo's interpretation of the first of the "Ten Words" in Decal. 155. Here Philo declares that God, as the Ruler, has expelled from the purest part of all that exists, namely heaven, oligarchy and mob-rule, which are produced by disorder and covetousness (ἐξ ἀταξίας καὶ πλεονεξίας).

On the other hand, the heavenly order also reaches down to earth, Spec. IV 232-237. The masters of natural philosophy have handed down the importance of equality (ἰσότης) in the order of heaven and earth. Equality makes the universe into a cosmos, cities into the best of all constitutions, a democracy; it makes bodies healthy and creates virtuous conduct in the souls.

The term equality, ἰσότης, was widely used to express the Greek sense of justice. It was a central principle for the cosmic and human order, especially in the Pythagorean-Platonic tradition.[1] The term did have different shades of meanings, as for instance numerical equality or proportional. The former means the distribution of things equally among men irrespective of merit; the latter means the distribution according to their individual merits or needs.

That Philo was well aware of this distinction can be seen from Heres 144-145. Both in Heres 191 and in Qu. in Gen. IV 102, Ex. 16, 18 is interpreted from the viewpoint of proportional equality. So also is the case in Leg. all. III 163.165.166, although the specific term ἰσότης is not used. The principal emphasis in the homily of Leg. all. III 162-168 is not to describe equality as such, but to exhort the Jews to stay within the limits of the heavenly measures: "Both in the case of manna then, and in the case of every boon which God confers upon our race, it is good to take what is fixed by strict measure and reckoning (ἐνάριθμον καὶ μεμετρημένον, cf. Ex. 16, 16.18), and not that which is above and beyond us; for to do this is to be overreaching (πλεονεξίας)," Leg. all. III 166.

In this context, the use of the term πλεονεξία approaches the Greek background of the idea of equality. It corresponds quite closely to its use in Plato's Gorgias, 508A for instance, where πλεονεξία describes the breaking of the equality which binds heaven and earth, gods and men, together in one commonwealth.[2] Thus in Leg. all. III 166 the term means to go beyond the heavenly measures embodied in the Jewish laws and practices and in that way to break the order of proportional equality.[3]

Leg. all. III 167 thus offers a concrete illustration of breaking the cosmic measures out of their equality, just as making the day into night and the light into darkness. Men go beyond these measures if they use their education just for the purpose of social and political success in the pagan environment.

---

[1] See the extensive discussion of the Greek concept of equality in R. Hirzel, *Themis, Dike und Verwandtes. Ein Beitrag zur Geschichte der Rechtsidee bei den Griechen*, Leipzig 1907, pp. 228-320. See also *Die Werke Philos* (Cohn, Heinemann, Adler, Theiler) V, p. 256, n. 1; *Philo* (Colson and Whitaker) IV, p. 570, n. on § 145; and E. Goodenough, *Light*, pp. 65 ff.; cf. H. A. Wolfson, *Philo* II, pp. 386-387 and F. Geiger, *Philon als sozialer Denker*, pp. 19 ff.

[2] *Plato*, with an English Translation by W. R. M. Lamb, V, (*Loeb*), London/New York 1925, pp. 470-471. See G. Delling, πλεονέκτης κτλ., *ThWb* VI, p. 267.

[3] Philo does not conceive this order in a static way. He thinks, rather, that within this order there is progress (προκοπή, Leg. all. III 165) away from the

This is the point to return to the question of the dualism between heaven and earth and soul and body, expressed in Leg. all. III 162.168. It is not, as is the case in the gnostic view of man and the world, that this material world, of which men are a part, is separated from a higher spiritual world above it.[1] The dualism of Leg. all. III 162-168 is, rather, that of the conflict between order and disorder: If earth, the body and human achievement as education are permitted to go beyond their measures, then the dualistic conflict appears. If they stay within these measures, then the heavenly order is realized on earth. The tendency towards disorder is, however, present in the perishable (§ 162: φθαρτοῖς) earth.

Philo combines the ethical dualism between heaven and earth with the dualism of Judaism and the pagan world. The Jews who have luxurious living and political careers as their objective, join in with the earthly, pagan disorder. There is therefore no inconsistency between the viewpoint of the homily of Mut. 253-263 and that of the homily of Leg. all. III 162-168, but the emphasis differs. If education, which is an adiaforon on the borderline between Jews and pagans, is rightly understood, then it has its virtue and there is difference, but no dualism between heaven and earth (Mut. 253-263). If, on the other hand, education is misused for the purpose of making a pagan career, then a cosmic and ethical disorder is created, resulting in a dualistic conflict between heaven and earth.

In spite of many differences, Philo has a cosmological orientation in common with the Palestinian Judaism. The Palestinian midrash regarded the Torah as the law of the world. The world is created according to the model of the preexistent Torah, etc.[2] The distinction made between heaven and earth also sometimes results in the Torah as a heavenly image.[3]

---

passions. Cf. the Stoic use of this term; see M. Pohlenz, *Die Stoa* I, p. 154 and II, p. 83.

[1] W. Bousset, *Hauptprobleme der Gnosis*, FRLANT X, Göttingen 1907, pp. 91 ff. 328 ff.; H. Leisegang, *Die Gnosis*, KT XXXII, Leipzig 1924, pp. 21-27; H. Jonas, *Gnosis und spätantiker Geist*, I (*Die mythologische Gnosis*), FRLANT LI (N.F. XXXIII), Göttingen 1934, pp. 98-102; *The Gnostic Religion. The Message of the Alien God and the Beginnings of Christianity*, Boston 1958, pp. 43-47, 51-56, etc.; J. Jervell, *Imago Dei*, pp. 140-161; C. H. Dodd, *The Interpretation*, pp. 103-107.

[2] Pirqe Aboth 3, 14; Tanhuma B, Bereshith 5; Siphre on Deut. 11,22; Gen R. 1, 1, etc. See the extensive list of references in J. Jervell, *Imago Dei*, p. 79.

[3] Aboth de Rabbi Nathan 39. See further M. J. Bin Gorion, *Die Sagen der*

In the apocrypha and pseudepigrapha this cosmic aspect is even more prominent, and interesting parallels to Philo's identification of the Jewish laws and the cosmic law occur. Thus the Testament of Naphtali chs. 2 and 3, describes the cosmic and ethical law as τάξις, order, so that sin becomes disorder, ἀταξία. Testament Naphtali 2, 3 even has the idea of cosmic measures. And this cosmic and ethical order is at the same time identical with the laws of Moses. The pagans have already corrupted this order of creation (Testament of Naphtali 3, 3).[1] In corresponding ways creation, ethics and the laws of Moses are united in several other of these writings as well.[2]

Although Philo develops his ideas of the cosmic and ethical order more in accordance with the higher level of Stoic philosophy and Platonic thought patterns, his ideas are to some degree parallel to the cosmological interpretation of the Torah found in the Palestinian midrash as well as the apocrypha and pseudepigrapha. At this point, the latter group of writings produce closer parallels to Philo, especially Testament Naphtali which, as the homily of Leg. all. III 162-168, has the idea of a cosmic and ethical order based on divine measures. There is in Philo, however, a stronger tendency towards a dualism between soul and body, heaven and earth than in the Palestinian traditions generally.[3] Accordingly he stresses much more the abstract cosmic principles beyond the concrete Torah.

This analysis of the heavenly measures in Leg. all. III 162-168 calls for a criticism of those scholars who overstress the dualistic element between heaven and earth, soul and body, in Philo's works.

Juden I. *Von der Urzeit*, 2nd ed., Frankfurt 1919, pp. 24-29; J. Bonsirven, *Le Judaisme Palestinien au temps de Jésus-Christ. Sa Théologie* I, (*Bibliothèque de Théologie Historique*), Paris 1934, pp. 250 f.; J. Jervell, *Imago Dei*, p. 80; See also L. Wächter, "Der Einfluss platonischen Denkens auf rabbinische Schöpfungsspekulationen," ZRG XIV, 1962, pp. 36-56.

[1] *The Greek Versions of the Testaments of the Twelve Patriarchs*, Ed. by R. H. Charles, Oxford 1908, pp. 145-150. See W. C. van Unnik, "Is I Clement 20 purely Stoic?" VigChr IV, 1950, pp. 186-187; S. Aalen, *Die Begriffe "Licht" und "Finsterniss" im Alten Testament, im Spätjudentum und im Rabbinismus*, SkrNVA 1951 I, Oslo 1951, pp. 173 f., and J. Jervell, *Imago Dei*, pp. 29 f.

[2] See W. C. van Unnik, VigChr IV, 1950, pp. 181-189; S. Aalen, "*Licht" und "Finsternis*", pp. 170-175. (cf. the criticism of some of Aalen's viewpoints by N. A. Dahl, "Begrepene "lys" of "mörke" i jödedommen. Opposisjonsinnlegg ved S. Aalens disputas 5.12. 1951 for den teologiske doktorgrad," NTT LIII, 1952, pp. 77 f.); J. Jervell, *Imago Dei*, pp. 31-37.

[3] Cf. R. Meyer, *Hellenistisches in der rabbinischen Anthropologie*, p. 32.

A few of them have made specific references to this homily to prove their point. Leisegang, to mention one, says, on the basis of Leg. all. III 162, that Philo tries to remove the pure heaven as far from the earthly matter as possible.[1] Goodenough interpreted the manna in Mut. 253-263 as "showers of refreshing" for the mystic during his struggle away from the somatic passions. In the same context Goodenough also refers to Leg. all. III 162-168, as well as to other instances where Philo expounds the manna miracle.[2]

Both scholars have overlooked the fact that the dualism of Leg. all. III 162ff. is basically one of order and disorder, and not a dualism of the spiritual quality versus matter as such.

God's care, men's trust

So far it is evident that Greek ideas were transformed by Philo to interpret Judaism especially with reference to the actual situation of the Jews in Alexandria. This transformation was given in the form of an exegesis of Ex. 16, 4, into which fragments from the haggadah about bread from heaven and earth and some Greek terminology were incorporated.

Philo (Leg. all. III 162-168), by means of Scripture and haggadah, has transformed the Greek ideas in still another way. They are seen within the framework of God's activity and men's faith or rather lack of faith. Hence Leg. all. III 162-168, with all its philosophical and ethical ideas, has a strong religious core.

In the quotation from Ex. 16, 4 (Leg. all. III 162), God is the one who rains bread from heaven (ἐγὼ ὕω — ἄρτους [ἐκ] τοῦ οὐρανοῦ). The exegete then says that God pours like rain the logoi from heaven (ὁ θεὸς ὀμβρήσῃ λόγοις ἐκ τῆς — φύσεως, ἣν οὐρανὸν κέκληκεν·) The logoi, i.e., the heavenly principles embodied in the laws and practices of the Jews, are therefore the gifts of God, as said in Leg. all. III 163-164. 166 (ἀγαθά, χάριτες, δωρεά).

Also other heavenly qualities are brought about by the activity of God: right reason, virtue, ethical perceptions (§§ 167-168) and the heavenly order of measures and portions (§§ 163.165-166). God is the dispenser or guardian of all these good things (§§ 163.166).

In Leg. all. III 162-168, therefore, Philo describes God's activity and providential care for the Jews, both now and in the future

---

[1] H. Leisegang, *Der Heilige Geist*, I, 1, p. 54, n. 5.
[2] E. Goodenough, *Light*, pp. 207-208.

(§ 164 καὶ νῦν καὶ ἀεί). God is the active dispenser and guardian of the heavenly order of the Jewish people.

The response of man is not just a question of conformity or non-conformity to a cosmic order embodied in laws and practices. It is rather a question of trust or usurpatory and disorderly disbelief.

This idea of disbelief was a feature common to the Palestinian haggadah and Philo's narrative on the manna in De vita Mosis. Expounding Ex. 16, 20 the haggadah in Ex. R. 25, 10 says that those who left over manna to the next day lacked faith (מחוסרי אמנה). Mek. Ex. 16, 27 gives the same characterization to those who went out to collect manna on the Sabbath. Just at the very same points in the narrative on manna Philo describes the people correspondingly by the words ἀπιστεῖν (Mos. II 261) and ἀπιστία (Mos. II 269). In the homily of Leg. all. III 162-168, therefore, Philo used this feature from the tradition about the manna and applied it to his ethical exhortations.

Although the terms ἀπιστία and ἄπιστος have kept the Jewish meaning of lack of trust and faith in God, the new context in the homily has, of course, influenced the concept. Stoic and Platonic ideas and thought-patterns have placed the concept within the context of the heavenly order reaching down to check the disorderly tendencies of the earth. Thus, lack of trust and faith here means that men rely upon themselves and the earthly elements rather than upon God and the heavenly order.[1]

This view of Leg. all. III 164 fits well to the example given by Philo in § 167: Those who do not trust God by relying upon the heavenly orders of the Jews are those who misuse education for the purpose of social and political success in the pagan environment. These people rely upon themselves and the earthly elements and go beyond the measures of the heavenly order.

---

[1] Cf. Leg. all. III 164. The idea of faith or lack of faith frequently has this meaning in Philo's works. See Praem. 28; Heres 93; Ebr. 40; Mut. 201; Abr. 269; Virt. 216-218. Cf. A. Schlatter, *Der Glaube im Neuen Testament. Eine Untersuchung zur neutestamentlichen Theologie*, Leiden 1885, pp. 83-105; R. Bultmann, πιστεύω κτλ., *ThWb* VI, pp. 202-203; C. H. Dodd, *The Interpretation*, pp. 62-64; H. A. Wolfson, *Philo* II, pp. 215-218; E. Goodenough, *Light*, pp. 400-401 (Pauline interpretation of faith in Philo's works); E. Bréhier, *Les Idées*, pp. 222 ff. (stressing the Stoic background combined with the element of ecstasis from the circles of the mysteries); Cf. the survey in H. Thyen, *ThR* XXIII, 1955, pp. 237-242. The viewpoint of Schlatter, Bréhier and Goodenough that faith in Philo represents the completed stage in man's progress does not apply to the homily of Leg. all. III 162-168.

CHAPTER SIX

THE UNIQUE VISION OF GOD IN JESUS, THE SON OF JOSEPH
JOHN 6, 31-58

Judaism as background for John 6

It is evident that both Philo and John draw on haggadic traditions about the manna (Ch. I), that they follow a common Jewish homiletic pattern (Ch. II), and employ midrashic methods, patterns, and terminology (Ch. III). In the two of Philo's homilies (Leg. all. III 162-168 and Mut. 253-263), however, non-Jewish (Greek) ideas about philosophy, encyclia, and cosmic order were apparent in the content. But Philo interpreted even these ideas within the context of the situation of the Jews in Alexandria and combined them with thoughts from the common Jewish heritage. Traces of the non-Jewish ideas were found in Palestinian traditions as well, an observation which shows that in different degrees Judaism as a whole—Palestinian Judaism included—was part of the Hellenistic world, with its oriental and Greek components (Chs. IV and V).

Philo interpreted the Jewish heritage along one line, whereas John interpreted it in another direction. John pre-supposed and re-interpreted among others the following facets of Judaism: 1) the identification of the wisdom and the Torah; 2) the identification of the manna with the Torah; and 3) the belief in Israel as the nation who sees God. Especially the development of the last point in Philo and John gives basis for the theory that both are partly side-branches of early Merkabah mysticism.[1]

With the exception of the identification of the manna with wisdom and Torah, John resembles other Jewish sources more than Philo. John has interesting similarities with ideas in the wisdom

---

[1]) H. Odeberg, *The Fourth Gospel*; G. Quispel, "L'Évangile de Jean et la Gnose," in *L'Évangile de Jean, RB* III, Lyon 1958, pp. 197-208, and N. A. Dahl, *Current Issues* (ed. W. Klassen and G. F. Snyder), pp. 124-142, have especially emphasized Jewish mysticism as background for John. On early Jewish mysticism in general, see G. D. Scholem, *Major Trends in Jewish Mysticism*, 3rd rev. ed., New York 1961, pp. 40-79; *Gnosticism, Merkabah Mysticism, and Talmudic Tradition*, New York 1960; L. Baeck, *Aus Drei Jahrtausenden*, pp. 244-255.

literature and aspects of rabbinic haggadah, reflecting also halakhic principles of agency. Furthermore, John draws on and interprets eschatological concepts which are found in Palestinian Judaism and in the New Testament in general.

In spite of the differences between John and Philo, they offer mutually illuminating parallels, since they both interpret Jewish traditions under strong influence of non-Jewish thought-categories and ideas. Hence, in the two homilies on the manna (Mut. 253-263 and Leg. all. III 162-168) Philo undercuts the Jewish idea that God acts in history, interpreting manna as cosmic principles which should govern the Jewish nation. On the basis of ideas from Greek philosophy Philo strives for order between (the spiritual) heaven and (the external) earth. The homily in John 6, 31-58, correspondingly, is a polemic against a gnosticizing tendency to draw a sharp distinction between the spiritual sphere and the external sphere. John opposed and was influenced by a docetic Christology and an understanding of the vision of God which was so general that it played down the importance of the external Torah and the unique role of Jesus Christ of history.

Bread, Torah and Sinai

The homily of John 6, 31-58 presupposes the giving of the Torah at Sinai as model. The midrashic supplement (italicized together with parallel phrases) in John 6, 33 offers an initial clue to the question: *"and gives life to the world"* (καὶ ζωὴν διδοὺς τῷ κόσμῳ). Similar phrases are frequently used about the Torah, especially in connection with the Sinai event. Among the parallels are: "The voice...*gave life to Israel* who accepted the Torah"; "God said to Moses: Say to Israel: The words of the Torah which I have given to you *are life unto you*"; "If the earth trembled when *He gave life to the world*" (שהוא נותן חיים על עולם).[1]

One striking observation can be made from these parallel phrases: According to some, the life was given to Israel and according to others—such as John 6, 33—the life was given to the world. The solution to this seeming difference lies in the fact that in Jewish literature and in the Fourth Gospel Israel was regarded as the center

---

[1] Tanhuma Shemoth 25 (Hebrew text and Greek translation in A. Schlatter, *Der Evangelist Johannes*, p. 173); Mek. Ex. 15, 26; Ex. R. 29, 9; cf. Deut. R. 7, 3.

of the world.¹ When life was given to Israel, it was eo ipso given to the world.

Against this background it is clear that John 6, 33, instead of saying that the words of the Torah at Sinai gave life to the world, transfers the role of the Torah to the bread from heaven: "For the bread of God is that which comes down from heaven, and *gives life to the world.*" In this way the words from the Old Testament quotation cited in 6, 31b ("bread...from heaven") have been paraphrased together with words from haggadic traditions about Torah and Sinai ("and gives life to the world").²

There are similar qualifications of "the bread" which betray the same background in the idea that Torah brings life. Thus, John 6, 51 testifies that "the bread" is given "for the life of the world". Furthermore, the phrase "the bread of life" (ὁ ἄρτος τῆς ζωῆς), 6, 35.48, seems to have been created with phrases about Torah as a model:³ "the law of life" (νόμος ζωῆς), Sirach 17, 11; 45, 5; cf. 4 Ezra 14, 30, and "words of life" (דברות של חיים), Ex. R. 29, 9, and "living words" (λόγια ζῶντα, cf. John 6, 51 ὁ ἄρτος ὁ ζῶν), Acts 7, 38. John 6, 63, "the words...are life" (τὰ ῥήματα — ζωή ἐστιν), and 6, 68, "the words of eternal life" (ῥήματα ζωῆς αἰωνίου), even suggest that John in a direct way reproduces such traditional phrases. Significantly enough, the parallel phrases about the Torah of life occur in contexts which describe the theophany at Sinai.

Since the bread from heaven has been given the function of the Torah at Sinai, John obviously reflects that the manna was identified with the Torah. The analysis of the homily, Mut. 253-263, showed that Philo also linked the manna with the laws of Moses, especially as they were read and interpreted on the Sabbath. In Mek. 13, 17 the same identification is made, since the Torah has been given the function of the manna: "I will 'lead them out' in the desert for forty years that they may eat the manna and drink the water of the well and (thereby) the Torah will be united (assimi-

---

[1] Cf. N. A. Dahl, *Das Volk Gottes*, pp. 77 f.; J. Jeremias, *Jesus' Promise to the Nations*, StBTh XXIV, London 1958, pp. 55-73; A. Fridrichsen, "Missionstanken i Fjärde Evangeliet," *SEA* II, 1937, pp. 139-53, and "La pensée missionnaire dans le Quatrième Évangile," *AMNTSU* VI, 1937, pp. 39-45; N. A. Dahl, *Current Issues* (ed. W. Klassen and G. F. Snyder), especially p. 129. See further discussion below on pp. 175-179.

[2] See the analysis on pp. 20 f. for other haggadic elements in the paraphrase developed in John 6, 33. Cf. also pp. 66 f.

[3] See p. 73 and nn. 3, 4.

lated) with their body."[1] John, therefore, follows a line of interpretation which was employed by Philo and also indicated in Palestinian haggadah.

The allusion to the Torah and the Sinai event is also clear in John 6, 45-46, which is a quotation from Is. 54, 13 followed by a brief exposition.[2] In rabbinic tradition Is. 54, 13 (about those "taught by God") is frequently cited to show that God Himself will teach the Torah in the future coming aeon. The quotation also occurs, however, with reference to the learning of the Torah in the present age. In Berakoth 64a it is used to show that the scholars of the Torah are taught by God, and the expression "taught by God" is used in CD 20, 4 by the Zadokite community to describe itself and its interpretation of the Torah. When Is. 54, 13 is quoted in John 6, 45 the idea intended is that those "taught by God" are men who have received the meaning of the Torah (directly) from God Himself.[3]

The brief exposition of Is. 54, 13 in John 6, 45b-46 elaborates upon the idea of teaching/learning by adding two central features from the theophany at Sinai, hearing and seeing. Those who are "taught by God" have "heard" the meaning of the Torah from God Himself.[4] According to Ex. 33, 20 there was a significant modification made at the theophany at Sinai. Moses was not allowed to see the face of God; for no man can see God and live. The same reservation is made in John 6, 45-46: those who are "taught by God" have "heard from God" without actually seeing Him.[5]

The statement, "Not that any one has seen the Father, etc.," in John 6, 46, has a close parallel in John 1, 18. Recent scholarship has shown convincingly that John 1, 14-18 interprets the theophany at Sinai, and gives thereby a strong support for the same understanding of John 6, 45-46.[6]

---

[1] See pp. 112-114.   [2] See pp. 70, 84-85.

[3] John 6, 45 indicates therefore that the exegesis of the Old Testament is itself regarded as revelation. A similar view is held by the Qumran community and Philo. See especially O. Betz, *Schriftforschung*, pp. 5, 118-119, 152-153; P. Volz, *Der Geist Gottes*, pp. 130 f.; R. M. Grant, *The Letter and the Spirit*, p. 34.

[4] On the "hearing" at Sinai, see Deut. 4, 12; 5, 24; 18, 16; Sirach 17, 13; 45, 5; Mek. Ex. 19, 2, etc.

[5] The exegetical pattern of reservation in John 6, 46 is analysed on pp. 84-85.

[6] See especially M. E. Boismard, *St. John's Prologue*, Westminster, Md. 1957, pp. 136-140; S. Schulz, *Komposition*, pp. 40 f.; N. A. Dahl, *Current*

The interpretation of John 6, 45-46 given here is confirmed by its context. In John 6, 41-42 "the Jews" object to Jesus' exposition of the Old Testament quotation cited in v. 31b. They cannot accept his identification with "the bread from heaven" in the quotation. In John 6, 45-46 Jesus then answers that those who share in the theophany at Sinai and have heard from God and thus learned the true meaning of the Torah will understand and accept his interpretation of the manna.

At this point John 5, 37-47 becomes an interesting parallel.[1] According to John 5, 39-40 the Jews misuse the scriptures because they interpret them without recognizing their testimony to Jesus. In John 6, 41-42, then, the Jews disagree with Jesus' exegesis of the manna because he says that it means himself. In 5, 37-47 the Jews, who refuse to interpret the scriptures Christologically and "come to" Jesus, prove that they have no share in the revelation at Sinai: "His voice you have never heard, his form you have never seen" (5, 37). The same ideas are stated in a positive way in John 6, 41-48. Those who accept a Christological interpretation of the scriptures (v. 41.48, "I am the bread") share in the theophany at Sinai: they have "heard" from God and learned the right understanding and therefore they "come to" Jesus (6, 45-46).

A comparison between the two passages reveals a surprising difference as well. John 5, 37 ff. says that the Jews who do not interpret the scriptures Christologically have never seen God's "form" at Sinai. It would be natural, then, to expect that in John 6, 41-48 those who had the right understanding of the scriptures would be said not only to have "heard" but also to have "seen" God's "form". Instead John 6, 46 declares emphatically that no man has ever seen God; only the son of God has seen Him. The reason for the seeming discrepancy must be that the Evangelist wants to show clearly that there is no vision of God apart from the Son, not even in the theophany at Sinai. John 6, 46 probably implies that God's "form" (εἶδος), 5, 37, was the Son of God. The men who share in the (preparatory) revelation at Sinai have seen God only

---

Issues (ed. W. Klassen and G. F. Snyder), p. 132, with numerous references to Jewish ideas on the vision and the ascent of Moses at Sinai in note 13, on p. 286: Sirach 45, 2-5; Jubilees 1; Ps-Philo, Ant. bibl. 12, 1; 4 Ezra 14, 5; Syriac Baruch 59, etc.; Cf. also E. M. Sidebottom, *The Christ*, p. 37.

[1] See N. A. Dahl, *Current Issues* (ed. W. Klassen and G. F. Snyder), pp. 132-133, who has shown that John 5, 37 ff. must be interpreted against the background of the theophany at Sinai.

through the Son, Jesus Christ, to whom they now come (5, 45b).[1]

At this point it is logical to conclude that the homily of John 6, 31-58 attributes to the "bread from heaven" the life-giving function of the Torah and alludes to the theophany at Sinai. Similar allusions to the theophany at Sinai are found in John 5, 37-47. The latter passage shows that the Jews, who misuse and misinterpret the scriptures, have no share in the (preparatory) revelation given to Israel at Sinai, and the homily in John 6 indicates that only those who share in the (preparatory) revelation at Sinai have the right understanding of the scriptures, in this case a quotation about the manna. John 6, 31-58 is therefore an elaboration upon and an illustration of the points discussed in 5, 37-47.[2]

Scholars like Odeberg, Billerbeck, Dodd, and Barrett have linked the "bread from heaven" with the concept of the Torah. They have pointed to the fact that in Judaism the Torah was described as bread, and Odeberg has made it evident that in Mek. 13, 17 the manna itself was identified with the Torah.[3] Barrett has, therefore, also suggested that in John 6, 33, etc. the life-giving function of the Torah has been transferred to the "bread from heaven".[4] All the scholars mentioned, however, have overlooked the allusions to the theophany at Sinai in John's exposition of the manna miracle.

Gärtner and Bultmann represent the scholars who have given alternative interpretations. The key to Gärtner's explanation is that he combines the manna miracle with the Passover proper, because he does not realize that John combines the manna miracle, the Torah,

---

[1] Cf. that Abraham and Isaiah and probably also Moses saw Jesus Christ, John 8, 56; 12, 41; 1, 17 and 5, 46. See especially N. A. Dahl, *Current Issues* (ed. W. Klassen and G. F. Snyder), pp. 131-134.

[2] The close connection between John 5, 37-47 and 6, 31-58 speaks against any re-arrangement of the sequence of chs. 5 and 6 in spite of the obvious geographical discrepancies (ch. 5 in Jerusalem; ch. 6 at the sea of Galilee, etc.). This observation supports the viewpoint that the Gospel forms a united whole in spite of all discrepancies. See our discussion above on p. 5, and further C. H. Dodd, *The Interpretation*, pp. 289-290 and C. K. Barrett, *St. John*, pp. 18-21, over against R. Bultmann, *Evanglium*, p. 154 and W. Wilkens, *Die Entstehungsgeschichte des vierten Evangeliums*, Zollikon 1958, p. 5, etc. Cf. the survey in W. F. Howard, *Criticism*, p. 303; cf. pp. 297-302.

[3] H. Odeberg, *The Fourth Gospel*, pp. 239-245, 255 (Odeberg identifies, however, too readily the concepts of "bread", "parnāsā" and manna); Str.-B. II, pp. 483 ff.; C. H. Dodd, *The Interpretation*, pp. 336 f.; C. K. Barratt, *St .John*, pp. 240 f.; cf. E. M. Sidebottom, *The Christ*, p. 130.

[4] C. K. Barrett, *St. John*, p. 241.

and the Sinai event.¹ Unfortunately Gärtner's analysis of the main body of John 6 is rather sketchy and inadequate. Ignoring the concepts of the Torah and the theophany at Sinai, Bultmann identifies the manna with the idea of revelation: the bread from heaven means the (gnostic) Revealer, who comes from heaven and brings life to the world (cf. John 6, 33)².

In John 6, 45-46 the scholars generally have overlooked the theophany at Sinai as the necessary clue for interpretation, and therefore suggested other solutions. Dodd interprets 6, 46 and the parallel in 1, 18 against the background of the vision of God in Jewish eschatological expectations and in Hellenistic mysticism.³ Bultmann finds that the same verses emphasize the author's conviction that God is not at man's disposal and is only available through revelation. The Oriental-Old Testament idea about the sovereignty and inaccessibility of God is here interpreted in a radical way and with the gnostic idea of revelation as accompaniment.⁴ Barrett's interpretation combines elements both from Dodd and Bultmann.⁵ More independent is Odeberg who interprets 6, 46 against the background of "Jewish-mystic-rabbinic" ideas with a sharp distinction made between the external and the spiritual spheres: "there is no knowledge of the spiritual world without entering into knowledge-communion with the spiritual world, and, in the last instance, with God, and such communion is given only in and through the Son." ⁶ Thus, although Odeberg realizes the connection between the manna and the Torah, he is not successful in

---

¹ B. Gärtner, *Passover*, pp. 18-19. In passing Gärtner mentions that together with the manna miracle, also the giving of the Torah at Sinai was emphasized in the Passover Haggada, p. 33, especially n. 1. He also refers to the combination of manna, Torah and life, etc., as outlined by Odeberg, but without making these ideas fruitful for his own interpretation, p. 41, and n. 3.

² R. Bultmann, *Evangelium*, p. 169. S. Schulz, *Komposition*, p. 95, rejects any connection between the manna and the concept of Torah with the surprising remark that the Torah was never directly called bread in Judaism. He therefore modifies Bultmann's interpretation by placing more emphasis on the passages on the manna in the Old Testament and their eschatological developments in Jewish traditions.

³ C. H. Dodd, *The Interpretation*, pp. 167, 338.

⁴ R. Bultmann, *Evangelium*, pp. 54-55; 172-173; "Untersuchungen zum Johannesevangelium B," *ZNW* XXIX, 1930, pp. 176 ff.; cf. the discussion and modification of Bultmann's interpretation in Th. Müller, *Das Heilsgeschehen im Johannesevangelium*, Zürich 1961, pp. 18-20.

⁵ C. K. Barrett, *St. John*, pp. 141, 245.

⁶ H. Odeberg, *The Fourth Gospel*, pp. 257-259.

showing the way these and associated ideas have made an impact upon this specific point in John 6.

Bread and Wisdom

Just as the bread from heaven was identified with the Torah, or rather replaced the Torah, in John, so also is it identified with another term for the Torah, namely wisdom. The ideas which clearly come from the Jewish wisdom traditions are centered around the words "to come", "to eat and drink" and "hunger and thirst".

The words, "he who comes to me", (ὁ ἐρχόμενος πρὸς ἐμέ) in John 6, 35, renders a stereotyped phrase which John combines with a variety of words and ideas (John 5, 40; 6, 37.44.45.65; 7, 37; cf. 6, 37 πρὸς ἐμὲ ἥξει). Of special interest is John 7, 37 because the phrase there has the form of an invitation in imperative form, "let him come [to me]" (ἐρχέσθω [πρός με]). [2]

The parallels in the Synoptics show that the phrase belongs to the common gospel tradition. Matt. 19, 14 says "Let the children come to me" (ἄφετε τὰ παιδία — ἐλθεῖν πρός με, cf. Mark 10, 14; Luke 18, 16). Luke uses the phrase both in 6, 47, "Every one who comes to me" (πᾶς ὁ ἐρχόμενος πρός με, Matt. 7, 24 differs.) and in 14, 26. "If any one comes to me" (εἴ τις ἔρχεται πρός με, cf. Matt. 10, 37, which differs). In spite of different wording, Matt. 11, 28, "Come to me" (Δεῦτε πρός με), is very significant, because it obviously points back to the invitations from wisdom in wisdom literature.[1]

Such phrases of invitation from the wisdom (and the teachers of wisdom) are found in Prov. 9, 5, "Come", (לכו/LXX Ἔλθατε) and Sirach 24, 19, "Come to me" (προσέλθετε πρός με). Although the imperative form is not given in John 5 and 6, it is explicitly stated in John 7, 37. John's dependance upon wisdom traditions is therefore certain.

John also agrees with wisdom traditions in associating "coming" with "eating" and "drinking". This is evident in John 6, 35 since the phrase "he who comes to me" is part of the exposition of "I am the bread of life" and is, moreover, associated with the cessation of hunger and thirst:

---

[1] ℵ*D b e omitts πρός με, but the longer reading gives the correct meaning, even if it should be secondary. See R. Bultmann, *Evangelium*, p. 228, n. 5.

[2] On Matt. 11, 28 and its relationship to the wisdom traditions, see especially N. A. Dahl, *Matteusevangeliet*, p. 157.

"I am the bread [cf. wisdom/Torah] of life;
he who comes to me shall not hunger,
and he who believes in me shall never thirst."

The following passages combine the same ideas:

"Come to me....
Those who eat me will hunger for more
and those who drink me will thirst for more" (Sirach 24, 19.21)
"Come, eat of my bread
and drink of the wine I have mixed" (Prov. 9,5)

Three observations are evident in these comparisons: First, Sirach 24, 21 identifies wisdom itself with food and drink, just as presupposed in John 6, 35. Second, the context of Sirach 24, 19.21 explicitly identifies wisdom with the Torah (v. 23), a combination which John 6, 35 also presupposed. In midrashic interpretations, moreover, Prov. 9, 5 is made to refer to the Torah.[1] Third, the promise in John 6, 35 is much more radical than that in Sirach 24, 21, since it tells about cessation of hunger and thirst instead of continuation.[2]

The idea of eating is central in the second half of the homily (John 6, 49-58), and is connected with the idea of drinking in vv. 53 ff. Fragments from haggadic traditions about the manna and the well and from eucharistic traditions have been employed in this section,[3] but it is evident that also ideas about wisdom have influenced it. The actual wording, John 6, 57, "he who eats me" (ὁ τρώγων με), is very similar to Sirach 24, 21, "Those who eat me" (οἱ ἐσθίοντές με). Hence the eating of the bread from heaven and the eating and drinking in the eucharist mean the eating and the drinking of wisdom (and the Torah).

In different ways it is evident in John 6, 49-58 that those who eat and drink are promised and actually receive eternal life, and will not die. The same promise is made in wisdom literature:

"All who hold her fast will live,
and those who forsake her will die" (Baruch 4, 1; cf. also Prov. 8, 35-36).

Both the life-giving function of the Torah and the promise of life associated with wisdom explain John's basis for interpreting bread

---

[1] See Gen. R. 43, 6; 54, 1; 70, 5; Ex. R. 47, 7; Num. R. 8, 9; 13, 15 and 16; Eccl. R. VII, 8 ≠ 1, etc. Cf. *Str.-B.* II, pp. 482-483.

[2] Further discussion of this point on p. 166.

[3] See the analysis on pp. 20-22, 90-92.

from heaven as the life-giving factor. In John, however, the idea of life has been further defined as eternal life (John 6, 40.47.54; cf. 6, 51.58).[1]

Although wisdom literature provides good material on the ideas of the wisdom being called food and drink, it does not give parallels to the Johannine identification of the *manna* and the wisdom. Such an identification, however, is suggested in Ex. R. 25, 7, where Ex. 16, 4 about the manna is combined with Prov. 9, 5 about the wisdom (and the Torah):

> "Another explanation of
> 'Behold, I will cause to rain bread from heaven for you.'
> (Ex. 16, 4).
> It is written,
> 'Come, eat of my bread, and drink of the wine which
> I have mingled'" (Prov. 9, 5).

In the homily of Mut. 253-263, Philo not only indicates the identification, but states it explicitly in his interpretation of Ex. 16, 4:[2]

> "And indeed it says
> 'Behold I rain upon you bread from heaven' (Ex. 16, 4).
> Of what food can he rightly say that it is rained
> from heaven, save of heavenly wisdom ...?"

A comparison between John 6, 31-58 and Mut. 253-263 shows that John has utilized the personal features of the wisdom (6, 35, "he who comes to me", etc.), while Philo has developed the impersonal aspects more fitting to the meaning of σοφία within Greek educational philosophy.

Among the personal features of wisdom is her self predication in sayings of the "I"-style. Within the context of the wisdom ideas in John 6, 31-58, the midrashic formula of "I am (the bread, etc.)", vv. 35.41.48.51, receives the force of such self predication. A similar description occurs in Prov. 8, 30 "I was beside him, like a master workman (אמון)"; and the simpler form in the paraphrase of this verse in Gen. R. 1, 1 comes even closer to John 6, 35: "I was the working tool (כלי אומנתו) of the Holy One." The allusions to the theophany at Sinai in John 6 have also given the "Ego eimi" sayings overtones from God's presentation of Himself,

---

[1] See the discussion of eschatological concepts on pp. 165 ff.
[2] See pp. 112-115.

as in Ex. 20, 2 "I am the Lord your God." This is the deeper meaning of the exegetical phrase "Ego eimi" by which the word "bread" in the Old Testament text "Bread from heaven he gave them to eat" (John 6, 31b) is identified with Jesus, the son of Joseph (vv. 41-42).

Summary. — In John the bread from heaven has been given the life-giving functions of Torah and wisdom. The presence of the bread is pictured with features from the theophany at Sinai and the invitation to eat and drink extended by wisdom. He who shares in the (preparatory) revelation at Sinai accepts the invitation and "comes to" wisdom/Jesus (John 6, 45). The midrashic formula of "I am" receives in this context the force of the self predication of wisdom with overtones from God's theophanic presentation of Himself.—By combining ideas about the Torah, the theophany at Sinai and the wisdom, John 6, 31-58 follows the lines suggested by the Prologue (1, 1-18) where the same combination has been made.[1]

Dodd and Barrett have no independent analysis of the influence of wisdom ideas on John 6, 31-58, apart from their discussion of the impact of the concept of Torah.[2] Schulz and Schlatter completely deny any influence of the wisdom idea on the Johannine concept of the manna and Hoskyns ignores the question.[3]

Bultmann, on the other hand, point out that the "coming" and the cessation of "hunger" and "thirst" (John 6, 35, etc.) come from wisdom tradition. He is not, however, distinct and precise in his analysis which brings all of these ideas into his main concept of a gnostic Revealer.[4]

Sidebottom has a more precise understanding of the wisdom traditions as background for John.[5] Having referred to the passages about wisdom in Sirach 24 and Prov. 9, Sidebottom writes: "... words that are appropriate to wisdom because of its very nature apply in an opposite sense to the rich food of Christ. 'I am the bread

---

[1] On the Torah, Sinai and wisdom in the Prologue, see especially the survey in S. Schulz, *Komposition*, pp. 31-36, 40-43, and W. F. Howard, *Christianity According to St. John*, London 1943, pp. 34-56, and the discussion of John 1, 1-18 in commentaries.

[2] C. H. Dodd, *The Interpretation*, pp. 83-84, 336-337; C. K. Barrett, *St. John*, p. 240.

[3] S. Schulz, *Komposition*, p. 95; A. Schlatter, *Der Evangelist Johannes*, p. 173; E. C. Hoskyns, *The Fourth Gospel*, ed. F. N. Davey, 2nd ed., London 1947, pp. 294 ff.

[4] R. Bultmann, *Evangelium*, p. 168, n. 4 and p. 228, n. 7.

[5] E. M. Sidebottom, *The Christ*, pp. 203-207, etc.

of life', he says, 'he that comes to me will not hunger, and he that believes in me will never thirst.'...Jesus, not Law or wisdom, is the living bread that finally satisfies."[1]

A comprehensive survey of the research on the "Ego eimi" formula in John would go beyond the scope of the present study. It suffices to answer a problem posed by Schulz in agreement with Grünweller and Dietrich. Schulz emphasizes that in Old Testament and Judaism such a formula is never connected with a metaphoric word like "bread", "vine", etc. In the Mandean literature, on the other hand, a combination of "I am" and metaphoric concepts occurs frequently. In his conclusion, therefore, Schulz follows with certain modifications scholars as Bauer, Bultmann and Schweizer, who find that the Johannine "Ego eimi" formula has its origin in non-Jewish gnostic circles.[2]

Schulz would have found another solution on his problem if he had realized that John, at least in 6, 35.41.48.51, employs a midrashic formula for identifying an Old Testament word, e.g. a metaphoric term, with a person in first person singular. Due to the ideas in the context, this formula is in John 6 given the function of the self predication of wisdom and the theophanic self presentation. Hence, in the homily of John 6, 31-58 the "Ego eimi" sayings can definitely be explained on the background of Old Testament and Judaism.

Bread and the commissioned agent

Still another concept qualifies the use of "bread from heaven" in the homily of John 6, 31-58, the concept of agency. John 6, 38 illuminates this point, because in it the exegetical paraphrase of the (italicized) words from the Old Testament text (v. 31b) and from the haggadah are supplemented to show that Jesus is the agent of God:

"For *I have come down from heaven* (καταβέβηκα ἀπὸ τοῦ οὐρανοῦ)
not to do my own will,
but the will of him who sent me (τοῦ πέμψαντός με)."

The phrases for the sending are: vv. 38.39, τοῦ πέμψαντός με, v. 44, ὁ πέμψας με, v. 46, ὁ ὢν παρὰ τοῦ θεοῦ and v. 57 ἀπέστειλέν με ὁ — πατήρ.

---

[1] *Ibid.*, p. 130.
[2] S. Schulz, *Komposition*, pp. 90-94, 119-124, with references in the footnotes. See further above on pp. 72-73.

THE UNIQUE VISION OF GOD IN JESUS 159

John frequently uses the term "he who sent me/him", ὁ πέμψας με (αὐτόν), in a technical and stereotyped way.[1] John 13, 16 introduces it into a halakhic statement with partial parallels in Matt. 10, 24 and in the rabbinic halakah:

> John 13, 16: "a servant is not greater than his master; nor is he who is sent greater than he who sent him."
> (οὐδὲ ἀπόστολος μείζων τοῦ πέμψαντος αὐτόν)
> Matt. 10, 24: "nor [is] a servant above his master." [2]
> Gen. R. 78, 1: "the sender is greater than the sent"
> (המשלח גדול מן המשתלח).

Furthermore, the term occurs in John 13, 20 in a statement which has a parallel in Matt. 10, 40 (cf. Matt. 18, 5; Mark 9, 37 and Luke 9, 48), and which reflects the halakhic rule that "an agent is like him who sent him": [3]

> John 13, 20: "he who receives any one whom I send receives me; and he who receives me receives him who sent me"
> (λαμβάνει τὸν πέμψαντά με).

On the basis of this technical halakhic use of the term ὁ πέμψας με, it is reasonable to interpret the statements about the sending in John against the background of the judicial rules for agency in the Jewish traditions.

In John 6, 38 the term ὁ πέμψας με is interwoven with the common Jewish and New Testament phrase "to do the will of God":[4] "to do the will of him who sent me." The same combination occurs in 4, 34, and shortened to "the will of him who sent me" (τὸ θέλημα τοῦ πέμψαντός με) in John 6, 39 and 5, 30.[5]

All the halakhic statements about agency presuppose that the agent identifies himself with the will and the intention of him who

---

[1] John 4, 34; 5, 23.24.30.37; 7, 16.18.28.33; 8, 16.18.26.29, etc. See the list of occurrences in K. Kundsin, *Charakter*, p. 203, and G. D. Kilpatrick, "Some Notes on Johannine Usage," *BT* XI, 1960, p. 176.

[2] Cf. Luke 6, 40. See the analysis in C. H. Dodd, "Some Johannine 'Herrnworte' with Parallels in the Synoptic Gospels," *NTSt* II, 1955/56, pp. 75-78.

[3] See Mek. Ex. 12, 3.6; Berakoth 5, 5; Qiddushin 41b-43a. Cf. *Str.-B.* I, p. 590; II, p. 558. See the discussion of the Synoptic parallels in C. H. Dodd, *NTSt* II, 1955/56, pp. 81-85.

[4] See Matt. 7, 21; 12, 50 par, etc.; Eph. 6, 6; Hebr. 10, 36; 13, 21, etc.; Siphre on Num. 5,18, etc. See further *Der tannaitische Midrasch Sifre zu Numeri*, translated by K. G. Kuhn, *RT*, Ser. 2, III, Stuttgart 1959, p. 51 and n. 22; p. 129 and n. 11; A. Schlatter, *Der Evangelist Matthäus, seine Sprache, sein Ziel, seine Selbständigkeit*, Stuttgart 1929, pp. 257 f.

[5] Cf. John 6, 40, "the will of my father" and 7, 19; 9, 31, to do "his will".

sent him.¹ This presupposition is explicitly formulated in the Mediaeval collection Shulhan Aruq, Hoshen Mishpat, 188, 5: "Stets wenn der Vertreter (שהשליח) von dem Willen des Vertretenen (מדעת המשלח) abweicht, ist das Vertretungsverhältnis gänzlich aufgelöst."² Thus John 6, 38, in accordance with the halakhic principles, tells that the Son came from heaven not to execute his own will, since he was an agent, but the will of the sender, the Father. Hence, also 6, 39-40 tells about this will of the Father.³

According to the halakhic rules the sender had to authorize the agent by transferring his own rights and the property concerned to the agent.⁴ The will of the sender, the Father, in John 6, 39, makes just this transfer clear: "This is the will of him who sent me, that all that he has given me (πᾶν ὃ δέδωκέν μοι, cf. v. 37) ..."⁵ The transfer is even more pointedly stated in John 17, 6: "thine they were, and thou gavest them to me" (σοὶ ἦσαν κἀμοὶ αὐτοὺς ἔδωκας).

Thus it may be said that the Father takes possession of his belongings (through the Son as agent), or that the Son acquires the property for himself in a lawsuit. These two aspects are expressed in 6, 44 and 12, 32, respectively. John 6, 44 runs: "No one can come to me (i.e. the agent) unless the Father who sent me (ὁ πέμψας με, i.e. the sender) draws (ἑλκύσῃ) him." John 12, 32, on the other hand, says: "and I [i.e. the Son]...will draw (ἑλκύσω) all men to myself."

In both places the verb ἑλκύειν, to draw or drag, occurs in juridical contexts.⁶ It renders with all probability the Hebrew משך, to draw,

---

[1] K. H. Rengstorf, ἀποστέλλω κτλ, *ThWb* I, p. 415, discussing Qiddushin 3,1: Das bedeutet aber, das ohne die enschlossene Unterordnung des Willens des Beauftragten unter den des Auftragsgebers ein geordneter Ablauf des Verfahrens nicht gewährleistet wird." The will of the sender is explicitly mentioned in Qiddushin 41b. See also M. Cohn, "Die Stellvertretung im jüdischen Recht," *ZvglR* XXXVI, 1920, pp. 132 and 134 f.

[2] M. Cohn, *ZvglR* XXXVI, 1920, p. 206.

[3] Cf. *ibid.*, pp. 140-142, and L. Auerbach, *Das jüdische Obligationsrecht* I (*Umriss der Entwicklungsgeschichte des jüdischen Rechts. Die Natur der Obligation*), Berlin 1870, p. 565, with references to the collections of Maimonides, etc. where it is explicitly formulated that the will of the sender makes the agency legal.

[4] L. Auerbach, *Obligationsrecht* I, pp. 567-569, M. Cohn, *ZvglR* XXXVI, 1920, pp. 165-167. On this basis the sender should say to the agent: "Go forth and take legal action so that you may acquire title to it and secure the claim for yourself," Baba Qamma 70a. (English translation in *The Babylonian Talmud, Sedar Nezikin* I, ed. by I. Epstein, London 1935, p. 402).

[5] Variants of the phrase occur in John 17, 2.6.7; cf. 13, 3. The authorization (ἐξουσία) is directly mentioned in John 17, 2; cf. Matt. 10, 1 par.

[6] Cf. our analysis of the halakhic style of John 6, 44, on pp. 83 f.

pull, seize.[1] The LXX frequently translates מָשַׁךְ by ἑλκύειν.[2] In the judicial terminology of Judaism מָשַׁךְ has received the technical meaning of "to take possession of" (by drawing or seizing an object).[3]

Against this background, John 6, 44 says that only those of whom the sender (through the agent) takes the actual possession are received by the agent, and nobody else. In 12, 32, then, the aspect of the transfer of the object is brought fully to the surface, so that the agent, after winning the lawsuit, takes the possession of the property for himself (ἑλκύσω πρὸς ἐμαυτόν). The halakhic statement about agency in Baba Qamma 70a closely resembles this thought of John 12, 32: "Go forth and take legal action...and secure the claim for yourself" לְנַפְשָׁךְ).[4]

Although John says that the Father, through His agent, the Son, takes possession of those who belong to Him, he nevertheless holds that this thought is linked to the idea of a willing response on their part. The response is evident in the phrase "he who believes in me", etc., John 6, 35.40.47. This phrase occurs with slight variation frequently in John and 1 John and is a stereotyped term, although the combinations and contexts vary.[5] The Johannine literature has here only promoted a common Christian phrase into a fixed and favorite term, since close parallels are found elsewhere in the New Testament.[6]

In the Johannine context of agency the concept of believing means to have confidence and trust in the Son, based on an acceptance of the claims made for his person.[7] It means, therefore, to accept the fact that the Son is the agent of the Father and is authorized to take the possession of those who belong to Him and believe.[8]

---

[1] So also A. Schlatter, *Der Evangelist Johannes*, p. 176 and R. Bultmann, *Evangelium*, p. 171, n. 7. These scholars have not, however, focused the attention upon מָשַׁךְ as a judicial term.

[2] Deut. 21, 3; Neh. 9, 30; Ps. 9, 30 (10, 9); Eccl. 2, 3; Cant. 1, 4, etc.

[3] Baba Metzia 4, 2; Baba Metzia 47a; 48a; 49a. Cf. *Mishnayoth* (Ph. Blackman) IV, p. 579.

[4] See p. 160, n. 4. (Hebrew text in *Der Babylonische Talmud mit Einschluss der vollständigen Mischnah*, by L. Goldschmidt, VI, Leipzig 1906, p. 258).

[5] John 2, 11; 4, 39; 7, 5.31.38.39.48; 8, 30, etc.; cf. 1 John 5, 10. See especially John 3, (15).16.36; 11, 25.26, etc.

[6] See Matt. 18, 6; Acts 10, 43; Phil. 1, 29. Cf. Acts 14, 23; 19, 4; Rom. 10, 14; Gal. 2, 16; 1 Pet. 1, 8.

[7] Cf. C. H. Dodd, *The Interpretation*, pp. 183-184 and R. Bultmann, *Evangelium*, p. 37, n. 4.

[8] To this judicial and personal meaning of faith in John, compare the different Jewish and Platonizing concept of faith in Philo. See p. 146.

The basic principle of the Jewish institution of agency is that "an agent is like the one who sent him". In general this rule means that the agent is like his sender as far as the judicial effects are concerned. There were, however, rabbis who developed it into a "juridical mysticism" saying that the agent is a person identical with his principal.[1] Thus not only his authority and function are derived from the sender, but also his qualities.[2]

John follows the line of "juridical mysticism" in his Christology and soteriology.[3] Therefore, the life of the Father as the sender is transferred to the agent, the Son: "For as the Father has life in himself, so he has granted the Son also to have life in himself" (5, 26). The "juridical mysticism" with the Father enables the Son to hand on the life of the Father to men, as said in John 6, 57: "As the living Father (i.e. the sender) sent me (as the agent), and I live because of the Father, so he who eats me will live because of me." According to John the source of life is God Himself. In this way 6, 57 develops the Old Testament and Jewish concept of "the living God", which is also used frequently elsewhere in the New Testament.[4]

The phrase "every one who sees the Son" (6, 40) is also explained by John's "juridical mysticism". John 6, 46 denies the possibility that any man has had the vision of God. Only the agent who is from God (ὁ ὢν παρὰ τοῦ θεοῦ) [5] has had the vision. In 6, 40 it is then said that the agent of the Father, the Son, who alone has seen Him, mediates this vision of the Father when people see the Son. This thought is explicitly stated in 14, 9: "He who has seen me has seen the Father." Again the basis for such ideas is the halakhic principle that the agent is like him who sent him.

Hence, the process of bringing the "bread from heaven" to "the world" in John 6, 31-58 is described by weaving it together with the concepts of Torah, wisdom and agency. The appearance and

---

[1] Qiddushin 43a: "he ranks as his own person" (הוה ליה כגופיה). (Translation in *The Babylonian Talmud* (I. Epstein), *Nashim* VIII, p. 216; Hebrew text in *Der Babylonian Talmud* (L. Goldschmidt) V, p. 845). Cf. also Sanhedrin 111b; Gittin 32.

[2] See M. Cohn, *ZvglR* XXXVI, 1920, pp. 137 f.

[3] The phrase of "juridical mysticism" as clue to central ideas in John is suggested by Théo Preiss, *Life in Christ*, StBTh XIII, London 1954, p. 25.

[4] Josh. 3, 10; 1 Sam. 17, 26.36; Ps. 42, 2; Dan. 6, 20; J. Berakoth 3b; J. Sanhedrin 26c; Matt. 16, 16; Acts 14, 15; 1 Thess. 1, 9; Rev. 7, 2, etc.

[5] Cf. John 7, 29, παρ' αὐτοῦ εἰμι.

presence of the bread are consequently pictured as theophany (Torah), invitation (wisdom) and "juridical mysticism" (agency). The formula of "I am (the bread, etc.)" in this context receives the force of the self predication of wisdom with overtones from God's theophanic presentation of Himself, in John, of course, through the representation by God's agent, the Son.[1]

The concept of the Torah and the theophany at Sinai explain the ideas of the "hearing" of God and the denial of the vision of God. The concept of wisdom (and Torah) have contributed the ideas of eating and drinking and the cessation of hunger and thirst. The halakhic concept of agency has solved the problem of the denial of the vision of God, because the mediating function of the agent has made it possible. The concept of agency also explains that those who belong to God are transferred to the Son, so that God through him takes possession of them. Those who belong to God accept the claim of the Son and believe/trust in him.

All three concepts, the Torah, the wisdom and the agent of the living God, are associated with the giving of life, and they explain therefore that this function has been attributed to the "bread from heaven".

Among the contemporary scholars, Dodd finds that the status and function of the Son as God's delegated representative recalls the language of the Old Testament prophets. Certain peculiarities, such as the Son's complete and uninterrupted dependence on the Father, and the dualism between a higher and lower sphere, suggest to him that this aspect of Jesus' human career is a projection of the eternal relation of the Son and the Father upon the field of time.[2]

Dodd's interpretation does not take seriously the idea of the Son being commissioned and sent, but rather dissolves it into an eternal and "Platonic" idea of relationship.

Bultmann, on the other hand, rightly places the commissioning and sending of the Son in the very center of the message of the Gospel. He also finds certain points of contact between the Johannine ideas and the prophets of the Old Testament. But John,

---

[1] For the idea of a heavenly being representing God in a theophany, cf. that the Torah, according to some traditions, were mediated by one or several angels, who spoke to the people on God's behalf. See Acts 7, 38.53; Gal. 3, 19; Hebr. 2, 2; Josephus Ant. XV 136; Jubilees 1, 27; 2, 1. See *Str.-B.* III, pp. 554 ff.

[2] C. H. Dodd, *The Interpretation*, pp. 254-262.

according to Bultmann, goes beyond the thought of a prophet and interprets gnostic mythology about divine and pre-existent agents, commissioned by the Father and sent to the world.[1]

It seems strange that Bultmann looks to Mandean and other gnostic sources for parallels without asking whether or not Jewish ideas of agency can explain the Johannine thoughts. This question is more natural since Matt. 10, 40 and par. describes Jesus as the commissioned agent of God, and John 13, 20 renders this saying in a form even more similar to rabbinic language than the Synoptics.[2]

The parallels in the other New Testament writings and in the rabbinic halakah encourage, therefore, the investigation of the extent to which John's Christology and soteriology are moulded on Jewish rules for agency. Rengstorf has made a promising beginning at this point, although he does not think that the idea of agency plays any central role in the Johannine idea of Jesus as the Son of God.[3] Also Preiss and Barrett draw attention to the similarities between John and the halakah at certain places.[4] Significantly enough, Preiss discusses the idea of the Son as commissioned by the Father within the wider framework of the juridical aspects of Johannine thought.[5] In spite of the works of these scholars, the field is open to examine the degree in which halakhic principles of agency are reflected in John.

The Christological and soteriological significance of the halakhic concept of agency as interpreted in John has not been developed by other scholars who largely draw on Judaism for background material, whether emphasizing "normative" traditions as those found in the Mekilta on Exodus (Schlatter) and in the Passover haggadah (Gärtner), or emphasizing mystical and esoteric traditions (Odeberg), wisdom traditions (Sidebottom) or secterian apocalyptic-gnostic traditions (Schulz).[6]

---

[1] R. Bultmann, *Evangelium*, pp. 187-188; "Die Bedeutung der neuerschlossenen mandäischen und manichäischen Quellen für das Verständniss des Johannesevangeliums," *ZNW* XXIV, 1925, pp. 104-109. Cf. E. Haenchen, "Der Vater, der mich gesandt hat," *NTSt* IX, 1962/63, pp. 208-216.

[2] Cf. R. Bultmann, *Evangelium*, p. 364, nn. 2, 4, 7.

[3] K. H. Rengstorf, *ThWb* I, pp. 403-405; 421-422; 435-436.

[4] Théo Preiss, *Life in Christ*, pp. 9-31; C. K. Barrett, *St John*, pp. 216, 474.

[5] The same emphasis on the judicial aspect of John's thought is found in N. A. Dahl, *Current Issues* (ed. W. Klassen and G. F. Snyder), pp. 137 ff.

[6] A. Schlatter, *Der Evangelist Johannes*; B. Gärtner, *Passover*; H. Odeberg, *The Fourth Gospel*; E. M. Sidebottom, *The Christ*; S. Schulz, *Menschensohn-Christologie*; and *Komposition*.

Bread and eternal life

The background of Torah, wisdom and the principle of agency have conferred upon the bread from heaven the function of giving life. Logically enough, therefore, terms for "life" at several places in the homily of John 6, 31-58 supplement words from the Old Testament text cited in v. 31b. The underscoring of the Old Testament words makes these supplementary terms more apparent: vv. 35.48, ὁ ἄρτος τῆς ζωῆς, v. 51 ὁ ἄρτος ὁ ζῶν, v. 51 (cf. v. 58) ἐάν τις φάγῃ ἐκ τούτου τοῦ ἄρτου, ζήσει εἰς τὸν αἰῶνα.

The last phrase (v. 51) suggests an eschatological setting of the Johannine concept of life, which the term "eternal life", ζωὴ αἰώνιος, confirms (vv. 40.47.54).[1] John's use of "eternal life" establishes a meaning within the thought pattern of "this aeon/world" and "the coming aeon/world". One example is 12, 25:[2] "he who hates his life in this world (ἐν τῷ κόσμῳ τούτῳ) will keep it for eternal life (εἰς ζωὴν αἰώνιον)."[3]

John follows here an eschatological terminology and thought pattern common to the Synoptics, Paul, Hebrews, Jewish apocalyptic literature and the rabbinic writings.[4] Mark 10, 30 (cf. Luke 18, 30) shows that the term ζωὴ αἰώνιος is closely tied to "the coming aeon": "...a hundredfold now in this time (ἐν τῷ καιρῷ τούτῳ),...and in the age to come (ἐν τῷ αἰῶνι τῷ ἐρχομένῳ) eternal

---

[1] ζωὴ αἰώνιος occurs also in John 3, 15.35; 4, 14.36; 5, 24.39; 6, 27.68; 10, 28; 12, 50; 17, 2.3. The single ζωή is frequently used as well (3, 36; 5, 24, etc.) with no basic difference in meaning. See H. Pribnow, *Die johanneische Anschauung vom "Leben". Eine biblisch-theologische Untersuchung in religionsgeschichtlicher Beleuchtung*, GThF IV, Greifswald 1934, pp. 27-31.

[2] Cf. also John 5, 39 which refers to a Jewish doctrine about the study of Torah and the life of the coming aeon, as seen from Pirqe Aboth 6, 7. See C. H. Dodd, *The Interpretation*, p. 146.

[3] The Synoptic parallels (Mark 8, 35 par., Matt. 10, 39) lack the reference to "this aeon/world" and "the coming aeon/world". See the discussion by C. H. Dodd, NTSt II, 1955/56, pp. 78-81 and commentaries on John 12, 25.

[4] See Matt. 12, 32; Mark 10, 30; Luke 16, 8; 18, 30; 20, 34 f.; John 8, 32; 9, 39; 12, 25.31; 13, 1; 16, 11; 18, 36; 1 John 4, 17; Rom. 12, 2; 1 Cor. 1, 20; 2, 6.8; 3, 18.19; 5, 10; 7, 31; 2 Cor. 4, 4; Gal. 1, 4; Eph. 1, 21; 2, 2; 1 Tim. 6, 17; 2 Tim. 4, 10; Tit. 2, 12; Hebr. 6, 5; Syriac Baruch 14, 13; 15, 7 f. 78; 16, 1; 44, 12.15; 48, 50; 51, 10.14; 4 Ezra 4, 2.27; 6, 9.55; 7, 12.47. 112.113; Slavic Enoch 50, 2.5; 66, 6.7.8; Pirqe Aboth 2, 7; Gen. R. 14, 5; Lev. R. 11, 9; Gittin 57a; Hagigah 15a; Mek. Ex. 16, 25, etc. See P. Volz, *Die Eschatologie der jüdischen Gemeinde im neutestamentlichen Zeitalter*, 2nd ed., Tübingen 1934, p. 65; Str.-B. IV, ?, pp. 799-976; H. Sasse, αἰών, ThWb I, pp. 204-207.

life (ζωὴν αἰώνιον)." The conclusion is that the life brought by the bread from heaven in accordance with ideas from Torah, wisdom and the agent of the living God receives in John the further qualification of being eternal life, i.e. life of the coming aeon.

This interpretation of the Johannine concept of life is confirmed by the fact that the homily of John 6, 31-58 also has other eschatological concepts which have their background in the Jewish apocalyptic and rabbinic traditions and the New Testament.

In v. 35b and v. 37 the following phrases betray their eschatological character: 1) "shall not hunger...shall never thirst" (οὐ μὴ πεινάσῃ — οὐ μὴ διψήσει πώποτε, v. 35) echoes Is. 49, 10 (LXX οὐ πεινάσουσιν οὐδὲ διψήσουσιν) which also receives an eschatological interpretation in Rev. 7, 16;[1] and 2) "I will not cast out" (οὐ μὴ ἐκβάλω ἔξω, v. 37) has close parallels in John 12, 31 and Luke 13, 28, both of which are eschatological statements. In John 12, 31 the ruler of this aeon (ὁ ἄρχων τοῦ κόσμου τούτου) is said to be thrown out at the judgment (ἐκβληθήσεται ἔξω). Luke 13, 28 tells about those who will be excluded from the kingdom of God (ὑμᾶς δὲ ἐκβαλλομένους ἔξω).[2]

The phrases "I should lose nothing" (μὴ ἀπολέσω ἐξ αὐτοῦ, v. 39) and "I will raise him up at the last day" (ἀναστήσω αὐτὸν ἐγὼ ἐν τῇ ἐσχάτῃ ἡμέρᾳ, v. 40, and with slight variations in vv. 39.44.54) have the same background. The first phrase renders the transitive form of the verb ἀπολλύειν, to lose, which usually occurs in the intransitive form, to perish, in the New Testament.[3] The eschato-

---

[1] See especially K. Schaedel, *Das Johannesevangelium und "die Kinder des Lichts"*, p. 188; C. K. Barrett, *St. John*, p. 243; A. Schlatter, *Der Evangelist Johannes*, p. 174; L. van Hartingsveld, *Die Eschatologie des Johannesevangeliums*, Assen 1962, p. 70. Cf. also C. H. Dodd, *The Interpretation*, p. 246 (John 6, 35 echoes Is. 49, 10).—R. Bultmann, *Evangelium*, p. 168, n. 4 does not explain the difference between John 6, 35 and Sirach 15, 4; 24, 21, and he ignores the eschatological allusion to Is. 49, 10 and Rev. 7, 16.

[2] Cf. variants of the same phrase in Matt. 8, 12; 22, 13; 25, 30. See also A. Schlatter, *Der Evangelist Johannes*, p. 175; C. K. Barrett, *St. John*, p. 244. —R. Bultmann, *Evangelium*, p. 172 does not discuss the parallel eschatological phrases in the Synoptics.

These parallels to John 6, 35.37 indicate that here stereotyped phrases from eschatological traditions ("shall not hunger...shall never thirst"; "I will not cast out") are fused together with other phrases ("he who comes to me"..."and he who believes in me"; "and him who comes to me") into midrashic statements of participial character. This observation militates against the viewpoint that vv. 35b and 37 as such are independent and fixed sayings from the tradition. See p. 79.

[3] The transitive form of the verb is also used in John 18, 9. Both in 6, 39

logical setting of this term is evident, since in John 3, 16 ff. it is associated with the idea of judgment and has as contrast the term eternal life (ζωὴ αἰώνιος; cf. also 10, 28). The eschatological usage of this word is widely present in the Synoptics, Paul, 2 Peter, James and Jude. To Paul the contrast to "perish" is "to be saved" (σώζεσθαι) in correspondance with John's "eternal life", and in Rom. 2, 12 the word "perish" is associated with judgment.[1]

It is commonly recognized that the phrase "I will raise him up at the last day" has its background in eschatological traditions. Belief in the final resurrection is widely maintained in apocalyptic and rabbinic Judaism, primarily championed by the Pharisaic school.[2] The New Testament shares this belief, and the term appearing in John 6, 39.40.44.45, ἀνιστάναι, is frequently used in this connection.[3]

The phrase ἐν τῇ ἐσχάτῃ ἡμέρᾳ which occurs in John 6, 39.40.44.54; 11, 24; 12, 48, has a parallel in Siphre on Deut. 34, 2 where "as far as the Western Sea (עד הים האחרן) is read as "until the last day" (עד היום האחרן).[4] In the plural form the phrase and its Hebrew equivalent are frequently used in the New Testament, LXX, apocalyptic and rabbinic traditions and the Qumran literature.[5]

---

and 18, 9 it is clear that the eschatological term is interpreted within the context of agency: God's judicial agent, the Son, shall not lose those whom God, the Father, has transferred to him. Odeberg's translation of ἐξ αὐτοῦ in John 6, 39 fits very well to this line of thought: "that ... I should not lose...*from Him*". H. Odeberg, *The Fourth Gospel*, p. 264.

[1] See 1 Cor. 1, 18; 2 Cor. 2, 15; 2 Thess. 2, 10; cf. John 3, 16-17; (cf. James 4, 12); Rom. 2, 12. For more detailed analysis and more references, see A. Oepke, ἀπόλλυμι κτλ, *ThWb* I, pp. 394-395.—It is commonly recognized that the Johannine concept of "lose" and "perish" comes from eschatological terminology. See R. Bultmann, *Evangelium*, p. 110, n. 5 and p. 174, n. 2; C. K. Barrett, *St. John*, p. 244; A. Schlatter, *Der Evangelist Johannes*, p. 175, etc.

[2] Is. 25, 6 ff.; Dan. 12, 2; 2 Maccabees 7, 9; Ethiopian Enoch 51, 1 ff.; Acts 23, 8; Sanhedrin 10, 1; Sotah 9, 15, etc. See K. Schaedel, *Das Johannesevangelium und "die Kinder des Lichts"*, pp. 121-123; C. K. Barrett, *St. John*, pp. 328 f.; P. Volz, *Die Eschatologie*, pp. 234 f.

[3] ἀνιστάναι: Mark 12, 23.25; Luke 16, 31; John 11, 23.24; 1 Thess. 4, 16; about Jesus' resurrection, Mark 8, 31; 9, 9, etc.; Acts 2, 24.32; 13, 33, etc.; 1 Thess. 4, 14, etc.

[4] *Sifré debé Rab* (ed. Friedmann), 357 (149a). Another rabbinic parallel is found in Ex. R. 52, 3. See A. Schlatter, *Der Evangelist Johannes*, p. 175.

[5] See G. Kittel, ἔσχατος, *ThWb* II, p. 695; F. Nötscher, *Zur theologischen Terminologie der Qumran-Texte*, BbB X, Bonn 1956, pp. 165 ff.

All these eschatological concepts have in John 6, 31-58 been associated with the bread from heaven on the basis of ideas about Torah, theophany, wisdom and agency; and they are not confined to future expectation. Instead they are seen as present realities. Thus eternal life is no longer the future life of the coming aeon. The promise that believers will neither hunger nor thirst (v. 35b) is fulfilled in the present. The eschatological judgment with the verdict that those who come to Jesus will neither be thrown out (v. 37) nor perish (v. 39) takes place in the present.

In agreement with John's emphasis on the present, 6, 32 says that the right interpretation of the verb ἔδωκεν (נתן) in v. 31b is the present tense "gives" (δίδωσιν / נוֹתֵן) and not past tense, "gave" (δέδωκεν / נָתַן). The corresponding philological exegesis in Mek. Ex. 15, 11 makes the Hebrew vocalization of participle עושה (cf. John 6, 32, נותן), "who does" wonders, refer to the eschatological time. John 6, 32, therefore, emphasizes that God gives the bread from heaven in the eschatological present.[1]

The homily of John 6, 31-58 makes one significant exception in the transformation of the traditional eschatological expectation into the present, namely, the ideas about the resurrection on the last day. There the future tense is maintained with full force (vv. 39.40. 44.54). The parallel statement in 5, 28 f. about the resurrection of those in the tombs shows that John keeps the Jewish and New Testament idea of the future general bodily resurrection. The Johannine thought is, therefore, that the eternal life which already is a reality in the present will include the bodily resurrection of life at the last day.[2]

The closest parallels to this tension between the present realization and future expectation in eschatology, are found in other New Testament books.[3] Paul, for example, describes "eternal life" as referring to the future in Rom. 2, 7; 5, 21; 6, 22 f.; Gal. 6, 8; 1 Cor.

---

[1] See pp. 64-65.
[2] The eternal life as a present possession and as the resurrection life at the last day, are just two aspects and stages of the same life, given by the Father through the Son. Therefore, it can be said that the resurrection life is also a present reality, as well as it is connected with the last day. See John 11, 23-27.
[3] See the survey in H. C. Kee, "The Development of Eschatology in the New Testament," *JBR* XX, 1952, pp. 187-193. As regards the Synoptics, see especially W. G. Kümmel, *Promise and Fulfillment. The Eschatological Message of Jesus*, StBTh XXIII, London 1957.

15, 20 f. 45 f.; 2 Cor. 5, 1 ff., etc. The believers, however, already possess this life in the present on the basis of Christ's death and resurrection, Rom. 6, 4.11; 8, 2.6.10, etc.[1] But John is the most radical of all in transforming the eschatological expectations into the present.

The ideas of eternal life and the last day will guide the survey of scholarship on the eschatology in John. Van Hartingsveld underestimates the present aspect when he tries to interpret eternal life within the context of the traditional future expectations in Judaism. He says believers in the present have eternal life only as a promise; they will receive it as their possession at the last day.[2]

Van Hartingsveld is, nevertheless, right insofar as he affirms that these eschatological expectations in Judaism form part of the background of the Johannine interpretation of life. This fact provides obstacles for those who attempt to understand John mainly within the framework of sectarian Judaism, as represented by the Qumrān literature, because here there are only rudiments of ideas as "the coming aeon" and "eternal life".[3] The connection between eternal life and resurrection is, moreover, not explicit in the Dead Sea Scrolls. Some scholars, as Schaedel and Schulz, still try to maintain the Qumran sect as background at this point by the weak statement that the idea of life in the sect belonged to Judaism in general,

---

[1] With regard to St. Paul's teaching about the present and future aspects of eternal life, see E. von Schrenk, *Die johanneische Anschauung vom "Leben" mit Berücksichtigung ihrer Vorgeschichte*, Leipzig 1898, pp. 38 ff.; cf. K. L. Schmidt, "Eschatologie und Mystik im Urchristentum," *ZNW* XXI, 1922, p. 289 and A. Schweitzer, *Die Mystik des Apostels Paulus*, Tübingen 1930, pp. 76-174.

[2] L. van Hartingsveld, *Die Eschatologie*, pp. 60, 264-265, etc.

[3] The thought pattern of "this aeon/world" and "the coming aeon/world" may be compared with phrases as "the days of the dominion of Belial" (I QS 2, 19) and the time of God (I QS 3, 23, etc.). See G. Baumbach, *Qumrān und das Johannes-Evangelium. Eine vergleichende Untersuchung der dualistischen Aussagen der Ordensregel von Qumran und das Johannes-Evangeliums mit Berücksichtigung der spätjüdischen Apokalypsen*, AVThR VI, Berlin 1958, pp. 39 ff. (p. 41; "Anklänge an die Lehre von den zwei Äonen"); cf. H. W. Huppembauer, *Der Mensch zwischen zwei Welten. Der Dualismus der Texte von Qumran (Höhle I) und der Damaskusfragmente*, AThANT XXXIV, Zürich 1959, p. 111.—The idea of eternal life occurs occasionally, as in I QS 4, 7 f., where it is listed among the blessings of the eschatological time, but the idea receives no distinct description. Cf. F. Nötscher, *Zur theologischen Terminologie*, pp. 150 f. and 157 f.; H. Ringgren, *Tro ock liv enligt Döda-havsrullarna*, Stockholm 1961, pp. 117-121.

where the concepts of eternal life and resurrection were central.[1]

In Dodd's judgment, John's radical stress in eternal life as a present reality relates the Fourth Gospel closely to Platonic ideas in Philo. Like Philo John means a life which has, properly speaking, neither past nor future, but is lived in God's eternal To-day. Eternal life is timeless. John knows, however, the popular expectation of a future general resurrection, but he regards it only as a truth of minor importance in comparison with the timeless quality of the present possession of eternal life.[2]

Dodd is right in pointing to the affinities between John and Philo because both lay the emphasis on the present. Dodd, however, plays down the differences between them, which are caused by the fact that John still takes the temporal categories seriously. This objection against Dodd's interpretation can be illustrated by their different interpretation of the manna. Both Philo (Leg. all. III 162-168 and Mut. 253-263) and John (6, 31-58) show their primary interest in the present movement of the bread from heaven to earth. John, however, thinks of the bread from heaven and eternal life within the perspective of the present together with the future last day, whereas Philo's interpretation of the manna makes no such temporal distinctions.

Bultmann denies any temporal meaning attached to the Johannine concept of life, even though he admits its background in Jewish eschatology. Life is rather to be interpreted from gnostic thinking: it means real life in contrast to the false and seeming life of this world.[3] This definition of life leads him of necessity to accept

---

[1] "Nach den bisherigen Ausführungen kann die Verwandtschaft der johanneischen Lebensvorstellung mit der jüdischen, in deren Rahmen auch die der Sekte gehört, kaum geleugnet werden." S. Schulz, *Komposition*, p. 109, paraphrasing K. Schaedel, *Das Johannesevangelium und "die Kinder des Lichts"*, p. 128; cf. H. Blauert, *Die Bedeutung der Zeit*, p. 178, where he rightly states the background of the Johannine concept of life: "Es ist grundsätzlich der gleiche, eschatologische Begriff jüdisch-urchristlicher Provenienz."—It should be added that in the Qumran literature published so far, there is no exposition of the manna.

[2] C. H. Dodd, *The Interpretation*, pp. 148, 150; cf. pp. 337-338, a similiar interpretation was given in J. Lindblom, *Das ewige Leben. Eine Studie über die Entstehung der religiösen Lebensidee im Neuen Testament*, Leipzig 1914, pp. 233-234.—On Philo's ideas, see especially E. Goodenough, "Philo on Immortality," *HThR* XXXIX, 1946, pp. 85-108, who discusses the variety of ideas on immortality found in his writings.

[3] R. Bultmann, *Evangelium*, p. 109, n. 2; see also ζάω κτλ, *ThWb* II, pp. 871-874, and *Theology* II, p. 11.

the viewpoint of "orthodox liberalism" that all futuristic eschatology in John—6, 39.40.44.54 included—are secondary adaptations to the popular eschatology of the Church. Hence, Bultmann draws the conclusion that a Church-minded "Redactor" has added these ideas of futuristic eschatology to the Gospel.[1]

But there is a large group of scholars who maintain that both the present and the future aspects of eschatology are integral parts of the Johannine thinking. Many of them find that the resurrection at the last day makes the concept of eternal life to include the bodily resurrection.[2] Some see the idea of future eschaton as the fulfillment of the present or as the final manifestation of the hidden Messiah and life in the present.[3] The relationship can also be stated in a more general way by the thought that the believers both possess life now and have a future hope.[4] Often the scholars who hold views like these just mentioned tend to give more weight to the future than John himself does.

Scholars such as Howard, Ruckstuhl, Baumbach and Blauert

---

[1] See R. Bultmann, ζάω κτλ, *ThWb* II, pp. 872-873; *Theology* II, p. 39, cf. p. 85, n. *; *Evangelium*, p. 162, cf. pp. 175-176.—Among the many scholars holding a similar view, see W. Bousset, *Kyrios Christos. Geschichte des Christusglaubens von den Anfängen des Christentums bis Irenaeus*, FRLANT XXI (N.F. IV), 3rd ed., Göttingen 1926, p. 177, n. 1; A. Faure, *ZNW* XXI, 1922, pp. 62 f.; E. Hirsch, *Studien zum vierten Evangelium*, pp. 62 f.; R. Bultmann, "Johannesevangelium," *RGG* III, 3rd ed., 1959, col. 841; K. Schaedel, *Das Johannesevangelium und "die Kinder des Lichts"*, pp. 98 ff.—See also our analysis above on pp. 110-111.

Other scholars reject the theory of editorial additions and leave the inconsistencies in John unsolved at this point: W. Bauer, *Das Johannes-Evangelium*, pp. 83, 93; W. Heitmüller, *Das Johannes-Evangelium*, SNT IV, 3rd ed., Göttingen 1918, pp. 83-84; G. H. C. Macgregor, *The Gospel of John*, MNTC, London 1928, pp. 146-147; M. Dibelius, "Johannesevangelium," *RGG* III, 2nd ed., 1929 cols. 355-356.

[2] J. H. Bernard, *St. John* I, pp. clix, 244-245; R. H. Strachan, *Fourth Gospel*, p. 188; E. Ruckstuhl, *Einheit*, pp. 164-167; cf. also J. Lindblom, *Das ewige Leben*, pp. 233-234.

[3] H. Pribnow, *Anschauung von "Leben"*, pp. 126-129; F. Mussner, ΖΩΗ. *Die Anschauung vom "Leben" im vierten Evangelium unter Berücksichtigung der Johannesbriefe*, MThS I, V, München 1952, p. 143: cf. G. Stählin, "Das Problem der Johanneischen Eschatologie," *ZNW* XXXIII, 1934, pp. 236-239, 243, 254 and E. Stauffer, "Agnostos Christos. Joh. 2, 24 und die Eschatologie des vierten Evangeliums," in *The Background of the New Testament and its Eschatology*, in honor of C. H. Dodd, pp. 281-229. See also A. Corell, *Consummatum Est. Eschatology and Church in the Gospel of St. John*, London 1958, p. 148, who regards the present life as an anticipation of the future life in its perfection.

[4] C. K. Barrett, *St. John*, p. 244.

hold that the idea of the last day in John keeps the eternal life within the framework of time.[1] Of special interest is the assertion of Ruckstuhl, that in John eternal life is unfolding itself in time up to the final close at the bodily resurrection on the last day.[2]

The analysis of John 6, 31-58 proposed here agrees with the viewpoint that the eternal life is a present reality which unfolds itself in time up to the final close at the bodily resurrection on the last day. Our discussion has, moreover, shown that this Johannine idea has been made possible by qualifying the life given by Torah, wisdom and the agent of the living God as the eschatological eternal life, and by transferring these concepts upon the bread from heaven.

The Johannine interpretation of past, present and future needs still further examination. As a key to this question, the thought pattern of the external aspect and the spiritual aspect of bread from heaven will be employed.

Bread, external and spiritual, given to Israel

What is the relationship between the bread from heaven given in the past and God's bread from heaven given in the present? The answer is that John places the events of the past in the external sphere and the bread from heaven of the present in the spiritual sphere.

The midrashic exposition in John 6, 31-32 is based on this distinction. The true meaning of the Old Testament text "Bread from heaven he gave (ἔδωκεν / נתן) them to eat" (v. 31b) is not the external event of the manna miracle in the past, but the spiritual bread of the present, as is demonstrated by the proper vocalization of the Hebrew verb: not past tense δέδωκεν / נָתַן, but present tense δίδωσιν / נֹתֵן (v. 32).[3] Verse 32 can therefore be paraphrased in the following way: Not the external sphere of the past in which Moses gave you the external bread from heaven, but the spiritual sphere of the present in which my Father gives you the true spiritual bread from heaven.

With different wording the same distinction occurs in John

---

[1] W. F. Howard, *Christianity*, p. 124; cf. p. 109; E. Ruckstuhl, *Einheit*, pp. 164-166; G. Baumbach, *Qumrān und das Johannes-Evangelium*, pp. 43-44 and p. 44, n. 1; H. Blauert, *Die Bedeutung der Zeit*, pp. 93-95. See also F. V. Filson, "The Gospel of Life," *Current Issues* (ed. W. Klassen and G. F. Snyder), p. 114.

[2] E. Ruckstuhl, *Einheit*, p. 165.

[3] See pp. 62-65.

6, 49-50.58: Your fathers ate the external manna in the wilderness and died, but a man may eat of the spiritual bread which comes down from heaven and not die (vv. 49-50); the spiritual bread is not like the external bread the fathers ate and died (v. 58). The association of death with the external events and persons of the past are also found in John 8, 53 stating that Abraham and the prophets died.

Since ideas from the Torah and the theophany at Sinai have been associated with the bread from heaven in the present, it is quite logical that the bread from heaven in the past also combines in itself the manna miracle and the giving of Torah at Sinai. This combination explains why Moses in John 6, 32 is introduced as subject of the verb, δέδωκεν (ἔδωκεν), although not suggested by the Old Testament text cited in v. 31b. The wording in v. 32, accordingly, is parallel to phrases about the giving of the Torah:

John 6, 32: οὐ Μωϋσῆς δέδωκεν ὑμῖν τὸν (ἄρτον ἐκ τοῦ οὐρανοῦ)
Not Moses gave you the (bread from heaven).
John 7, 19: οὐ Μωϋσῆς ἔδωκεν ὑμῖν τὸν νόμον;
Did not Moses give you the Law?
John 1, 17: ὅτι ὁ νόμος διὰ Μωϋσέως ἐδόθη
For the Law was given through Moses

John 6, 31-32 shows, therefore, that both the manna miracle and the giving of Torah at Sinai belong to the external events of the past.

Although the bread from heaven in the present has been associated with ideas from Torah (giving of life, theophanic hearing and vision) and wisdom (invitation, eating and drinking), it is not directly identified with Torah and wisdom as such.[1] Instead, the ideas from Torah and wisdom attributed to the bread from heaven describe the spiritual reality to which the external manna and Torah of the past point. And since the ideas from Torah and wisdom have been given eschatological qualification as eternal life, cessation of hunger and thirst, etc., also the eschatological ideas employed are spiritually understood.

Philo, correspondingly, distinguishes between the external bread —the bread from earth—and the spiritual bread, the manna in Leg. all. III 162-168 and Mut. 253-263. He does not, however, apply this distinction to the past and present aspects of history, as John does.

---

[1] Cf. the quotation from E. M. Sidebottom, cited above on pp. 157 f.

Philo is therefore not interested in the manna miracle as an external event of the past, but devotes his whole attention to the ever-present spiritual manna, an idea which he applies to the concrete situation of Judaism in Alexandria.[1]

Schlatter, Cullmann, Gärtner and van Hartingsveld have tried to interpret the relationship between the past and present in John 6, 31 ff. on the basis of the Jewish expectation that the manna miracle in the desert would be repeated in the Messianic age.[2] This interpretation is, however, inadequate, since it ignores or minimizes the distinction between the external bread and the spiritual bread.

Other scholars ignore the temporal aspect of past and present. They refer to the Messianic expectations of the manna as background material, but find that John is only interested in the difference between external and spiritual bread. Thus Bultmann thinks that the bread given by Moses describes worldly and seeming goods and the wish for objective criteria as condition for accepting the divine revelation. The true bread from heaven, on the other hand, means God's revelation, or rather, God's Revealer, which comes in a way different from the "Jewish" and worldly expectations.[3] Dodd places the bread given by Moses in the phenomenal and temporal sphere, whereas the true spiritual bread belongs to the timeless eternal reality.[4]

Odeberg denies that the idea of external bread is found in John 6, 31-34. John draws here rather a distinction between two inter-

---

[1] See chs. IV and V.

[2] A. Schlatter, *Der Evangelist Johannes*, p. 172; (cf. *Str.-B.* II, p. 481); O. Cullmann, *Early Christian Worship*, StBTh X, London 1953, pp. 96-97; cf. A. Corell, *Consummatum Est*, p. 65; L. van Hartingsveld, *Die Eschatologie*, pp. 69-70. B. Gärtner, *Passover*, pp. 20-25, uses the Jewish pattern of three ages: the manna in the desert for the Mosaic age, Jesus' feeding of the people in the Messianic age and the feast in God's kingdom, the eucharistic bread. On pp. 21-22, Gärtner indicates a distinction between a materialistic and a spiritual understanding of the bread, but does not develop its principal importance.

The same eschatological interpretation occurs in modified form in E. C. Hoskyns, *The Fourth Gospel*, pp. 293-294; H. Strathmann, *Das Evangelium nach Johannes*, NTD IV, 8th ed., Göttingen 1955, p. 120; S. Schulz, *Komposition*, pp. 95-98, 118.

[3] R. Bultmann, *Evangelium*, p. 169; cf. the similar interpretation by E. Schweizer, *EGO EIMI*, pp. 135, 153-154, who gives more emphasis to Jesus' criticism of the human ideas and expectation.

[4] C. H. Dodd, *The Interpretation*, pp. 335-336; cf. W. F. Howard, *Christianity*, pp. 189, who modifies Dodd's interpretation by rightly emphasizing the positive significance of temporal categories in John.

pretations of the spiritual bread: the one, manna, is linked to a specific event and a specific figure in history, Moses, whereas the other, the divine food, the parnāsā, is always present and is given *now*.[1]

Barrett has developed a more nearly accurate interpretation. He characterizes the manna miracle of the past as a shadow of the true bread from heaven in the present, and finds that the contrast also implies the difference between the secondary and transient revelation of the Mosaic law and the true bread from heaven as the substance itself.[2]

According to John 6, 32 both the external bread of the past and the spiritual bread of the present are given to "you", which interprets "them" in the text, v. 31b. Verse 36 motivates this exposition by Jesus: "But I said 'you', because you have seen [me] and yet do not believe."[3] The meaning is that the manna/Torah and also the true bread form heaven, the Son of God, were given to Israel because its history was the place where God revealed himself.

John's use of the word "to see", v. 36 (ἑωράκατε), shows that it refers to theophanic visions in the history of Israel: Abraham saw (εἶδεν) the day of the Son of God (8, 56); Nathanael is to see (ὄψεσθε) what Jacob/Israel saw in his vision at Bethel (1, 49-51). The phrase, "we have beheld (ἐθεασάμεθα) his glory" (1, 14), alludes to the theophany at Sinai (cf. also 1, 18; 5, 37 and 6, 46). Isaiah saw (εἶδεν) the glory of the Son (12, 41), and John the Baptist saw (ἑώρακα) the Son of God (1, 32-34). With John the Baptist the actual seeing of the Son began, while the preceding visions had the character of previews. Against this background the "you" (ὑμῖν) in John 6, 32-33 implies that both the preparatory theophanic events in the past and the actual realization of the spiritual theophany in the true bread/the Son of God took place in Israel, the center of the world.[4]

John 6, 36 continues "and yet do not believe". John accuses Israel of distorting all the visionary events by not accepting the true bread/the Son of God in her midst. The criticism by "the

---

[1] H. Odeberg, *The Fourth Gospel*, pp. 255-257.
[2] C. K. Barrett, *St. John*, pp. 240-241; cf. R. Strachan, *The Fourth Gospel*, pp. 186, who emphasizes the inferior and temporary character of the manna in the past against the superior (and spiritual) bread of the present.
[3] See pp. 74-75. The reading με gives the correct meaning, even if it may have been lacking in the original text as in ℵ A it sy^sc.
[4] See pp. 148 f.

Jews" (vv. 41.52) expresses their rejection. John regularly uses the term, "the Jews", to designate the opponents of Jesus and his disciples (5, 15-18; 6, 41.52; 7, 1; 13, 33; 18, 12, etc.). In other words, Israel is called "the Jews" insofar as she rejects the Son of God and interprets the Old Testament history recorded in the scriptures apart from the spiritual reality to which it points. "The Jews" may be called externalists, because they absolutize the external manna miracle and giving of Torah in the past and make them self-sufficient as ends in themselves. In the words of 9, 22.28.39-41 the "disciples of Moses" in the synagogue who saw became blind.

The contrasting group to those who saw and yet did not believe (6, 36) is pictured in 6, 37-40, especially in v. 40: "every one who sees the Son and believes in him". Who are these who see and believe? They are those who are given (transferred) from the Father to the Son (vv. 37.39). God's elect ones who belong to Him are the ones who have the vision of the Son (and the Father) and accept his claim and put their trust in him. John 6, 44-46 expresses the same idea: those who belong to God and are "drawn" by Him, have had their true Sinai experience and "heard" from God. Therefore they are prepared for coming to the Son who is the only mediator of the vision of God.[1]

John seems here to have abandoned the idea that the historical Israel is the chosen people of God for the more general idea of an elect or predestined group of people outside Israel. Such a conclusion, however, is hardly correct, as can be seen from John's understanding of the ones given by the Father to the Son. It is important that Nathanael, "an Israelite indeed", is the type for those given by God, since his name means "God gives" or "God has given" (1, 45-51). And John 17 adds the information that those given to the Son by the Father (17, 2. 6. 9) consist of the disciples and all who will believe in the Son through their word (17, 20). Parallel distinctions in John, as "this fold" and "other sheep that are not of this fold" (10, 16) and "the nation" together with "the children of God who are scattered abroad" (11, 51-52), show that Nathanael represents the elect ones within the nation of Israel and all those chosen from outside Israel shall be gathered together with them.[2]

---

[1] See pp. 150, 160-161, 162.
[2] See further discussion of these and similar ideas in John in N. A. Dahl, *Current Issues* (ed. W. Klassen and G. F. Snyder), pp. 124-142.

Hence, the people of Israel has been divided into two groups. They are "Jews" insofar as they make the scriptural event of the manna miracle and the giving of Torah at Sinai self-sufficient in themselves and therefore reject their true spiritual meaning, the Son of God. They have seen, and yet they do not believe (6, 36). On the other hand are the true Israelites, typified in Nathanael, who recognize the right meaning to which the scriptural events point, and therefore also accept the Son of God. They are given to the Son by the Father and they see the Son and believe in him (6, 37-40; cf. 6, 44-46). All God's chosen ones outside Israel join together with the true Israelites to have the same vision.

Philo again and again describes Israel as the nation which sees God, because etymologically the very name Israel means "he who sees God".[1] Both to Philo and John the vision belongs to the spiritual sphere. Philo ties it, however, to the empirical Jewish nation,[2] whereas John makes the vision refer to the elect ones within (the true Israelites) and outside (God's children abroad) the empirical Jewish nation.

John's affinities to the Merkabah mysticism are especially apparent in connection with the idea of the vision of God. Thus the thought that the heavenly Son (and agent) of God is the One who has seen God, John 1, 18 and 6, 46, is a striking parallel to the idea of Israel as a heavenly figure, "he who sees God." Both Philo (Conf. 145-147) and a gnostic text from Nag Hammadi provide evidence for this Jewish concept. Of special interest is the gnostic text in which traditions from Merkabah mysticism and gnostic ideas are closely interwoven.[3] Furthermore, John's idea that the vision of God mediated through the Son is the true meaning of the theophany at Sinai in the past may be compared with the idea that in the Merkabah men could participate in the meal (Ex. 24, 11) and the ascent at Sinai.[4]

---

[1] See p. 115, nn. 1 and 2.
[2] See pp. 116-118.
[3] See the gnostic text No. 40 discussed and partly translated by J. Doresse, *The Secret Books of the Egyptian Gnostics*, New York 1960, p. 167: "Near to Sabaoth stands a first-born who is named Israel, "the man who sees God." Cf. also pp. 176 f. The text shows influence from Jewish Merkabah traditions. More details and references in N. A. Dahl, *Current Issues* (ed. W. Klassen and G. F. Snyder), p. 136, nn. 21, 22.
[4] See Hagigah 14b. Cf. G. G. Scholem, *Major Trends*, p. 9: "To the mystic, the original act of Revelation to the community—the, as it were, public revelation of Mount Sinai, to take one instance—appears as something

Scholars, generally, have not interpreted John's understanding of vision and disbelief/belief (6, 36.40) against the background of the theophanic events and the appearance of the Son of God in the history of Israel. Instead, they limit the scope to an external and inadequate seeing of the Son in contrast to a true vision of the Son.[1] More to the point is the interpretation by Bauer, who rightly thinks that John 6, 36 deals with the unbelief of the Jews. He finds, however, that this idea does not fit into the thoughts of the discourse, and suggests that vv. 36-40 may be a secondary addition.[2]

As to "the Jews" the viewpoints range from Bultmann's idea that they represent "the world" in its hostility to God and do not refer to the empirical Jewish nation,—to the viewpoint of Lütgert and Bornhäuser that they represent the group that is faithful to the Torah within Israel.[3] The analysis of John 6 given here supports Dahl, who bases his interpretation on the idea that Israel is the center of the world: the world's enmity, opposition to God, gets its concentrated expression through the Jews because in their history God had revealed himself.[4] Dahl sees, further, that Nathanael is the representative of the true Israelites with whom shall be united those who belong to God outside Israel. He adds, moreover, that Paul in some respects has a similar conception: the kernel of the Church is those Israelites who believe in Christ (Rom. 11, 16-22; Eph. 2, 11-22).[5]

---

whose true meaning has yet to unfold itself; the secret revelation is to him the real and decisive one."

[1] R. Bultmann, *Evangelium*, p. 173 and C. K. Barrett, *St. John*, p. 243: external and materialistic understanding of the feeding miracle. H. Odeberg, *The Fourth Gospel*, pp. 257, 263: The corruption of man's own inclination causes him to shut himself against the spiritual world; although he sees externally he does not really see. C. H. Dodd, *The Interpretation*, pp. 185-186, 337, n. 2: mere physical vision in contrast to the life-giving vision of faith.

[2] W. Bauer, *Das Johannes-Evangelium*, p. 93.

[3] R. Bultmann, *Evangelium*, pp. 59-60; W. Lütgert, "Die Juden im Johannes-evangelium," *Neutestamentliche Studien G. Heinrici zu seinem 70. Geburtstag*, Leipzig 1914, pp. 147-154, and K. Bornhäuser, *Das Johannes-evangelium, eine Missionsschrift für Israel*, BFchrTh, Ser. 2, XV, Gütersloh 1928, pp. 19-23.

[4] N. A. Dahl, *Current Issues* (ed. W. Klassen and G. F. Snyder), pp. 129, 135.—J. Jocz, "Die Juden im Johannesevangelium," *Judaica* IX, 1953, pp. 129-142, has a similar viewpoint, but develops it with less precision: "the Jews" are those of Israel who do not believe in the Christ, while those who believe, whether Jews or pagans, are the true Israel and not "Jews" in the Johannine sense.

[5] N. A. Dahl, *Current Issues* (ed. W. Klassen and G. F. Snyder), pp. 136-137.

Recent attempts by Robinson, van Unnik and van Hartingsveld seek to interpret John within the context of Judaism only. According to them, the Gospel is addressed to the Jews of the Diaspora. These scholars, however, discuss inadequately John's concept of election and of the relationship between "the Jews" and "the world". A thorough analysis of the points would have shown that the distinction between Judaism in Palestine and in the Diaspora provides an insufficient understanding of John's ideas and purpose.[1]

Perishable and imperishable food; flesh and spirit

There is a hermeneutical principle implied in the midrashic exposition of John 6, 31 ff.: an Old Testament passage ("Bread from heaven he gave them to eat", v. 31b) shall not be interpreted within its own external meaning of the past ("not Moses gave you the bread from heaven", v. 32b), but on the basis of the present spiritual reality to which it points ("but my Father gives you the true bread from heaven", v. 32b). Again John 6, 31 ff. elaborates ideas in 5, 37-47, since the same hermeneutical principle is stated in 5, 39-40: the scriptures do not contain their true meaning in themselves; their meaning is rather found in the Son to which they bear witness.

Furthermore, John develops this hermeneutical principle into a theological one, and as such he applies it both to the works of Jesus and to anthropology. A conditioned dualism follows as a logical consequence of the distinction between the external and spiritual spheres: If the external factors are made self-sufficient and are used against the spiritual sphere, then the external sphere is misused for evil. If, on the other hand, these external factors are used to point beyond themselves to the spiritual reality of the Son, then they serve their proper and good function.

The dualistic tension between the external and spiritual spheres is illustrated in John 6, 26-27: "you seek me, not because you saw signs, but because you ate your fill of the loaves. Do not labor

---

[1] J. A. T. Robinson, "The Destination and Purpose of St. John's Gospel," *NTSt* VI, 1959/60, pp. 117-131; W. C. van Unnik, "The Purpose of St. John's Gospel," in *The Gospels Reconsidered. A Selection of Papers read at the International Congress on the Four Gospels in 1957*, Oxford 1960, pp. 167-196; L. van Hartingsveld, *Die Eschatologie*. See the convincing criticism of Robinson's and van Unnik's thesis by R. Schnackenburg, "Die Messiasfrage im Johannesevangelium," *Neutestamentliche Aufsätze*. Festschrift für Prof. J. Schmid zum 70. Geburtstag, Regensburg 1963, pp. 240-264.

for the food which perishes, but for the food which endures to eternal life." The external event of the feeding miracle (6, 1-14) was meant to point beyond itself to the spiritual food which endures to eternal life, but the people distorted it by thinking that the meal of the perishable food had its end and meaning in itself.[1]

Significantly enough, this interpretation of the feeding miracle makes it an integral part of the thoughts which bind 5, 36-47 and 6, 31-58 together, since the feeding miracle offers an example of the works mentioned in 5, 36: "for the works which the Father has granted me to accomplish, these very works which I am doing, bear me witness that the Father has sent me." [2] The works (5, 36), exemplified with the feeding miracle (6, 1 ff.), and the scriptures (5, 39-40), exemplified with the exposition of the quotation about the manna (6, 31 ff.), are two independent and parallel witnesses to the Son.[3] The manna miracle is therefore not a type in the past which is fulfilled in the present by the feeding miracle, as many scholars believe.[4] If the term type is to be used, the manna miracle and the feeding miracle are two independent and external types both of which are fulfilled in the spiritual sphere of the Son of God.

Whereas the preceding context of the homily of John 6, 31-58 provided illustration for external and spiritual interpretations of the

---

[1] The same understanding of the feeding miracle, John 6, 1-14, is indicated in vv. 15-21. According to v. 15, the feeding miracle brought the people to the non-spiritual and external wish to make Jesus king. For the disciples, on the other hand, it resulted in a theophanic encounter with the Son of God, vv. 16-21.

[2] The sequence of chs. 5 and 6 is therefore not due to dislocation. See above, p. 152, n. 2. The term "works", ἔργα, John 5, 36; 9, 3; 10, 25.32.37 f.; 14, 10-11, and in singular, 4, 34; 7, 21, refers primarily to the miracles of Jesus both as external manifestations and spiritual activity by the Son on behalf of the Father. At some places, e.g. John 4, 34, the concept may have the more comprehensive meaning of the mission of the Son in its totality.— See C. K. Barrett, *St. John*, p. 63, and his comments made to the passages concerned.

[3] The homily on the manna, John 6, 31 ff., is therefore not a discourse which draws out the symbolic significance of the narrative about the feeding miracle, as C. H. Dodd (*The Interpretation*, pp. 333 ff.) thinks. In spite of the failure of R. Bultmann's analysis of John 6 (*Evangelium*, pp. 155 ff. and 161 ff.) he is therefore right in stressing that in the discourse on the manna ideas are developed independently of the feeding miracle.

[4] Against the typological interpretations attempted by H. Ludin Jansen, "Typologien i Johannesevangeliet," *NTT* XLIX, 1948, pp. 144-158; H. Sahlin, *Zur Typologie des Johannesevangeliums*, *AUU* 1950: IV, Uppsala 1950, pp. 21-25; B. Gärtner, *Passover*, pp. 17-18; etc.

works of Jesus, the context following after the homily shows that the concept of the external and spiritual spheres are applied to anthropology. John 6, 63 is the key word:

It is the spirit (τὸ πνεῦμα) that gives life,
the flesh (ἡ σάρξ) is of no avail (ὠφελεῖ οὐδέν).

A close parallel occurs in 3, 6:

That which is born of flesh is flesh.
and that which is born of the Spirit is spirit.

Besides the term "flesh" (σάρξ, 1, 14; 3, 6; 6, 51.52.63; 17, 2) John also has the expression "flesh and blood" (σάρξ καὶ αἷμα, 6, 53. 54.55; cf. 1, 13). These terms do not refer to the lower (e.g. physical) part of man within a dichotomic anthropology, but to man as a whole. John here employs concepts from Old Testament and Judaism. In Judaism the expression "flesh and blood" (בשר ודם) signifies man and the sphere of his activity in contrast to God and heavenly powers and the sphere of their activity.[1]

John has interpreted these ideas within the thought-category of spiritual and external spheres. To the spiritual sphere belong God (1, 13), Logos (1, 14), the Son (17, 1-2), the spirit (3, 6; 6, 63), spiritual and divine (re)birth (1, 13; 3, 6) and life-giving power (6, 63). To the external sphere of man and his activity, John lists mainly the fact of human birth from a woman (1, 13; 3, 4.6) in connection with his characterization of man as flesh.

There is no dualism between the two spheres as such, but rather a sharp distinction. Rightly understood, the external sphere of man as flesh points to the spiritual sphere, as can be seen from the parallellism between the external and spiritual births (3, 3-7). Man and his activity, however, are ineffective in producing any life-giving effects in the spiritual sphere, just because they belong to the external sphere (6, 63).[2]

---

[1] See Sirach 14, 18; 17, 31; Nazir 9, 5; Sotah 8, 1, and the text from Ex. R. 25, 6 (cf. Mos. I 201-202) analysed on p. 10; other rabbinic evidences in Str.-B. I, pp. 141, 725-726, 730-731, etc.; A. Schlatter, *Der Evangelist Matthäus*, pp. 108, 230, 505. See also J. Jeremias, *The Eucharistic Words*, p. 143, nn. 4, 5.—In the New Testament: Matt. 16, 17; 1 Cor. 15, 50; Gal. 1, 16; Eph. 6, 12; Hebr. 2, 14.—For the use of the term flesh alone, see especially A. Schlatter, *Der Evangelist Johannes*, pp. 22-23, 318.—E. Schweizer, πνεῦμα κτλ, *ThWb* VI, p. 391, n. 353, points out that the distinction between flesh and spirit as two different spheres has determined the LXX translation of Num. 16, 22 and 27, 16: "the God of the spirits of all flesh" has been translated into "the God of the spirits *and* all flesh".

[2] See especially C. K. Barrett, *St. John*, p. 175 on John 3, 6 and p. 350

Philo makes a similar distinction between the external earthly sphere and the heavenly and spiritual sphere (Mut. 258-260). There is a certain parallelism between the spheres, because Philo speaks about both bread from earth and bread from heaven. But he puts the main emphasis on the difference between the human effort of producing bread on the earthly level and God's exclusive self-acting in showering manna on the heavenly level. The main difference between John and Philo at this point is that John understands man in his totality in the external sphere of flesh, whereas Philo follows a dichotomic anthropology and links the spiritual sphere to the souls of man.[1]

The following lists of the external and spiritual factors in John 5, 36-6, 63 will summarize this discussion. The idea of the external sphere is applied to

A. the scriptures:
 1. the scriptures, misunderstood as having life in themselves (5, 39).
 2. the scriptural passage about the bread from heaven, misunderstood as only referring to the manna miracle and the giving of the Torah in the past (6, 31-32.49.58).

B. the works assigned to the Son:
 1. (his works misunderstood as having their end in themselves, and not understood as witness; implied in 5, 36).
 2. the feeding miracle, misunderstood as being performed to fill the stomachs of the people,—as food which perishes (6, 1-14.26-27)

C. man and his activity:
 1. "the flesh is of no avail" (6, 63)

The idea of the spiritual sphere is connected with

A. the scriptures:
 1. the Son and agent of God, who brings life, to whom the external scriptures, rightly understood, bear witness (5, 38-40)
 2. the true bread from heaven which the Father gives, the same as the Son and agent of the Father; the scriptural passage about the bread/Torah, properly understood, points to this lifegiving reality (6, 31-33.38, etc.)

---

for comment on the phrase ὠφελεῖτε οὐδέν in 12, 19 with reference to 6, 63. Barrett finds the meaning to be "effecting nothing". Cf. E. M. Sidebottom, *The Christ*, pp. 128-129.

[1] Cf. pp. 118 ff.

B. the works assigned to the Son:
  1. the Son and his commission from the Father, to whom his works, correctly understood, bear witness (5, 36)
  2. the food which endures to eternal life, to which the external feeding miracle, rightly understood, points (6, 1-14.26-27).

C. man and his activity:
  1. "It is the spirit that gives life", a spiritual reality sharply distinct from the external sphere of man (6, 63); (the sphere of man can, however, point to the spiritual sphere, as seen from John's interpretation of human and spiritual births, 3, 3-8).

Since John applies the distinction between the external and the spiritual spheres not only to the scriptures and the works of Jesus, but to anthropology as well, the danger of docetic Christology is a logical consequence. Jesus, belonging to the ineffective external sphere of man as "flesh", could only point to and bear witness to the spiritual sphere of the Son of God, but not be the Son of God himself.

It is of great importance that 1 and 2 John give clear evidence for a docetic distinction: the divine and spiritual figure of the Son of God and the Christ cannot belong to the external sphere of "the flesh" and be identical with the historical person Jesus. The answer in 1 John 2, 22; 4, 2.3.15; 5, 1.5 and 2 John v. 7 is that the Son of God is, indeed, a man in "flesh", namely Jesus. The answer of the homily of John 6, 31-32 is the same. In Jesus as "flesh and blood" the distinction between the external and the spiritual spheres have been removed: "The Word became flesh", John 1, 14.

Incarnation proves docetic spiritualists to be externalists

There are some inconsistencies in the homily of John 6, 31-58, and the problem of docetic Christology gives a clue to their solution. One of the inconsistencies becomes evident when 6, 34 is compared with 6, 25-27. Although the people according to 6, 25-27 understood the feeding miracle in an external way as only perishable food, in 6, 34 they nevertheless accept the spiritual interpretation of the bread from heaven (6, 32-33) and ask: "Lord, give us this bread always."

In a similar way there is a contradiction between 6, 41-42 and 5, 39. When "the Jews" thought that "eternal life" was found within the external scriptures themselves (5, 39), their exegetical objection to the interpretation of the bread from heaven should have been something like this: The true bread, which gives life, does not refer to any spiritual reality beyond the boundaries of the external Torah, since life is found in Torah itself. Instead, according to 6, 41-42, "the Jews" accept the spiritual understanding of the bread from heaven, but deny that it is identical with Jesus, the son of Joseph, who belongs to the external sphere.

Finally, the same inconsistency occurs when 6, 52 is compared with 6, 32a: On the basis of the „Jewish" interpretation that the bread from heaven referred to the (external) manna miracle and the giving of the Torah in the past (v. 32a), the question of "the Jews" could have been: How can bread exist outside the Torah and the concrete events recorded in it? The question in 6, 52, however, runs very differently: "How can this man give us flesh to eat?"

How can these inconsistencies be explained? The answer is that John tries to show that the docetic spiritualists in the Church are like "Jewish" externalists, because both reject the Incarnate One as the only mediator between God and man. This interpretation is supported by the fact that according to 6, 41 "the Jews murmured", but 6, 60-61 tells that the "disciples murmured". The disciples were just like the Jews in their objection.

The people (and the docetists) ask for the spiritual bread from heaven (6, 34) because it is not yet identified with the earthly Jesus, and they therefore thought it could be found outside the Incarnate One. But as soon as Jesus says "I am the bread of life" (6, 35), he not only echoes the self predication of wisdom, but he also identifies the bread with himself. In their self assertion, "the Jews" used the Torah to reject Jesus, and consequently it is also a "Jewish" exegesis to say (as do the docetists) that the spiritual bread from heaven cannot be one and the same with Jesus, the son of Joseph, and him as a historical being, "flesh" and "blood" (6, 41-42.52 ff.).

Over against "the Jews" and "the disciples" who reject Jesus, John pictures God's elected Israelites and disciples who understand that the bread from heaven is, indeed, identical with Jesus in "flesh". Therefore 6, 65 refers to the true disciples who are transferred to the Incarnate Son, just as 6, 37.39.44 tells about the true Israelites transferred and given from the Father to the Son.

Hence, John 6 reflects the actual situation in the Johannine Church. The threat comes from gnostic docetism. John follows the gnostic line of thinking to a large extent, since the emphasis on the spiritual meaning of the scriptures leads in a logical way to a spiritual and docetic Christology. It is therefore most probable that 6, 31-33 (not external, but spiritual bread) illustrates the midrashic exegesis employed by the gnostics in the Johannine Church.[1] John agrees with exposition, but makes one basic modification: the spiritual bread is identical with Jesus, the Son of Joseph.

The gnostic docetism undercut with necessity the exclusive connection between Jesus and the vision of God, and gave the vision of the spiritual realities a more general character. John 6, 46 criticizes this relativism by emphasizing that the Son of God, being identical with Jesus in flesh, is the only on who has seen God and the only one who can mediate this vision.[2]

The anti-docetic polemic in 1 and 2 John shows that docetists existed in the Johannine environment. Dahl has pointed out that these gnostics seem to be much of the same type as those of the Ignatian letters. The gnostics criticized by Ignatius developed also their spiritualistic and docetic Christology from exegesis of the Old Testament. They thereby rejected the Incarnate One. Ignatius, moreover, labelled these ideas "Jewish".[3]

The terms of "flesh" (John 6, 51-52) and "flesh and blood" (6, 53.54.55.56), then, mean man and his activity as a historical being and thus only elaborate the explicit reference to Jesus, the son of Joseph in 6, 42. Correspondingly, in 1, 14 the term, "flesh", is used and in 1, 17 this human being is specified as "Jesus Christ". Some of the stages in Jesus' career are indicated in 6, 31-58: 1) the incarnation, e.g. vv. 42-43 ("I have come down"—as Jesus); 2) Jesus as the son of Joseph, whose parents were well known in Galilee (v. 42), and 3) his death, where Jesus says that he will give himself as human being ("flesh") for the life of the world (v. 51).[4]

All the spiritual concepts of the homily, then, are tied to the

---

[1] The docetists may also have used the quotation from Is. 54, 13, cited in John 6, 45, to support their own spiritual exegesis and revelations: they were taught by God directly.
[2] The same polemic is found in John 1, 18 and 3, 13. See N. A. Dahl, *Current Issues* (ed. W. Klassen and G. F. Snyder), p. 141.
[3] *Ibid.*, p. 142, n. 28. Dahl refers to E. Molland, "The Heretics Combatted by Ignatius of Antioch," *JEH* V, 1954, pp. 1-6.
[4] The term "the Son of Man" added to the word pair of "flesh" and "blood" in John 6, 53 comprises both the spiritual and heavenly aspect and

incarnation. From the traditions about the manna, some of these concepts are: bread from heaven, food and drink and eat and drink;[1] from the traditions about Torah come ideas as the giving of life and the theophanic vision of God;[2] the traditions of wisdom have contributed the concepts of invitation and of eating and drinking and of self predication (cf. "I am the bread of life", v. 35, etc.);[3] and together with the idea of the Son as the agent of the Father goes the concepts of election, faith, and the "juridical mysticism" by which the Son fully represents the Father;[4] and finally come the eschatological concepts of eternal life, no hunger or thirst, etc.[5] This whole spiritual sphere is one with Jesus, as "flesh and blood", as said in 6, 51: "the [spiritual] bread...is my flesh".

The cultic background of John's thoughts are also indicated by the terms "flesh and blood": the giving of the flesh for the world (6, 51) and eating the flesh and drinking the blood (6, 52 ff.) draw on eucharistic terminology and ideas.[6] The purpose is not to give doctrinal instruction about the eucharist as such, but rather to use the eucharistic ideas to throw light upon the reality of the incarnation. Since ideas about eating and drinking of manna, the well, and of wisdom are woven into the eucharistic terminology, John's point can be formulated in this way: the eating and drinking in the eucharist mean eating and drinking the Son as manna and water from the well and also as God's wisdom; to eat and drink in this way, however, is not a spiritual experience apart from Jesus as "flesh and blood". Eating and drinking in the eucharist means that the believers become united with the historical Jesus. They participate in Jesus' historical existence, the life of the Incarnate One. This identification of "flesh" and "blood" (6, 53-56) with Jesus Christ as person is supported by 6, 57, "he who eats *me*."

---

the external and human aspect of John's Christology. The following three elements seem to form the background of the Johannine Son of Man: the apocalyptic Son of Man of Daniel 7, 13-14 (cf. John 5, 27); the human figure in the Merkabah passage of Ezech. 1, 26; and also Chritian re-interpretation of the term. See indications for such an interpretation in N. A. Dahl, *Current Issues* (ed. W. Klassen and G. F. Snyder), pp. 136-137 and 141, n. 27.

[1] See pp. 20-22.
[2] See pp. 148-154.
[3] See pp. 154-158.
[4] See pp. 158-164.
[5] See pp. 165-172.
[6] See pp. 90-92.

John, therefore, moves directly from the historical Jesus, the son of Joseph, whose parents were known in Galilee, to this same Jesus being encountered in the Church in a cultic way. John, however, is aware of a distinction between the period of the Incarnate Son before his return to the Father through death and resurrection and the post-resurrection period of the Church. In the period of the Church after his departure, the docetic danger will be even worse, because of the scandalon of his death. This distinction becomes clear when 6, 43 is combined with 6, 61-62: If the Jews/disciples take offense in the period of the Incarnate One who has come down from heaven, the offense will even be greater when, through death, he has ascended to the place where he was before.[1]

So far the concept of "flesh" and "flesh and blood" in 6, 51 ff. have been discussed while ignoring the use of "flesh" in 6, 63, which seems to express a contradicting idea. Although 6, 51 says that the spiritual bread is external flesh, the sharp distinction between the sphere of flesh and the sphere of the spirit is maintained in 6, 63. The solution to this problem is that 6, 63 reports the kind of docetic anthropology which the homily of 6, 31-58 combats. John 6, 63 itself supports this interpretation, since the sentence "the words that I have spoken to you are spirit and life" gives a Christological modification to the docetic anthropology. A paraphrase of the whole verse is as follows:

> Although it is true, as claimed by the docetists,[2] that the life-giving activity belongs to the spiritual sphere, and the human sphere and the activity of man are ineffective in this respect, the words that *I*, Jesus, the Incarnate One, have spoken are spirit and life in spite of the fact that I am flesh.

The emphatic "I" (ἐγώ) alludes therefore to the midrashic formula of "Ego eimi" (6, 35.41.48.51), which identifies the spiritual

---

[1] See the similar interpretation of John 6, 62 in R. Bultmann, *Evangelium*, p. 341; E. Schweizer, *EvTh* XII, 1952/53, p. 357.—Other scholars defend the opposite point of view, namely, that Jesus' death will not sharpen but rather remove the offence: W. Bauer, *Das Johannes-Evangelium*, p. 97; E. C. Hoskyns, *The Fourth Gospel*, pp. 300-301; R. H. Strachan, *The Fourth Gospel*, p. 197, etc.

[2] Thus the contrast between flesh and spirit in John 6, 63 reproduces ideas propagated by the gnostic docetists, just as does the distinction in 6, 32 between the external bread of Moses of the past and the spiritual bread of God in the present. Cf. R. Bultmann, *Evangelium*, p. 341, n. 9, who finds that 6, 63a sounds like a quotation.

bread with the Jesus of flesh and blood. Peter expresses the same idea when he confesses that the Jesus of flesh is the spiritual and divine being and has the words of eternal life (6, 66 ff.).

The reference to Jesus' words (6, 63.68) supplement the reference to the eucharist (6, 51 ff.): Just as the Christians in the time of the Church are united with the Incarnate One by means of the eucharist, so they also hear his words of life, as illustrated by the homily of 6, 31-58. Hence, there is no conflict between Word and Sacrament in John 6, because both lead to the Incarnate One.[1]

In a way corresponding to that of John, Philo (Mut. 253-263) interprets manna and wisdom in a cultic context, since they are present especially on the Sabbath day. Manna and wisdom are thus tied to the laws of Moses.[2] There are, however, two important differences to be noticed. Whereas Philo binds manna and wisdom to the laws of Moses, John connects them with Jesus about whom Moses spoke. And to Philo the manna and wisdom describe God's cosmic activity reaching for man in the cult, but according to John, the cultic meal of the eucharist unites man with God's activity in history, in Jesus, the Incarnate One. Paul also associates the manna and the water of the well with the eucharist in 1 Cor. 10, 3.[3]

In connection with the homily of John 6, 31-58, a final question is necessary: John has overcome the threat of docetic Christology, but has he also been able to solve the underlying problem of a docetic anthropology? Does regenerated man still live under the conditions of man as "flesh"? The answer is, Yes. As "flesh" he still must die, but the resurrection of life when those in the tombs shall come out (5, 28-29) shows that the life-giving activity of the spirit also includes man's sphere of "flesh". Hence, the references to the resurrection at the last day (6, 39.40.44.54) are integral and necessary parts of John's thinking and draws the line from anti-docetic Christology to an anti-docetic anthropology and soteriology.

---

[1] E. Lohse, "Wort und Sakrament in Johannesevangelium," *NTSt* VII, 1960/61, pp. 110-125, discusses John on the basis of the later tension between Word and Sacrament, and finds that the aspect of the Word is central to this thinking. The Sacrament only makes the Word more articulate, and the materialistic teaching of the eucharist in John 6, 51b-58 shows that this passage is an interpolation.

[2] See pp. 112-114.

[3] See H. Lietzmann, *An die Korinther I-II*, HNT IX, 4th ed., (by W. G. Kümmel), Tübingen 1949, p. 44; cf. J. Jeremias, *The Eucharistic Words*, pp. 157-158.

At the last day, the distinction between flesh and spirit, drawn sharply in 6, 63, will finally be removed, and the spiritual and external spheres will be one and the same.

The eucharistic references in John 6 are among the questions most debated by New Testament scholars. The following critical survey must therefore be limited to the most typical interpretations which have been suggested.[1] Odeberg attempts a very spiritualistic exegesis which approaches a docetic Christology and makes him deny any reference to the eucharist in John 6, 51-58. The term "flesh and blood" (vv. 53 ff.) only expresses the fact that the spiritual organism is as real as the earthly organism. The word "flesh" in v. 51, however, has a different meaning, since it says directly that "the bread" is "flesh". This verse refers therefore to the incarnation: Jesus' earthly appearance, his σάρξ, may be defined as the vehicle for the spiritual reality. By this vehicle Jesus speaks words that are received by the ears and minds of earthly men.[2]

More widespread is the approach which develops a sharp contrast between personal union with Jesus Christ through faith and a materialistic and mechanical sacramentalism. Among the recent champions of this viewpoint are Bultmann, Bornkamm and Lohse. They all find that John 6, 51b-58, in contrast to the preceding section, advocates the eucharist as φάρμακον ἀθανασίας in the Ignatian sense and therefore must be an interpolation. And the word-pair, "flesh" and "blood", which is also used by Ignatius, characterizes the elements of the eucharist in a rather materialistic way. Lohse explicitly bases his interpretation on the general tension between Word and Sacrament in the Church.[3]

The main objection to these viewpoints is that they fail to take account of the idiomatic character of the expression "flesh and blood" which is a typical Jewish term for man as distinct from God.

---

[1] See also surveys in Ph.-Menoud, *L'évangile de Jean*, pp. 53-54; C. Vollert, "The Eucharist: Quest for Insights from Scripture," *ThSt* XXIII 1962, pp. 183-206.

[2] H. Odeberg, *The Fourth Gospel*, pp. 260-261.

[3] R. Bultmann, *Evangelium*, pp. 162, 174-176; *Theology* I, pp. 147 f.; G. Bornkamm, *ZNW* XLVII, 1956, pp. 161-169; E. Lohse, *NTSt* VII, 1960/61, pp. 110-125. Cf. A. Wikenhauser, *Das Evangelium nach Johannes*, *RNT* IV, 2nd ed., Regensburg 1957, pp. 135-136. See further above on p. 25. Against these scholars should also be mentioned that the idea of faith is absent not only in John 6, 51b-58, but in the larger section of vv. 49-58. The reason is, that the word "to eat" is in the center of the midrashic exposition from v. 49 and onwards. See p. 35.

These scholars also overlook the fact that the anti-docetic polemic ties the reference to Jesus as son of Joseph (6, 42) and "flesh" and "blood" (6, 51 ff.) together. John's answer to the docetic threat is therefore not sacramental materialism, but a stress on Jesus as a historical man, "the Word became flesh" (1, 14). In his anti-docetic thinking John therefore follows Jewish thought categories more closely than Ignatius. Moreover, they have not seen that ideas from wisdom/Torah, manna/the well and the Son as God's agent are woven into 6, 51b-58, just as in 6, 31-51a. Thus, verse 55 does not, as Bultmann, Bornkamm and Lohse think, certify that Jesus' flesh and blood are real food and drink, but instead restates the ideas from vv. 35 and 41-42 by saying that Jesus as "flesh and blood" is the spiritual manna and the spiritual water from the well.[1] These ideas, of course, are different from the suggested "medicine of immortality".

Another group of scholars—Cullmann, Corell, Wilkens, and Léon-Dufour—not only regard John 6, 51b-58 an integral part of the larger discourse, but find in it the central idea. According to Cullmann, the main point of the discourse on the manna (6, 26-65) is the unity between the historical appearance of Jesus and the presence of the risen Christ in the eucharist of the church. Subordinate to this basic motive, John also wants to combat docetic heresy and therefore puts the emphasis on the material character of the sacrament. The life-giving activity of the spirit (6, 63) and faith must, however, go together with the eating of the flesh.[2]

Cullmann and the other sacramentalists, however, bring to the foreground that which really forms the background for John 6. The homily of 6, 31-58 and its context are not, as Cullmann thinks, intended to give eucharistic teaching in a direct way.[3] Terms and

---

[1] See p. 92.

[2] O. Cullmann, *Early Christian Worship*, pp. 93-102. A. Correll, *Consummatum Est*, pp. 63-67, draws heavily on Cullmann's study and thinks that to John the eucharist is the continuation of the incarnation. W. Wilkens, *Die Entstehungsgeschichte des vierten Evangeliums*, pp. 20-24, stresses that "flesh" and "blood" give a very materialistic characterization of the eucharistic elements. Faith is, however, still a condition for receiving the blessings of the eucharist.—X. Léon-Dufour, *RSR* XLVI 1958, pp. 481-523, thinks that Jesus' discourse on the bread of life simultaneously deals with eating by faith and eating by the sacrament of the eucharist. Cf. a similar line of thinking in E. C. Hoskyns, *The Fourth Gospel*, pp. 304-307.

[3] Cf. R. Schnackenburg, "Die Sakramante im Johannesevangelium," *Sacra Pagina* II, Paris 1959, pp. 239-243, who holds a moderate Roman

phrases from eucharistic and other traditions are rather employed to throw light upon the historical basis of Christology against gnostic docetism. The use of eucharistic traditions which John makes here, of course, presupposes that he has a high regard for the eucharist itself.

The importance of the anti-docetic motive in John 6 has been emphasized by Schweizer and indicated by Dahl. Schweizer rejects, with some hesitation, the theory that 6, 51b-58 is an interpolation, and formulates the main concern of the passage in this way: the meaning of the eucharist is to guarantee the reality of the incarnation, even to the death on the cross, against all docetic spiritualization. "Flesh" and "flesh and blood" refer here to the Incarnate One, and it is not stated in John that the "flesh" of Jesus is identified with the element of the eucharist. Instead, eucharist is a witness to the incarnation. Schweizer correctly observes that already 6, 41-42 betrays an anti-docetic tendency, when the identification of the spiritual bread with Jesus is questioned by the Jews.[1]

The interpretation offered here is in general agreement with that of Schweizer and Dahl. The new insight is that ideas from traditions about manna and the well, and wisdom and halakhic principles of agency have been interwoven with the eucharistic phrases in a midrashic paraphrase. These ideas are associated with eating of the flesh and drinking of the blood.

But Schweizer's interpretation of John 6, 63 is incorrect. Together with many other scholars he regards this verse as a needed modification of the endearing words about eating flesh and drinking blood in 6, 51b-58.[2] Bornkamm rightly connects 6, 63 with the parallel statement about "flesh" and "spirit" in 3, 6 and concludes that the verse does not deal with the flesh of the Son of man (6, 53) at all. It refers instead to the contrast between human flesh and

---

Catholic position: for John the eucharist takes the salvation once performed by Jesus in incarnation and crucifixion, represents it, and applies it to all believers. The self-revelation of Jesus stands in the foreground of the Gospel; the Church and the sacraments stand in the background.

[1] E. Schweizer, *EvTh* XII, 1952/53, pp. 361-362; *ThLZ* LXXIX, 1954, col. 591; "Abendmahl," *RGG* I, 3rd ed., Tübingen 1957, col. 12; N. A. Dahl, *Current Issues* (ed. W. Klassen and G. F. Snyder), p. 142.

[2] E. Schweizer, *EvTh* XII, 1952/53, pp. 357 ff.; πνεῦμα κτλ, *ThWb* VI, pp. 439-440 and σάρξ κτλ, *ThWb* VII, pp. 140-141; "Abendmahl," *RGG* I, 3rd ed., 1957, col. 12. A survey of similar viewpoints by other scholars are given by G. Bornkamm, *ZNW* XLVII, 1956, p. 165.

divine spirit.[1] According to Bornkamm, then, 6, 63 deals with anthropology rather than Christology.

Bornkamm is correct at this point, but he errs by failing to discuss anthropology and Christology together. If he had examined them together, he would have realized that the distinction between the sphere of man and the divine sphere of the spirit in 6, 63 leads to a docetic Christology. The homily of 6, 31-58 develops an antidocetic Christology as the answer: the spiritual bread from heaven is identical with Jesus, the son of Joseph, a historical human being ("flesh and blood"), with whom the elected believers are united through the mediation of the eucharist and the words of Jesus. The docetic spiritualists, therefore, are like "Jewish" externalists, because they believe the bread from heaven to be found outside the Incarnate One. Furthermore, in the bodily resurrection at the last day (6, 39.40.44, 54) the anthropological and soteriological distinction between flesh and spirit (6, 63) will finally be removed, and the spiritual and external spheres will be one and the same.

---

[1] G. Bornkamm, *ZNW* XLVII, 1956, pp. 167-168. Bornkamm's observation that the word pair in John 6, 63 is πνεῦμα/σάρξ and not as in 6, 53 ff. σάρξ/αἷμα has no weight since "flesh and blood" is an elaborate expression for "flesh". Corresponding terms to the "flesh/spirit" in 6, 63 and 3, 6 are rather "of the flesh/of God" in 1, 13; "flesh/the Word" in 1, 14; and "flesh (and blood)/the bread" in 6, 51 ff.

PERIODICALS, SERIES, ETC.

AB	Archiv für Begriffsgeschichte, Bonn.
AMNTSU	Arbeiten und Mitteilungen aus dem neutestamentlichen Seminar zu Uppsala, Uppsala.
ASNU	Acta seminarii neotestamentici Upsaliensis, Uppsala.
AO	Der alte Orient, Leipzig.
ATA	Alttestamentliche Abhandlungen, Münster i. W.
AThANT	Abhandlungen zur Theologie des Alten und Neuen Testaments, Zürich.
AThD	Acta Theologica Danica, Aarhus.
AUL	Acta Universitatis Latviensis (Latvijas Universitates Raksti, Teologijas Fakultates Serija), Riga.
AUU	Acta Universitatis Upsaliensis, Uppsala.
AVThR	Aufsätze und Vorträge zur Theologie und Religionswissenschaft, Berlin.
BA	The Biblical Archeologist, New Haven, Conn.
BASOR	Bulletin of the American Schools of Oriental Research, New Haven, Conn.
BbB	Bonner biblische Beiträge, Bonn.
BFchrTh	Beiträge zur Förderung christlicher Theologie, Gütersloh.
BGgrPhR	Beiträge zur Geschichte der griechischen Philosophie und Religion, Berlin.
BGPhM	Beiträge zur Geschichte der Philosophie des Mittelalters, Münster i. W.
BhTh	Beiträge zur historischen Theologie, Tübingen.
BIAO	Bulletin de l'Institut français d'Archéologie Orientale, Cairo.
BSAA	Bulletin de la Société d'Archéologie d'Alexandrie, Alexandria.
BT	The Bible Translator, Amsterdam.
BWANT	Beiträge zur Wissenschaft vom Alten und Neuen Testament, Leipzig/Stuttgart/Berlin.
Cahiers	Cahiers théologiques de l'actualité protestante, Neuchâtel/Paris.
CBQ	The Catholic Biblical Quarterly, Washington, DC.
ChrW	Die Christliche Welt, Marburg.
CPJ (Tcherikover and Fuks)	Corpus Papyrorum Judaicarum I-II, ed. by V. A. Tcherikover and A. Fuks, Cambridge, Mass.
CN	Coniectanea neotestamentica, Lund.
CW	The Classical World, New York.
DTT	Dansk Teologisk Tidsskrift, Copenhagen.
EJ	Encyclopaedia Judaica, Berlin.
Entretiens	Entretiens sur l'Antiquité Classique. Fondation Hardt, Vandoeuvres/Genève.
ET	The Expository Times, Edinburgh.
EvTh	Evangelische Theologie, München.
Exp	The Expositor, London.
FRLANT	Forschungen zur Religion und Literatur des Alten und Neuen Testaments, Göttingen.
GthF	Greifswalder theologische Forschungen, Greifswald.

Gymnasium	Gymnasium. Zeitschrift für Kultur der antike und humanistische Bildung, Heidelberg.
HAAT	Kurzgefasstes, exegetisches Handbuch zu den Apokryphen des Alten Testamentes, Leipzig.
HAT	Handbuch zum Alten Testament, Tübingen.
HklAW	Handbuch der klassischen Altertums-Wissenschaft, München.
HNT	Handbuch zum Neuen Testament, Tübingen.
HCNT	Hand-Commentar zum Neuen Testament, Freiburg i. B.
Hermes	Hermes. Zeitschrift für klassische Philologie, Berlin/Wiesbaden.
HThR	The Harvard Theological Review, Cambridge, Mass.
HUCA	Hebrew Union College Annual, Cincinnati.
ICC	The International Critical Commentary, Edinburgh.
JclPh	Jahrbücher für classische Philologie, Leipzig.
JBL	Journal of Biblical Literature, Philadelphia.
JE	The Jewish Encyclopedia, NewYork/London.
JEH	Journal of Ecclesiastical History, London.
JFS	Jahresbericht des jüdisch-theologischen Seminars "Frankel'scher Stiftung", Breslau.
JHI	Journal of the History of Ideas, New York.
JJSt	Journal of Jewish Studies, London.
JNESt	Journal of Near Eastern Studies, Chicago.
JQR	Jewish Quarterly Review, Philadelphia.
JThSt	Journal of Theological Studies, Oxford.
Meyer	Kritisch-exegetischer Kommentar über das Neue Testament (Begr. von H. A. W. Meyer), Göttingen.
KT	Kröners Taschenausgabe, Leipzig.
LD	Lectio Divina, Paris.
Loeb	The Loeb Classical Library, London/New York.
MGWJ	Monatschrift für Geschichte und Wissenschaft des Judentums, Breslau.
MNTC	The Moffat New Testament Commentary, London.
MThSt	Münchener Theologische Studien. 1: Historische Abteilung, München.
NAG	Nachrichten von der Akademie (formerly: königlichen Gesellschaft) der Wissenschaften in Göttingen, Phil.-hist. Klasse, Göttingen.
NJklA	Neue Jahrbücher für das klassische Altertum Geschichte und deutsche Literatur, Leipzig/Berlin.
NT	Novum Testamentum, Leiden.
NTD	Das Neue Testament Deutsch, Göttingen.
NTSt	New Testament Studies, Cambridge.
NTT	Norsk Teologisk Tidsskrift, Oslo.
Pauly-W.	Paulys Realencyclopädie der klassischen Altertumswissenschaft, fortgeführt von Wissowa-Kroll, etc., Stuttgart.
Philologus	Philologus. Zeitschrift für das klassische Altertum, Leipzig/Berlin.
PhU	Philologische Untersuchungen, Berlin.
PSSLAa	Publications de la Société des Sciences et des Lettres d'Aarhus. Serie de Théologie. (Det laerde Selskabs Skrifter. Teologiske Skrifter), Copenhagen.
RB	Recherches Bibliques, Lyon.

RGG	Die Religion in Geschichte und Gegenwart, Tübingen.
RNT	Regensburger Neues Testament, Regensburg.
RQ	Revue de Qumran, Paris.
RSR	Recherches de Science Religieuse, Paris.
RT	Rabbinische Texte, Stuttgart.
SAB	Sitzungsberichte der Preussischen Akademie der Wissenschaften, Phil.-hist. Klasse, Berlin.
SAW	Sitzungsberichte der keiserlichen Akademie der Wissenschaften, Phil.-hist. Klasse, Wien.
SBU	Symbolae Biblicae Upsalienses, Uppsala.
SEA	Svensk Exegetisk Aarsbok, Uppsala.
SF	Studia Friburgensia, Freiburg i.d. Schweiz.
SJHLD	Schriften der jüdisch-hellenistischen Literatur in deutscher Übersetzung, Breslau.
SkrNVA	Skrifter utgitt av Det norske videnskapsakademi i Oslo. 2: hist.-fil. klasse, Oslo.
SNT	Die Schriften des Neuen Testaments, Göttingen.
SO	Symbolae Osloenses, Oslo.
StBTh	Studies in Biblical Theology, London.
STDJ	Studies on the Texts of the Desert of Judah, Leiden.
StGKA	Studien zur Geschichte und Kultur des Altertums, Paderborn.
Str.-B.	Kommentar zum Neuen Testament aus Talmud und Midrash von H. L. Strack und P. Billerbeck, München.
StVF (Arnim)	Stoicorum veterum fragmenta, coll. H. von Arnim, Leipzig.
TBA	Tübinger Beiträge zur Altertumswissenschaft, Stuttgart.
ThB	Theologische Blätter, Leipzig.
ThLZ	Theologische Literaturzeitung, Halle/Berlin.
ThR	Theologische Rundschau, Tübingen.
ThSt	Theological Studies, Baltimore, Md.
ThWb	Theologisches Wörterbuch zum Neuen Testament, ed. G. Kittel, Stuttgart.
ThZ	Theologische Zeitschrift, Basel.
TStJThS	Texts and Studies of the Jewish Theological Seminary of America, New York.
TU	Texte und Untersuchungen zur Geschichte der altchristlichen Literatur, Leipzig.
UNT	Untersuchungen zum Neuen Testament, Leipzig.
VigChr	Vigilia Christianae, Amsterdam.
WSt	Wiener Studien. Zeitschrift für klassische Philologie, Wien.
WUNT	Wissenschaftliche Untersuchungen zum Neuen Testament, Tübingen.
YJS	Yale Judaica Series, New Haven, Conn.
ZAW	Zeitschrift für die alttestamentliche Wissenschaft, Giessen/Berlin.
ZNW	Zeitschrift für die neutestamentliche Wissenschaft, Giessen/Berlin.
ZRG	Zeitschrift für Religions- und Geistesgeschichte, Köln.
ZThK	Zeitschrift für Theologie und Kirche, Tübingen.
ZvglR	Zeitschrift für vergleichende Rechtswissenschaft, Stuttgart.

REFERENCE WORKS[1]

Biblia hebraica, ed. R. Kittel, 4th ed., Stuttgart 1949.
Septuaginta, ed. A. Rahlfs, I-II, Stuttgart 1935.
Novum testamentum Graece, ed. E. Nestle, 17th ed., Stuttgart 1941.
Huck, A., Synopse der drei ersten Evangelien, 9th ed. (by H. Lietzmann), Tübingen 1936.
The Holy Bible. Revised Standard Version, New York 1953.

Flavii Josephi Opera, ed. B. Niese, I-VII, Berlin, 1887-1845.
Josephus, With an English Translation by H. St. Thackeray and R. Marcus, I-VIII, (Loeb), London 1926-1963.
Philo, With an English Translation by F. H. Colson and G. H. Whitaker, I-IX, (Loeb), London 1929-1941.
Philo. Supplements I-II, translated by R. Marcus, (Loeb), London 1953.

מדרש רבה על חמשה הומשי תורה וחמש מגילות I-V, Jerusalem 1949.
Midrash Rabbah. Translated into English with Notes, Glossary and Indices under the Editorship of H. Freedman and M. Simon, I-X, London 1939.
Mekilta de-Rabbi Ishmael. By J. Z. Lauterbach I-III, Philadelphia 1949.

Bauer, W., Griechisch-deutsches Wörterbuch zu den Schriften des Neuen Testament, 4th ed., Berlin 1952.
Bruder, C. H., Concordantiae omnium vocum Novi Testamenti Graeci, Göttingen 1913.
Gesenius, W., Hebräisches und aramäisches Handwörterbuch über das Alte Testament, (F. Buhl), 17th ed., Berlin/Göttingen/Heidelberg 1949.
Hatch, E. and Redpath, H. A., A Concordance to the Septuagint and the other Versions of the O.T. (including the apocryphal Books), I-II. Supplement, Oxford 1897-1906.
Jastrow, M., A Dictionary of the Targumim, the Talmud Babli and Yerushalmi, and the Midrashic Literature I-II, New York 1950.
Kassovsky, H. J., Concordantiae totius Mischnae I-II, Frankfurt à.M. 1927.
Leisegang, H., Indices ad Philonis Alexandrini Opera. Philonis Alexandrini Opera (ed. Cohn and Wendland) VII, Berlin 1926.
Levy, J., Wörterbuch über die Talmudim und Midraschim I-IV, 2nd ed. (by H. L. Fleischer and L. Goldschmidt), Berlin/Wien 1924.
Liddell, H. G., and Scott, R., A Greek-English Lexicon, 9th ed. (by H. Stuart Jones,etc.), Oxford 1958.
Moulton, J. H. and Milligan, G., The Vocabulary of the Greek Testament, illustrated from the papyri and other non-literary sources, London 1930.

---

[1] Books used without explicit reference being made except in special cases.

INDEX OF AUTHORS[1])

Aalen, S. *144*
Adler, M. *28 f.*, *44*, 60, 103, 108, 111, 112, 123, 125, 127, 131, 134, 135, 142
Alfonsi, L. *131*
Anderson, A. *25*
Apelt, M. *4*, 102
Aptowitzer, V. *41*, 42
Arnaldez, R. *13*, 140
Arnim, H. von *4*, *102*, *108*, 122, 123, 124, 131, 138, 195
Auerbach, L. *160*

Bacher, W. *52*, 56, *57*, *62*
Baeck, L. *56*, 147
Barrett, C. K., *3*, *27*, *29*, *38*, *40*, *42*, 74, 92, 94, 152, 153, 157, 164, 166, 167, 171, 175, 178, 180, 181
Bauer, W. *74*, *97*, 171, 178, 187, *196*
Baumbach, G. *169*, 172
Becker, H. *68*, *72*, *79*, *86*, *97*
Bell, H. I. *125*, *126*
Bentwich, N. *117*
Bernard, J. H. *97*, 171
Betz, O. *25*, 150
Billerbeck, P. *73*, *114*, *118*, 152, 155, 163, 165, 174, 181, 195
Billings, Th. H. *128*, 129, 139
Bin Gorion, M. J. *143*
Blackman, Ph. *83*, 110, 161
Blauert, H. *5*, *79*, *86*, *96*, *97*, *170*, 172
Bloch, Ph. *53*, 54, 56
Boismard, M. E. *150*
Bonsirven, J. *62*, *144*
Borgen, P. *13*, *24*, *26*, *27*, *35*, *40*, *42*, *45*
Bormann, K. *139*
Bornhäuser *178*
Bornkamm, G. *25*, 93, 189, 191, 192
Boughton, J. S. *113*

Bousset, W. *4*, *25*, *28*, *56*, 103, *143*, *171*
Bréhier, E. *103*, 105, 111, 123, 140, 146
Brown, R. E. *45*
Brownlee, W. H. *24*, 41, *76*, 83
Bruder, C. H. *196*
Buhl, F. *196*
Bultmann, R. *4*, *6*, *25*, 26, *28*, *38*, *44*, *68 f.*, 72, 74, 75, 78, 79, 85, 86, 93, 95, 96, 97, *146*, 152, *153*, 154, 157, 161, *164*, 166, 167, 170, *171*, 174, 178, 180, 187, 189
Bury, R. G. *129*
Burney, C. F. *27*, 40, 42, 64, 84

Capelle, W. *131*, *132*
Carpenter, J. E. *25*
Charles, R. H. *17*, *144*
Cherniss, H. *104*
Cohen, H. *139*
Cohn, L. *15*, *28*, 29, 60, 102, 103, 106, 108, 111, 112, 123, 125, 127, 131, 134, 135, *139*, 142, 196
Cohn, M. *160*, 162
Colson, F. H. *44*, *55*, *81*, *101*, *102*, 103, 105, 106, 108, 109, 112, 115, 116, 120, 123, 124, 125, 129, 130, 134, 135, 142, 196
Corell, A. *171*, 174, 190
Cullmann, O. *174*, 190

Dahl, N. A. *13*, *24*, *42*, *45*, *64*, *115*, 117, 118, *129*, 130, 134, 135, *144*, 147, 149, 150, 151, 152, 154, 164, 176, 177, 178, 185, 186, 191
Daniélou, J. *19*, 60
Daube, D. *3*, *46*, *61*
Deissmann, A., *56*
Delling, G. *142*
Dibelius, M. *25*, *56*, 171
Diels, H. *133*

---

[1]) The number of the page on which a work is cited for the first time appears in italics.

INDEX OF AUTHORS

Dodd, C. H. *19*, *72*, 97, 114, 139, 143, 146, 152, 153, 157, *159*, 161, 163, 165, 166, 170, 171, 174, 178, 180
Doresse, J. *177*
Dobschütz, E. v. *4*, *25*
Drummond, J. *116*

Eckart, K.-G. *54*
Elbogen, I. *56*, 57
Elliger, K. *25*
Epstein, I. *160*, 162
Ewald, H. 29

Faure, A. *27*, 171
Feldman, L. H. *13*, 29, 100
Festugière, A. J. *99*
Fichtner, J. *17*
Filson, F. V. *172*
Fitzmyer, J. A. *61*, 62
Franke, A. H. *27*
Frankel, Z. 29, *55*, 56, 59, *60*
Freedmann, H. *53*, 54, 196
Freudenthal, J. 29, *57*, *133*
Fridrichsen, A. *149*
Friedmann, M. *115*, *126*, 167
Fuks, A. *110*, 125, 126, *193*

Gärtner, B. *22*, *27*, *45*, 153, *164*, 174, 180
Geiger, F. *126*, 140, 142
Gesenius, W. *196*
Ginzberg, L., *8*, *19*, 22, *115*, *130*, *133*,
Goldschmidt, L. *161*, 162
Gomperz, Th. *106*
Goodenough, E. R. *3*, *111*, 114, 116, *117*, 119, *120*, 123, 125, 127, 136, 137, 140, 142, 145, 146, *170*
Goppelt, L. 29
Grant, R. M. *60*, 150
Gressmann, H. *56*
Grimm, C. L. W. *17*
Guilding, A. *27*, 55
Gummere, R. M. *102*
Gutbrod, W. *116*

Habermann, A. M., *76*, 83
Hadas, M. *61*
Hadot, P. *103*
Haenchen, E. *3*, *5*, *55*, *164*
Hanson, R. P. C. *19*
Harris, R. *27*

Hartingsveld, L. v. *166*, 169, 174, 179
Hatch, E. *196*
Hegermann, H. *104*, 114, 121, 140
Heinemann, I. *19*, *28*, 29, *60*, 102, 103, 108, 111, *112*, 123, 125, 127, 131, 134, 135, 142, 160, 162
Heinisch, P. *60*
Heinrici, G. *178*
Heitmüller, W. *171*
Helmbold, W. C. *104*
Highet, G. *107*
Hirsch, E. *25*, 171
Hirzel, R. *142*
Hoskyns, E. C. *157*, 174, *187*, 190
Howard, W. F. *3*, *4*, *5*, 152, *157*, 172, 174
Huck, A. *196*
Hühn, E. *27*
Huppembauer, H. W. *169*

Jaeger, W. *106 f.*, *129*
Jansen, H. Ludin, *180*
Jastrow, M. A. *196*
Jellinek, A. *8*, 22
Jeremias, J. *5*, 20, *25*, 44, 45, 74, 96, *149*, 181, 188
Jervell, J. *100*, 118, 129, 136, 140, 143, 144
Jocz, J. *178*
Jonas, H. *116*, 120, 140, *143*
Jülicher, A. *4*, *6*, *56*, 75

Käsemann, E. *25*
Kaminka, A. *61*
Kaplan, M. M. *13*
Kassovsky, H. J. *196*
Katz, P. *19*, 20
Kee, H. C. *168*
Kilpatrick, G. D. *73*, *74*, *159*
Kittel, G. *115*, *167*, 195
Kittel, R. *196*
Klassen, W. *42*, 147, 149, 151, 152, 164, 172, 176, 177, 178, 185, 186, 191
Kleinknecht, H. *138*
Knox, W. L. *55*
Köster, H. *13*
Kranz, W. *129*, 132
Kroll, J. *132*
Kümmel, W. G. *168*
Kuhn, K. G. *74*, *159*
Kundsin, K. *72*, *75*, 159

INDEX OF AUTHORS

Lamb, W. R. M. *142*
Lauterbach, J. Z. *196*
Lechner, M. *102*
Lehmann, M. R. *41*
Lehrmann, S. M. *53*
Leisegang, H. 29, *103*, 115, 116, 120, *122*, 129, 133, *140*, *143*, 145, *196*
Léon-Dufour, X. 68, 82, 190
Lepape, A. *125*
Levy, J. *196*
Lewald, H. *61*
Lewy, H. *104*, 119, 120, 140
Lewy, I. *62*
Liddell, H. G. *93*, 119, 196
Lieberman, S. 60, *110*
Lietzmann, H. *188*, *196*
Lindars, B. 27
Lindblom, J. *170*, 171
Loewe, R. *73*
Lohmeyer, E. 5, 29
Lohse, E. *188*, 189
Loisy, A. 25
Lütgert, W. *178*

Macgregor, G. H. C. *171*
Mangey, T. 106
Mann, J. 56
Marcus, R. *13*, *138*, *196*
Marcus, S. *110*
Markland, 15
Marmorstein, A. 55, 60
Maybaum, S. *51*, 52, 54
Meister, R. *123*
Menoud, Ph.-H. 4, 5, 189
Messel, N. *117*
Mette, H. J. *102*
Metzger, B. M. *62*
Meyer, R. *110*, 129, 130, 144
Michaelis, W. *115*
Michel, O. 96
Milligan, G. H. *93*, 196
Molland, E. *185*
Mondésert, J. *13*, 140
Montefiore, C. G. *105*
Moore, G. F. 3, 56, 127, 133
Moulton, J. H. *93*, 196
Müller, Th. *153*
Mussner, F. *171*

Nauck, W. *89*
Nestle, E. *196*
Neugebauer, F. *72*

Niese, B. *196*
Nilsson, M. P. *132*
Noack, B. 6, 26, 27, 42, 68, 74, 79, 80, 84, 86, 97, 98
Nötscher, F. *167*, 169
Norden, E. *103*

Odeberg, H. *64*, 96, 114, 147, 152, 153, 164, 167, 175, *178*, 189
Oepke, A. *167*

Pascher, J. *114*, 116, 120, 140
Pepin, J. *19*, 60
Pohlenz, M., *102*, 111, 117, *122*, 128, 129, 13*1*, 132, 135, 140, 143
Pouilloux, J. *13*, 140
Preiss, T. *162*, 164
Pribnow, H. *165*, 171

Quispel, G. *147*

Rabin, Ch. *89*
Rad, G. von *13*
Rahlfs, A. *17*, 196
Redpath, H. A. *196*
Reinhardt, K. *129*
Reitzenstein, R. *100*, *116*
Rengstorf, K. H. *160*, 164
Richter, W. *102*
Ringgren, H. *140*, *169*
Robinson, J. A. T. *179*
Rosenzweig, A. *62*
Ruckstuhl, E. 4, 5, 6, 20, 26, 28, 68, 76, 94, 96, *171*, 172

Sahlin, H. *180*
Sandmel, S. *13*, 103
Sandys, J. *105*
Sasse, H. *165*
Sauneron, S. *12*
Schaedel, K. 25, 40, 41, 65, 72, 73, 166, 167, 170, 171
Schlatter, A. 84, 85, *131*, 133, *146*, 148, 157, *159*, 161, 164, 166, 167, 174, 181
Schmid, J. *179*
Schmid, W. 60
Schmidt, H. *129*
Schmidt, K. L. *169*
Schnackenburg, R. *179*, *190*
Schneider, J. 29
Scholem, G. D. *147*, 177
Schrenk, E. von *169*

Schürer, E. *56*
Schürmann, H. *93, 97*
Schulz, S. *5, 40, 41, 56, 65, 68 f., 72, 73, 79, 86, 96, 97, 150, 153, 157, 158, 164, 170, 174*
Schwartz, E. *25, 138, 139*
Schweizer, E. *5, 20, 25, 68, 72, 74, 75, 76, 94, 96, 174, 181, 187, 191*
Schweitzer, A. *169*
Scott, R. *93, 119, 196*
Scott, W. *104, 129, 132*
Sidebottom, E. M. *3, 151, 152, 157, 158, 164, 173, 182*
Siegfried, C. *60, 63, 101, 103, 109, 111*
Silbermann, L. H. *25*
Simon, M. *53, 54, 196*
Skard, E. *129*
Smend, F. *27*
Smith, M. *56*
Snyder, G. F. *42, 147, 149, 151, 152, 164, 172, 176, 177, 178, 185, 186, 191*
Spitta, F. *25*
Staerk, W. *140*
Stählin, G. *171*
Stählin, O. *60*
Stauffer, E. *171*
Stein, E. *13, 19, 53, 55, 60, 115, 117*
Stendahl, K. *27, 29, 41, 42, 74*
Strachan, R. H. *97, 171, 175, 187*
Strack, H. L. *73, 114, 118, 152, 155, 163, 165, 174, 181*
Strathmann, H. *174*

Tcherikover, V. *110, 125, 126, 193*
Thackeray, H. St. *196*

Theiler, W. *29, 60, 103, 108, 111, 112, 123, 125, 127, 131, 134, 135, 142, 160, 162*
Theodor, J. *57*
Thompson, J. M. *25*
Thyen, H. *5, 29, 52, 54, 55, 60, 120, 146*
Torczyner, H. *62*
Treitel, L. *19, 60, 100*

Unnik, W. C. van *144, 179*

Verbeck, W. *25, 171*
Völker, W. *13, 29, 99, 100, 103, 105, 111, 117*
Vollert, C. *189*
Volz, P. *116, 150, 165, 167*

Wächter, L. *144*
Wellhausen, J. *25*
Wendland, P. *4, 15, 20, 42, 56, 60, 106, 111, 123, 131, 196*
Whitaker, G. H. *44, 81, 101, 103, 106, 109, 112, 115, 116, 120, 123, 124, 125, 129, 130, 134, 135, 142, 196*
Wikenhauser, A. *189*
Wilkens, W. *152, 190*
Windisch, H. *56, 97, 120, 134*
Wolfson, H. A. *102, 103, 105, 108, 111, 114, 117, 119, 122, 123, 127, 133, 139, 142, 146*
Wyttenbach, D. *106*

Zeller, E. *111*
Zunz *56, 57*

INDEX OF REFERENCES

I. OLD TESTAMENT

Genesis (Gen.)

1, 26 f.	100
2, 6	74, 75
2, 11	65
2, 19	84
3, 13	49
3, 14	44, 48
3, 14-15	49, 50
3, 15	44
4, 8	63
12, 1	64
12, 3	49
12, 7	49
15, 5	49
15, 6	47, 49, 50, 51
16	39
17, 1	70, 71
17, 5	49
17, 16	81, 134
17, 18	43
17, 19	31, 38, 39, 43, 44, 48
17, 20	38, 39, 43
17, 20 f.	33, 39
17, 21	39, 43
17, 22	85
18, 18	49
28, 12	49, 64
29, 31	32
31, 10-11	49
37, 7	49, 50
38, 6-7	49
38, 7	50, 88

Exodus (Ex.)

6, 7	49
12, 2	81
12, 4	30, 38
15, 8	49
15, 11	64
15, 26	70
16	40, 41
16, 2	40, 41
16, 4	7, 8, 14, 15, 16, 18, 21, 24, 30, 32, 35, 36, 38, 39, 41, 42, 44, 53, 54, 62, 65, 71, 76, 90, 101, 102, 107, 110, 112, 118, 121, 122, 123, 126, 127, 128, 130, 136, 137, 141, 145, 156
16, 13-15	44, 47, 49, 50
16, 15	40, 41, 42, 47, 65, 66, 67, 68, 90
16, 16	39, 141, 142
16, 16 ff.	39
16, 18	39, 141, 142
16, 20	146
16, 23 ff.	111
20, 2	157
22, 3	88
22; 5	70
24, 11	177
33, 20	150

Leviticus (Lev.)

1, 6	49
2, 14	48, 49, 50
18, 5	49
19, 9	49
19, 32	49
25, 4 f.	112
26, 10	49
26, 12	49

Numbers (Num.)

11, 16	49
16, 22	181
21, 17	7, 8
21, 18	89
27, 16	181
31, 28	49

Deuteronomy (Deut.)

1, 17	49
4, 2	42
4, 12	150
5, 24	150
6, 6	42
8, 3	15, 16, 18
8, 15	72
8, 16	89
9, 23	62
10, 15	135
11, 4	41
11, 11	7
18, 16	150
19, 17	49
21, 3	161
21, 23	49
27, 26	49
28, 14	42
28, 49	73
33, 2	71
33, 14	8
33, 28	8

Joshua (Josh.)

3, 10	162

I Samuel (I Sam.)

2, 5	81
17, 26	162
17, 36	162

Nehemiah (Neh.)

9, 15	40, 41
9, 30	161

INDEX OF REFERENCES

Psalms (Ps.)	
7, 10	72
10, 9 (9,30)	161
32, 1-2	49
41 (40), 10	93
42, 2	162
78 (77), 24	40, 41, 68
78, 25	63
104, 14	7
105 (104), 40	41
(131), 16-17	72
135, 6	53

Proverbs (Prov.)	
8, 30	156
8, 35-36	155
9	157
9, 5	154, 155, 156

Songs of Songs (Cant.)	
1, 4	161

Ecclesiastes (Eccl.)	
2, 3	161

Isaiah (Is.)	
6, 10	64
11, 10	72
25, 6 ff.	167
40, 3	72
43, 9	41
49, 10	166
54, 12	84
54, 13	38, 40, 66, 70, 82, 84, 85, 86, 150, 185
56, 5	41

Lamentations (Lam.)	
1, 16	73

Ezechiel (Ezech.)	
1, 26	186

Daniel (Dan.)	
6, 20	162
7, 13-14	186
12, 2	167

Hosea (Hos.)	
9, 10	115
12, 6	53

Habakkuk (Hab.)	
2, 4	49

II. NEW TESTAMENT

Matthew (Matt.)	
6, 10	94
7, 21	159
7, 24	154
8, 12	166
10, 1	160
10, 24	159
10, 37	154
10, 39	165
10, 40	159, 164
11, 28	154
12, 32	165
12, 50	159
13, 1-9	46
13, 10 ff.	46
16, 16	162
16, 17	181
18, 5	159
18, 6	161
19, 14	154
22, 13	166
25, 30	166
26, 26	91, 92
26, 27-28	92

Mark	
6, 31-44	45
6, 45-54	45
8, 1-10	45
8, 11-13	45
8, 14-21	45

8, 27-30	45
8, 31	167
8, 31-33	45
8, 35	165
9, 9	167
9, 37	159
10, 14	154
10, 30	165
12, 23	167
12, 25	167
14, 23-24	92

Luke	
6, 31	94
6, 40	159
6, 47	154
9, 48	159
13, 28	166
14, 26	154
16, 8	165
16, 31	167
18, 16	154
18, 30	165
20, 34 f.	165
22, 19	91

John	
1, 1-18	157
1, 13	181, 192
1, 14	175, 181, 183, 185, 190, 192
1, 14-18	150
1, 15	74
1, 17	152, 173, 185
1, 18	66, 150, 153, 175, 177, 185
1, 23	72
1, 32-34	175
1, 49-51	175
1, 51	64
2, 11	161
2, 24	171
3, 2	83
3, 3-7	181
3, 3-8	183
3, 4	181
3, 6	181, 191, 192
3, 13	185
3, 15	161, 165
3, 16	161
3, 16 ff.	167
3, 16-17	167
3, 35	165
3, 36	161, 165
4, 12-14	96
4, 14	165
4, 15	69
4, 34	76, 159, 180
4, 36	165
4, 39	161
4, 42	92
5	154, 180

INDEX OF REFERENCES

5, 15-18	176	
5, 23	159	
5, 24	159, 165	
5, 26	162	
5, 27	186	
5, 28 f.	168	
5, 28-29	188	
5, 30	159	
5, 35	72	
5, 36	180, 182, 183	
5, 36-47	180	
5, 36-6, 63	182	
5, 37	151, 159, 175	
5, 37 ff.	151	
5, 37-47	151, 152, 179	
5, 38-40	182	
5, 39	165, 182, 183	
5, 39-40	151, 179, 180	
5, 40	154	
5, 45	152	
5, 46	152	
6	22, 26, 27, 35, 42, 44, 45, 55, 67, 68, 74, 85, 97, 99, 114, 152, 153, 154, 156, 158, 178, 180, 185, 188, 189, 190	
6, 1 ff.	180	
6, 1-14	180, 182, 183	
6, 1-15	45	
6, 1-26	44	
6, 1-30	45	
6, 14	92	
6, 15	180	
6, 15-21	180	
6, 16-21	180	
6, 16-24	45	
6, 23	96	
6, 25-27	183	
6, 25-34	45	
6, 25-59	55	
6, 26	45, 74, 96	
6, 26-27	46, 179, 182, 183	
6, 26-29	46	
6, 26-65	190	
6, 27	26, 46, 165	
6, 27 ff.	44, 46	
6, 27-51	26	
6, 27-58	29	
6, 29	75	
6, 30	45, 69	
6, 30-33	68, 69, 78	
6, 31	21, 22, 23, 25, 26, 27, 33, 35, 37, 38, 39, 40, 41, 42, 46, 61, 62, 63, 64, 65, 66, 67, 68, 69, 71, 72, 73, 74, 77, 78, 79, 80, 82, 83, 84, 86, 87, 89, 90, 92, 95, 96, 97, 98, 149, 151, 157, 158, 165, 168, 172, 173, 175, 179	
6, 31 ff.	38, 174, 179, 180	
6, 31-32	63, 65, 115, 172, 173, 182, 183	
6, 31-33	37, 41, 61, 63, 65, 67, 70, 79, 85, 182, 185	
6, 31-34	174	
6, 31-40	85	
6, 31-51	96, 190	
6, 31-58	1, 2, 14, 20, 22, 23, 26, 28, 29, 33, 35, 37, 38, 40, 42, 43, 45, 46, 47, 49, 51, 52, 54, 55, 56, 57, 59, 61, 66, 68, 69, 70, 89, 91, 96, 97, 98, 99, 147, 148, 152, 156, 157, 158, 162, 165, 166, 168, 170, 172, 180, 183, 185, 187, 188, 190, 192	
6, 32	26, 27, 33, 40, 41, 61, 62, 63, 64, 65, 66, 67, 68, 74, 76, 78, 168, 172, 173, 175, 179, 184, 187	
6, 32 ff.	66	
6, 32-33	40, 62, 67, 69, 80, 90, 175, 183	
6, 32-35	23	
6, 32-48	35, 42, 87, 95	
6, 32-51	25	
6, 32-58	42	
6, 33	20, 33, 38, 40, 41, 61, 62, 63, 65, 66, 67, 68, 88, 148, 149, 153, 152	
6, 34	33, 66, 69, 70, 77, 78, 79, 80, 183, 184	
6, 34-40	69, 72, 79, 80, 86	
6, 35	26, 33, 66, 67, 68, 69, 70, 71, 72, 73, 75, 77, 78, 79, 82, 88, 90, 97, 149, 154, 155, 156, 157, 158, 161, 165, 166, 168, 184, 186, 187, 190	
6, 35 ff.	70	
6, 35-40	69, 77	
6, 35-60	45	
6, 36	33, 69, 70, 74, 75, 78, 79, 175, 176, 177, 178	
6, 36-37	71, 75, 90	
6, 36-40	78, 79, 178	
6, 37	26, 33, 69, 70, 79, 154, 160, 166, 168, 176, 184	
6, 37-40	176, 177	
6, 38	20, 21, 23, 33, 69, 71, 75, 78, 79, 82, 88, 158, 159, 160, 182	
6, 38 ff.	71	
6, 38-40	75	
6, 39	33, 69, 75, 76, 77, 78, 95, 122, 158, 159, 160, 166, 167, 168, 171, 176, 184, 188, 192	
6, 39-40	75, 160	
6, 40	34, 69, 75, 76, 77, 78, 79, 95, 122, 156, 159, 161, 162, 165, 166, 167, 168, 171, 176, 178, 188, 192	
6, 41	20, 23, 34, 40, 41, 72, 73, 79, 80, 78, 82, 86, 88, 151, 156, 158, 176, 184, 187	
6, 41 ff.	21	
6, 41-42	151, 157, 183, 184, 190, 191	
6, 41-46	78, 85	
6, 41-48	80, 81, 82, 83, 85, 86, 98, 151	

Suppl. to Novum Test., X

INDEX OF REFERENCES

Reference	Pages	Reference	Pages	Reference	Pages
6, 42	21, 23, 34, 80, 86, 88, 185, 190	6, 51 ff.	90, 96, 97, 187, 188, 190, 192	6, 71-72	45
6, 42-43	185	6, 51-52	185	7	29
6, 43	34, 40, 41, 80, 187	6, 51-58	25, 35, 38, 90, 91, 92, 94, 96, 97, 188, 189, 190, 191	7, 1	176
6, 43-48	82			7, 5	161
6, 44	26, 34, 77, 78, 80, 82, 83, 84, 85, 86, 154, 158, 160, 161, 166, 167, 168, 171, 184, 188, 192	6, 52	34, 87, 89, 91, 95, 97, 101, 128, 176, 181, 184	7, 16	159
				7, 18	159
				7, 19	159, 173
				7, 21	180
				7, 22	84
		6, 52 ff.	184, 186	7, 28	159
6, 44-46	176, 177	6, 52-57	87, 89, 90	7, 29	162
6, 45	26, 34, 38, 40, 66, 70, 71, 80, 84, 86, 90, 150, 154, 157, 167, 185	6, 52-58	23, 95	7, 31	161
		6, 53	21, 22, 34, 87, 89, 91, 95, 97, 181, 185, 191	7, 33	159
				7, 37	154
				7, 38	161
				7, 39	161
6, 45-46	66, 84, 85, 150, 151, 153	6, 53 ff.	155, 189, 192	7, 40	92
		6, 53-56	186	7, 48	161
6, 45-51	176	6, 54	21, 22, 34, 77, 78, 87, 89, 91, 92, 93, 95, 97, 156, 165, 166, 167, 168, 171, 181, 185, 188, 192	8, 16	159
6, 46	34, 66, 79, 80, 84, 85, 86, 150, 151, 153, 158, 162, 175, 177, 185			8, 18	159
				8, 26	159
				8, 29	159
				8, 30	161
				8, 32	165
6, 47	34, 68, 80, 82, 156, 161, 165	6, 54 ff.	37	8, 53	173
		6, 55	21, 22, 34, 87, 89, 91, 92, 95, 97, 181, 185, 190	8, 56	152, 175
6, 47 f.	26			9, 3	180
6, 47-48	86			9, 22	176
6, 47-51	78	6, 56	21, 22, 34, 87, 89, 91, 92, 93, 95, 97, 185	9, 28	176
6, 48	26, 34, 66, 67, 72, 73, 79, 80, 82, 86, 88, 98, 149, 151, 156, 158, 165, 187			9, 31	159
		6, 57	21, 22, 34, 87, 89, 90, 92, 93, 94, 95, 97, 155, 158, 162, 186	9, 39	165
				9, 39-41	176
				10	29
6, 48-51	23			10, 16	176
6, 49	21, 22, 34, 35, 38, 86, 87, 88, 95, 96, 98, 182, 189	6, 57-58	92, 94	10, 25	180
		6, 58	20, 21, 22, 34, 37, 38, 46, 87, 88, 89, 92, 93, 94, 95, 96, 97, 156, 165, 173, 182	10, 28	165, 167
				10, 32	180
6, 49 ff.	37			10, 36	74
6, 49-50	97, 173			10, 37 f.	180
6, 49-51	87, 97			11, 23	167
6, 49-58	35, 42, 86, 95, 155, 189	6, 59	46, 56	11, 23-27	168
		6, 60 ff.	46	11, 24	167
6, 50	20, 34, 38, 75, 78, 87, 88, 95, 97, 98, 122	6, 60-61	184	11, 25	161
		6, 60-65	46	11, 26	161
		6, 61-62	187	11, 51-52	176
6, 50-51	88	6, 61-70	45	12, 14	61
6, 51	20, 34, 38, 40, 41, 64, 66, 67, 72, 73, 78, 79, 85, 86, 87, 88, 89, 90, 91, 92, 93, 94, 95, 96, 97, 149, 156, 158, 165, 181, 185, 186, 187	6, 62	187	12, 19	182
		6, 63	149, 181, 182, 183, 187, 188, 189, 190, 191, 192	12, 25	165
				12, 31	165, 166
				12, 32	160, 161
		6, 65	83, 154, 184	12, 40	64
		6, 66 ff.	188	12, 41	152, 175
		6, 68	149, 165, 188	12, 48	167

INDEX OF REFERENCES

12, 50	165	10, 14	161	2, 11-22	178
13	181	11, 16-22	178	6, 6	159
13, 1	165	12, 2	165	6, 12	181
13, 3	160				
13, 16	159	*1 Corinthians (1 Cor.)*		*Philippians (Phil.)*	
13, 18	93	1, 18	167	1, 29	161
13, 20	159, 164	1, 20	165		
13, 33	176	2, 6	165	*1 Thessalonians*	
14, 9	162	2, 8	165	*(1 Thess.)*	
14, 10-11	180	3, 18	165		
15, 12	75	3, 19	165	1, 9	162
15, 13	56	5, 10	165	4, 9	84
16, 11	165	7, 31	165	4, 14	167
17	176	10, 1 ff.	21	4, 16	167
17, 1-2	181	10, 1-4	21, 22, 91, 92		
17, 2	160, 165, 176, 181	10, 3	188	*2 Thessalonians*	
		11	91	*(2 Thess.)*	
17, 3	75, 165	11, 23 ff.	90, 92		
17, 6	160, 176	11, 23-24	91	2, 10	167
17, 7	160	11, 24	93		
17, 9	176	11, 27	91, 92	*1 Timothy (1 Tim.)*	
17, 20	176	11, 27 ff.	92, 95, 97	6, 17	165
18, 9	166, 167	11, 27-28	96		
18, 11	96	11, 27-29	91	*2 Timothy (2 Tim.)*	
18, 12	176	11, 28	91		
18, 36	165	11, 29	91	4, 10	165
		15, 20 ff.	169		
Acts		15, 45 ff.	169	*Titus (Tit.)*	
2, 24	167	15, 49	94		
2, 32	167	15, 50	181	2, 12	165
7, 38	149, 163				
7, 51	94	*2 Corinthians (2 Cor.)*		*Hebrews (Hebr.)*	
7, 53	163	2, 15	167	2, 2	163
10, 43	161	4, 4	165	2, 14	181
13, 33	167	5, 1 ff.	169	6, 5	165
14, 15	162			10, 36	159
14, 23	161	*Galatians (Gal.)*		13, 21	159
19, 4	161	1, 4	165		
23, 8	167	1, 9	94	*James*	
		1, 16	181	4, 12	167
Romans (Rom.)		2, 16	161		
2, 7	168	3, 6-29	47, 48, 49, 50, 52	*1 Peter (1 Pet.)*	
2, 12	167	3, 7	48	1, 8	161
4, 1-22	47, 49, 50, 52	3, 16	64		
4, 3	47	3, 19	163	*1 John*	
4, 23-25	48	3, 29	48	2, 22	183
5, 21	168	6, 8	168	3, 11	75
6, 4	169			3, 23	75
6, 11	169	*Ephesians (Eph.)*		4, 2	183
6, 22	168	1, 21	165	4, 3	183
8, 2	169	2, 2	165	4, 15	183
8, 6	169				
8, 10	169				

4, 17	165	5, 10	161	Revelation (Rev.)	
5, 1	183	II John		2, 23	72
5, 3	57	6	75	7, 2	162
5, 5	183	7	183	7, 16	166
				22, 16	72

III. PHILO

De Opificio Mundi		127, 129, 136, 137,		82-85	50
(*Opif.*)		141, 142, 143, 144,		80-81	50
27	131	145, 146, 147, 148,		86	50
48	134		170, 173	87	48, 49
72	120	III 163	30, 39, 133,	186	66
114	131		134, 135, 141, 142,		
135	129		145	*Quod Deterius Potiori*	
149	84, 85	III 163-164	35, 145	*Insidiari Soleat* (*Deter.*)	
		III 163-167	35	47-48	63, 64, 98
Legum Allegoriae		III 163-168	36	84-85	129
(*Leg. all.*)		III 164	30, 146	85	129, 132
I 2	134	III 165	30, 38, 141, 142	145	102
I 28	74	III 165-166	35		
I 43	130	III 166	31, 71, 98, 123,	*De Posteritate Caini*	
I 67	64, 65, 98		125, 141, 142, 145	(*Post.*)	
I 88	132	III 166-167	35	63	115
II 86	89	III 167	31, 122, 123,	102	20, 42
III 65	48		124, 127, 133, 135,	115	132
III 65-75	47, 48, 49, 50, 98		142, 146	142	136
III 68	48, 50	III 167-168	35, 76,	163	132
III 69	50		125, 127, 129, 136, 145	165	132
III 69 ff.	48	III 168	1, 15, 16, 18,	*De Gigantibus* (*Gig.*)	
III 71	88, 98		31, 36, 37, 47, 122,	62	130, 131
III 75	48, 50		124, 127, 128, 129,		
III 75-76	48		133, 137, 139, 143	*Quod Deus Immutabilis*	
III 104	130	III 169	41, 47, 66	*Sit* (*Immut.*)	
III 135	105	III 169 f.	44	100	77
III 148	124	III 169-173	47, 49, 52	144	115
III 161	44, 129	III 169-174	50		
III 161-181	44, 45	III 173	47, 66	*De Agricultura* (*Agr.*)	
III 162	1, 15, 16, 18, 21, 29, 35, 37, 38, 39, 40, 44, 47, 62, 66, 122, 127, 128, 129, 130, 131, 132, 137, 138, 139, 143, 145	III 182	44	5 f.	119
				9	106
		De Cherubim (*Cher.*)		13 ff.	106
		4	130	17 ff.	106
		128	136	44	134
				88	134
III 162 ff.	145	*De Sacrificiis Abelis et Caini* (*Sacr.*)		130	136
III 162-168	1, 2, 16, 28, 29, 35, 38, 39, 42, 44, 46, 47, 49, 51, 52, 54, 57, 76, 98, 99, 100, 118, 122, 123, 124, 126,	49 ff.	124	*De Plantatione* (*Plant.*)	
		76	48	14	129, 131
		76-79	50	17	129
		76-87	47, 48, 49, 50	20-22	129
		78	103		

INDEX OF REFERENCES

22	132
53	132
127	130

De Ebrietate (Ebr.)

33	124
36	135
37	134
40	146
73	132
91	102
208	132

De Sobrietate (Sobr.)

8	109
33	136

De Confusione Linguarum (Conf.)

91	115
92	115
145-147	177
154	132
176 ff.	129

De Migratione Abrahami (Migr.)

1	64
14	134
43	64
53 f.	115
104	134
178	131

Quis Rerum Divinarum Heres Sit (Heres.)

86 f.	131
93	146
125	101
144-145	142
191	39, 142
283	129, 131

De Congressu Quaerendae Eruditionis Gratia (Congr.)

2-3	109
11	110
12	101
14	101
20	110
20 ff.	108
22	110
34-36	103
35	109
170	1, 15, 16
170-174	18, 29, 42
173	15, 16, 17, 21
173-174	1, 15
174	15, 17

De Fuga et Inventione (Fug.)

137	21
137-139	41
139	41, 66
139 f.	115
170	106
170 ff.	107
171	106
180	12, 16
212-213	109

De Mutatione Nominum (Mut.)

47	70
66 ff.	131
88	103
141	81, 82, 83, 98
142	81, 82
142-144	81, 83, 98
143	81
144	81
150	134
201	43, 146
201-232	43
233-251	43
252-253	43
253	31, 36, 38, 39, 43, 48
253-255	35
253-263	1, 2, 28, 29, 31, 35, 36, 38, 39, 42, 43, 44, 46, 48, 49, 51, 54, 57, 98, 99, 100, 101, 103, 104, 105, 106, 107, 108, 109, 110, 111, 114, 115, 117, 118, 119, 121, 122, 123, 124, 141, 143, 145, 147, 148, 149, 156, 170, 173, 188
254	31, 121
255	32, 36, 39, 48, 101, 103, 109, 119
255-260	35, 121
255-263	35, 105
256	32
257	32, 101, 106, 119
258	16, 32, 101, 104, 105, 115, 116, 119, 120, 121
258 ff.	114, 120
258-259	15, 16, 21, 127
258-260	1, 14, 15, 18, 101, 120, 182
259	9, 16, 21, 32, 38, 40, 62, 90, 101, 106, 119, 120, 122
259 f.	120
259-260	111, 112, 113
260	16, 32, 106, 112, 119
261	33, 39
261-263	35
262	33
263	33, 36, 38, 39, 43, 101, 102, 104, 107, 113, 119
264 ff.	43
270	85

De Somniis (Somn.)

I 21	131
I 146	129
I 167-168	103
II 10	103
II 17	49
II 17 ff.	50
II 17-20	49
II 17-30	47, 48, 49, 50
II 21	49, 50
II 30	49
II 127	56
II 135	137
II 135 ff.	136
II 222	72

De Abrahamo (Abr.)

52	103
52-53	113
53	105
251	108
269	146

INDEX OF REFERENCES

De Josepho (Jos.)		*De Specialibus Legibus (Spec.)*		43-47	136
1	103			47	137
31	137	I 242	83, 84	80 ff.	56
		I 303	135	81	112
		I 342	134		
De Vita Mosis (Mos.)		II 13	137, 138	*De Vita Contemplativa (Cont.)*	
I 21-32	126	II 39-222	112		
I 30-31	125	II 61-62	56	30-31	56
I 35	126	II 62	113	72	134
I 76	103	II 92	125		
I 114-115	11	II 105	106	*De Aeternitate Mundi (Aet.)*	
I 116-117	12	II 107	106		
I 117	12, 16, 21	II 166	132	4	134
I 201-202	7, 9, 10, 11, 13, 16, 181	II 199	21, 22	7-9	132
		III 1 ff.	130		
I 202	11	IV 86-91	125	*In Flaccum (Flac.)*	
I 205	113	IV 172	125		
II 184	124	IV 232-237	141	130-134	124
II 195	12			130-145	124
II 195-196	115	*De Virtutibus (Virt.)*		135 ff.	124
II 215	56, 112	97	106		
II 216	113	127	136	*Hypothetica (Hypoth.)*	
II 258	9	216-218	146	7, 10-19	112
II 261	146			7, 12-15	56
II 263-264	113	*De Praemiis et Poenis (Praem.)*			
II 267	8, 9, 10, 11, 13, 16, 17, 101	27	103	*De Legatione ad Gaium (Legat.)*	
II 269	146	28	146	1-7	116, 117
		57	94, 95	312	56
		65	94, 95, 96		
De Decalogo (Decal.)		65-66	113	*Quaestiones et Solutiones in Genesin (Qu. in Gen.)*	
13	137, 138	66	113		
17	138	152	125	III 19	108
40	113			III 21	108
134	129	*Quod Omnis Probus Liber Sit (Probus.)*		IV 8	131
155	141			IV 102	142
158-164	112	43-46	137	IV 140	138

IV. VARIOUS JEWISH AND CHRISTIAN WRITINGS

MIDRASH RABBAH

Genesis Rabbah (Gen. R.)		70, 5	155	24, 53, 54, 57, 61, 116	
1, 1	143, 156	78, 1	159		
8, 11	118, 130			25, 3	17, 53
12, 8	130	*Exodus Rabbah (Ex. R.)*		25, 6	7, 9, 10, 11, 12, 13, 14, 16, 24, 53, 57, 61, 181
14, 3	118, 130	3, 17	94		
14, 5	165	15-52	53		
21, 5	130	25	53	25, 7	114, 156, 181
43, 6	155	25, 2	7, 8, 9, 10, 12, 13, 14, 16, 20, 21,	25, 10	146
54, 1	155			29, 9	148, 149

INDEX OF REFERENCES

30, 16	130	*Numbers Rabbah* (*Num. R.*)		7, 3	148
38, 3	77, 78				
41, 3	118	7, 4	130	*Ecclesiastes Rabbah* (*Eccl. R.*)	
47, 7	155	8, 9	155		
52, 3	167	13, 15	155	VII, 8 § 1	155
		13, 16	155	VII, 29 § 1	130
Leviticus Rabbah (*Lev. R.*)		14, 12	133		
		Deuteronomy Rabbah (*Deut. R.*)		*Lamentations Rabbah* (*Lam. R.*)	
11, 9	165				
20, 10	118	7, 2	118	I, 16 § 45	73

Other Midrashim

Mekilta on Exodus (*Mek. Ex.*)		19, 7	71	*Siphre on Deuteronomy* (*Siphre on Deut.*)	
		19, 11	118		
12, 1	82	22, 3	88	11, 22	143
12, 2	80, 82, 83	22, 5	70	32, 2	126, 130
12, 3	159	*Midrash Psalms* (*Midrash Ps.*)		34, 2	167
12, 6	159				
13, 17	2, 114, 149, 152	105 § 1	118	*Tanhuma Shemoth*	
13, 21	85	*Pesiqta Rabbati*			
15, 5	82				
15, 11	64, 65, 168	43	130	25	148
15, 26	70, 148	*Petirat Moses*			
16, 4	7, 8, 9, 10, 12, 13, 14, 16, 20, 21, 24, 61, 63, 64	8, 9, 12, 13, 14, 16, 21, 22		*Pequde*	
				3	133
		Seder Eliahu Rabbah			
16, 25	165	27	115	*Tanhuma B. Bereshith*	
16, 27	146				
16, 28	22	*Siphre on Numbers* (*Siphre on Num.*)			
17, 9	64			5	143
19, 2	150	5, 18	159	17	130

Mishnah

Berakoth		*Sotah*		*Sanhedrin*	
5, 5	159	8, 1	181	10, 1	167
8, 8	83	9, 15	167		
Bikkurim		*Qiddushin*		*Pirqe Aboth*	
1, 5	83	3, 1	160	2, 7	165
				3, 14	136, 143
Nazir		*Baba Metzia*		3, 18	110
9, 5	181	4, 2	161	6, 7	165

Babylonian Talmud

Berakoth		*Taanith*		15a	165
64a	150	7a	127	16a	130
Yoma		*Hagigah*		*Gittin*	
75	17	14b	177	32	162

57a	165	Baba Qamma		48a	161
		70a	160, 161	49a	161
Qiddushin					
41b	160			Sanhedrin	
41b-43a	159	Baba Metzia			
43a	162	47a	161	IIIb	162

JERUSALEM TALMUD

Berakoth (J. Berakoth)		Sanhedrin (J.Sanhedrin)	
3b	162	26c	162

ABOTH DE RABBI NATHAN

37	130
39	143

SHULHAN ARUQ

Hoshen Mishpat	
188, 5	160

APOCRYPHA AND PSEUDEPIGRAPHA

Baruch		66, 8	165	3 Maccabees	
4, 1	155			3, 9	135
		4 Ezra		Sirach	
Baruch, Syriac		4, 2	165	14, 18	181
14, 13	165	4, 27	165	15, 4	166
15, 7 f.	165	6, 9	165	17, 11	149
15, 78	165	6, 55	165	17, 13	150
16, 1	165	7, 12	165	17, 31	181
44, 12	165	7, 47	165	24	157
44, 15	165	7, 112	165	24, 19	154, 155
48, 50	165	7, 113	165	24, 21	155, 166
51, 10	165	14, 5	151	24, 23	155
51, 14	165	14, 30	149	45, 2-5	151
59	151			45, 5	149, 150
		Jubilees			
Enoch, Ethiopian		1	151	Testament of Naphtali	
51, 1 ff.	167	1, 27	163	2, 3	144
Enoch, Slavic		2, 1	163	3, 3	144
50, 2	165			Wisdom (Wisd.)	
50, 5	165	2 Maccabees		16, 20	17
66, 6	165	7, 9	167	16, 20 ff.	17
66, 7	165	15, 12	135	16, 25	17

DEAD SEA SCROLLS

Manual of Discipline		4	76	4, 12 f.	76
(I QS)		4, 2	76	5, 13	83
2, 19	169	4, 2 f.	75, 78	Damascus Document	
3	76	4, 2-3	76	(CD)	
3,18	76	4, 3	76	3, 7	62
3, 23	169	4, 6 f.	76	4, 4	89
3, 26	76	4, 7 f.	169	20, 4	84, 150

Josephus

Contra Apionem		Antiquitates Judaicae	
I 32	135	XV 136	163
		XVIII 159 f.	125
Bellum Judaicum		XVIII 259	125
VI 47	131	XX 100	125

Pseudo Philo

Liber Antiquitatum Biblicarum (Ant. Bibl.)
12, 1   151

Barnabas

Barnabas
21, 6   84

V. GREEK AND LATIN AUTHORS

Aristotle

Analytica Posteriora		Metaphysica		Ethica Nicomachea	
75b 24	132	992b 17	132	1168b 32	135
85b 18	132				

Cicero

De natura deorum		De republica		Tusculanae disputationes	
II 17	132	VI 17	132	I 41	131
II 56	132			I 42 ff.	132
				I 60	132
				II 5	106

Diogenes Laertus

VII 89   122
VII 127   122

Pindar

The Olympian Odes
IX 100 ff.   104

Plato

Gorgias		Phaedo		Protagoras	
508A	142	84AB	129	313C	129
Laws		Phaedrus		Timaeus	
III 686B	135	246DE	129	90A-C	128
		247CD	129		
		248BC	129		

Plutarch

Moralia		De liberis educandis	
106D	132	2B	106
973E	104, 105	7D	108
991E ff.	104, 105		
992A	104		

Seneca

Ad Lucilium Epistulae Morales		LXXXVIII 20	102	De Ira	
		LXXXVIII 21-28	102	III 6, 1	132
LXXXVIII	102	XLIX 16	132		

INDEX OF SUBJECTS

I. STYLE AND HERMENEUTICS

A is B   89, 92-93, 95
Addition   4, 77-78, 88, 135, 171, 178; see Supplement
Allegory   18-19, 50, 60, 95, 108, 116
Appendix   48, 53, 77

Bridge, Literary   43-44, 70, 79, 88-89; see Transition

Causal Clause   74-75, 78
Closing Statement   34-38, 42, 47-53, 56, 87, 96, 128; see Conclusion
Combination, of Old Testament Verses   20, 41-42
Comment   4, 6, 26, 28, 68, 75, 89-91
Commentary   3-6, 20, 27, 44, 46, 53, 96, 98-100, 108
Comparison   94-95
Compilation   1, 24, 54, 57
Conclusion   36-37, 48, 82, 85, 86, 88-89, 94-96, 107; see Closing Statement
Conditional Statement   77, 83, 85, 88-91, 95-96, 98
Confirmation, of Old Testament Text, 62, 64, 67, 98; see Contrast
Context   14, 29, 39-40, 43, 45-46, 54, 69, 73, 78, 100, 105-106, 110, 113, 120, 133, 135, 137, 141-142, 146, 151, 155, 157-158, 160-161, 163, 180-181, 190
Contrast, Pattern of   62-65, 67, 69, 71, 80, 85; see Confirmation and Correction
Correction, of Old Testament Text   62-64, 67, 98; see Contrast
Cycle of Traditions   45, 69

Debate, Pattern of   80, 82, 85-86, 98
Definition   68, 75-77, 88, 95, 122
Dialogue   26, 66, 68
Diatribe   55, 60

Digression   43
Discourse   4, 26, 44-46, 68, 85, 178, 180, 190
Displacement   45; see Dislocation
Dissertation   28
Dislocation   180; see Displacement

Ego Eimi   68, 72-73, 78-79, 88, 97, 156-158, 187; see I am, Index II
Etymology   2, 115-117, 177
Evangelist   4, 26, 28, 44, 68, 78, 95-97, 151
Exegesis, Exegetical, *passim*, esp. Chs. I-III
Explicative Statements   63, 67, 70, 76-77, 79, 88-89, 95, 122
Exposition, *passim*, esp. Chs. I-III

Final Clause   71-72, 75, 78, 80
Form Criticism   6, 56, 59, 78-79, 85-86, 95, 98
Formula   51, 61-62, 66, 72-73, 78-79, 84, 88, 93-94, 156-158, 163, 187
Fragment, *passim*, esp. Chs. I-III
Fusion   59, 79, 86, 90, 166

Gloss   4, 91, 93, 96
Greek, see Index II

Haggadah, *passim*, esp. Chs. I-III
Halakah   2-3, 8, 84, 148, 159, 160-164, 191; see Judicial
Hellenistic, see Index II
History, of Tradition   2, 26, 54, 57, 59
Homily, *passim*, esp. Ch. II

Interpolation   4, 19-20, 25, 35, 37-38, 53, 90, 96, 188-189, 191
Introductory Formula, of Old Testament Quotation   61-62, 84, 136

Judicial, see Index II; see also Halakah, Index I

INDEX OF SUBJECTS

Lecture 28, 55-56
Linguistic Characteristics, Exegesis 4-5, 59
Literary Criticism 4, 29
Logion 6, 26, 68, 79, 86, 97

Method, Exegetical, Midrashic, etc. 1, 3-4, 14, 23-25, 28-29, 41, 50, 59-62, 67, 71, 95, 98-101, 108, 127-128, 130, 132, 134, 137, 147
Midrash Midrashic, *passim*, esp. Chs. I-III

Narrative 44, 46, 53, 180

Opening Statement 34-38, 47-49, 51-53, 128
ὅτι *recitativum* 74

Palestinian, see Index II
Parallelism (Poetic), 28
Paraphrase, *passim*, esp. Chs. I-III
Participial Statement 70-71, 77-79, 84-85, 88-91, 94-96, 166
Parashah 55
Pericope 1, 39, 42-43, 51-55
Philological Exegesis 40, 57, 62, 64-65, 67, 69-70, 79-80, 85, 115, 168
Preaching 55
Preface 36, 48-49
Proem, Proemial Text 51-53, 56; see Subordinate Quotation
Prohibition 83, 85
Pronouns, Change of 41, 66-67, 78-79

Qumran, see Index II
Quotation, from Old Testament, *passim*, esp. Chs. I-III

Rabbinic, see Index II
Redactor 4, 25, 38, 171
Reference, 74-75, 78-79, 82, 86, 88
Relative Statement 70-71, 77-78, 90
Replacement of Word 67, 90, 95, 98, 100-102, 107, 112, 127-128, 137

Reservation, Statement of 84-85, 150
Revelatory Discourse (*Offenbarungsreden*) 4, 26, 28, 44, 68, 79, 97

School 3, 28, 31-33, 101-103, 106-109, 113, 118, 123-124, 167
Self Predication, see Index II; see also Ego Eimi, Index I
σημεῖα-*Quelle* 44
Septuaginta 19 f.
Sermon 28-29, 52, 57, 100
Sidra 53
Sitz im Leben 55-56
Source 3-6, 26-28, 40, 44-45, 58, 60, 79, 86, 97
Stereotype, In Use of Tradition 1, 52, 54, 99, 159, 161, 166
Stoic, see Index II
Style 4-6, 26, 59-60, 75-76, 78, 82, 84-86, 91, 94-96
Subject, Grammatical 65, 67, 90, 173
Subordinate Quotation from Old Testament 38-40, 42, 47, 49, 51-53, 82, 122; see Proem
Supplement 66-67, 71-72, 75, 87-88, 98, 100, 128, 130, 132, 134, 148, 158, 165; see Addition
Synagogue 2-3, 28, 46, 55-56, 99, 113, 118, 176
Synoptics, see Index II

Targum 13
Teaching, Teacher, see Index II
Testimonies 55
Text, Old Testament, *passim*, esp. 38-57, 61-97
Tradition, Traditional, *passim*, esp. 1-6, 11-18, 21-29
Transition, Literary 44, 46, 62; see Bridge
Type, Typology 180

Vocalization, of Hebrew 64, 67, 115, 168, 172

II. THEOLOGY AND PHILOSOPHY

Abraham 43, 47-48, 51, 85, 94, 103-104, 108-109, 113, 173, 175
Aeon 150, 165-166, 168-169; see Age
Age 150, 165, 174; see Aeon

Agency, Agent 2, 148, 158-168, 172, 177, 182, 186, 190-191; see Sender
Agriculture 9, 105-107, 118-119
Air 7-11, 16, 130, 132

INDEX OF SUBJECTS

Alexandria 1-2, 11, 13, 28, 55, 108, 110-111, 121, 124-127, 141, 145, 174
Anthropology, Anthropological 118, 120, 129, 131, 133, 136, 147, 179, 181-183, 187-188, 192; see Man
Apocalyptic 164-167, 186
Apocrypha 144
Aristotle 131-132, 135

Baptist, John the 72-73, 78, 175
Believe 33-34, 47, 51, 69, 77, 80, 158, 161, 163, 166, 168-169, 171, 175-178, 186, 191-192; see Faith and Trust
Body 2, 48, 50, 88, 91, 114, 120, 130, 138, 141, 143-144, 150, 168, 171-172, 192
Bread, *passim*.

Career, Pagan 2, 122-126, 143
Christology, see Jesus Christ
Church 2-4, 25, 28, 54-55, 57, 114, 117, 171, 178, 184-186, 188-191
Citizenship 126
Cosmos 2, 118, 120, 122, 127-128, 131, 133, 135-139, 141-144, 146-148, 188; see World
Cynics 102

Day 30-31, 35, 71, 87, 123-124, 127, 142; The Last Day: 34, 69, 77-78, 80, 87, 166-169, 171-172, 188-189, 192; Day of the Son: 175
Decay 15, 36, 130-131, 133
Democracy 141
Diaspora 22, 179
Disorder 141, 143-146
Docetism 2, 148, 183-185, 187-192
Dualism 118-120, 128, 130, 132-134, 143-145, 163, 179, 181

Earth, *passim*, esp. 2, 7-18, 106-107, 118-121, 127-134, 142-146, 148, 170, 173, 182, 184, 189
Education 2, 100-110, 113, 115, 118-121, 123-129, 137, 141-143, 156
Egypt, Egyptian 7, 10-13, 22, 74, 108, 125, 140
Election 176, 179, 184, 186, 192
Element, Physical 8, 10, 131-133
Emancipation 126, 133
Empirical 2, 117, 135-136, 177-178
Encyclia 2, 99-103, 105-111, 113, 115, 117-121, 123-125, 147

Epicureans 102
Equality 2, 141-142
Eschatology 2, 65, 67, 73, 148, 153, 156, 165-174, 186
Essenes 112
Ether, Ethereal 44, 130-132
Ethics, Ethical 124, 128, 131, 133, 137, 143-146
Eucharist 3, 25, (38), 90-93, 95-97, 114, 155, 174, 186, 188-192
External 2, 31, 122-125, 128-129, 137-138, 148, 153, 172-176, 178-189, 192

Faith 30, 47-48, 145-146, 161, 178, 186, 189-190; see Believe and Trust
Father, (God), *passim*, esp. 65-67, 90, 94, 150, 159-164, 167-168, 172, 176, 179-180, 182-184, 186-187
Flesh (and Blood) 34, 77, 87, 89, 92, 120, 179, 181-192

Gnosis, Gnostic 2-4, 28, 116, 120, 140, 143, 148, 153, 157-158, 164, 170, 177, 185, 187, 191
God, *passim*, esp. 2, 10, 50, 65-66, 84, 90, 94, 110, 113, 116-120, 130, 134, 138-151, 153, 156-159, 162-164, 166-170, 172, 174-178, 182, 184-189
Greek 2, 18-19, 59-61, 64, 67, 83, 93, 100, 103-107, 110, 113, 115, 118-124, 126-127, 129-130, 133, 140-142, 145, 147-148, 156

Hagar 32, 36, 39, 104, 108-109
Haggadah, see Index I
Halakah, see Index I
Heaven, Heavenly, *passim*, esp. 116-122, 127-146, 148-149, 151-153, 155-166, 168, 170, 172-175, 177, 179, 181-187, 192
Hellenistic 3-4, 18, 28, 51-52, 54-55, 93, 99, 102, 113, 131-132, 147, 153
Hermetica 104, 129, 132
History, Historical 2, 95, 148, 173, 175-176, 178, 183-192

I am 33-34, 72-73, 78, 80, 88, 151, 154-158, 163, 184, 186; see Ego Eimi, Index I; see also Self Predication, Index II
Ignatius 185, 189, 190
Imperishable 132

INDEX OF SUBJECTS

Incarnation 183-192
Inconsistencies 99, 105, 107-108, 141, 143, 171, 183-184
Individualistic 133-137
Intuition 37, 105, 107
Isaac 33, 43, 94, 103, 108-109 113,
Ishmael 43, 104, 108-109
Isocrates 123
Israel, Israelites 2, 7, 61, 71, 83, 115-118, 130, 135-136, 147-149, 152, 172, 175-178, 184

Jacob 94, 103, 113, 175
Jesus Christ 2, 33-34, 37, 57, 66, 69, 73-74, 78-80, 86, 90, 147-148, 151-152, 157-158, 163-164, 167-169 174-176, 178-180, 183-192
Jews, Jewish 2-4, 26-28, 34, 51-52, 54-55, 73-74, 76-78, 80, 84, 89, 107-123, 125-127, 130, 133-148, 151-154, 159, 161-162, 164-166, 168, 170, 174, 176-179, 183-185, 187, 189-192
Judaism 1-3, 22, 51, 54-55, 89, 107-113, 115, 117-118, 121, 130, 133, 137, 143, 145, 147, 152-153, 158, 161, 164, 167, 169, 174, 179, 181
Judicial 84, 89, 159, 161-162, 164, 167; see Halakah and Juridical
Juridical 162-164, 186; see Halakah and Judicial
Justice 2, 113, 138, 141

Knowledge 15, 30-31, 36, 107, 110, 124, 127-128, 138, 153

Law, Laws 2, 31, 35, 76, 84, 89, 112-115, 118, 122, 125-127, 134, 136-146, 149, 158, 173, 175, 178, 188; see Torah
Learning, Learner 31-34, 36, 80, 85, 104-105, 113-114, 150-151
Life 33-34, 37, 45, 61, 66, 69, 73-74, 77-78, 80, 87-88, 94, 127, 148-150, 152-158, 162-163, 165-173, 178, 180-188, 190
Logos, Logoi 114, 117, 137-141, 145; see Word
Lord 47-48, 53, 65, 71, 73, 84-85, 88, 91, 157, 183

Man 118, 120-123, 128-130, 133, 135-136, 142-143, 146, 181-184, 189, 192; see Anthropology

Mandean 28, 158, 164
Manna, *passim*.
Matter, Material 132-133, 140, 143, 145, 188-190
Measures 30-31, 141-146
Merkabah, see Mysticism
Mind 31-32, 75, 81, 88, 135, 138
Moses 2, 14, 22, 32-33, 37, 47, 61, 65-67, 81, 84-85, 94, 113-115, 118, 126, 134, 140, 144, 148-151, 172-176, 179, 187-188
Mysticism, Mystery 2-3, 19, 111, 113-114, 116-117, 120, 127, 138, 140, 145-147, 153, 162-164, 177, 186

Nation, the Jewish 2, 33, 109, 115-118, 133-137, 139, 147-148, 176-178; see People, the Jewish
Nature 103-107, 113-114, 118-120, 130, 133, 136, 138-141

Office 31, 123-125
Oligarchy 141
Order, Cosmic, Heavenly 2, 7-8, 11, 13, 122, 141-148, 179, 180, 182, 184, 187

Palestine, Palestinian 1-3, 6, 8, 11, 13-14, 16-17, 19, 21-22, 24, 41, 51-56, 59-64, 69-70, 78, 80, 82, 84-85, 94, 98-99, 110, 114-115, 118, 126, 127, 129-130, 133, 136, 140, 143-144, 146-147, 150, 179
People, the Jewish 134-135, 146, 163, 176; see Nation, the Jewish
Peripatetics 131
Perish, Perishable 131-132, 143, 166-168, 179-180, 182-183
Philosophy, Philosopher 2, 19, 31, 59, 99-103, 105, 107-109, 111-113, 117-124, 127, 131, 135, 139-141, 145, 147-148, 156
Physics, Physical 2, 130-133, 178, 181
Plato, Platonic 2, 103, 120, 123, 127-130, 132, 135-136, 139-142, 144, 146, 161, 163, 170
Political 123-127, 135-136, 142-143, 146
Practice 43, 103, 105, 113-114, 120, 136-137, 139, 142, 146
Principle, Cosmic, Heavenly 2, 137-139, 141, 144-145, 148

INDEX OF SUBJECTS

Providence 145
Pseudepigrapha 144
Pythagoras, Pythagorean 103, 120, 141

Qumran 41, 61, 74, 76, 89, 95, 150, 167, 169-170

Rabbinic 6, 42, 54, 59-60, 64, 114, 130, 148, 150, 153, 159, 162, 164-167, 181
Reason, the Right, etc. 122-124, 126-130, 133, 136-137, 145
Resurrection 167-172, 188, 192
Revelation, Revealer 110, 120, 150-153, 157, 174-175, 177-178, 185, 191
Roman 123, 125, 131

Sabbath, Sabbathical 14, 33, 106-107, 111-114, 117-118, 146-147, 149, 188
Sarah 31-32, 35, 36, 39, 81, 108-109
Scripture 47, 57, 100, 111, 117, 132, 136, 138, 140-141, 145, 151-152, 176-177, 179, 180, 182
See 33-34, 69, 77, 80, 84, 115-118, 150-151, 162, 175-178, 185; see Vision
Self Predication 80, 156-158, 163, 184, 186; see I am
Selftaught 103-107, 109, 113, 118-120
Sender, Sent 33-34, 69, 71, 75, 77, 80, 83, 87, 94, 158-160, 162-164, 180; see Agency
Shekinah 118
Sign 45, 69
Sinai 2, 71, 118, 148-153, 156-157, 163, 173, 175-177
Son of God 34, 69, 77, 90, 94, 151-153, 160-164, 167-168, 175-180, 182-187, 190
Son of Man 34, 87, 185-186, 191
Sophist 123-124
Soteriology 162, 164, 188, 192
Soul 2, 14-15, 29-32, 36, 44, 62-63, 66, 71, 81, 102, 111, 116, 119-120, 123, 128-130, 133-139, 141, 143-144, 182
Spirit, Spiritual, Spiritualize 2, 114-116, 134-135, 137, 143, 145, 148, 153, 172-192
Stoic 2, 60, 102, 109, 122-123, 126-131, 133, 135-136, 138, 139-141, 143-144, 146
Sublunar Sphere 130, 132
Supralunar Sphere 130, 132
Synagogue, see Index I
Synoptics 45-46, 69, 91-93, 154, 159, 164-168

Teaching, Teacher 32-34, 36, 56-57, 80, 84, 101, 103-110, 113-114, 118, 120, 134, 150, 154, 185
Theophany 2, 149-153, 156-158, 163, 168, 173, 175-178, 180, 186
Time, Timeless 77, 163, 165, 168, 170, 172, 174

Torah 2, 71, 77, 110, 114, 130, 136, 139, 143-144, 147-157, 162-163, 165-166, 168, 172-173, 175-177, 182, 184, 186, 190; see Law
Transcendence 139-140
Trust 2, 30, 145-146, 161, 163, 176; see Believe and Faith

Virtue 14, 32-33, 36, 43, 63, 76, 81, 101-103, 105, 107, 109, 111, 113, 117-124, 126-129, 133, 136, 138, 143, 145
Vision 2, 14, 111, 114-118, 120, 138, 147-148, 151, 153, 162-163, 173, 175-178, 185-186; see See

Wisdom 2, 14-15, 32, 89, 100-103, 105, 107, 109-114, 118-120, 134, 139-140, 147, 154-158, 162-166, 168, 172-173, 184, 186, 188, 190-191
Witness 179-180, 182-183
Word, Words 15, 29-30, 44, 47, 62, 128, 137-141, 148-149, 176, 183, 187-190, 192; see Logos
World 7-8, 10, 33-34, 37, 47, 61, 66, 87, 140, 143, 148-149, 153, 162, 164-165, 169-170, 174-175, 178-179, 185-186; see Cosmos
Works, of Jesus 179-183

Supplements to
NOVUM TESTAMENTUM

Editorial Staff: C. K. BARRETT, A. F. J. KLIJN, J. SMIT SIBINGA.
Editorial Secretary: H. J. DE JONGE.

1. **Peterson, P. M.** Andrew, brother of Simon Peter. His history and legends. Repr. of the first (1958) ed. 1963. (viii, 70 p., 4 geneal. tabl.) (D) [01581 7]
cloth Gld. *22.—/24.—
2. **Strobel, A.** Untersuchungen zum eschatologischen Verzögerungsproblem auf Grund der spätjüdisch-urchristlichen Geschichte von Habakuk 2,2 ff. 1961. (xxxii, 305 p.) [01582 5] *cloth* Gld. *60.—/72.—
3. **Iersel, B. M. F. van.** 'Der Sohn' in den synoptischen Jesusworten. Christusbezeichnung der Gemeinde oder Selbstbezeichnung Jesu? 2., durchges. Aufl. Mit einem Nachtrag. 1964. (xxiv, 202 p.) (D) [01583 3]
cloth Gld. *32.—/36.—
5. **Klijn, A. F. J.** The Acts of Thomas. Introduction. Text. Commentary. 1962. (xii, 304 p.) *reprint under consideration*
6. **Neotestamentica et Patristica.** Eine Freundesgabe Herrn Professor Dr. OSCAR CULLMANN zu seinem 60. Geburtstag überreicht. 1962. (xx, 331 p., 1 portr.) [01586 8] *cloth* Gld. *64.—/76.—
8. **De Marco, A. A.** The tomb of Saint Peter. A representative and annotated bibliography of the excavations. 1964. (x, 261 p.) [01588 4]
cloth Gld. *64.—/76.—
9. **Loos, H. van der.** The Miracles of Jesus. Reprint of the first (1965) ed. 1968. (xvi, 748 p.) [01589 2] *cloth* Gld. *80.—/92.—
13. **Moore, A. L.** The Parousia in the New Testament. 1966. (viii, 248 p.) (D) [01593 0] *cloth* Gld. *72.—/84.—
15. **Quispel, G.** Makarius, das Thomasevangelium und das Lied von der Perle. 1967. (viii, 126 p.) [01595 7] *cloth* Gld. *40.—/48.—
16. **Pfitzner, V. C.** Paul and the Agon motif. Traditional athletic imagery in the Pauline literature. 1967. (x, 222 p.) (D) [01596 5] *cloth* Gld. *48.—/56.—
17. **Bellinzoni, A.** The sayings of Jesus in the writings of Justin Martyr. 1967. (x, 152 p.) [01597 3] *cloth* Gld. *40.—/48.—
18. **Gundry, R. H.** The use of the Old Testament in St. Matthew's Gospel. With special reference to the Messianic hope. Reprint of the first (1967) ed. 1975. (xvi, 252 p.) [04278 4] *cloth* Gld. *76.—/88.—
19. **Sevenster, J. N.** Do you know Greek? How much Greek could the first Jewish Christians have known? 1968. (viii, 197 p.) [03090 5]
cloth Gld. *76.—/84.—
20. **Buchanan, G. W.** The consequences of the Covenant. 1970. (xx, 343 p., 2 [1 fold.] sketchmaps) [01600 7] *cloth* Gld. *96.—/116.—
21. **Klijn, A. F. J.** A survey of the researches into the Western text of the Gospels and Acts. Part 2: 1949-1969. 1969. (xii, 86 p.) [01601 5]
cloth Gld. *32.—/40.—

22. **Gaboury, A.** La structure des Évangiles synoptiques. La structure-type à l'origine des synoptiques. 1970. (x, 226 p., 19 tables) [01602 3]
cloth Gld. *64.—/72.—

23. **Gaston, L.** No stone on another. Studies in the significance of the Fall of Jerusalem in the synoptic gospels. 1970. (x, 537 p.) [01603 1]
cloth Gld. *116.—/32.—

24. Studies in John. Presented to Professor Dr. J. N. SEVENSTER on the occasion of his seventieth birthday. 1970. (viii, 220 p., portr.) [03091 3]
cloth Gld. *64.—/72.—

25. **Story, C. I. K.** The nature of truth in 'The Gospel of Truth', and in the writings of Justin Martyr. A study of the pattern of orthodoxy in the middle of the second Christian century. 1970. (xxiv, 247 p.) [01605 8]
cloth Gld. *84.—/96.—

26. **Gibbs, J. G.** Creation and Redemption. A study in Pauline theology. 1971. (xii, 194 p.) [01606 6]
cloth Gld. *64.—/72.—

27. **Mussies, G.** The morphology of koine Greek as used in the Apocalypse of St. John. A study in bilingualism. 1971. (xvi, 386 p., 2 fold. tabl.) (D) [02656 8]
cloth Gld. *108.—/120.—

28. **Aune, D. E.** The cultic setting of realized eschatology in early Christianity. 1972. (x, 242 p.) (D) [03341 6]
cloth Gld. *76.—/88.—

29. **Unnik, W. C. van.** Sparsa collecta. Collected Essays. Part 1. Evangelia, Paulina, Acta. 1973. (x, 409 p.) [03660 1]
cloth Gld. *144.—/180.—

30. **Unnik, W. C. van.** Sparsa collecta. Collected Essays. Part 2. I Peter, Canon, Corpus Hellenisticum, Generalia. 1980. (viii, 332 p.) [06261 0]
cloth Gld. *84.—/96.—

31. **Unnik, W. C. van.** Sparsa collecta. Collected Essays. Part 3. Patristica, Gnostica, Liturgica.
in preparation

32. **Nicol, W.** The sēmeia in the fourth gospel. Tradition and redaction. 1972. (x, 155 p.) (D) [03477 3]
cloth Gld. *52.—/60.—

33. Studies in New Testament and early Christian literature. Essays in honor of ALLEN P. WIKGREN. Ed. by D. E. AUNE. 1972. (viii, 274 p., portr.) [03504 4]
cloth Gld. *76.—/88.—

34. **Hagner, D. A.** The use of the Old and New Testaments in Clement of Rome. 1973. (xii, 393 p.) [03636 9]
cloth Gld. *92.—/108.—

35. **Gunther, J. J.** St. Paul's opponents and their background. A study of apocalyptic and Jewish sectarian teachings. 1973. (x, 323 p.) [03738 1]
cloth Gld. *96.—/116.—

36. **Klijn, A. F. J.** and **G. J. Reinink.** Patristic evidence for Jewish-Christian sects. 1973. (x, 313 p.) [03763 2]
cloth Gld. *96.—/112.—

37. **Reiling, J.** Hermas and Christian prophecy. A study of the eleventh mandate. 1973. (viii, 197 p.) [03771 3]
cloth Gld. *60.—/68.—

38. **Donfried, K. P.** The setting of Second Clement in early Christianity. 1974. (x, 240 p., some tables) [03895 7]
cloth Gld. *64.—/72.—

39. **Roon, A. van.** The Authenticity of Ephesians. 1974. (x, 447 p.) [03971 6]
cloth Gld. *132.—/156.—

40. **Kemmler, D. W.** Faith and human reason. A study of Paul's method of preaching as illustrated by 1-2 Thessalonians and acts 17, 2-4. 1975. (xii, 225 p.) [04209 1] *cloth* Gld. *84.—/88.—

41. **Sevenster, J. N.** The roots of pagan Anti-Semitism in the ancient world. 1975. (viii, 235 p.) [04193 1] *cloth* Gld. *88.—/96.—

42. **Pancaro, S.** The law in the Fourth Gospel. The Torah and the Gospel, Moses and Jesus, Judaism and Christianity according to John. 1975. (xvii, 571 p.) [04309 8] *cloth* Gld. *132.—/156.—

43. **Clavier, H.** Les variétés de la pensée biblique et le problème de son unité. Esquisse d'une Théologie de la Bible sur les textes originaux et dans leur contexte historique. 1976. (xvi, 424 p.) [04465 5] *cloth* Gld. *124.—/152.—

44. Studies in New Testament language and text. Essays in honour of GEORGE D. KILPATRICK on the occasion of his sixty-fifth birthday. Ed. by J. K. ELLIOTT. 1976. (x, 400 p., frontisp.) [04386 1] *cloth* Gld. *128.—/150.—

45. **Panagopoulos, J.** (ed.). Prophetic Vocation in the New Testament and Today. 1977. (viii, 248 p.) [04923 1] *cloth* Gld. *50.—/56.—

46. **Klijn, A. F. J.** Seth in Jewish, Christian and Gnostic literature. 1977. (viii, 145 p.) [05245 3] *cloth* Gld. *68.—/84.—

47. Miscellanea Neotestamentica, I. Studia ad Novum Testamentum Praesertim Pertinentia a Sociis Sodalicii Batavi c.n. Studiosorum Novi Testamenti Conventus Anno MCMLXXVI Quintum Lustrum Feliciter Complentis Suscepta. Edenda Curaverunt Curaverunt T. BAARDA, A. F. J. KLIJN, W. C. VAN UNNIK. 1978. (ix, 211 p.) [05685 8] *cloth* Gld. *92.—/104.—

48. Miscellanea Neotestamentica, II. 1978. (ix, 201 p.) [05686 6]
cloth Gld. *92.—/104.—

49. **O'Brien, P. T.** Introductory thanksgivings in the letters of Paul. 1977. (xii, 309 p.) [05265 8] *cloth* Gld. *64.—/76.—

50. **Bousset, D. W.** Religionsgeschichtliche Studien. Aufsätze zur Religionsgeschichte des Hellenistischen Zeitalters. Hrsg. von A. F. VERHEULE. 1979. (x, 314 p.) [05845 1] *cloth* Gld. *120.—/128.—

51. **Cook, M. J.** Mark's treatment of the Jewish leaders. 1978. (xii, 104 p.) [05785 4] *cloth* Gld. *28.—/32.—

52. **Garland, D. E.** The intention of Matthew 23. 1979. (xii, 225 p.) [05912 1
cloth Gld. *64.—/80.—

53. **Moxnes, H.** Theology in conflict. Studies in Paul's understanding of God in Romans. 1980. (xiv, 319 p.) [061401 1] *cloth* Gld. *76.—/88.—

54. **Clark, K. W.** The Gentile Bias and other essays. Selected by J. L. SHARPE III. With a foreword by H. ANDERSON. 1980. (xiv, 229 p., 7 fig.) [06127 4]
cloth Gld. *68.—/76.—

Prices marked with an asterisk are for subscribers to *Novum Testamentum*.

1981. Prices are subject to change without notice.

E. J. Brill — P.O.B. 9000 — 2300 PA Leiden — The Netherlands

MEDE VERKRIJGBAAR DOOR BEMIDDELING VAN DE BOEKHANDEL

www.ingramcontent.com/pod-product-compliance
Lightning Source LLC
Chambersburg PA
CBHW050844230426
43667CB00012B/2140